The Women of Hammer Horror

ALSO BY ROBERT MICHAEL "BOBB" COTTER
AND FROM MCFARLAND

*The Complete Misfits Discography: Authorized Releases and Bootlegs,
Including Recordings by Danzig, Samhain and The Undead* (2019)

*Vampira and Her Daughters: Women Horror Movie Hosts
from the 1950s into the Internet Era* (2017)

*Caroline Munro, First Lady of Fantasy: A Complete Annotated
Record of Film and Television Appearances* (2012)

Ingrid Pitt, Queen of Horror: The Complete Career (2010; paperback 2018)

*A History of the Doc Savage Adventures in Pulps, Paperbacks,
Comics, Fanzines, Radio and Film* (2009; paperback 2016)

*The Great Monster Magazines: A Critical Study of the Black and
White Publications of the 1950s, 1960s and 1970s* (2008; paperback 2019)

The Mexican Masked Wrestler and Monster Filmography
(2005; paperback 2008)

The Women of Hammer Horror

A Biographical Dictionary and Filmography

ROBERT MICHAEL "BOBB" COTTER
Foreword by Veronica Carlson

McFarland & Company, Inc., Publishers
Jefferson, North Carolina

The present work is a reprint of the illustrated case bound edition of The Women of Hammer Horror: A Biographical Dictionary and Filmography, *first published in 2013 by McFarland.*

LIBRARY OF CONGRESS CATALOGUING-IN-PUBLICATION DATA

Cotter, Bobb.
The women of Hammer Horror : a biographical dictionary and filmography / Robert Michael "Bobb" Cotter ; foreword by Veronica Carlson.
p. cm.
Includes bibliographical references and index.

ISBN 978-1-4766-8513-7
softcover : acid free paper ∞

1. Hammer Film Productions — History.
2. Motion picture actors and actresses — Biography — Dictionaries.
3. Horror films.   4. Women in motion pictures.   I. Title.
PN1999.H3C68 2021   791.43'61640941—dc23   2013017965

BRITISH LIBRARY CATALOGUING DATA ARE AVAILABLE

© 2021 The Estate of Robert Michael "Bobb" Cotter. All rights reserved

No part of this book may be reproduced or transmitted in any form or by any means, electronic or mechanical, including photocopying or recording, or by any information storage and retrieval system, without permission in writing from the publisher.

On the cover: Valerie Leon in a publicity still from the 1971 Hammer film *Blood from the Mummy's Tomb* (Author's collection)

Printed in the United States of America

*McFarland & Company, Inc., Publishers
Box 611, Jefferson, North Carolina 28640
www.mcfarlandpub.com*

Dedicated to Dad, Brownie, Ingrid Pitt, Davy Jones, and Elvis (R.I.P.).
Also to my wonderful wife Cheryl, Lucky the Wonder Dog, and Brian Wilson.

With thanks to Eide's Entertainment, the Usual Gang of Idiots,
Richard Klemensen, and Kevin Flynn.

And with special thanks to Veronica Carlson; John Del Margio,
the Rare Horror/Sci-Fi Movie Collector for Hire (jddmld@aol.com);
Mel Bridgeman, the Finest Photo and Lobby Card Reproductions on eBay
(pokepyn@comcast.net); and Paul C. Riggie (The Reception).

Table of Contents

Foreword by Veronica Carlson 1

Introduction 3

THE ACTRESSES 7

Hammer Film Credits 201

Bibliography 235

Index 237

Foreword by Veronica Carlson

I am delighted to have been asked to contribute this foreword to Bobb Cotter's *The Women of Hammer Horror*. I regret that I actually worked with so few of these actresses—without exception, they were lovely to know: Barbara Ewing, Marion Mathie, Kate O'Mara, Maxine Audley, Gwen Watford, and Helen Goss. But I have had the privilege of meeting many more—Linda Hayden, Stephanie Beacham, Martine Beswick, Caroline Munro, Mary Collinson, Madeline Smith, Valerie Leon, Yvonne Monlaur, Suzanna Leigh, Yutte Stensgaard, Virginia Wetherell—all through attending conventions, thanks to the devotees of Hammer Films.

The first time I met Bobb was at one of these conventions, the second was at another after he had just completed, and published, his biography of Ingrid Pitt, who had only recently passed away. It was a revealing and heart-stopping moment, as we both shared fond memories of this vibrant lady. She was fearless and exuberant in all she did. As we finished speaking, I recalled my beautiful first meeting with Ingrid. She and I met, coincidentally, for breakfast. Conversation flowed easily—she spoke of her war years, amazingly candidly, and with no glimpse of self-pity. I was mesmerized and totally fascinated, but horrified at what she had had to endure. So (I remember thinking as I left to go to my room)—*that* is what makes this woman so exceptional, and gave her such energy and passion for life and freedom. That courage and bravery never flagged or waned. Tony Rudlin, Ingrid's beloved husband, kindly sent me a photo of Ingrid; in it, she is serene, and as always, beautiful. I have it framed, and it sits on my desk as I write. Bobb's book on Ingrid's life is a must-read.

Caroline Munro was another Lady of Hammer that I met through attending conventions. I feel in her a soulmate, and in times gone by. She and her lovely stepdaughter Tami Hamalian have often proved to be staunch support systems for me. I shall always be grateful to them for their kindness and generosity with their time. Caroline is one of the loveliest people I've ever met, and one of the gentlest. I have many happy memories of our times together, especially when we were with Ingrid or Martine. But the one memory that edges out all others, for pride of place for me, happened at a convention hosted by Donald Fearney at Bray Studios in England. I live in the States, and "The Don" kindly invited me, along with my oldest son Adam, to attend. He had previously met my parents, so he kindly invited them and my younger sister Elizabeth, as well.

I was very busy signing autographs out in the lovely gardens, Adam occasionally bringing me refreshments; it was a beautiful, warm day. When I had some time to see how my parents were faring (as it was getting a bit late), they told me they had been "royally looked after" by none other than Caroline Munro! They were beaming from ear to ear. Father had his sweet sherry and smoked salmon; Mother had vodka and tonic and all kinds of delicious snacks. They were singing her praises for days afterwards, and often were to reminisce on their "wonderful day at Bray," and Caroline: "Eh! She treated us like she was our daughter," they would both say. Thank you, Donald, for making such wonderful memories possible. Thank you, Caroline, I shall *never* forget your kindness.

Another great memory I think of as the Day She Upstaged Me. We were attending a Q & A session, along with Yvonne Monlaur and Linda Hayden. I was asked when I first got the acting bug and at what age I said, "When I was cast as the Virgin Mary at the age of 6." Caroline (having been asked the same question) said, "When I was cast as Jesus at the age of 13!" It brought the house down.

Martine Beswick is enormous fun to be with, though I don't get to spend much time with her as I would like. Apparently, we both enjoyed being read to as children—and we discovered our minds saw very powerful pictures—something like Todd A O images. Ridiculous, wonderful fun!

After reading through Bobb's fine manuscript about the Ladies of Hammer, I was disappointed to learn that some have wished (or chosen) to distance themselves from their movies. I simply, or naively, thought that the passage of time would cause them to be forgotten. That changed when I was living in a large apartment overlooking beautiful Skull Creek. It had a rogue fire alarm. After the fifth false alarm—the fifth time evacuating, waiting for the fire trucks, waiting for the all-clear—I decided to ignore it if it happened again. It did. As usual, heart-rate up, I dashed out to look—sniffing the air, looking again, deciding it was safe, dashing back in—back to my easel. After about three minutes, a *loud* banging on my door. I opened it and looked up into the face of an exasperated fireman: "Ma'am, don't you know to leave the building when the alarm rings?" "Well, if it goes off all the time, officer..." "Ma'am, I don't care HOW many times it goes off...." A short pause, then, "Ma'am, I've just been watching you on television back at the firehouse—you're Veronica Carlson!" He smiled and said, "Miss Veronica, you can either walk out, or I can carry you out over my shoulder." I walked out. The fireman had been watching *Frankenstein Must Be Destroyed.*

The philosopher Andre Gide said it best: "Our acts are attached to us, as its glimmer is attached to phosphorous. They consume us, it is true, but they make our splendour." Bobb Cotter has created his own "splendour" by giving the fans of Hammer a truly invaluable reference book of "Hammer Horror Heroines" that is a delight to read.

Veronica Carlson is one of Hammer's legendary leading ladies, and starred in three of their genre classics: *Dracula Has Risen from the Grave, Frankenstein Must Be Destroyed,* and *The Horror of Frankenstein.* A very successful artist, her work is in both private and corporate collections throughout the United States and Europe. She lives on Hilton Head Island with her husband and three children.

Introduction

"Well, yes, and here we go again." — Hunter S. Thompson

"Repetition is a form of change." — Brian Eno

The freakish, mutant, alien overlords at McFarland generally require that the preface or introduction to any given book explain the whys and wherefores of that particular work, and so this one shall — in time. But I think that, particularly in the age of the Internet, it would be proper to segue into that with a thought or two on the whys and wherefores of books, period. For instance, by the time you get finished reading this sentence, this book will be out of date. It's the nature of the beast, somewhat akin to the Populuxe notion of planned obsolescence.

Those thoughts stem from an email exchange the author had with his esteemed colleague Mr. Joe Bob Briggs, in which we discussed the intransigence of what we do. Not in terms of our opinions, but in the very nature of the beast itself. Unlike the fluid and ever-changing Internet, once we write it down, or more precisely, the day the book is published, it's obsolete. No matter how up-to-date the information is, it will be subject to change that afternoon. But in a sense, it has always been such; it's just that now the rapidity of the change is so much faster. Perhaps some would argue that, because of that technology and method of gathering and distributing information, books themselves are obsolete. As one might expect, I'd argue that they're not; despite the omniscience of the mighty Internet, its all-pervading power can be neutered in the blink of an eye — as soon as the electricity goes off. Or, because of choice or circumstances or other reasons, some people just don't have computers. I think it's for those reasons and those people that books will continue to survive, and as they have always done build upon themselves and others in our ongoing studies of whatever subject a book addresses. At any rate, it's time to move on.

So, yes, here we do indeed go again; repetition as change, another variation on the theme; the theme of Hammer films. And although the author's love for them has inspired my most recent two books, on Ingrid Pitt and Caroline Munro, this is the first time that I've tackled the subject directly. That in itself is a daunting task; some mighty fine books have already addressed the subject, so the thought has to be, well, how it can be approached in a way that offers a different slant or new information on the subject? For instance, one may wonder at the inclusion of full credits for the films discussed, since, say, McFarland's *Hammer Films: An Exhaustive Filmography* lists the same. For two reasons, then: first, since the book was published in the '90s, it doesn't include any of the films from the resurgent Hammer, and secondly, well, we're all human, and sometimes we make mistakes, just I surely have — of course, we all try not to and hope that we don't, but thankfully, again, we're all human (at least sort of) and we do, and so hopefully this goes towards correcting any inadvertent omissions. This is not done in the spirit of superiority or one-upmanship, it's done merely to try and make sure all the facts are out there, and straight. For it's a continuous process, as alluded to in the opening paragraphs; once a book is done, it's set in stone, and this one is just another in a building process in the ever-evolving library of information concerning our beloved Hammer films. Plus, I think it's very important to have credits, because there are so many cooks involved in the making of a film, and films always come down to so much more than just a director or actors or whomever, and everybody deserves their share of the credit for making an idea a reality. I think, in this case, it also helps to remind us how important women were on both sides of the camera.

That being said, this book, much like life, cannot provide an equal distribution of wealth. Some actresses have lengthy, detailed entries, while others have little more than their name and the role or roles they played for Hammer — sometimes the only movie they were ever in at all — and thus, sadly, their lives and careers are largely undocumented. For comparison's sake, also included in the actresses' filmographies are their other contributions to the horror, sci-fi and fantasy genres.

This book isn't the first to focus on the women of Hammer; *Hammer Glamour* tackled the subject in a gorgeously mounted, oversized volume. But if there was any problem with it at all, it was that it just wasn't enough; out of the hundreds of actresses that appeared in Hammer films, only about 50 or 60 were covered, and then only the most gorgeous. Some major stars and equally proficient character players were left out of the mix, a somewhat lopsided picture of the kind of talent that went into these films. For example, resulting in Bette Davis and Joan Fontaine had been among Hollywood's most beautiful actresses in their primes, but by 1966, their glamour had faded and so they had to rely on their talent, of which they both possessed immense reserves. Raquel Welch in 1966, on the other hand, had exactly two things going for her, both of which were covered by her famous fur bikini in *One Million Years B.C.*, which only helped to cement Hammer's reputation as a purveyor of female exploitation — which they absolutely were, as they themselves were often the first to admit. At the same time that they were pushing Ms. Welch's bust line to the forefront of cinemas around the world, they were also making wonderful films like *The Nanny* and *The Witches* that showed that art need not take a back seat to commerce. In short, you'll get no argument here that Hammer indeed often featured "the most beautiful girls in the world" in their potboilers, just that they also, as often as not, featured talents that had little to do with how much skin was showing.

Which brings us to the question of the role of women in Hammer films and with it, the broader question of the reflection of their roles in society — but that's the subject of a whole other book, and certainly by a much wiser head than mine. Instead, let's take a look at the role of Hammer films in society and how those women's roles are defined within that. Taken more or less as a whole, are Hammer films reactionary or radical? On the surface (and perhaps below much of it), they are terribly reactionary, as personified by their Terminally Twerpy young leading men that had to be shown the Way and the Truth by the Wise Guiding Hand of the upper or ruling class. As Simon Winder says of the James Bond novel *Moonraker* in *The Man Who Saved Britain*: "Fleming's fantasy cuts both ways — attractively, it implies that the establishment is a farce and even a Nazi loony can get into it; unattractively, it implies an almost emetic loathing — a nightmare in which things that do not belong (and it could be humans like socialists or ghouls like the inheritance tax) are secretly stalking even the inner sanctums of British life. I would like to think that [Hugo] Drax's story is a satire about the former, but fear it is more plausibly about the latter." And obviously much the same thing can be said about Hammer, if not most horror films made up until the late '60s or mid–'70s; monsters, standing in for perceived social ills, certainly cause much damage and concern, but in the end are always vanquished by traditional values. But, as with the intertwining of art and commerce, the best-laid plans of mice and conservatives can often go awry, and that which was previously intended only to exploit can sometimes unintentionally illuminate. For all their effort to showcase the attractiveness of the established order (as well as lay down a warning as to what one could expect when one attempted to dismantle that order), Hammer, as well as Universal and the others, just as often as not did exactly the opposite of what they intended and shows the establishment for the farce it most often is.

And so it goes with the women involved with the films, again on both sides of the camera, both of which were male-dominated worlds. Actually, it was harder on the technical side; any pretty face could be plopped in front of the always-willing camera with no regard as to whether or not she could actually act. But if you were a female in any aspect of production, you had better be pretty damned good at what you did and had to work twice as hard. And of course, on the other side of the camera, the women were performing in roles that were by and large written by men, and so even when they are strong and independent, they are still doing so from a male perspective of what a strong and independent woman is. Does this invalidate the portrayals? I would argue not, because, as stated previously, the intention and the result sometimes have an ornery habit of avoiding each other completely. True, the women were performing in roles ascribed to them by men, but more often than not, the actress playing it was not playing the game and the force of those personalities come through in their portrayals, no matter how stereotypical they might seem or be. And again, more often than not, the very propriety that was ascribed in their roles, in order to maintain the status quo, was, attractively, seemingly a not-so-subtle jab at that propriety. In either case, on both sides of the camera, the women behind Hammer had to overcome scores of obstacles; some professionally, many more personally, some so tragic they could not overcome them. But, like women always have, they persevered and carved out an everlasting place for themselves, both in cinema history and life, and that makes all of them, to me, heroic. Hence the title; regardless of whether or not they actually played that specific role in the film, or if she was even in a movie, each and every last one of them, be she a Vampire Lover or a Tong Room Girl, or producer Aida Young or Continuity Girl Tilly Day, will always be the Hammer Heroines.

THE ACTRESSES

Omitted vital dates are unknown

Acosta, Carolina
FILM: *Beyond the Rave*, 2008 (DJ)

Adair, Jan
FILM: *Demons of the Mind*, 1972 (First Girl)
Other genre credits: FILM: *A Clockwork Orange*, Warner Brothers, 1971 (Bible Fantasy Handmaiden)

Adams, Joyce
FILM: *Quatermass 2*, 1957 (Woman MP)

Adcock, Sally (1949–)
BIRTHPLACE: London, England.
FILM: *Countess Dracula*, 1971 (Bertha the Goat Girl)

Addams, Dawn (1930–1985)
REAL NAME: Victoria Dawn Addams; BIRTHPLACE: Felixstowe, Suffolk, England.
FILMS: *The Two Faces of Dr. Jekyll* (a.k.a. *House of Fright*), 1960 (Kitty Jekyll); *The Vampire Lovers*, 1970 (The Countess)

BIOGRAPHY—Dawn Addams was born to an officer of the R.A.F. and a mother who died while Dawn was still a young child. Her film career seemed destined for greatness, but her early promise never quite panned out. She had substantial roles in the controversial Hollywood production *The Moon Is Blue* and such A-list titles as *The Robe* and Chaplin's *A King in New York*, and was a popular leading lady in European films of the late '50s which led to her work for Hammer in Terence Fisher's *The Two Faces of Dr. Jekyll*, a tale of two-faced "respectable" society. As Jekyll's faithless wife, she fulfills a stereotypical role as yet another in a long line of terrifically vivacious, beautiful women married to antisocial, obsessive scientists (the viewer always wonders just how they ever hooked up to begin with). But unlike the sympathetic Valerie Hobson in *WereWolf of London* and Frances Drake in *The Invisible Ray*, she is shown to be as morally bankrupt as any of the other principals. She makes a spectacular exit; she awakes in her corset and stockings after being raped by Hyde, and then discovers her lover's snake-topped corpse with a piercing scream. She wanders to the balcony, distraught, and takes a swan-dive through the skylight to the party below, spoiling the festive atmosphere. But even though she was more than adequate in her lead role as Kitty Jekyll, she's somehow more effective in her limited screen time as the mysterious countess in *The Vampire Lovers*, whose function is to procure potential victims for Carmilla. Her relationship to Carmilla is not specified; she describes her both as her daughter and her niece, and, indeed, there may not be any relation at all. The same can be said of her in relation to the equally mysterious Man in Black — is she his slave? Is she his wife (or one of them)? Is she a vampire? Is he a vampire, or merely an agent of the Devil? If so, then is she merely a sub-contractor? These questions are never answered, but Addams' performance makes the viewer want to ask them. *The Vampire Lovers* and *The Vault of Horror* were her last films, although she remained steadily employed in television until the time of her retirement, which was followed a few short years later by her death at the much-too-young age of 54.

Other genre credits: FILMS: *Riders to the Stars*, Ivan Tors Productions, 1954 (Susan Manners); *The 1,000 Eyes of Dr. Mabuse*, CEI Incom, 1960 (Marion Menil); *Zeta One*, Tigon British Film Productions, 1969 (Zeta); *The Vault of Horror*, Amicus Productions, 1973 (Inez) TELEVISION: *Star Maidens*: "The Trial," "Test for Love," "What Have They Done to the Rain?" "The End of Time," "The Enemy," 1976 (President Clara)

Dawn Addams was much more beautiful than either of *The Two Faces of Dr. Jekyll* in this on-set publicity pose (courtesy Mel Bridgeman).

Adderley, Diane

TELEVISION: *Hammer House of Horror*: "Carpathian Eagle," 1980 (Police Woman)

Ainger, Indira

FILM: *The Woman in Black*, 2012 (Little Girl on Train)

Aird, Jane (1926–1993)

BIRTHPLACE: Scotland.

FILMS: *The Quatermass Xperiment*, 1955 (Mrs. Lomax); *X: The Unknown*, 1956 (Vi Harding); *Quatermass 2*, 1957 (Mrs. McLeod)

BIOGRAPHY — The first wife of actor Guy Rolfe (*Stranglers of Bombay*), Aird's career only lasted ten years and encompassed a handful of credits. Three of them came as solid support in Hammer's first two *Quatermass* films and their faux-*Quatermass* film, *X: The Unknown*. All three are man's films, with very little for the few females to do except play very stereotypical roles, but she was particularly effective as the grieving mother in *X: The Unknown*.

Other genre credits: FILM: *The Day the Earth Caught Fire*, Pax Films, 1961 (The Nanny)

Aitchison, Peggy (1921–1990)

BIRTHPLACE: London, England.

TELEVISION: *Hammer House of Mystery and Suspense*: "Paint Me a Murder," 1985 (Bag Lady)

BIOGRAPHY—Her first role did not come until she was 42 years old, but for the next 25 years, she was one of Britain's most dependable television actresses. Her part in the last of the Hammer television series was one of the last roles she would play before her retirement three years later, followed shortly by her death. She also does nice comic turns in *That'll Be the Day* (1973) and the film most American audiences would recognize her from, *The Great Muppet Caper* (1981).

Alexander, Julie (1938–2003)

BIRTHPLACE: Fulham, London, England.

FILM: *The Terror of the Tongs*, 1961 (Beautiful Girl)

BIOGRAPHY—Like Caroline Munro, Julie Alexander was a top-drawer London model prior to her film career, but unlike Caroline, Ms. Alexander did not have a lasting career in fantasy films; in fact, she didn't have much of a celluloid career at all. The year after lending her statuesque form to *The Terror of the Tongs*, she married a theatrical accountant and retired from acting.

Alison, Dorothy (1925–1992)

REAL NAME: Dorothy Dickson; BIRTHPLACE: Broken Hill, New South Wales, Australia.

FILMS: *Journey into Darkness*, 1969 (Mrs. Latham); *Dr. Jekyll and Sister Hyde*, 1971 (Mrs. Spencer)

TELEVISION: *Journey to the Unknown*: "Paper Dolls," 1968 (Mrs. Latham)

BIOGRAPHY—This long-serving British character actress did two Hammer horrors: an episode of *Journey to the Unknown* and a nice turn in *Dr. Jekyll and Sister Hyde* as a clueless mother whose children take after her.

Other genre credits: FILMS: *See No Evil*, Columbia, 1971 (Betty Rexton); *The Amazing Mr. Blunden*, Hemdale Film, 1972 (Mrs. Allen) TELEVISION: *The Veil*: "Jack the Ripper," 1958 (Judith Durst)

Allen, Audrey

FILM: *Creatures the World Forgot*, 1971 (Prehistoric Woman)

Anderson, Daphne (1922–)

REAL NAME: Daphne Scrutton; BIRTHPLACE: London, England.

FILMS: *Cloudburst*, 1951 (Kate); *Night Creatures*, 1961 (Mrs. Rash)

TELEVISION: *Hammer House of Horror*: "Growing Pains," 1980 (Matron)

BIOGRAPHY—Daphne Anderson went to school in Kensington and then studied dancing with Zelia Raye. She made her stage debut in 1937 and her first film in 1949, going on to appear with such legends as Charles Laughton in *Hobson's Choice* and Marilyn Monroe in *The Prince and the Showgirl*. Her roles for Hammer span nearly thirty years: She was in the noir *Cloudburst* in 1951 and ten years later was solid in *Night Creatures* as the level-headed, good-natured wife of the bad-natured innkeeper who tries to rape Yvonne Romain. She brought back a touch of the company's golden age when she appeared on *Hammer House of Horror* in a bit part as the Matron who can't see that the stuffed rabbit-toting young boy adopted by Barbara Kellerman is going through just a wee bit more than a phase. She retired after her performance in the television series *Performance*.

Other genre credits: TELEVISION: *The Avengers*: "Man in the Mirror," 1963 (Betty Brown); *Suspense*: "The Men from the Bush," 1963 (Birdie); *Haunted*: "Many Happy Returns," 1967 (Ginny Granger)

Anderson, Kayla

FILM: *Let Me In*, 2010 (Newscaster)

Anderson, Lesley

FILM: *Countess Dracula*, 1971 (Gypsy Dancer)

Anderson, Margaret (1930–)

BIRTHPLACE: Plymouth, Devon, England.
FILM: *The Quatermass Xperiment*, 1955 (Maggie)
TELEVISION: *Hammer House of Horror*: "Witching Time," 1980 (Sister)

Andipa, Maria

FILM: *The Two Faces of Dr. Jekyll*, 1960 (Gypsy Girl)
Other genre credits: TELEVISION: *The Avengers*: "Death Dispatch," 1962 (Conchita)

Andress, Ursula (1936–)

BIRTHPLACE: Ostermundigen, Bern, Switzerland.
FILM: *She*, 1965 (Ayesha, "She Who Must Be Obeyed")
BIOGRAPHY—Ursula Andress, the archetypal Euro-Jet-Set Bombshell, was one of the forerunners of the type of celebrity who is "famous for being famous." Never classically trained, she more or less fell into acting by falling into bed with an actor after running away from home at 17. She then began doing bit parts in Italian sex comedies and entered into a series of high-profile relationships with actors such as James Dean and Marlon Brando, who was responsible for her getting a contract with Paramount. At this stage, her acting career fizzled, but another romance sizzled, this time with actor-photographer John Derek. An advertisement with one of her photos was seen by director Terence Young, who cast her in the first James Bond film, *Dr. No*, and of course, the rest is history, with Andress becoming the ultimate "Bond Girl." And although she may be the first listed in this book, she's not the first or the last "Bond Girl" to also be a "Hammer Heroine."

Honey was the gateway to worldwide fame for Andress, and led directly to her getting the role of Ayesha in Hammer's "spectacle-on-a-budget" version of H. Rider Haggard's classic novel *She*. Hammer was able to capitalize on making a film featuring "The Most Beautiful Woman in the World" (as she was billed by John Derek in the press and on the posters for the film) because of Seven Arts (who financed the film), and capitalize they did, especially when Andress appeared in a 1965 *Playboy* spread shot by Derek to promote the film. A great financial success, the film featured some wonderful performances from pros Peter Cushing, Christopher Lee, and Andre Morell in support of Andress, who, by her own admission, was not that much of an actress. The scenes of her aging caused her great consternation both before and during the filming. Her success in this, her first starring role, was due to her incen-

Ursula Andress and Rosenda Monteros decide how to divvy up John Richardson in *She* (courtesy Mel Bridgeman).

diary beauty and sheer presence, both of which were at their height in this film. (Her voice was dubbed by the same woman, Monica "Nikki" van der Zyl, who dubbed her in *Dr. No*.) But her regal disdain may have indeed been real disdain; she later disowned the film (although, to be fair, she later disowned *all* her films), claimed that she was forced to do it by Derek, and called it cheap, saying that the only things she liked were the costumes and the fact that she was photographed beautifully. Despite her personal feelings about the role of Ayesha, for Hammer fans, Ursula Andress will always be She-Who-Must-Be-Obeyed — Gladly.

Other genre credits: FILMS: *Dr. No*, Eon Productions, 1962 (Honey); *The 10th Victim*, Compagnia Cinematografica Champion, 1965 (Caroline Meredith); *Casino Royale*, Columbia Pictures, 1967 (Vesper Lynd/James Bond 007); *The Mountain of the Cannibal God*, Dania Film, 1978 (Susan Stevenson); *Clash of the Titans*, MGM, 1981 (Aphrodite) TELEVISION: *Thriller*: "La Strega," 1962 (Luana)

Anthony, Jane

FILM: *Dracula A.D. 1972*, 1972 (Debby Girl)

Anthony, Olga

FILMS: *Scars of Dracula*, 1970 (Girl at Party); *Captain Kronos, Vampire Hunter*, 1974 (Lilian)

Other genre credits: *The Mutations*, Cyclone/Getty, 1974 (Bridget)

Apple, Gwendolyn

FILM: *Let Me In*, 2010 (Girl in Pool)

Archer, Barbara Janet (1925–)

BIRTHPLACE: London, England.
FILM: *Dracula*, 1958 (Inga)

Arrighi, Nike (1947–)

BIRTHPLACE: Nice, France.
FILMS: *The Devil Rides Out*, 1968 (Tanith Carlisle), *Countess Dracula*, 1971 (Fortune Teller)

BIOGRAPHY—There is precious little biographical information available about the female lead of *The Devil Rides Out*. Her career only lasted for eight years; she first appeared in the television mini-series *Ransom for a Pretty Girl* in 1966 and last in the 1974 film *Stavisky*; but in those years she not only appeared in the two Hammer films listed, but standout episodes of *Out of the Unknown*, *The Saint*, and *The Prisoner*, as well as Truffaut's *Day for Night*. What is known is that the reason she retired was due to her marriage to Paolo Borghese (whom she met when she was 15, but did not marry until 1977); Borghese died in 1999. At last report she was living in a 17th century Borghese palace near Rome. Oscar-winning designer Luciana Arrighi is her sister.

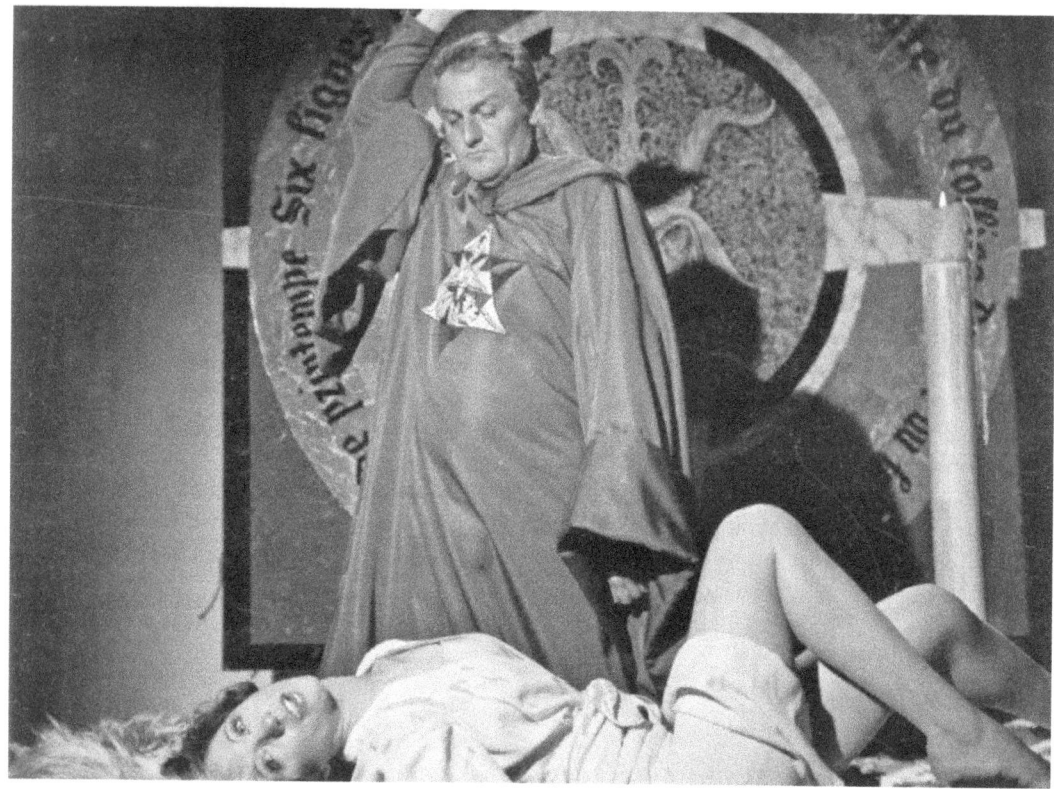

Nike Arrighi goes under Charles Gray's knife in a scene not actually included in *The Devil Rides Out*.

The Devil Rides Out is a Hammer classic, and Arrighi is one of the myriad reasons, holding her own against the commanding presences of heavyweights Christopher Lee and Charles Gray. But her character Tanith is definitely overpowered by the events of the film, and she splendidly portrays the struggle between the forces in contest for her very soul, particularly through wonderfully expressive eyes. She is a different type of Hammer heroine, beautiful but not buxom, and she possessed an ethereal quality that lent itself well to her character, who exists almost in a dream state, constantly buffeted about by forces that she has no control over — and who care nothing about her as an individual, only what place she represents in their respective visions of order. The only influence Tanith has on events is after she dies and while she is dead — power which disappears after she has been resurrected and taken her place in the accepted order. Her career may have been short, but at least it included this film, for which she will be long remembered.

Other genre credits: TELEVISION: *Out of the Unknown*: "The Machine Stops," 1966 (Airship Attendant)

Asher, Jane (1946–)

BIRTHPLACE: Marylebone, London, England.

FILMS: *The Big Deadly Game*, 1954 (Little Girl); *The Quatermass Xperiment*, 1955 (Little Girl)

TELEVISION: *Journey to the Unknown*: "Somewhere in a Crowd," 1968 (Marielle)

BIOGRAPHY — Gorgeous Jane Asher, sister of the Peter of Peter and Gordon, started her career as an in-demand child actress and got "Hammered" three times, most memorably as the little girl who almost gets consumed by the rapidly changing Richard Wordsworth in *The Quatermass Xperiment*, but who is spared by his last vestige of humanity. She went on to have a substantial career and is still active; she is also president of Britain's National Autism Society. She was briefly Paul McCartney's fiancée.

Other genre credits: FILMS: *The Masque of the Red Death*, Alta Vista Productions, 1964 (Francesca); TELEVISION: *Tales of the Unexpected*: "The Last of the Midnight Gardeners," 1984 (Jane)

Asherson, Dorothy Renee (1915–)

BIRTHPLACE: Kensington, London, England.

FILM: *Rasputin, the Mad Monk*, 1966 (Tsarina)

BIOGRAPHY — Renee Asherson's small part in *Rasputin, the Mad Monk* belies a large reputation as one of Britain's most respected actresses of television, screen, and particularly of the Shakespearean stage. She made her debut at the age of 20 in *Romeo and Juliet*, after having attended the Webber Douglas School of Dramatic Art. The next year she was playing opposite Laurence Olivier in *Henry V*. Her part in *Rasputin* was originally supposed to have been much larger, which is the reason they were able to persuade her to do the film, but due to cost overruns, many of her scenes had to be cut, a situation about which she was not pleased. She remained active until her last film appearance, which came in 2001 in *The Others*, starring Nicole Kidman.

Other genre credits: FILMS: *The Day the Earth Caught Fire*, Pax Films, 1961 (Angela); *Theater of Blood*, Cineman Productions, 1973 (Mrs. Maxwell); *The Others*, Cruise/Wagner Productions, 2001 (Old Lady)

Atwood, Kitty (1893–Unknown)

FILMS: *The Curse of the Werewolf*, 1961 (Midwife); *The Witches*, 1966 (Mrs. McDowall)

Kitty Atwood was a veteran British character actress who is best remembered by Hammer fans as the woman who delivered little Leon in *The Curse of the Werewolf*.

Other genre credits: TELEVISION: *The Avengers*: "Death of a Batman," 1966 (Edith Wrightson)

Aubrey, Angharad

FILM: *The Nanny*, 1965 (Susie Fane)

Aubrey-Smith, Debbie

FILM: *Creatures the World Forgot*, 1971 (Prehistoric Woman)

Audley, Maxine (1923–1992)

BIRTHPLACE: London, England.

FILMS: *Hell Is a City*, 1960 (Julia Martineau); *Frankenstein Must Be Destroyed*, 1969 (Ella Brandt)

BIOGRAPHY—Maxine Audley was very active in television, films, and especially the stage. She made two films for Hammer, first as the estranged wife of Stanley Baker in *Hell Is a City*, and another wife nine years later in *Frankenstein Must Be Destroyed*. In the latter she is shocked to be visited by her husband and finding out he's not exactly the man she married.

Other genre credits: FILMS: *Peeping Tom*, Michael Powell Theatre, 1960 (Mrs. Stephens); *The Brain*, Central Cinema Company Film, 1962 (Marion Fane) TELEVISION: *The Voodoo Factor*: "The Malayan," "The Professor," "The Spiders," 1959; "The Elixir," "The Missing Factor," "Operation Lifeboat," 1960 (Marion Whittaker); *Out of This World*: "Little Lost Robot," 1962 (Dr. Susan Calvin); *Space: 1999*: "The Last Enemy," 1976 (Theia)

Aukin, Liane (1936–)

BIRTHPLACE: London, England.

FILMS: *The Phantom of the Opera*, 1962 (Maria); *The Devil Rides Out*, 1968 (Satanist)

BIOGRAPHY—Liane Aukin was a British character actress with 20 titles to her credit in a career that lasted 17 years. Most of these titles were for television; her two Hammers are her only two feature film credits. In *The Phantom of the Opera*, she is the diva terrorized by Herbert Lom into quitting the opera, thus clearing the path for Heather Sears; her screen time is limited but her scream time results in one of the most full-throated, ear-piercing howls in Hammer History. *The Devil Rides Out* finds her as just one of the gang of devil-worshippers that, as in all of Hammer's Satanist films, seems to be no more debauched than the attendees of any typical Oasis concert. She retired in 1976 to devote her time to writing.

Other genre credits: TELEVISION: *Out of the Unknown*: "The Fox and the Forest," 1965 (Sarah Kirsten/Susan Travis); *The Avengers*: "All Done with Mirrors," 1968 (Miss Tiddiman)

Babus, Hulya

FILM: *Countess Dracula*, 1971 (Belly Dancer)

Baddeley, Hermione (1906–1986)

REAL NAME: Ruby Hermione Youlanda Clinton-Baddeley; BIRTHPLACE: Broseley, Shropshire, England.

FILM: *Women Without Men*, 1956 (Grace)

TELEVISION: *Journey to the Unknown*: Mrs. Kass, "Eve," 1968

BIOGRAPHY—A descendent of Revolutionary War general (on the losing side) Sir Henry Clinton, Hermione Baddeley was one of Britain's most popular character actresses, playing her first role at the dawn of sound in 1928. She was nominated for a Tony and an Oscar, and along the way provided solid support in such family classics as *Mary Poppins*. She tallied two Hammer films; the first was the undistinguished *Women Without Men*. But in the *Journey to the Unknown* episode "Eve" she really hit a home run: a hilarious turn as a frumpy, saucy, oversexed landlady who keeps trying to lure charming, young, and bonkers Dennis Waterman downstairs for a bit of action, but he only has eyes for the shop dummy who appears to him as Carol Lynley. Baddeley had previously appeared with Lynley in the Jean Harlow biopic *Harlow*. She played her last role in 1985, and passed away the following year.

Other genre credits: FILM: *Scrooge*, George Minter Productions, 1951 TELEVISION: *Bewitched*: "I Get Your Nanny, You Get My Goat," 1967 (Elspeth); *Batman*: "The Great Train Robbery," "The Great Escape," 1968 (Frontier Fanny); *Rod Serling's Night Gallery*: "Lindemann's Catch/A Feast of Blood/The Late Mr. Peddington," 1972 (Mrs. Gray); *The Bionic Woman*: "Black Magic," 1976 (Aunt Tess); *The New Adventures of Wonder Woman*: "A Date with Doomsday," 1979 (Mrs. Thrip)

Baker, Carrie

FILM: *Dracula Has Risen from the Grave*, 1968 (First Victim)

BIOGRAPHY—The term "biography" in this case is a misnomer, because I know practically nothing about Baker, other than the fact that *Dracula Has Risen from the Grave* was her first film. What is known is that she makes one of the most stunning and shocking entrances of any Hammer Heroine, bar none, as she's the corpse hanging upside down in place of the clapper in its unforgettable opening scene. This nightmarish, Sadean imagery was naturally used as a promotional aspect of the film, along with the blackly humorous (or merely foolish, depending on your point of view) tagline "Ring out the news—*Dracula Has Risen from the Grave!*"

Balfour, Penny

FILM: *The Resident*, 2011 (Drug Addict)

Other genre credits: FILMS: *Arthur and the Invisibles*, Europa Corporation, 2006 (Rose); *Arthur and the Revenge of Maltasard*, Europa Corporation, 2009 (Rose); *Arthur 3: The War of the Two Worlds*, Europa Corporation, 2010 (Rose)

Bankhead, Tallulah (1902–1968)

REAL NAME: Tallulah Brockman Bankhead; BIRTHPLACE: Huntsville, Alabama, USA.

FILM: *Fanatic*, 1965 (Mrs. Trefoile)

BIOGRAPHY—Tallulah Bankhead is a legendary star of the proverbial "stage, screen, and television," primarily the stage. Her legend was built as much on her personality as it was her not-inconsiderable acting ability, a personality that had the capability to flabbergast a town built of, by, and for outsized personalities and flamboyant excess. Her two most lasting contributions to pop culture are her role in Alfred Hitchcock's classic *Lifeboat* (1944; for which she won that year's New York Film Critics Circle Award for Best Actress) and the pronunciation of her trademark "*Dah*-ling!" which passed into the popular vernacular, recognizable enough to be lampooned by Bugs Bunny. It was her use of this expression that was one of the prime reasons that the title of *Fanatic* was changed to *Die! Die! My Darling!* For U.S. release (reportedly, Miss Bankhead was not amused).

Although Bette Davis must surely rate the top honors in Hammer's "Avenging Grannies" series, Miss Bankhead's Mrs. Trefoile is not far behind; she's a religious fanatic who imprisons and torments Stefanie Powers. And like Bette Davis, Miss Bankhead proved to be quite a handful on the set, although she was not the elemental force of nature that was Bette Davis, and she left the cast and crew with as many fond memories as painful ones. Director Silvio Narizzano felt her performance a bit too camp. True, she does tend to chew the scenery dread-

Tallulah Bankhead (right) and Yootha Joyce (left) try to shove some religion down the throat of Stefanie Powers in *Fanatic*.

fully, but enjoyably, as only an actor of her caliber could, and that's what *makes* the film — after all, she *is* a *Fanatic*! Bravura and "camp" it may be, but her performance never becomes high camp or self-parodying, and the threat to Powers' character is palpable in one of Hammer's best thrillers. The film and its U.S. title were immortalized in song by legendary horror-punk band The Misfits in their *Die! Die! My Darling!*

Barclay, Mary (1916–2008)

REAL NAME: Mary Biddulph; BIRTHPLACE: Williton, Somerset, England.
FILM: *Rasputin, the Mad Monk*, 1966 (Superior Lady)
Other genre credits: FILM: *The Headless Ghost*, Merton Park Studios, 1959 (Lady Ambrose)

Barker, Lucy

FILM: *Beyond the Rave*, 2008 (Psychiatrist)
Other genre credits: TELEVISION: *When Evil Calls* (Mini-Series): 2006 (Miss Nibb)

Barker, Lucy May (1992–)

BIRTHPLACE: Cleethorpes, Lincolnshire, England.
FILM: *The Woman in Black*, 2012 (Nursemaid)

Baron, Lynda (1939–)

BIRTHPLACE: Urmston, Greater Manchester, England.
FILM: *Hands of the Ripper*, 1971 (Long Liz)
BIOGRAPHY—This veteran British character actress of stage and screen trained at the Royal Academy of Dance, and made her first screen appearance in 1963. She's best-remembered for her role as the buxom Nurse Gladys in the Britcom *Open All Hours*, and has performed with three different Doctors in *Doctor Who*, spanning the very first to the most recent. She's also quite memorable in her *Hands of the Ripper* bit, for two reasons: as the buxom hooker "Long Liz," she bears the name and profession of an actual victim of Jack the Ripper, and she's on the receiving end of one of the most famous Hammer Horror murders of all time, the legendary hatpin-in-the-eye sequence that still hurts to watch. She's still active, with both eyes focused on the future.
Other genre credits: TELEVISION: *Doctor Who*: "A Holiday for the Doctor," 1966 (Voice of Singer); "Enlightenment" (Parts 3 and 4), 1983 (Captain Wrack); "Closing Time," 2011 (Val)

Barrese, Sasha (1981–)

BIRTHPLACE: Maui, Hawaii, USA.
FILM: *Let Me In*, 2010 (Virginia)
BIOGRAPHY—Gorgeous Sasha Barrese is the daughter of model and part-time actress Katherine Barrese and, like her *Let Me In* co-star Chloe Grace Moretz, she began her modeling and acting experience at a very early age, making her film debut along with her mother in 1989. She has a memorable supporting role in *Let Me In* as the woman who lives in the same block of flats as Moretz, who attacks her and turns her into a vampire. As Barrese lies in the hospital bed after the attack, a detective questions her boyfriend, and we can see her moving in the background; when the nurse walks in on her, she is sucking the blood from her own arm. The nurse doesn't see this and opens the curtains, whereupon Barrese bursts into flame and takes the unfortunate nurse with her. She's still active, and at the time of this writing, actually still lives with her mother.

Other genre credits: FILMS: *Hellraiser: Inferno*, Dimension Films, 2000 (Daphne Sharp); *The Ring*, DreamWorks SKG, 2002 (Teenage Girl #1) TELEVISION: *Paranormal Girl* (Movie), 2002 (Kelly Billingham); *Supernatural*: "Sin City," 2007 (Casey)

Barry, June (1935–)

BIRTHPLACE: Lancashire, England.
FILM: *The Terror of the Tongs*, 1961 (Tong Room Girl)
Other genre credits: TELEVISION: *Out of the Unknown*: "The Last Lonely Man," 1969 (Rowena Hale)

Barry, Mary Rose

FILM: *The Terror of the Tongs*, 1961 (Tong Room Girl)
Note: Her only film.

Barry, Michelle

FILM: *Moon Zero Two*, 1969 (Dancer)
Other genre credits: TELEVISION: *Doctor Who*: "Temple of Secrets," 1965 (Servant Girl)

Bartok, Eva (1927–1998)

REAL NAME: Eva Ivanova Marta Szoke; BIRTHPLACE: Budapest, Hungary.
FILMS: *Spaceways*, 1953 (Dr. Lisa Frank); *Break in the Circle*, 1955 (Lisa)

BIOGRAPHY — Eva Bartok is yet another actress in this book whose real life is as fascinating as any of her movie roles. She lived a fairly normal childhood until the Nazis came to power in Hungary, at which point her father disappeared, and she married a Hungarian Nazi officer so that she and her mother would not be sent to a concentration camp. The marriage, which she later described as a series of brutal rapes worse than death, was annulled at war's end. She escaped Hungary by marrying producer Alexander Paal; the union ended only two years later, but not before she had made inroads into the film industry. She became a leading lady with Burt Lancaster's *The Crimson Pirate*. This performance caught the eye of Hammer, and not long after, she was featured in two of their films: *Break in the Circle*, a film noir, and her sole genre effort for the company, *Spaceways*. *Spaceways* plays out more "soap opera" than "space opera," and for all its interplanetary aspirations, remains rather painfully earthbound. Bartok plays the type of strong, smart (and by extension, terribly sexy) woman scientist that was becoming a fixture of American sci-fi films of the time. But of course, it was required that these women with brains show that they were, underneath all that intelligence, "still a woman," and so she's required to fall in love with Howard Duff, a resolutely wooden, colorless actor who is not helped by lines like: "It's an old story, Lisa ... a guy with a one-track mind, nothing but rockets in his head, meets a beautiful woman with ... something entirely different in hers." She never fulfilled her early promise as an actress, but managed to keep herself in the headlines due to her number of marriages and high-profile affairs, including one with Frank Sinatra, whom she later claimed was the father of her daughter. But it soon became all too much for her to take, and four years after appearing in the certified classic *Blood and Black Lace*, she retired from films. She traveled first to Jakarta to find serenity, and then to Honolulu, where she opened a school teaching the Subud philosophy. She passed away in London in 1998.

Other genre credits: FILMS: *The Gamma People*, Warwick Film Productions, 1956 (Paula Wendt); *Blood and Black Lace*, Emmepi Cinematografica, 1964 (Contessa Cristina Como)

Bates, Samantha
FILM: *Creatures the World Forgot*, 1971 (Prehistoric Woman)

Baumann, Sue
FILM: *Moon Zero Two*, 1969 (Dancer)
Note: Her only film.

Beacham, Stephanie (1947–)
BIRTHPLACE: Barnet, England.
FILMS: *Dracula A.D. 1972*, 1972 (Jessica Van Helsing)
TELEVISION: *Hammer House of Mystery and Suspense*: "A Distant Scream," 1986 (Rosemary Richardson)

BIOGRAPHY—Like the Beach Boys' Brian Wilson, gorgeous Stephanie Beacham is completely deaf in her right ear and has only 75 percent capacity in her left, but that didn't stop her from becoming one of the big and small screen's busiest and most recognizable actresses. One of four children, she attended a Catholic girls' school, studied mime in France and trained

Christopher Lee looks like the cat that's eaten the cream in this publicity photograph from *Dracula A.D. 1972*, surrounded by (clockwise from top left) Stephanie Beacham, Marsha Hunt, Janet Key and Caroline Munro (courtesy Paul C. Riggie).

at RADA. She wanted to teach dance movement to deaf children, but a modeling career intervened and she soon began landing acting jobs in films and on television shows like *Jason King*. She starred opposite Marlon Brando in *The Nightcomers* (1971), in which she had a nude scene. This naturally brought her to the attention of Hammer, and the next year she was starring opposite Cushing and Lee in *Dracula A.D. 1972*. Since *A.D. 1972* is a bunch of old men's vision of "swinging" youth culture, then it follows that Ms. Beacham's role is their vision of a "liberated" young woman of the '70s, "free" to do and say as she pleases, but "confused" and shallow, thinking of little but "kicks." In fact, her last words to Van Helsing are "I'm sorry," which of course is her apology for her part in the preceding events, but can also be taken be taken as an apology for both her generation and gender. That being said, Jessica Van Helsing is the most mature of her group and the most skeptical of the amount of "kicks" to be found in Johnny Alucard's black mass. But of course, if she didn't go along, there'd be no story, so go along she does — in some of the most naff fashions and spouting risible "hip" dialogue. But due to her acting chops (and perhaps *because* of those fashions and dialogue), she manages to rise above, and create a memorable Hammer Heroine. She proved her versatility by going on to such polar-opposite roles as the saintly title character *Sister Kate* and villainous Sable Colby in *The Colbys* and *Dynasty*, as well as a goodly amount of genre work. The Golden Globe nominee never got too big for Hammer, though, and made a very happy return in 1986 to star in an episode of *Hammer House of Mystery and Suspense* with David Carradine. She is still quite beautiful and quite active in her chosen profession, as well as giving of herself as a spokeswoman for the American Speech, Language and Hearing Association. She also serves on the Board of Directors for Free Arts for Abused Children.

Other genre credits: FILMS: *The Devil's Widow*, Commonwealth United Entertainment, 1970 (Janet Ainsley); *The Nightcomers*, Elliot Kastner — Jay Kanter — Alan Ladd Jr. Productions, 1971 (Miss Jessel); *...And Now the Screaming Starts!*, Amicus Productions, 1973 (Catherine Fengriffen); *Schizo*, Heritage, 1976 (Beth); *Inseminoid* (a.k.a. *Horror Planet*), Jupiter Film Productions, 1981 (Kate); *The Witches Hammer*, Amber Pictures, 2006 (Madeline) TELEVISION: *UFO*: "Destruction," 1970 (Sarah); *Star Trek: The Next Generation*: "Ship in a Bottle," 1993 (Countess Bartholomew); *SeaQuest 2032*: "To Be or Not to Be," "The Devil's Window," "Treasure of the Mind," "Games," "Treasures of the Tonga Trench," "Brothers and Sisters," "Give Me Liberte," "Knight of Shadows," "Bad Water," "The Regulator," "SeaWest," "Photon Bullet," 1993; "Better Than Martians," "Nothing But the Truth," "Greed for a Pirate's Dream," "Whale Song," "The Stinger," "Hide and Seek," "The Last Lap at Luxury," "Abalon," "Such Great Patience," "The Good Death," "Higher Power," 1994 (Dr. Kristin Westphalen)

Beale, Erica

FILM: *Lust for a Vampire*, 1971 (Schoolgirl)

Bel Geddes, Barbara (1922–2005)

BIRTHPLACE: New York City, USA.
TELEVISION: *Journey to the Unknown*: "The Madison Equation," 1969 (Inga Madison)
BIOGRAPHY — The daughter of Norman Bel Geddes, blond, beautiful Barbara Bel Geddes first came to prominence on Broadway in 1946, and the following year made her film debut in *The Long Night* with Henry Fonda. Say what you will about Alfred Hitchcock, but he kept her working while she was under investigation by the House Un-American Activities Committee. She will be forever remembered by genre fans for her performance in Hitchcock's classic *Vertigo*, as the woman hopelessly, futilely in love with James Stewart. She'll be remembered by others for her role in TV's *Dallas*; she did over 200 episodes from 1978 through

1990, and won numerous awards, including an Emmy and Golden Globe. She added a real touch of class to her starring role in *Journey to the Unknown*'s "The Madison Equation," in which she plays computer genius Inga Madison. Bel Geddes retired in 1990 to pursue a career as a fine artist; she also authored two children's books and created a greeting card line. She died of lung cancer in 2005.

Other genre credits: FILM: *Vertigo*, Alfred Hitchcock Productions–Paramount Pictures, 1958 (Midge Wood) TELEVISION: *Alfred Hitchcock Presents*: "The Foghorn," 1958 (Lucia Clay); "Lamb to the Slaughter," 1958 (Mary Maloney); "The Morning of the Bride," 1959 (Helen Brewster); "Sybilla," 1960 (Sybilla Meade)

Bell, Ann (1940–)

BIRTHPLACE: Wallasley, Cheshire, England.
FILMS: *The Witches*, 1966 (Sally Benson)
TELEVISION: *Journey to the Unknown*: "Somewhere in a Crowd," 1968 (Ruth Searle)
Other genre credits: FILMS: *Dr. Terror's House of Horrors*, Amicus Productions, 1965 (Ann Rogers); *Fahrenheit 451*, Anglo Enterprises, 1966 (Doris); *The Shuttered Room*, Seven Arts Productions, 1967 TELEVISION: *The Avengers*: "The Deadly Air," 1961 (Barbara Anthony); *Out of This World*: "Divided We Fall," 1962 (Jean Bailey); *Mystery and Imagination*: "The Flying Dragon," 1966 (Countess de St. Valyre)

Bennett, Jill (1931–1990)

REAL NAME: Nora Noel Jill Bennett; BIRTHPLACE: Penang, the Straits Settlements, in Malaysia.
FILM: *The Nanny*, 1965 (Aunt Penelope Fane)
BIOGRAPHY — Trained at the Amersham Repertory and RADA, Jill Bennett made her first stage appearance in 1949, and her first film appearance in *The Long Dark Hall*. She was married at one time to playwright John Osborne; she starred in several of his plays, and won two awards for her role in his "Time Present." She was also a talented author herself. She is unforgettable as Aunt Pen in *The Nanny*, as the woman who dies when Bette Davis withholds her heart medication from her. Her death is especially upsetting because she is the only one in the movie who is not nuts in some way, the only one who has any grasp on reality. The firm-jawed beauty was also quite effective in her role as Peter Cushing's wife in *The Skull*. She was also a Bond Girl, playing the wonderfully named Jacoba Brink in *For Your Eyes Only*. She was active in all the aforementioned areas of performance until her untimely, tragic death in 1990; her suicide stemmed from a lifelong battle with depression and the traumatizing effects of her marriage to Osborne.

Other genre credits: FILMS: *The Skull*, Amicus Productions, 1965 (Jane Maitland); *The Haunting of Julia*, Canadian Film Development Corporation, 1977 (Lily Lofting); *For Your Eyes Only*, Eon Productions, 1981 (Jacoba Brink) TELEVISION: *Worlds Beyond*: "The Barrington Case," 1987

Benson, Lindy (1953–)

BIRTHPLACE: Muswell Hill, London, England.
FILM: *To the Devil a Daughter*, 1976 (Second Girl)

Bentinck, Anna

FILMS: *Vampire Circus*, 1972 (Schoolgirl); *To the Devil a Daughter*, 1976 (Isabel)

Benton, Barbi (1950–)

REAL NAME: Barbara Lynn Klein; BIRTHPLACE: New York City, New York, USA.

TELEVISION: *Hammer House of Mystery and Suspense*: "And the Wall Came Tumbling Down," 1985 (Caroline Trent)

BIOGRAPHY—Large-breasted American model, actress, singer, and interior decorator Barbi Benton is a former "*Hee-Haw* Honey" (kind of like a Bond Girl, except with more corn starch), *Playboy* cover girl, and girlfriend of big-time monster fan Hugh Hefner, who lent her two most valuable assets to several low-budget genre efforts, including a role in the "And the Wall Came Tumbling Down" episode of the third Hammer television series, *Hammer House of Mystery and Suspense*. She plays a paranormal researcher that is every Briton's wet dream of American stereotypes: brash, arrogant, loud, and aggressive, doing what could be construed as a parody of Jane Fonda, if only Ms. Benton could act. She is still active, although most of her appearances since 1986 have been as herself, capitalizing on her association with *Playboy*. She is happily married to a man convicted of tax fraud, and believes that mink are born to be turned into fur coats, because it's so much better than not being born at all. She is reportedly considering embarking on a new career in neurosurgery.

Other genre credits: FILMS: *Hospital Massacre*, Golan-Globus Productions, 1982 (Susan Jeremy); *Deathstalker*, Aries Cinematografica Argentina, 1983 (Codille)

Berova, Olinka (1943–)

REAL NAME: Olga Schoberova; BIRTHPLACE: Prague, Czech Republic.

FILM: *The Vengeance of She*, 1968 (Carol/Ayesha)

BIOGRAPHY—Poor Olinka. She only had to follow "The Most Beautiful Woman in the World," Ursula Andress, in the sequel to the hit *She*. The sequel had been announced quickly after the original became a success, and it was reported that Andress would reprise her role of Ayesha, but by the time the cameras rolled, She-Who-Must-Be-Obeyed became She-Who-Refused-to-Do-the-Sequel. And so yet another *Playboy* alum (March 1964's Berova) became yet another Hammer starlet, courtesy of some cordial persuasion by Fox. (She was featured on the *Playboy* cover as well as a pictorial inside, "The Girls of Russia and the Iron Curtain Countries"; she was the first Czech to appear in the magazine.) The star power may have dropped when Andress was replaced by Berova, but in actuality, the acting power did not, not that much. Andress had a barrelful of haughty self-confidence, but she herself admitted she was not much of an actress, and so the only real loss is in regal bearing and sheer presence; physically, the match could not have been much closer. The problem was, the sequel was nowhere near a match to the original. The story,

Olinka Berova looks to the heavens for talent other than what's on display (or not) in *The Vengeance of She* (courtesy Mel Bridgeman).

unlike Ms. Berova, had precious little "oomph"; sorely missed were Christopher Lee (killed in the first film), Peter Cushing (slated for a cameo which was not filmed), and even Bernard Cribbins. And then it has the nerve completely to waste Andre Morell, (who had been in *She*, but as a different character) and Noel Willman in bit parts, an offense compounded by the fact that it was the last Hammer film for both. The only wit on display comes in the in-joke form of lettering on the side of a truck proclaiming it to be a vehicle belonging to Bertera & Company, which was the last name of production manager Dennis Bertera. Berova made 22 films in several different countries in 22 years; her first screen appearance was a bit part in *We Were 10* (1963), and her last was in the action film *Vrak* (1984). She once again lives in Prague, under her real name, her screen career a thing to be thought of always, but never indulged in again.

Other genre credits: FILMS: *Voyage to the End of the Universe*, Filmov Studio Barrandov, 1964 (Crew Member); *Who Wants to Kill Jessie?* Ceskoslovensky Statni Film, 1966 (Jessie)

Beswick, Martine (1941–)

BIRTHPLACE: Port Antonio, Jamaica.

FILMS: *One Million Years B.C.*, 1966 (Nupondi); *Slave Girls* (a.k.a. *Prehistoric Women*), 1967 (Queen Kari); *Dr. Jekyll and Sister Hyde*, 1971 (Sister Hyde)

BIOGRAPHY—She is a stunningly beautiful woman and more-than-accomplished actress who has appeared in A-list productions, Z-grade horror films and everything else in between. But Martine Beswick will, either fairly or unfairly, probably be remembered best for being involved in two of the most famous catfights in cinema history. Although many Internet profiles list her as a British actress (her father was British, her mother Portuguese), Martine absolutely defines herself as Jamaican. It has also been reported that she won the beauty pageant title of Miss Jamaica; she admits to having competed, but she is quick to correct it by frankly (and gleefully) admitting that she didn't win because she partied too hard. The IMDb credits her with having appeared in the title sequence of *Dr. No* as one of the shapely silhouettes, but this isn't so, although she did audition for the film, and the director, Terence Young (who was to become a lifelong friend), guaranteed her that she would be in the next one—something she took with a grain of salt at the time. Young ultimately proved as good as his word, and she achieved cinematic immortality by engaging in Catfight #1 in a scene in *From Russia with Love*. Her status as one of the most iconic of the Bond Girls was cemented with her appearance as the ill-fated Paula in *Thunderball*, a heavily publicized part that led directly to her first role with Hammer in *One Million Years B.C.*, which she won solely on the strength of her being a Bond Girl; no audition needed, thank you.

While it was *Thunderball* that got her the part in the classic Hammer-Harryhausen collaboration, it was obviously the earlier Bond that was the inspiration for her similar moment in *One Million Years B.C.*—and while it doesn't contain the sadistic undercurrent of the scene in *From Russia with Love*, it has a more distinct visual contrast between its two combatants, the feral, dark-haired "Bad Girl" and star Raquel Welch's fair-haired "Good Girl." She and Welch did not get along well, but there was none of the true animosity that she felt towards her other catfight co-star, Aliza Gur, in *From Russia with Love*. The producers wanted to use body doubles for the sequence, but Martine and Welch insisted on doing it themselves. Martine is saved from the normal consequence of battle, which would be death, by Welch's Loana showing the brutal Rock Tribe its first example of compassion; unfortunately, that demise has only been delayed, and Martine is ultimately swallowed by the Earth in the film's climactic volcanic upheaval. But Martine got along well with one of her other co-stars, John Richardson, and the film saw the beginning of a relationship that lasted for the next six years; she still describes Richardson as the love of her life.

Are you being served? Martine Beswick certainly is, by an unidentified slave girl in *Prehistoric Women* (courtesy Paul C. Riggie).

It has been suggested in some quarters that many Hammer films, with their stock actors and characters, oftentimes stock scenarios, and marketing techniques, seem like an enormous self-parodic mass, full-blooded (literally) versions of *Carry On*, or a crazy-house mirror of the standard costume drama. If one accepts this theory, then *Slave Girls* can be seen as the biggest put-on of all; in fact, later, producer-director-writer Michael Carreras himself suggested that the only thing missing from the film were word balloons and opticals like "ZAP!" and "POW!" It has also been suggested that the film is "unwatchable," but this is simply not true; *Prehistoric*

Women is always eminently watchable, if only in sheer and utter disbelief (or, let's be honest, for all the gorgeous girls). Martine herself calls it one of the worst films ever, absolute nonsense, but does concede that it was a great deal of fun to make. The over-the-top approach to the film often left cast and crew in hysterics, such as the time when Carreras asked Martine to stroke the horn of the rhino statue. Martine certainly looks like she's having a grand time; it is a bravura performance that leaves no piece of scenery unchewed, whether it's stroking that horn, throwing a tantrum, savage lust, unfettered cruelty, or her both erotic and bizarre "mating dance" for the hero, like a demented Jurassic stripper, a Bizarro World "exotic dancer." The film is loaded with symbolism, for those who wish to find it, but Martine finds great amusement in the fact that anybody would make the effort. Indeed, if one over-analyzes, the results can range from the ludicrous to the possibly even mean-spirited — such as a tribe of "independent" and "strong" women that trivializes and makes slaves of men, but worships a phallic symbol that ultimately penetrates and kills Kari. There are also scenes of eye-rolling, dancing blacks who wait in eager anticipation for the sacrifice of another white "bride." But this delirious shambles is too silly to be racist and so chaotic as to make camp seem too kind a definition.

If one is looking for Freudian folderol, one need look no further than *Dr. Jekyll and Sister Hyde*. Martine's performance as Kari had been powerful, but also a caricature; here, she sinks her teeth into a more complex characterization. Her reaction to the first transformation is priceless: the look of shock when she sees her face in the mirror, then increasing delight as she discovers how complete the transformation has been, and then agony as she begins to change back. But the delight she takes in becoming her new self is nothing compared to the delight she takes in evil; she's one of Hammer's most memorable monsters. *Sister Hyde* was filled with screenwriter Brian Clemens' customary droll, sly and twisted wit, such as the scene where Martine seduces and kills Jekyll's randy associate, and when she tells Susan Brodrick how fond her "brother" is of her, and then in the same motion caresses Brodrick's brother's (facial) cheek, and tells him how fond she is of him.

Martine went on to do a great deal more genre work, but in the 1990s she more or less retired from actively seeking roles, and is now strengthening her legacy with appearances in documentaries and at fan conventions and simply enjoying life, as she has always done.

Other genre credits: FILMS: *From Russia with Love*, Danjaq/Eon Productions, 1963 (Zora); *Thunderball*, Eon Productions, 1965 (Paula); *Thirty Dangerous Seconds*, 1972; *Seizure*, Astral Bellevue Pathe, 1974 (Queen of Evil); *The Offspring*, Conquest Productions, 1987 (Katherine White); *Cyclone*, Cinetel Films, 1987 (Waters); *Evil Spirits*, 1990 (Vanya); *Trancers II*, Full Moon Entertainment, 1991 (Nurse Trotter); *Critters 4*, New Line Cinema, 1992 (Voice of Angela); *Night of the Scarecrow*, Republic Pictures, 1995 (Barbara) TELEVISION: *Rod Serling's Night Gallery*: "The Last Laurel," 1971 (Susan Davis); *Strange New World* (Movie), 1975 (Tana); *The Six Million Dollar Man*: "Outrage in Balinderry," 1975 (Julia Flood); *Shali Giba*, "The Thunderbird Connection," 1976 (Shali Giba); *The Next Step Beyond*: "Woman in the Mirror," 1978; *Devil Dog: The Hound of Hell* (Movie), 1978 (Woman with Red Hair); *The Powers of Matthew Star*: "Swords and Quests, 1983 (Katya).

Betts, Kirsten; a.k.a. Kirsten Lindholm (1943–)

REAL NAME: Kirsten Lindholm Andreassen; BIRTHPLACE: Odense, Denmark.

FILMS: *Crescendo*, 1970 (Catherine); *The Vampire Lovers*, 1970 (Vampire Girl); *Lust for a Vampire*, 1971 (Peasant Girl); *Twins of Evil*, 1971 (Young Girl)

BIOGRAPHY — Gorgeous blonde Kirsten Betts (one of a host of names) is another Hammer Heroine whose career was short and sweet; nearly every appearance she made on screen was for the company. Her first was as the former wife of James Olson in *Crescendo*; all he's got is a photograph and he realizes she's not coming back any more, which prompts Jimmy's mother to try and turn Stefanie Powers into another Kirsten. More importantly, she is one of the continuity links between all three films of the Karnstein Trilogy, although she plays a different character in each; perhaps it would be more proper to say that she's a member of a very small Karnstein "stock company." Her most memorable part in the three is in *The Vampire Lovers*, as the Karnstein descendant who attempts to seduce Douglas Wilmer until he lops her noggin off in a powerful, horrific prologue. In *Lust for a Vampire*, she is the peasant girl kidnapped and sacrificed in a blood ritual. She dies violently a third time in *Twins of Evil*, as she's burned at the stake by Sgt. Peter Cushing and his Howlin' Puritans. She looked as though she was on the right track to a steady career, but in 1971, she literally left it all behind when she became an adherent of Kundalini yoga; she moved to California with her husband and became a practicing Sikh. She then moved to Hawaii and became a faith healer. She now teaches yoga in New Zealand. She has undergone another name change, to Elandra Kirsten Meredith, and she is also known by her Sikh religious name of Vikram Kaur Khalsa.

Other genre credits: TELEVISION: *UFO*: "Timelash," 1971 (Actress)

Birthistle, Eva (1974–)

BIRTHPLACE: Bray, Ireland.
FILM: *Wake Wood*, 2011 (Louise)

BIOGRAPHY—Classic Irish beauty Eva Birthistle studied at the Gaiety School of Acting, and has twice won the Irish Film and Television Award as Best Actress. She played the female lead in *Wake Wood*, another offering from the New Hammer (although technically it was an independent film that Hammer did not produce, just distribute). The film itself wears its influences on its sleeve: It's an Irish mash-up of *The Wicker Man* and *Pet Sematary*, with a dash of *The Omen* and other Creepy Little Kid movies for seasoning. The movie tells of grieving parents who participate in a pagan ritual to return their dead daughter to life for three days and ... well, you know how things like that always turn out. Birthistle is quite good as the mourning but not entirely truthful mother, but her performance is somewhat obscured by some very disturbing visuals, mostly centered on dogs and other animals, so be forewarned. Birthistle recently married.

Other genre credits: FILMS: *Reverb*, Reverb Productions, 2008 (Maddy); *The Daisy Chain*, Subotica Productions, 2008 (Cat); *The Children*, Vertigo Films, 2008 (Elaine)

Black, Isobel (1943–)

BIRTHPLACE: Edinburgh, Scotland.
FILMS: *The Kiss of the Vampire*, 1963 (Tania); *Twins of Evil*, 1971 (Ingrid Hoffer)

BIOGRAPHY—Isobel Black is the daughter of novelist and screenwriter Ian Stuart Black. Her career is much like that of her *Kiss of the Vampire* co-star Jennifer Daniel: Both spent the great majority of their careers in television, and both made two other feature films besides their efforts for Hammer. She only has a few scenes as Tania in *Kiss* but she makes each one unforgettable. She is first seen on the stairs, stealing furtive glances at their just-arrived guests, the hint of a smile on her lips and a foreboding twinkle in her eye. We soon see why: While her father, sister and brother put on an appearance of normality and entertain Daniel and her husband, Black steals out to the cemetery and reveals her (and their) true nature as she scoops dirt from a grave: "Why have you not been to see us, my sweet? Why have you waited so long? You know how much we've missed you ... you should not be lying here all alone." Her reverie is interrupted by Clifford Evans' vampire hunter, whose wrist she promptly sinks her fangs into, her wonderful eyes afire, and she runs away laughing to the safety of the castle.

Isobel Black is about to put the bite on Edward de Souza in this lobby card from *The Kiss of the Vampire* (courtesy Mel Bridgeman).

Much later, after Ms. Daniel has been kidnapped, her husband steals into the castle to rescue her. He surprises Tania in her bed and, thinking her to be an ally, believes she will help him find his wife. She does, but of course also leads him into the trap of the vampires — and then, as his wife looks on, she walks up to him slowly and then rips his shirt open, baring his chest and her fangs, and lights up again as she prepares to sink them into him. (Out of the whole family, Tania is the one who most seems to enjoy being a vampire.) Normally, scenes like this would steal the picture (and they come close), but the whole cast is excellent so these scenes are two gems among many. In *Twins of Evil*, she went from vampire to vampire's victim as the schoolmistress Ingrid. She retired in 1990 after her appearance in the television series *Castle of Adventure*.

Other genre credits: TELEVISION: *Invisible Man*: "The White Rabbit," 1959 (Collette); *Witch Wood* (Movie), 1964 (Katrine Yester); *The Avengers*: "Silent Dust," 1965 (Clare Prendergast); *Mystery and Imagination*: "The Curse of the Mummy," 1970 (Margaret Trelawney)

Blackman, Honor (1927–)

BIRTHPLACE: Plaistow, Newham, London, England.

FILMS: *The Glass Tomb*, 1955 (Jenny Pelham); *Danger List*, 1959 (Gillian Freeman); *To the Devil a Daughter*, 1976 (Anna)

Honor Blackman (left) advises Nastassja Kinski to change her habits in *To the Devil... a Daughter*.

BIOGRAPHY—The daughter of a statistician, an international movie star and a certified pop culture icon, Honor Blackman was there for both the Alpha and Omega of Hammer. Hammer films were a stop on the way up to that international stardom: Her roles in Hammer noir movies were among the many she essayed in similarly routine crime thrillers before becoming a household name in Britain as Mrs. Gale in *The Avengers* and a worldwide one as Pussy Galore in *Goldfinger*. She was also in the original company's last horror film. She's not well served in any respect in *To the Devil a Daughter*: As the female half of a "swinger" couple enlisted to protect Nastassja Kinski, she wears some of the most mortifying fashions in film history, and on top of that, she dies by a long-handled metal comb through the skull; no fun for anyone, then. Fortunately for her (and unfortunately for Hammer), not many people saw *To the Devil a Daughter* on its original release (and not many more want to now), and so remains a blip on an otherwise distinguished career. She is also quite fondly remembered by genre fans for her role as Hera, Queen of the Gods, in the Ray Harryhausen classic *Jason and the Argonauts*. As of this writing, she is still alive and well, dividing her time between acting and activism; Ms. Blackman is heavily involved in the campaign to move Great Britain out of the Middle Ages and replace its monarchy with an elected head of state. This puts her at odds with fellow Hammer alum and confirmed Monarchist Joan Collins.

Other genre credits: FILMS: *Daughter of Darkness*, Victor Hanbury Productions, 1948 (Julie Tallent); *Jason and the Argonauts*, Columbia Pictures, 1963 (Hera); *Goldfinger*, Eon Productions, 1964 (Pussy Galore); *Fright*, Fantale Films, 1972 (Helen); *The Cat and the Canary*,

Grenadier Films, 1978 (Susan Sillsby); *Tale of the Mummy*, Seventh Voyage, 1998 (Captain Shea); *Cockneys vs. Zombies*, Tea Shop & Film Company, 2011 (Peggy) TELEVISION: *Invisible Man*: "Blind Justice," 1959 (Katherine Holt); *The Avengers*: "Mr. Teddy Bear," "Propellant 23," "Bullseye," "The Mauritius Penny," "Death of a Great Dane," "Death on the Rocks," "Traitor in Zebra," "The Big Thinker," "Death Dispatch," 1962; "Intercrime," "Immortal Clay," "Warlock," "The Golden Eggs," "The White Dwarf," "Conspiracy of Silence," "Six Hands Across a Table," "Killer Whale," "Brief for Murder," "The Undertakers," "Man with Two Shadows," "The Nutshell," "Death of a Batman," "November 5," "The Gilded Cage," "Second Sight," "The Medicine Man," "The Grandeur That Was Rome," "The Golden Fleece," "Don't Look Behind You," "Death a la Carte," "Dressed to Kill," 1963; "The White Elephant," "The Little Wonders," "The Wringer," "Mandrake," "The Secrets Broker," "Trojan Horse," "Build a Better Mousetrap," "The Outside-In Man," "The Charmers," "Concerto," "Esprit de Corps," "Lobster Quadrille," 1964 (Cathy Gale); *Orpheus in the Underworld* (Movie), 1983 (Juno/Empress Eugenie); *Doctor Who*: "The Trial of a Time Lord," Parts 9, 10, 11, 12, 1986 (Professor Lasky); *Dr. Terrible's House of Horrible*: "Lesbian Vampire Lovers of Lust," 2001 (Transeet Van Eyre)

Blair, Isla (1944–)

BIRTHPLACE: Bangalore, India.
FILM: *Taste the Blood of Dracula*, 1970 (Lucy Paxton)
TELEVISION: *Hammer House of Mystery and Suspense*: "Tennis Court," 1985 (Eileen)
BIOGRAPHY — Indian-born, the daughter of a tea planter of British descent, lovely Isla Blair demonstrated a flair for the performing arts at an early age, and attended the Royal Academy of Dramatic Arts. Her first stage appearance was in the classic comedy *A Funny Thing Happened on the Way to the Forum*, and her first film role was a genre picture, *Dr. Terror's House of Horrors*. (It would have been *A Hard Day's Night*, but her scene was cut.) She gives a memorable performance in *Taste the Blood of Dracula* as the count's pawn in his scheme of revenge against three upper-class hypocrites, in a role that somewhat recalls that of Barbara Shelley in *Dracula, Prince of Darkness*. As the more mature friend of Linda Hayden, recently engaged, she too is taken before the younger girl and becomes a vampire; she gets a particularly nice scene after she comes to life when her father (one of the hypocrites) cannot bring himself to stake her. Blair and Hayden corner the ill-fated pater, Hayden holding him down while Blair turns the tables and kills him with the stake, an evil smile curling her lips. But she is killed by Dracula when he has no more use for her, and the next we see of Blair is her corpse floating in Black Park Lake; but the illusion is rather destroyed when Hayden's boyfriend pulls her out of the lake and she grabs his waist! She returned to Hammer Films in 1985 for an appearance in their third and last television series, *The Hammer House of Mystery and Suspense*, in which she gives an affecting, emotional performance as a woman torn between two lovers, who carries with her a terrible secret and guilt. And she is actress enough (and still beautiful enough) to be able to play herself as a young woman, adding gravitas to an episode of a series which did not always possess it. She has continued to appear in genre-related material; she is married to actor Julian Glover, and in their joint appearance in *Indiana Jones and the Last Crusade*, their characters were also married.

Other genre credits: FILMS: *Dr. Terror's House of Horrors*, Amicus Productions, 1965 (Pretty Girl); *Indiana Jones and the Last Crusade*, Paramount Pictures, 1989 (Mrs. Donovan). TELEVISION: *The Avengers*: "A Funny Thing Happened on the Way to the Station," 1967 (Bride); *The Canterville Ghost* (Movie), 1975 (Lady Stutfield); *Alien Attack* (Movie), 1976, (Alien); *Space: 1999*: "War Games," 1975 (Alien); "Journey to Where," 1976 (Carla); *Blake's 7*: "Duel,"

1978 (Sinofar); *Doctor Who*: "The King's Demons," 1983 (Isabella); *The Quatermass Experiment* (Movie), 2005 (Blaker)

Blair, Joyce (1932–2006)

REAL NAME: Joyce Ogus; BIRTHPLACE: London, England.
FILM: *Journey to Murder*, 1971 (Betty)
TELEVISION: *Journey to the Unknown*: "Do Me a Favor and Kill Me," 1968 (Betty)

Blake, Ann (Died 1973)

FILM: *The Curse of Frankenstein*, 1957 (A Wife)

Blake, Anne (1913–1973)

FILMS: *Scream of Fear*, 1961 (Marie); *The Curse of the Werewolf*, 1961 (Rosa Valiente)
Other genre credits: FILMS: *The Private Life of Sherlock Holmes*, Compton Films, 1970 (Madame) TELEVISION: *Quatermass and the Pit*: "The Wild Hunt," 1959 (Woman Journalist)

Blake, Beverly

FILM: *Creatures the World Forgot*, 1971 (The Young Mistress)

Blare, Amber

FILM: *Taste the Blood of Dracula*, 1970 (Bordello Girl)

Blythe, Domini Miranda (1947–2010)

BIRTHPLACE: Upton, Cheshire, England.
FILM: *Vampire Circus*, 1972 (Anna Mueller)
BIOGRAPHY—A British-born actress who later immigrated to Canada, Blythe graduated from the Central School of Speech and Drama and made her stage debut in *Oh Calcutta*. This prepared her for her first feature film role as Anna Mueller in *Vampire Circus*, in which she also gets naked. But her role as the vampire's mistress raises many questions. It's a deliciously perverse performance in a deliciously perverse film, in which she receives sexual gratification from the seduction and death of a little girl before receiving sexual gratification from the vampire. Then after the angry villagers stake the count, they form a gauntlet to beat her. When her husband saves her, she spits in his face for his trouble and runs back into the castle to receive the vampire's dying instructions. But at no time is there ever any evidence of her actually *being* a vampire. The audience *assumes* that she perishes or is trapped when the angry villagers blow up the castle, although there is some question to this as her last shot shows her running towards an opening that had not, as yet, blown up. But whether she survives the blast seems immaterial at the climax, when the gypsy woman (Adrienne Corri) transforms into Blythe as she dies — this despite her having not actually being portrayed as a vampire or shown to have any other proclivities towards supernatural abilities. This was her only genre effort.

Boht, Margo

FILM: *Scars of Dracula*, 1970 (Landlord's Wife)
Other genre credits: TELEVISION: *Doomwatch*: "Invasion," 1970 (Woman); "You Killed Toby Wren," 1970 (Woman)

Boize, Sandra

FILM: *Hysteria*, 1965 (English Girl)

Bond, Sidonie

FILM: *Demons of the Mind*, 1972 (Mrs. Zorn)
Other genre credits: TELEVISION: *The Avengers*: "How to Succeed ... at Murder," 1966 (Annie)

Borgo, Marianne

TELEVISION: *Hammer House of Mystery and Suspense*: "The Corvini Inheritance," 1985 (Madame Roulier)
BIOGRAPHY—Beautiful Marianne Borgo is a still-active French character actress who has done much of her work in that country. She has a small role in "The Corvini Inheritance" as the posh wife of the man who wants to sell a cursed jewelry collection.

Borland, Katie

FILM: *Beyond the Rave*, 2008 (Tina)

Boshier, Joan

FILM: *Creatures the World Forgot*, 1971 (Prehistoric Woman)

Boulting, Ingrid; a.k.a. Ingrid Brett (1947–)

BIRTHPLACE: Transvaal, South Africa.
FILMS: *The Witches*, 1966 (Linda Rigg); *Journey to Murder*, 1971 (Vera Verdew)
TELEVISION: *Journey to the Unknown*: "The Killing Bottle," 1969 (Vera Verdew)
BIOGRAPHY—Flaxen-haired Ingrid Boulting is the niece of director-writer-producer Roy Boulting. She moved to London at age eight, later training with the Royal Ballet Company and becoming a much-photographed model. Her first screen role came in 1966, and later that year she appeared for Hammer as the virginal Linda in *The Witches*, where she's seemingly an innocent but, like the "sacrificial lamb" (and the whole village) in *The Wicker Man*, she's not only in on it, but into it. Boulting's youthful beauty allowed her to play a 12-year-old girl at the age of 19. And she didn't look a day older two years later when she returned to the company to play the female lead in the *Journey to the Unknown* episode "The Killing Bottle." It's one of the series' more ridiculous installments, due entirely to Roddy McDowall's incredibly over-the-top portrayal of a heterosexual hipster whose dialogue, like that in *Dracula A.D. 1972*, comes off as some geezer's idea of what "the kids" talk like, and quickly crosses the line between camp and cosmically bad. She played her last role in 2006 in *Conversations with God*; she is now an artist and yoga instructor.
Other genre credits: TELEVISION: *The Twilight Zone*: "Ye Gods," 1985 (Woman)

Bowers, Lally (1917–1984)

REAL NAME: Kathleen Bowers; BIRTHPLACE: Oldham, Lancashire, England.
FILM: *Dracula A.D. 1972*, 1972 (Matron Party Hostess)
Other genre credits: FILM: *Screamtime*, Salon Productions, 1986 (Mrs. Kingsley) TELEVISION: *The Avengers*: "The Undertakers," 1963 (Mrs. Renter); *Mystery and Imagination*: "Uncle Silas," 1968 (Lady Ilbury); *Tales of the Unexpected*: "Georgy Porgy," 1980 (Miss Elphinstone); "A Sad Loss," 1983 (Alicia Hawksworth)

B

Brackenbury, Pat

FILM: *Dr. Jekyll and Sister Hyde*, 1971 (Helen)

Bradshaw, Irene

FILM: *Dr. Jekyll and Sister Hyde*, 1971 (Yvonne)
Other genre credits: TELEVISION: *The Avengers*: "One for the Mortuary," 1961 (Maid); "The Golden Eggs," 1963 (Diana DeLeon); "Murdersville," 1967 (Maggie)

Brahms, Penny

FILM: *Dracula A.D. 1972*, 1972 (Hippie Chick)
Other genre credits: FILMS: *The Ambushers*, Columbia Pictures, 1968 (Slaygirl); *2001: A Space Odyssey*, MGM, 1968 (Stewardess); *The Private Life of Sherlock Holmes*, Compton Films, 1970 (Girl)

Brandon-Jones, Una

TELEVISION: *Hammer House of Horror*: "The House That Bled to Death," 1980 (Mrs. Clements)
Other genre credits: TELEVISION: *Supernatural*: "Lady Sybil," 1977 (Miranda)

Brauns, Marianne

FILM: *X: The Unknown*, 1956 (Zena)
BIOGRAPHY—Marianne Brauns was a British character actress with eleven television and film credits in ten years. She does a sexy turn in *X: The Unknown* as Zena, a nurse who gets to play doctor with one of the house physicians. X makes the doc its dinner as Zena screams.

Brennan, Sheila

FILM: *The Curse of the Werewolf*, 1961 (Vera)
Other genre credits: TELEVISION: *Out of the Unknown*: "The Last Witness," 1965 (Mrs. Kemball)

Brett, Anna

FILM: *Dr. Jekyll and Sister Hyde*, 1971 (Julie)

Briars, Shevaun

TELEVISION: *Hammer House of Mystery and Suspense*: "Last Video and Testament," 1984 (Nurse)

Brodrick, Susan (1946–)

BIRTHPLACE: London, England.
FILMS: *Journey to Midnight*, 1971 (Rose Parkington); *Countess Dracula*, 1971 (Chambermaid); *Dr. Jekyll and Sister Hyde*, 1971 (Susan)
TELEVISION: *Journey to the Unknown*: "Poor Butterfly," 1969 (Rose Parkington)
BIOGRAPHY—Unlike many performers who profess to have been drawn to the art from the time of the cradle, Susan Brodrick had no such ambitions, and was not bitten by the bug until the age of 15. She won a place at London's Central School of Dramatic Art, and while in attendance there that she won her first movie role, as the girl in the antique shop in the

classic thriller *Blow Up*. She then joined the famous repertory company Everyman Theatre in Liverpool; a year later she returned to London, where she added more films and television shows to her CV. Her first appearance for Hammer was in the *Journey to the Unknown* episode "Poor Butterfly" that was later edited together with "The Indian Spirit Guide" to create the film *Journey to Midnight*. In it she gives a spirited performance as a ghost who's been reincarnated to recreate a tragedy, but is having a hard time accepting her (second) fate. She's very ethereal (fitting, since she's a ghost) and manages to evoke sympathy despite the conclusion which is telegraphed, oh, about as many years in advance as the first time she died. She played the supporting role of Teri the chambermaid who becomes the first victim of Ingrid Pitt's bloodlust in *Countess Dracula*. Her best turn for the company was as the comically naïve and clueless almost-girlfriend of Ralph Bates in *Dr. Jekyll and Sister Hyde*, who nearly meets a sticky end at the hands of Hyde, but instead survives to see her *objet d'amour* hurl himself from a ledge to kill the ever-more dominant other half of his personality. Her last role was in *The Winter's Tale* (1981), at which time she apparently lost the bug as quickly as she found it.

Brody, Estelle (1900–1995)

BIRTHPLACE: New York City, New York, USA.
FILM: *Never Take Sweets from a Stranger*, 1960 (Eunice)
Other genre credits: TELEVISION: *The Martian Chronicles*: "The Expeditions," 1980 (Mrs. Black)

Brousse, Liliane

FILMS: *Paranoiac*, 1963 (Francoise); *Maniac*, 1963 (Annette Beynat)

Brown, Barbara (1940–)

BIRTHPLACE: London, England.
FILM: *The Terror of the Tongs*, 1961 (Helena)

Bruce, Angela (1951–)

BIRTHPLACE: Leeds, Yorkshire, England.
FILM: *Man at the Top*, 1973 (Joyce Harvey)
TELEVISION: *Hammer House of Horror*: "Charlie Boy," 1980 (Sarah)
BIOGRAPHY—Born in Leeds to a West Indian father and a British mother, Angela Bruce originally wanted to become a nurse, but after failing her exams decided to become an actress (who would go on to portray a number of nurses). She made her film debut with Hammer, in *Man at the Top*, and she returned seven years later to essay the female lead in the *Hammer House of Horror* episode "Charlie Boy," a fairly routine story about an African fetish (to whom Bruce gives the nickname of the title) that causes the deaths of people that her lover has had issues with, and then starts working overtime (big surprise there). Bruce is solid as the woman who plants the suggestion in the first place and then spends the rest of the episode not believing the mounting evidence until it's too late.
Other genre credits: TELEVISION: *Red Dwarf*: "Parallel Universe," 1988 (Deb Lister); *Doctor Who*: "Battlefield," 1989 (Brigadier Winifred Bambera); *The Ghost Hunter*: various episodes, 2000 (Mrs. Justin)

Bruce, Brenda (1918–1996)

BIRTHPLACE: Manchester, England.
FILM: *Nightmare*, 1963 (Mary Lewis)

BIOGRAPHY—British actress Brenda Bruce had a long and distinguished career (some 60 years) on screen, television and the stage with the Royal Shakespeare Company. She won a BAFTA Award as Best Actress in 1963, the year that she appeared in her only Hammer film, *Nightmare*. In it, she essays the role of Jennie Linden's strict but fair and genuinely caring teacher Mary Lewis, who uses the same tactics on Linden's guardian that he and his lover (Moira Redmond) use to drive Linden over the edge, with even more effective results.

Other genre credits: FILMS: *Peeping Tom*, Michael Powell Theatre, 1960 (Dora) TELEVISION: *Late Night Horror*: "William and Mary," 1968 (Mary Pearl); *Doctor Who*: "Paradise Towers," Parts 1, 2, and 3, 1987 (Tilda)

Bryan, Dora (1923–)

REAL NAME: Dora May Broadbent; BIRTHPLACE: Southport, Lancashire, England.

FILM: *Hands of the Ripper*, 1971 (Mrs. Golding)

BIOGRAPHY—Dora Bryan began performing in pantomimes as a child and joined the Oldham Repertory as a teenager, spending the next eight years there. Her first film role was in 1947 and in 1961 she won a BAFTA Award as Best Actress for *A Taste of Honey*; in 1963 she had a hit on the pop music charts with "All I Want for Christmas Is a Beatle." She gives a fine performance as a phony medium who becomes the first victim of Angharad Rees in *Hands of the Ripper*; she has a picturesque, almost Dr. Phibes–like demise in which she is impaled on a door with a poker. She reportedly was a great help to Rees and kept her in stitches as well. In one scene, Rees had to speak with Bryan, who was off-camera and had already changed her costume. Bryan recited her lines perfectly while fixing her makeup, and it was all Rees could do to keep a straight face. Bryan retired in 2000 and is, at the time of this writing, wheelchair-bound and in ill health.

Other genre credits: FILMS: *Mother Riley Meets the Vampire*, Fernwood Productions, 1952 (Tilly); *Screamtime*, Salon Productions, 1986 (Emma)

Buono, Cara (1971–)

BIRTHPLACE: Bronx, New York, USA.

FILM: *Let Me In*, 2010 (Owen's Mother)

Other genre credits: FILMS: *Hulk*, Universal Pictures, 2003 (Edith Banner); *From Other Worlds*, Belladonna Productions, 2004 (Joanne); *Cthulhu*, Arkham Northwest Productions, 2007 (Dannie Marsh) TELEVISION: *Stephen King's Dead Zone*: "Ego," "Big Top," "Interred," "Numb," "Transgressions," "Ambush," 2007 (Sheriff Anna Turner)

Burgess, Vivienne (1914–1999)

BIRTHPLACE: Weston-Super-Mare, Somerset, England.

TELEVISION: *Hammer House of Mystery and Suspense*: "In Possession," 1985 (Mrs. Jessica Prentice)

Burke, Marie (1894–1988)

REAL NAME: Marie Rosa Holt; BIRTHPLACE: London, England.

FILMS: *Bad Blonde*, 1953 (Mother Vecchi); *The Snorkel*, 1958 (Daily Woman); *The Man Who Could Cheat Death*, 1959 (Woman at Private View); *The Terror of the Tongs*, 1961 (Maya)

Other genre credits: FILMS: *Séance on a Wet Afternoon*, Beaver Films, 1964 (Woman at First Séance); *Devils of Darkness*, Planet Film Productions, 1965 (Old Gypsy Woman)

Burnett, Ruth; a.k.a. Ruthie Barnett (1959–)

BIRTHPLACE: Brighton, England.
TELEVISION: *Hammer House of Mystery and Suspense*: "The Corvini Inheritance," 1985 (Second Female Model)
BIOGRAPHY—A former Miss Brighton and model, she had a very short career; she appeared in only four titles, one of which was an episode of *Hammer House of Mystery and Suspense* as a model. She also did three episodes of the classic comedy *The Young Ones* and appeared with Tony Perkins in *Edge of Sanity*, where Perkins turns his patented twitchy nut routine loose on the Jekyll and Hyde story.
Other genre credits: FILM: *Edge of Sanity*, Allied Vision, 1989 (Margo)

Burrell, Sheila (1922–2011)

BIRTHPLACE: Blackheath, London, England.
FILMS: *The Man in Black*, 1949 (Janice); *Cloudburst*, 1951 (Lorna Dawson); *The Rossiter Case*, 1951 (Honor); *Women Without Men*, 1956 (Bates); *Paranoiac*, 1963 (Aunt Harriet)
BIOGRAPHY—A busy British character actress (and cousin of Laurence Olivier), Sheila Burrell had a career of over 50 years on stage, screen and television. She made five films for Hammer, including her first three film appearances. In all three, she was a "bad girl": In *The Man in Black*, she's a scheming stepdaughter in league with her murdering mother; in *Cloudburst*, she co-stars with Elizabeth Sellars (*The Curse of the Mummy's Tomb*) and gets around to the murdering personally. In *The Rossiter Case*, she plays a slore who tries to steal her wheelchair-bound sister's husband, and she livens up the rather tame women-in-prison entry *Women Without Men* (released in the U.S., with added and deleted footage, as *Blonde Bait*) with a memorable freak-out. Her fearsome finale was as Aunt Harriet in *Paranoiac*, where she knows what Oliver Reed did ten summers ago, and will go to great lengths to ensure that knowledge stays within the family. When she was bad, she was very, very good indeed.
Other genre credits: FILMS: *Afraid of the Dark*, Les Films Ariane, 1991 (Meg) TELEVISION: *Out of the Unknown*: "The Naked Sun," 1969 (Minnim); *The Avengers*: "Bizarre," 1969 (Mrs. Jupp); *Tales of the Unexpected*: "The Tribute," 1983 (Lady Eleanor Benson); *The Young Indiana Jones Chronicles*: "Paris, October 1916," 1993 (Lady # 1)

Burton, Audrey

FILM: *The Terror of the Tongs*, 1961 (Tong Room Girl)

Butler, Shirley

FILM: *Never Take Sweets from a Stranger*, 1960 (Mrs. Nash)

Byron, Kathleen (1921–2009)

REAL NAME: Kathleen Elizabeth Fell; BIRTHPLACE: London, England.
FILMS: *The Gambler and the Lady*, 1952 (Pat); *Twins of Evil*, 1971 (Katy Weil)
BIOGRAPHY—British character actress Kathleen Byron trained at the Bristol Old Vic, with her first film appearance coming in 1938. She did everything from B-movies to the A-list pictures *The Elephant Man* and *Saving Private Ryan*, with her most memorable role coming in *Black Narcissus* (1947). She played two roles for Hammer, nearly twenty years apart: In *The Gambler and the Lady*, she plays the spurned lover of a nightclub owner who adds insult to his injury by running him over with a car after he's been shot. She's the complete opposite in *Twins of Evil* as the compassionate, long-suffering, level-headed wife of the fanatical Gustav Weil (Peter Cushing). She retired in 2001 and passed away eight years later.

Other genre credits: FILMS: *Burn, Witch, Burn*, Independent Artists, 1962 (Evelyn Sawtelle); *One of Our Dinosaurs Is Missing*, Walt Disney Productions, 1975 (Colonel's Wife/) TELEVISION: *The Avengers*: "Pandora," 1969 (Miss Faversham); *Menace*: "The Haunting," 1973 (Madame Ordine); *Supernatural*: "Night of the Marionettes," 1977 (Elsbeth); *Blake's 7*: "Weapon," 1979 (Clonemaster Fen); *Frighteners*: "Rose Cottage," 1997 (Bessie Hammond)

Caclough, Sally

FILM: *Slave Girls*, 1967 (Amazon)

Calder-Marshall, Anna (1947–)

BIRTHPLACE: Kensington, London, England.
TELEVISION: *Hammer House of Horror*: "The Two Faces of Evil," 1980 (Janet Lewis)
BIOGRAPHY—The daughter of novelist Arthur Calder-Marshall, Anna Calder-Marshall is another mainstay of (mostly) British television and some feature films. Notable among the former are her Emmy-winning performance (Best Supporting Actress) in *Male of the Species*, an NBC-TV movie, and a starring role in *Pussycat, Pussycat I Love You*, for which she received a Golden Globe nomination. (It also featured fellow Hammer Heroines Veronica Carlson and Madeline Smith.) Her sole turn for Hammer came in a somewhat confusing episode of *Hammer House of Horror*, "The Two Faces of Evil": She conveys mounting confusion, paranoia and hysteria in a story that starts out like a maniac-on-the-loose scenario, then shifts gears into doppelgangers and ends it all like *Invasion of the Body Snatchers*; what had been a fairly cohesive story of a woman's husband being replaced by the killer who looks just like him suddenly has doubles of everybody in sight with no explanation as to why. Still, Calder-Marshall handles herself nicely, especially in the scenes when she finds out that her husband isn't quite himself and a like scene with their son. Still active in television, she is married to one actor, David Burke, and is the mother of another, Tom Burke.
Other genre credits: TELEVISION: *Animated Epics: Beowulf*, 1998 (Voice of Queen Wealtheow); *Doctor Who: Scream of the Shalka*, 2003 (Voice of Mathilda Pierce)

Calvert, Ruth

FILM: *The Terror of the Tongs*, 1961 (Tong Room Girl)
Other genre credits: TELEVISION: *Doctor Who*: "The War Machines" (Part One), 1966 (Inferno Customer)

Cameron, Isla (1930–1980)

BIRTHPLACE: Scotland
FILM: *Nightmare*, 1963 (Mother)
BIOGRAPHY—Scottish actress Isla Cameron also had a successful career as a folk singer. She was featured in *The Innocents* along with one of her co-stars from *Nightmare*, Clytie Jessop, and cuts a memorable figure as well as a song. She has a brief but very memorable bit in *Nightmare* as the mad mother in the literal nightmare that the film opens with, laughing maniacally and exhorting her daughter Jennie Linden to join her in madness.
Other genre credits: FILM: *The Innocents*, 20th Century–Fox, 1961 (Anna)

Capes, Marialla

FILM: *The Terror of the Tongs*, 1961 (Tong Room Girl)

Carby, Fanny (1925–2002)

BIRTHPLACE: Sutton, Surrey, England.
TELEVISION: *Journey to the Unknown*: "The Indian Spirit Guide," 1969 (Housekeeper); *Hammer House of Mystery and Suspense*: "A Distant Scream," 1986 (Mrs. Kimble)
Other genre credits: TELEVISION: *Out of the Unknown*: "Tunnel Under the World," 1966 (Miss Mitkin)

Cardew, Jane

FILM: *Demons of the Mind*, 1972 (Second Girl)
Other genre credits: FILM: *The Flesh and Blood Show*, Peter Walker Heritage Limited, 1972 (Lady Pamela)

Carita (1942–)

REAL NAME: Carita Jarvinen; BIRTHPLACE: Sipoo, Finland.
FILM: *The Viking Queen*, 1967 (Salina, the Viking Queen)
BIOGRAPHY—Carita was as mysterious as she was beautiful, and biographical details are sketchy. According to Hammer's press release, "Six years ago, she was a young peasant girl in the country of 80,000 frozen lakes... [A]t 17 she wanted to become a dress designer, but she

No man could teach Carita how to act, not even Don Murray in this lobby card from *The Viking Queen* (courtesy Mel Bridgeman).

was spotted by photographers and became a cover girl by 20. She landed in Paris a bit later and a film mogul noticed her. She had six months' training in New York, and then was signed up on a seven-year contract." So that Hammer could publicize *The Viking Queen* as her first film, they neglected to mention that she had been in one other movie. But it certainly was her first and only starring role, so the artistic license is granted. And although at times she seems overwhelmed, especially by the combined experience and talents of the supporting cast, she does not acquit herself that badly, and that same supporting cast shoulders the load in the moments when her inexperience shows. She was reportedly more than game, even taking chariot-driving lessons. Unlike similar actresses in similar circumstances, she is not responsible for the film's ultimate failure. In retrospect, it is not hard to see why *The Viking Queen* failed: Like Hammer's earlier *The Phantom of the Opera*, it didn't have enough of a budget to match whatever lofty ambitions they might have had to raise them a level above the standard horror film, and not enough Hammer Horror to satisfy the monster kids. Therefore it appealed to few in either audience. She only made one other film appearance, in *The Green Ray* (1986), and today she is happily retired from both acting and modeling and lives in Paris.

Carlson, Veronica (1944–)

BIOGRAPHY — REAL NAME: Veronica Mary Glazer; BIRTHPLACE: Yorkshire, England.

FILMS: *Dracula Has Risen from the Grave*, 1968 (Maria Mueller); *Frankenstein Must Be Destroyed*, 1969 (Anna Spengler); *The Horror of Frankenstein*, 1969 (Elizabeth Heiss)

BIOGRAPHY — Although born in England, Veronica Carlson spent much of her childhood in Germany, where her father, a member of the RAF, was stationed. Veronica was a model early in her career and, like more than a few Hammer actresses, was invited to audition for the company based on photographs that Sir James Carreras saw in a magazine.

Her signing by Hammer was greatly heralded, and she received quite a build-up before playing her most iconic role, that of Maria Mueller in *Dracula Has Risen from the Grave*. Maria is an archetypal woman-child; young enough to still keep her doll in bed, but old enough to know better — if you know what I mean. This is particularly evident in the scene where she's seduced (and then vampirized) by Dracula: She is "to die for" (no pun intended) as she turns on the light in bedroom eyes that express the welling-up of long-repressed passion, and the screen begins to sizzle when Dracula begins to nuzzle. Cut to Veronica's hand forcefully shoving the doll from her bed onto the floor; no symbolism there. But this fairly obvious, er, climax is counterbalanced by some of the most iconic and powerful images in the entire Hammer Dracula series: Veronica's midnight stroll through the forest in her flowing white nightgown, Dracula's tears of blood in the climax, and the scene where those eyes and mouth are wide open as he has that redwood tree of a stake sticking out of his chest in a River Thames of Kensington Gore.

Paul, the Young Male Lead, is an atheist who cannot bring himself to say the requisite prayers when Dracula is impaled (a new twist inserted in this film for that sole purpose). The Hammer Young Male Lead was usually a total knob, made to appear even more so in order to emphasize the wisdom of the establishment — and certainly Paul's attitude is a concession to the more modern attitudes of the young at the time it was made. What is surprising and pleasing is that Paul is not portrayed as a fool for his beliefs, nor does he renounce them and "see the light." Both he and Maria's uncle, the monsignor (Rupert Davies), are seen as honorable men of radically different views who ultimately come to respect each other, have faith in each other and can work together. But really, Paul is no more impudent than the title itself, wonderfully cheeky in the, er, vein of the Bardot parody of *Frankenstein Created Woman*, but altogether quite a bit more daring in its mocking of the Resurrection. Although the core of Hammer was solidly establishment, they never lost sight of how to shock the rest of it.

But sometimes even Hammer went a little too far. *Frankenstein Must Be Destroyed* was the fourth of the series, by which time the character of Peter Cushing's baron had undergone some fairly unpleasant personality changes — most egregiously when he rapes Veronica's character of Anna Spengler. Cushing's Frankenstein had been a ruthless murderer and would stop at nothing to gain his ends — but never a rapist. The scene gave true friends Veronica and Cushing much apprehension; it was done at the last moment when it was decided that the film wasn't quite "sexy" enough, although why the producers thought rape was "sexy" is anybody's guess. Still, they performed the scene as directed, like the professionals they were.

Veronica plays a character quite different from the one in *Dracula Has Risen from the Grave* in this most harsh of Frankenstein films: No longer the innocent woman-child to be corrupted, she is corrupt from the beginning. Although she appears in the beginning to be an attractive young woman who runs a boarding house for her mother, another typical virginal heroine, we soon find that her lover, Karl, steals and sells drugs (from the asylum where he is employed as a doctor) to pay for her mother's care. And therein probably lies the reason that director Terence Fisher called the film the one nobody else seems to care for: It's just not very much fun. There's not even a traditional romantic clinch or chance at redemption for Anna or Karl; she is stabbed by Frankenstein after giving the "monster" the same. An unrelentingly downbeat film, *Frankenstein Must Be Destroyed* contains Veronica's most powerful and accomplished Hammer performance.

But if nobody else seemed to care for *Frankenstein Must Be Destroyed*, then where does

Veronica Carlson has no idea what Peter Cushing has planned for her in *Frankenstein Must Be Destroyed* (courtesy Paul C. Riggie).

that leave *The Horror of Frankenstein*? As producer, director and writer Jimmy Sangster put it, that was simply the one nobody liked, an opinion which still holds somewhat true to this day. Its chief sins appear to be that it (a) is a satire of the beloved *Curse of Frankenstein*, and (b) does not feature Peter Cushing as Frankenstein. But as Veronica astutely points out, the film was ahead of the game on both counts: a parody featuring a "Young Frankenstein" years before Mel Brooks' film of the same name. And although she would have preferred a role with more substance, like Anna in the previous film, she had a wonderful time making it, and gives a marvelous comedic performance — so impossibly naïve and good that she makes Maria Mueller look like Zena the barmaid. Although, truth to tell, she is not much more naïve than Hazel Court in this film's inspiration *The Curse of Frankenstein*; it is such subtle parody and such a comedic performance that indeed it almost seems played straight, a real tribute to her skills. Her best scene comes at the climax, after she has been attacked by Dave Prowse's monster, and she has led the gendarmes to the lab. They cannot find the monster, which has been given a hot acid shower by an unwitting little girl after being hidden by Frankenstein. "Well, perhaps he's gone now," she says in her best blank tone, while wonderful Ralph Bates wearily nods in agreement. And while second-billed Kate O'Mara gets practically all the really meaty, big and bouncy bits (and Veronica admits she would have loved to play her part), they wouldn't have worked as well without Veronica playing her role as only she could. So what if it's more *Carry On* than *Curse of*? It's a very funny film, and doesn't deserve to be treated as the black sheep of Hammer's Frankenstein family.

In 1975, after her appearance in an episode of the television series *Public Eye*, Carlson more or less removed herself from the acting world, although she did pop up in a couple of productions in the ensuing decades. She got married and concentrated on raising her family and on her career as an artist, at which she has become very successful. Still beautiful, gracious and outgoing, she has also become a favorite at fan conventions, where her fans still might get a glimpse of her acting magic; for instance, at the Monster Bash convention in June 2011, she was featured in a recitation of "Dracula's Guest" along with fellow Hammer heroines Caroline Munro and Yvonne Monlaur, a once-in-a-lifetime show that none who attended will ever forget.

Other genre credits: FILMS: *The Ghoul*, Tyburn Film, 1975 (Daphne Welles Hunter); *Old Dracula*, World Film Services, 1975 (Ritva); *Black Easter*, Sleepy Hollow Productions, 1994; *Freakshow*, Crimson Productions, 1995 (Grace Harmsworth)

Carvana, Lorraine

FILM: *The Curse of the Werewolf*, 1961 (Servant Girl as a Child)

Cashfield, Katy (1937–)

BIRTHPLACE: London, England.
FILM: *The Terror of the Tongs*, 1961 (Tong Room Girl)
Other genre credits: FILMS: *Jack the Ripper*, Mid Century Film Productions, 1959 (Blond Girl) TELEVISION: *Doctor Who*: "The Rescue," 1964 (Thal)

Casson, Maxine

FILM: *Twins of Evil*, 1971 (Schoolgirl)

Castle, Susan

FILM: *The Brides of Dracula*, 1960 (Elsa)
Other genre credits: TELEVISION: *The Avengers*: "Hunt the Man Down," 1961 (Nurse Wyatt)

Chandler, Vivienne (1947–)

BIRTHPLACE: Nice, France
FILMS: *Lust for a Vampire*, 1971 (Schoolgirl); *Twins of Evil*, 1971 (Schoolgirl)
BIOGRAPHY—This foxy French character actress made her first appearance on television in 1970, soon followed by a short stint for Hammer, where she played schoolgirls in two films from the Karnstein Trilogy (she grew up real quick in *A Clockwork Orange*). She retired in 1997 to pursue a still-successful career as a photographer and is a member of the Royal Photographic Society.
Other genre credits: FILMS: *A Clockwork Orange*, Warner Brothers, 1971 (Handmaiden in Bible Fantasy); *Star Wars: Return of the Jedi*, Lucasfilm, 1983 (X-Wing Fighter Pilot) TELEVISION: *The Frighteners*: "Night of the Stag," 1972 (Caroline)

Chanter, Doreen (c. 1953)
Chanter, Irene (c. 1953)

FILM: *Twins of Evil*, 1971 (Schoolgirl)
BIOGRAPHY—The Collinson twins were not the only set of sisters in *Twins of Evil*; Doreen and Irene Chanter were siblings as well, musically and professionally known as the Chanter Sisters. They have provided backing vocals for a number of major rock acts, including the legendary Roxy Music.

Chasan, Debbie

TELEVISION: *Hammer House of Mystery and Suspense*: "Child's Play," 1986 (Sarah Preston)
BIOGRAPHY—In her acting debut, Debbie Chasan gave a fine performance as the petulant, somewhat mysterious daughter in the "Child's Play" episode of *Hammer House of Mystery and Suspense*. It appears to have been her first role and her last.

Chevreau, Cecile

BIRTHPLACE: London, England.
FILMS: *Spaceways*, 1953 (Vanessa Mitchell); *Paid to Kill*, 1954 (Joan Peterson)

Chilcott, Barbara (1923–)

BIRTHPLACE: Newmarket, Ontario, Canada.
FILM: *Stop Me Before I Kill!* 1960 (Baroness de la Vailion)
Other genre credits: TELEVISION: *Invisible Man*: "Behind the Mask," 1959 (Maria); *The Twilight Zone*: "The Curious Case of Edgar Witherspoon," 1988 (Mrs. Milligan)

Christie, Helen Mary (1914–1995)

BIRTHPLACE: British India.
FILMS: *Rasputin, the Mad Monk*, 1966 (First Tart); *Lust for a Vampire*, 1971 (Miss Simpson)
BIOGRAPHY—A British character actress of stage, screen and television, she made her film debut in 1947. She has a bit part in *Rasputin, the Mad Monk* as a lady of easy virtue, and a more substantial one in *Lust for a Vampire* as Miss Simpson, the principal of the girls' school that Yutte Stensgaard turns into a personal lunch counter. The welfare of the students is Miss Simpson's chief concern — except when they start getting murdered, when her chief concern is to preserve the image of the school.

Church, Suzanne (1951–)

TELEVISION: *Hammer House of Mystery and Suspense*: "Child's Play," 1986 (Giant Space Mother)

BIOGRAPHY—This attractive British character actress appeared primarily on the television (she had a nice bit in *Fawlty Towers*) but also in a few feature films (*The Great Muppet Caper*). She has a wee bit part in "Child's Play" as an alien mother who must deal with her bratty daughter not taking care of her toys—which in this case means an Earth family who suffer dire consequences when she doesn't, such as suffocating or being attacked by a melted Mars bar. She's had no credits since 2007.

Churcher, Melinda

FILMS: *Lust for a Vampire*, 1971 (Schoolgirl); *Beyond the Rave*, 2008 (worked as a dialogue coach)

Other genre credits: FILM: *Horror House*, Tigon British, 1969 (Young Girl)

Cilento, Diane (1933–2011)

BIRTHPLACE: Brisbane, Queensland, Australia.

FILMS: *Dead on Course*, 1952 (Jeanette); *Stop Me Before I Kill!* 1960 (Denise Colby)

BIOGRAPHY—Born in Australia and educated at RADA, Diane Cilento was signed to a movie contract almost immediately after graduation. Her star rose quickly; she was nominated for a 1956 Tony Award for *Tiger at the Gates* and a 1963 Academy Award for *Tom Jones*. Steely-eyed Cilento was featured in two Hammers: the yawn-inducing *Dead on Course* and the only slightly more interesting *Stop Me Before I Kill!*, which can be seen as kith and kin to Hammer's "psychological" thrillers, only less convoluted. In *Stop Me Before I Kill!* she plays the newlywed wife of a race car driver, and they crash en route to their honeymoon hideaway. As a result of the accident, every time they embrace, he feels an unspeakable urge to kill her (always a sure mood-killer). Enter an evil psychiatrist who wants Diane, and takes to convincing her distraught hubby that he's already chopped her up into little pieces. Cilento passed away from cancer in 2011.

Other genre credits: FILMS: *Z.P.G.*, Sagittarius Productions, 1973 (Edna Borden); *The Wicker Man*, British Lion, 1973 (Miss Rose) TELEVISION: *Late Night Horror*: "Kiss of Blood," 1968 (Lady Sannox); *Thriller*: "Spell of Evil," 1973 (Clara)

Clare, Diane (1938–)

REAL NAME: Diane C.O.G. Dirsztay; BIRTHPLACE: London, England.

FILM: *The Plague of the Zombies*, 1966 (Sylvia Forbes)

BIOGRAPHY—Diane Clare was descended from William (Buffalo Bill) Cody on her mother's side, and her father, Baron A Dirsztay, was the son of Olga Berger, prima ballerina of the Vienna Opera. Clare began appearing in movies at the age of two; she first received an on-screen credit in 1958. She was no stranger to genre films by the time she played the lead in *The Plague of the Zombies*: She had already appeared in Robert Wise's classic *The Haunting*, and had a featured role in *Witchcraft*. *Plague* co-star Jacqueline Pearce claims that Clare annoyed Andre Morell tremendously, and perhaps this is supported by the weight he gives to the line "I think it would have been better had you been drowned at birth." But if Morell's true feelings were communicated with this line, then it's equally fair to say that Ms. Clare's own natural quality of innocence comes through in her portrayal of Sylvia, an island of purity in dark, sordid waters. She retired from show business only two years after making *The Plague of the Zombies*; she married novelist and playwright Barry England and devoted herself to her family, and the marriage has survived happily into the present day. Her last two genre appearances, which were also her last two film roles, were in *The Beast of Morocco* and the legendarily bad *The Vulture*, which would be enough to make the greatest actor or actress question their career choice.

Other genre credits: FILMS: *The Haunting*, Argyle Enterprises, 1963 (Carrie Fredericks); *Witchcraft*, Lippert Films, 1964 (Amy Whitlock); *The Vulture*, Homeric Films, 1967 (Trudy Lutens); *Beast of Morocco*, Associated British-Pathe, 1968 (Chantal) TELEVISION: *The Avengers*: "Death at Bargain Prices," 1965 (Julie Thompson)

Clarke, Melita

FILM: *Lust for a Vampire*, 1971 (Schoolgirl)
Other genre credits: FILM: *Queen Kong*, Cine-Art Munchen, 1976 (Crew Girl)

Clay, Rachel

FILM: *The Damned*, 1963 (Victoria)
Other genre credits: FILM: *The Monster of Highgate Ponds*, Halas and Batchelor Cartoon Films, 1961 (Sophie)

Clayton, Lynn

TELEVISION: *Hammer House of Mystery and Suspense*: "Paint Me a Murder," 1985 (Secretary)

Cleveland, Carol (1942–)

BIRTHPLACE: London, England.
FILMS: *Moon Zero Two*, 1969 (Hostess); *Journey to Murder*, 1971 (Lisa)
TELEVISION: *Journey to the Unknown*: "Do Me a Favor and Kill Me," 1968 (Lisa)
BIOGRAPHY—The beautiful and brilliant comedienne Carol Cleveland was born in London and trained at RADA. The year after graduation, she played her first part in *Dixon of Dock Green*, and then alternated between television and feature films (including *A Countess from Hong Kong*). Her two roles for Hammer came in the form of a bit part in *Journey to the Unknown* and another in the bizarre *Moon Zero Two*, where she plays a hostess employed on an intra-moon transportation system. Cleveland soon became known and loved the world over for her work in the Monty Python series and movies; she is still active in films and television, and her own one-woman stage show, "Carol Cleveland Reveals All."

Other genre credits: FILM: *Old Dracula*, World Film Services, 1975 (Jane) TELEVISION: *The Avengers*: "A Touch of Brimstone," 1966 (Sarah Bradley)

Clune, Anne

FILM: *Hands of the Ripper*, 1971 (First Cell Whore)
BIOGRAPHY—This British character actress with a propensity for portraying prostitutes also had a bit part in *A Hard Day's Night*.
Other genre credits: FILMS: *The Hands of Orlac*, Pendennis Films, 1960 (Cell Whore); *The Oblong Box*, American International, 1969 (Whore)

Cole, Linda

FILM: *Journey to Midnight*, 1971 (Lady Hamilton)
TELEVISION: *Journey to the Unknown*: "Poor Butterfly," 1969 (Lady Hamilton)

Coleman, Bula

FILM: *She*, 1965 (Handmaiden)

Collier, Patience (1910–1987)

REAL NAME: Renee Ritcher; BIRTHPLACE: London, England.
FILM: *Countess Dracula*, 1971 (Julie)
Other genre credits: TELEVISION: *The Avengers*: "Crescent Moon," 1961 (Senora Mendoza); *Mystery and Imagination*: "Uncle Silas," 1968 (Madame de la Rougierre)

Collings, Lisa

FILM: *Captain Kronos, Vampire Hunter*, 1974 (Vanda Sorell)
Other genre credits: FILM: *The Mutations*, Cyclone/Getty Pictures, 1974 (Prostitute)

Collins, Joan (1933–)

BIRTHPLACE: Paddington, London, England.
FILM: *Fear in the Night*, 1972 (Molly Carmichael)
BIOGRAPHY—Joan Collins, the Princess of Posh Pablum, was born the year that the original *King Kong* was released, which is appropriate since her reputation, both personal and professional, easily looms as large.

Fear in the Night finds her in a role both stereotypical and typical of many of her other roles: the cruel, scheming bitch who's having an affair with the heroine's husband; the vivacious, sexy woman who's married to her complete opposite for his money, who wants the money and no longer has any use for him. Of course, there's a reason she's got these roles, and that's because she's frightfully good at them, and she makes the most of her relatively limited screen time. In fact, she makes her entrance by shooting and killing a bunny rabbit! Of course, after she perpetrates such a heinous act, the audience knows she's capable of anything, and indeed she is; and what really makes it work is the sheer, unmitigated delight which Ms. Collins takes in her evil ways. For instance, when Judy Geeson is kidnapped in the climax, Ralph Bates brings her to Collins, who is busy digging the eye out of a sculpture of Judy with a large

Be afraid. Be very afraid. Joan Collins starred in *Fear in the Night*.

knife; she laments that she can't get "the right simpering expression" and then slaps Geeson across the face, warning, "Next time it'll be the hand with the knife!" When Geeson tries to escape, Bates tells her he doesn't want her to get hurt, to which Collins replies, "Oh, I do!" Of course, Collins gets hers in the end — or does she? By way of flashbacks and exposition, she is shown to be Geeson's "one-armed" assailant (except for once when it was Bates), and she is also seemingly (accidentally) shot dead by Bates. But when Bates tries to hang Geeson in the schoolyard, he is thwarted (and summarily killed) by a one-armed assailant. Is it the cuckolded, one-armed Peter Cushing, who has discovered the plot and has so skillfully manipulated Bates into killing his faithless wife, or is it Collins' last hurrah? The assailant is never shown.

Collins' career stalled somewhat in the '70s, when she took to slumming in a goodly number of television shows and genre films, including *The Devil Within Her*, in which she was once again paired with Ralph Bates. But it was resuscitated with appearances in films based on novels by her sister Jackie Collins and what is probably her best-known role as part of the cast of the famous prime-time soap opera *Dynasty* (which also included *Dracula A.D. 1972* alum Stephanie Beacham). She is still quite active, quite striking, and still very much her own woman.

Other genre credits: FILMS: *Inn of the Frightened People*, George H. Brown Productions, 1971 (Carol Radford); *Tales from the Crypt*, Amicus Productions, 1972 (Joanna Clayton); *Dark Places*, Glenbergh, 1973 (Sarah Mandeville); *Tales That Witness Madness*, World Film Services, 1973 (Bella Thompson); *The Devil Within Her*, The Rank Organization, 1975 (Lucy Carlesi); *Empire of the Ants*, Cinema 77, 1977 (Marilyn Fryser) TELEVISION: *The Man from U.N.C.L.E.*: "The Galatea Affair," 1966 (Baroness Bibi De Chasseur/Rosy Schlagenheimer); *Star Trek*: "City on the Edge of Forever," 1967 (Sister Edith Keeler); *Batman*: "Wail of the Siren," "Ring Around the Riddler," 1967 (The Siren); *The Danny Thomas Hour*: "The Demon Under the Bed," 1967 (Myra); *Space: 1999*: "Mission of the Darians," 1975 (Kara); *The Fantastic Journey*: "Turnabout," 1977 (Queen Halyana); *Tales of the Unexpected*: "Neck," 1979 (Natalia Turton); "A Girl Can't Always Have Everything" (Suzy Starr), "Georgy Porgy," 1980 (Clara Duckworth/Julia Roach)

Collinson, Madeline (1952–)
Collinson, Mary (1952–)

BIRTHPLACE: Sliema, Malta
FILM: *Twins of Evil*, 1971 (Frieda and Maria Gellhorn)
BIOGRAPHY — The gorgeous Collinson twins were raised on Malta, mostly by their mother, and began modeling at the age of 14 or 15; they moved to London at 16 to pursue that career. They were "discovered" by Victor Lowndes at a party and an assignment for *Playboy* soon followed; they shot to celebrity as the magazine's first-ever identical twin Playmates in the October 1970 issue. This got the attention of Hammer execs, and soon they were slated to star in Hammer's third installment of the Karnstein Trilogy, *Twins of Evil*. Rebounding from the *Lust for a Vampire* debacle, Hammer produced a latter-day classic of horror and hypocrisy, with Peter Cushing at his most fanatically righteous as Gustav Weil, who burns innocent girls that he and his men suspect of being vampires. Weil also happens to be the twins' uncle. The twins were not entirely new to the film world, but these were their first major roles, and they acquit themselves very nicely, their performances reflecting the naughty-nice contrast that was part of their real-life personalities. Madeline has the showier part, but until she gets her head lopped off, it's Mary who has to undergo the most physical and psychological abuse from her uncle, even being mistaken for her wayward sibling and nearly burned at the stake, while

Madeline gets to have all the fun, willingly and callously exploiting her sister's more submissive nature. It may have had exploitation at its heart of hearts, but like *The Vampire Lovers*, it manages to rise above its baser inspirations. It's a piece with real substance, and this is in large part due to the Collinson twins, who were as good-bad, virtuous-vile, and sexy-sexy as anybody could hope for. But the novelty soon wore off, for both them and the audience; they made their last film in 1973, and retired from modeling (another profession that has never been kind as a woman gets older) in 1978. Madeline married an RAF officer and had three children; she lives in Malta and is involved with cultural and educational activities. Mary has lived with an "Italian gentleman" for over 20 years now and has two daughters with him. Both she and her sister consider *Twins of Evil* (along with the *Playboy* shoot, naturally) the highlights of their brief career.

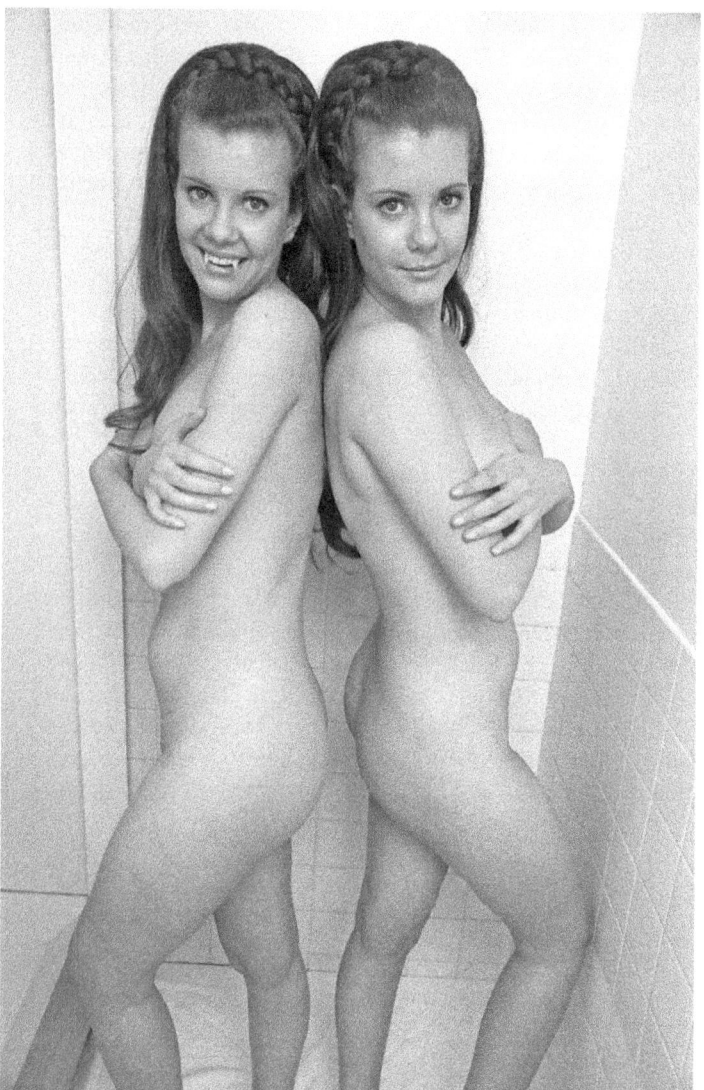

Bum's the word! Madeline and Mary Collinson in a, er, behind-the-scenes photograph from *Twins of Evil*.

Compton, Fay (1894 – 1978)

REAL NAME: Virginia Lilian Emmeline Mackenzie Compton; BIRTHPLACE: West Kensington, London, England.

FILM: *Journey to Midnight*, 1971 (Queen Victoria)
TELEVISION: *Journey to the Unknown*: "Poor Butterfly," 1969 (Queen Victoria)
BIOGRAPHY — One of Britain's most acclaimed stage actresses, Fay Compton is the grandmother of Tracy Reed. Her Fay Compton School of Dramatic Arts has trained many a famous actor. She made her first movie before the talkies, and went on to appear in such esteemed productions as Orson Welles's *Othello*. She has an imperious part in *Journey to the Unknown* as a costume party Queen Victoria, playing it so haughtily and sternly as to make one believe she really is. Her last film role was in 1970, and she passed away eight years later.
Other genre credits: FILM: *The Haunting*, Argyle Enterprises, 1963 (Mrs. Sanderson)

Connell, Maureen (1931–)

BIRTHPLACE: Nairobi, Kenya.
FILM: *The Abominable Snowman*, 1957 (Helen Rollason)
BIOGRAPHY—Maureen Connell's career was short, sweet, and a bit mysterious as well. From her first screen role in 1954's *The White Huntress* to a part in television's *Secret Agent* in 1964, she was fairly active in both film and television, and then she didn't make another appearance until *Skyjacked* in 1972. And perhaps this was what happened to Maureen Connell. As the lead (in fact, only) female in *The Abominable Snowman*, she fills a standard role, the long-suffering wife of Peter Cushing, who wonders why he'd rather trudge around in sub-zero temperatures risking death at the claws of a legendary monster rather than spend time with her, a loaf of wine and a jug of bread—and so do we. But no shrinking violet is she, and Connell makes the most of her limited screen time. She is concerned and distraught over her husband's single-minded pursuit, but supportive, level-headed, and quite plucky, too. Ultimately she's the one who pulls Cushing's fat out of the fire—or to be more precise, his nearly frozen bum out of the snow.

Connolly, Ella

FILM: *Wake Wood*, 2011 (Alice)

Cook, Jacqui

FILM: *Captain Kronos, Vampire Hunter*, 1974 (Barmaid)

Cook, Vera

FILMS: *The Brides of Dracula*, 1960 (Landlord's Wife); *Never Take Sweets from a Stranger*, 1960 (Mrs. Demarest); *The Shadow of the Cat*, 1961 (The Mother); *Cash on Demand*, 1962 (Mrs. Fordyce); *The Kiss of the Vampire*, 1963 (Anna)
BIOGRAPHY—Vera Cook had a late-starting career that spanned twenty years, but only encompassed fifteen roles, fully a third of which were for Hammer. She filled matronly roles in keeping with her advancing dignity. Her last film role was in another permanent piece of the pop culture fabric, the Beatles' *Help!*

Cordeau, Sonya

FILM: *The Phantom of the Opera*, 1962 (Yvonne)

Corri, Adrienne (1930–)

REAL NAME: Adrienne Ricciboni; BIRTHPLACE: Edinburgh, Scotland.
FILMS: *The Viking Queen*, 1967 (Beatrice); *Journey into Darkness*, 1971 (Terry Lawrence); *Moon Zero Two*, 1969 (Elizabeth Murphy); *Vampire Circus*, 1972 (Gypsy Woman)
TELEVISION: *Journey to the Unknown*: "The New People," 1968 (Terry Lawrence)
BIOGRAPHY—The very smart and very sexy Adrienne Corri was Scottish-born, to Italian parents, and harbored no burning desire to act; she claims that she gravitated to the profession because it afforded her the chance to earn money while staying her "naturally lazy self," but her very busy life and career contradict this self-deprecating statement. She has been a major presence on the British stage, is an expert on Gainsborough (and written a book on him as well), and appeared in both Oscar-winning films (*Dr. Zhivago*) and significant genre efforts. Despite her feisty personality both in real life and generally on-screen, in *A Clockwork Orange*, she plays a meek writer's wife who is gang-raped by Alex and his Droogs to the tune of "Singin' in the Rain." It's her best-remembered genre role.

Adrienne Corri and Anthony Corlan aren't clowning around with Lynne Frederick in this shot from *Vampire Circus*.

The words most often used to describe Corri are "feisty" and "fiery" (she reportedly once gave a rude theatre audience the two-fingered salute and told them to go fuck themselves), and she is all of that and more in her first effort for Hammer, *The Viking Queen*. So much so that one wonders why the superior actress didn't play the lead (played instead by the beautiful but wooden Carita). Her next role for the company was in a rarely seen, yet classic, episode of Hammer's first television series *Journey to the Unknown* (which then became half of the feature film *Journey into Darkness*), playing the doomed swinger Terry in a combination of *Rosemary's Baby* (except there's no baby) and *The Devil Rides Out* (except the Devil doesn't show up in person). In the "space western" *Moon Zero Two* she makes an eye-popping entrance in space bra and panties, and then changes into an only slightly more subtle mini-skirt and thigh-high boots. By this time the viewer has abandoned any sense of caring about the plot of this otherwise odorous otherworldly oater, only to rail at that plot when it dictates that Adrienne buys the lunar farm.

Fortunately for Hammer Horror fans, she saved the best for last: her top-billed role in the great *Vampire Circus*. As the mysterious "Gypsy Woman," she has one of the best opening lines of Hammer or any other horror film: When asked by one of the townspeople why the gypsies have come, she cackles, "To steal the money from dead men's eyes! Hahahahahahahaha!" Along with her co-star Domini Blythe, she gives a magnificently perverse performance, even loving up on her own son and daughter ... which makes her sudden self-sacrifice at the climax all the more inexplicable, almost as much as when she turns into Blythe when she dies. But this in no way diminishes the delicious evil of her performance and the obvious delight which she takes in it. Her last feature film role was in 1979, although she continued to act on stage and television, making her last appearance on television in 1992.

Other genre credits: FILMS: *Devil Girl from Mars*, Danziger Productions, 1954 (Doris); *Corridors of Blood*, Amalgamated Productions, 1958 (Rachel); *The Tell-Tale Heart*, Danziger Productions, 1960 (Betty Clare); *A Study in Terror*, Compton Films, 1965 (Angela); *A Clockwork Orange*, Warner Brothers, 1971 (Mrs. Alexander); *Madhouse*, American International Pictures, 1974 (Faye Carstairs Flay) TELEVISION: *Invisible Man*: "Crisis in the Desert," 1959 (Yolanda); *One Step Beyond*: "The Confession," 1961 (Sarah); *UFO*: "The Square Triangle," 1970 (Liz Newton); *Doctor Who*: "The Leisure Hive," 1980 (Mena); *Shades of Darkness*: "The Demon Lover," 1986 (Delia Graham)

Costello, Deirdre

BIRTHPLACE: Elland, Yorkshire, England.
FILM: *Demons of the Mind*, 1972 (Magda)
Other genre credits: FILM: *The Doctor and the Devils*, Brooksfilms, 1985 (Nelly) TELEVISION: *Jack the Ripper*: 1988 (Annie Chapman)

Court, Hazel (1926–2008)

BIRTHPLACE: Sutton Coldfield, Warwickshire, England.
FILMS: *The Curse of Frankenstein*, 1957 (Elizabeth); *The Man Who Could Cheat Death*, 1959 (Janine Du Bois)

BIOGRAPHY—The lushly beautiful, crimson-tressed "Horror Queen" (the title of her autobiography) Hazel Court was the daughter of a noted cricketer, and studied drama at the Birmingham Repertory Theatre as well as the Alexandra Theatre (also in Birmingham). Her first film appearance came in 1944 with a bit part in *Champagne Charlie*, and two years later, she won a British Film Critics Award for her sympathetic performance as the crippled girl in *Carnival*. She married fellow actor Dermot Walsh in 1949, and they co-starred in her first genre film, *Ghost Ship*, in 1952; two years later came the second, the cult favorite *Devil Girl from Mars*.

Many of the actresses featured in this book only made as few as one film for Hammer, and yet they made an impression that has endured the test of time. Hazel Court made two, of course, and her impact was doubled in that she appeared in the film that started it all for Hammer, *The Curse of Frankenstein* (playing Elizabeth), making her the mother of all Hammer Horror Heroines. She was also the mother of Sally Walsh, her daughter by Dermot Walsh, who played Elizabeth, as a young girl in the film. The theory has been advanced, as stated previously, that the Hammer films, for all their nasty shocks and the conviction with which the films were played, could be seen almost as having a laugh, albeit subtly in many cases (and others not so). For instance, obviously *The Horror of Frankenstein* is not to be taken seriously, but what of Hazel Court's role in the movie that it was a remake-parody of? This is not to say that she played it for comedic effect, or even tongue-in-cheek, but the role itself is so archly stereotypical that the question almost becomes inevitable. Hazel's Elizabeth, who has been promised to her cousin Baron Frankenstein in marriage, is not a stupid woman, but she is so blissfully unaware of any situation that the role, like the film, can be seen not as a re-imagining or updating of the Universals that were their inspiration, but the slyest form of what the Britons would call "taking the piss." Take the scenes where, instead of a heartbreaking

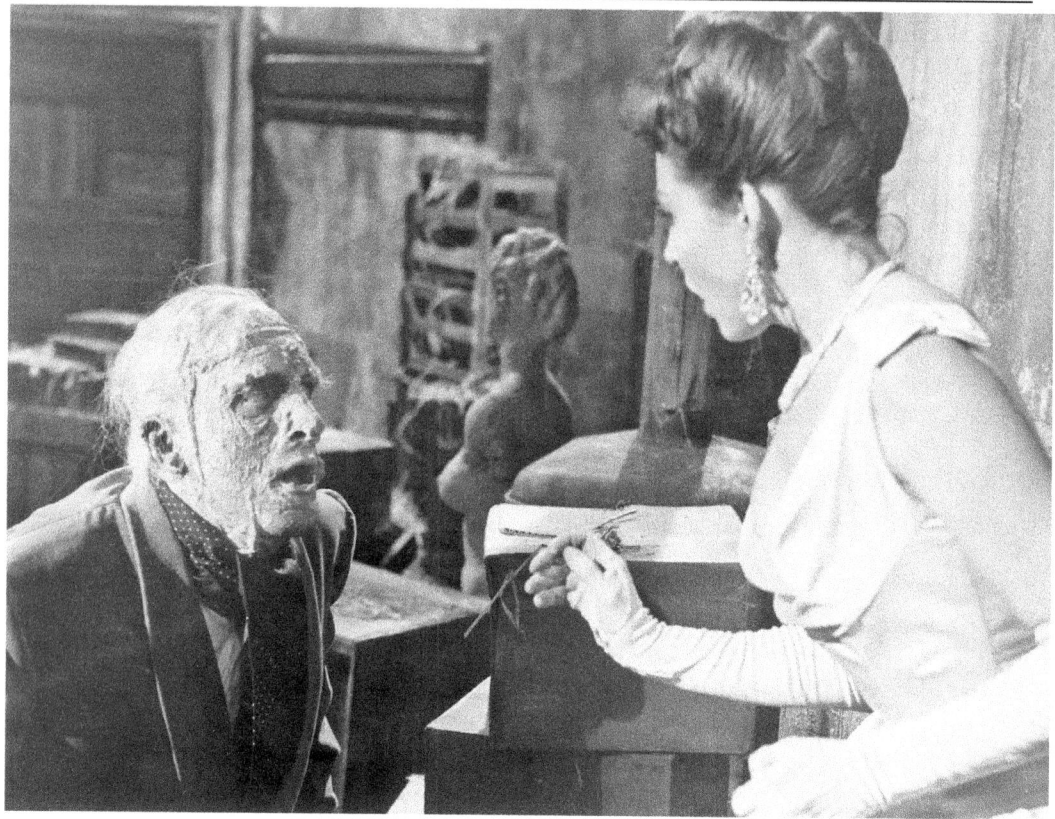

Anton Diffring begs Hazel Court to save him from his sweaty makeup appliance in *The Man Who Could Cheat Death*.

interlude in *Bride of Frankenstein* with a blind hermit, Christopher Lee's creature polishes off a blind man without so much as a by-your-leave; or Peter Cushing's "Pass the marmalade" scene a darkly humorous parallel to the similar scene in *Son of Frankenstein*. And so the character of Elizabeth can be seen as the piss-take on the impossibly virginal and shrill heroines of those two films, particularly Valerie Hobson in *Bride*, who breaks down in hysterics at the drop of lederhosen. Taken in this vein, Hazel's part can be seen not as the stereotypical helpless heroine, but the archetypal "English Rose" afloat in a sea of bloody (literally) cheek.

Her role as Janine in *The Man Who Could Cheat Death* had a bit more meat (and quite a bit more flesh) to it — her entrance in a blue gown with a neckline plunging to Antarctica, and her later nude scene for the "European" version, which is unfortunately lost footage, although a photo exists. And she's not virginal; she has already been the lover of Anton Diffring's Bonner, arrives at the party with her current squeeze Christopher Lee, and then cuts out on him to cut back to Diffring. But while she's wise in the ways of love, Janine shares with *Curse*'s Elizabeth the distressing trait of not being able to smell something fishy even if there were a whale in the room. On the whole, though, it's a solid, impassioned performance that makes it a shame that this was her last role for Hammer.

But one can hardly argue with the credits she amassed afterwards; *Doctor Blood's Coffin* and her three films for Roger Corman, which made her a household name with American horror fans as well as the British. And then, all of a sudden she disappeared — not completely, as she did nine years of television after that, including an episode of *The Wild Wild West* that capitalized on her "Horror Queen" image, "The Night of the Returning Dead." After her divorce from Walsh, she permanently moved to America and remarried, this time to American actor-director Don Taylor, and after her last TV appearance in 1972, retired for real (save for a cameo in *Omen III: The Final Conflict*), to concentrate on her family and develop as a sculptor, plus make much-appreciated appearances at fan conventions. She passed away from a heart attack in 2008.

Other genre credits: FILMS: *Ghost Ship*, Vernon Sewell Productions, 1952; *Devil Girl from Mars*, Danziger Productions, 1954 (Ellen Prestwick); *Doctor Blood's Coffin*, Caralan Productions, 1961 (Linda Parker); *The Premature Burial*, American International Pictures, 1962 (Emily Gault); *The Raven*, 1963 (Lenore Craven); *The Masque of the Red Death*, 1964 (Juliana); *Omen III: The Final Conflict*, 20th Century–Fox Film Productions, 1981 (Champagne Woman at Hunt) TELEVISION: *Invisible Man*: "The Mink Coat," 1959 (Penny Page); *Alfred Hitchcock Presents*: "The Crocodile Case," 1958 (Phyllis Chaundry); "The Avon Emeralds," 1959 (Lady Gwendolyn Avon); "Arthur," 1959 (Helen Braithwaite); "The Pearl Necklace," 1961 (Charlotte Jameson Rutherford); *Thriller*: "The Terror in Teakwood," 1961 (Leonie Vicek); *Twilight Zone*: "The Fear," 1964 (Charlotte Scott)

Cowling, Brenda Rose (1925–2010)

BIRTHPLACE: Islington, London, England.

TELEVISION: *Hammer House of Horror*: "The Two Faces of Evil," 1980 (Nurse Davies)

BIOGRAPHY—One of Britain's most in-demand character actresses was born in London and trained at RADA. She spent a goodly amount of time treading the boards until she made her film debut in 1950 in *Stage Fright*. She appeared in such diverse pictures as *Octopussy* and Pink Floyd's *The Wall* and played a sinister nurse in an episode of *Hammer House of Horror*. She retired in 2006 following a stroke and passed away four years later.

Other genre credits: FILMS: *Jabberwocky*, Python Films, 1977 (Mrs. Fishfinger); *Octopussy*, United Artists/Eon Productions, 1983 (Schatzi) TELEVISION: *The Avengers*: "The Medicine Men," 1963 (Masseuse)

Craig, Wendy (1934–)

BIRTHPLACE: Sacriston, County Durham, England.

FILM: *The Nanny*, 1965 (Virginia Fane)

BIOGRAPHY—This beloved British leading lady and character actress attended the Durham High School for Girls and made her screen debut in 1955; she won a BAFTA Award for Best Actress in 1969. She made one film for Hammer, *The Nanny*, in which she plays the mother of problem child William Dix. Her character is little more than a child herself, completely dependent on Bette Davis's nanny, and pays for that dependence when Davis poisons her and tries to blame Dix. The tacked-on "happy ending" shows her reunited and reconciled with the little Dix, although he still has obvious issues, her daughter and now Aunt Pen are dead, the nanny is a nut, and her husband doesn't give a toss about her—I guess it all depends on your definition of a happy ending. Craig later created and starred in a television series called *Nanny*, which was totally unrelated to the movie. At the time of this writing, she is still active.

Other genre credits: TELEVISION: *Out of the Unknown*: "Satisfaction Guaranteed," 1966 (Claire Belmont)

Crane, Hilary

BIRTHPLACE: Liverpool, England.

TELEVISION: *Hammer House of Mystery and Suspense*: "Mark of the Devil," 1984 (Carla)

BIOGRAPHY—A British character actress, she has worked almost exclusively in television; she plays a guest at an engagement party in the "Mark of the Devil" episode of *Hammer House of Mystery and Suspense*.

Crawford, Joan (1905–1977)

REAL NAME: Lucille Fay Lesueur; BIRTHPLACE: San Antonio, Texas, USA.

FILMS: *Journey to the Unknown*, 1969 (Hostess); *Journey to Murder*, 1971 (Hostess)

BIOGRAPHY—Joan Crawford was a legendary American leading lady, an Oscar and Golden Globe winner who appeared in some of the best films of all time (*Mildred Pierce*), some of the worst (*Trog*), and certainly one of the campiest (*Johnny Guitar*). She made her first film in 1925, and two years later starred with Lon Chaney in *The Unknown*. She had an intense rivalry with Bette Davis, which carried over to the screen in the classic *What Ever Happened to Baby Jane?* She was at the end of a career that influenced both fashion and how women viewed themselves when she made her appearances for Hammer; unfortunately, unlike Davis, she wasn't able to lend her prodigious, if diminished, talent to any of their proper films. Instead she was wasted in two "hostess" roles introducing mashed-up segments of their first television series, *Journey to the Unknown*. She retired after her episode of *The Sixth Sense*, and soon withdrew from public life altogether. The years, alcoholism and numerous other factors finally took their toll in 1977.

Other genre credits: FILMS: *The Unknown*, MGM, 1927 (Nanon Zanzi); *What Ever Happened to Baby Jane?* Associates and Aldrich Company, 1962 (Blanche Hudson); *Strait-Jacket*, William Castle Productions, 1964 (Lucy Harbin); *I Saw What You Did*, William Castle Productions, 1965 (Amy Nelson); *Berserk*, Herman Cohen Productions, 1967 (Monica Rivers); *Trog*, Herman Cohen Productions, 1970 (Dr. Brockton) TELEVISION: *The Man from U.N.C.L.E.*: "The Five Daughters Affair," 1967 (Amanda True); *Rod Serling's Night Gallery*: "Night Gallery," 1969 (Miss Menlo); *Beyond the Water's Edge* (Movie), 1972 (Allison Hayes); *The Sixth Sense*: "Dear Joan, We're Going to Scare You to Death," 1972 (Joan Fairchild)

Crosby, Mary (1959–)

BIRTHPLACE: Los Angeles, California, USA.

TELEVISION: *Hammer House of Mystery and Suspense*: "Child's Play," 1986 (Ann Preston)

BIOGRAPHY—The daughter of Bing Crosby and Kathryn Grant (*The 7th Voyage of Sinbad*), the lovely Mary Crosby made her acting debut at the age of eight in 1967 on *The Danny Thomas Hour*. She graduated high school at 15 and studied at the American Conservatory Theatre. Her best-known role is that of Kristin on the primetime soap opera *Dallas*; she was the one who shot J.R. A few years later, she starred in the "Child's Play" episode of *Hammer House of Mystery and Suspense*, in which a small family unit (mother, dad, and daughter) awakes to find their house enclosed by an unbreakable substance, and it's all they can do to keep from breaking down themselves. She gives a fine performance, at times hysterical but never lapsing into mere histrionics; her confusion and fear at the unexplainable events are vividly portrayed. More's the pity, then, that her efforts are somewhat undermined by a twist ending straight out of EC or Marvel Comics, in which the family is actually the literal plaything of alien life. She is still active in a career that has lasted practically her whole life.

Other genre credits: FILM: *The Ice Pirates*, JF Productions, 1984 (Princess Karina) TELEVISION: *The Danny Thomas Hour*: "The Demon Under the Bed," 1967 (Joan); *Freddy's Nightmares*: "Lucky Stiff," 1989 (Greta Nordhoff-Roscoe); "Easy Come, Easy Go," 1990 (Greta Ross); *Lois & Clark: The New Adventures of Superman*: "Neverending Battle," 1993 (Monique); *Star Trek: Deep Space Nine*: "Profit and Loss," 1994 (Natima Long)

Crosdale, Vera P.

FILM: *Creatures the World Forgot*, 1971 (Cave Girl)

Crow, Angela

BIRTHPLACE: Manchester, England.
FILMS: *X: The Unknown*, 1956 (Woman); *The Shadow of the Cat*, 1961 (The Daughter)
Other genre credits: FILMS: *Morons from Outer Space*, Thorn EMI Screen Entertainment, 1985 (Woman in Car) TELEVISION: *Doomwatch*: "Sex and Violence," 1970 (Mrs. Hastings); *Jack the Ripper* (Movie), 1988 (Liz Stride); *Tales of Mystery and Imagination*: "The Black Cat," 1995

Crowley, Amelia

FILM: *Wake Wood*, 2011 (Mary Brogan)

Cruikshank, Martha Ann "Marty" (1943–)

BIRTHPLACE: London, England.
FILM: *Journey to Midnight*, 1971 (Diana)
TELEVISION: *Journey to the Unknown*: "Poor Butterfly," 1969 (Diana)

Crutchley, Rosalie (1920–1997)

BIRTHPLACE: London, England.
FILMS: *Creatures the World Forgot*, 1971 (Old Crone); *Blood from the Mummy's Tomb*, 1971 (Helen Dickerson)
BIOGRAPHY — This distinguished, Mediterranean-featured British character actress trained at the Royal Academy of Music, made her stage debut in the 1930s and her screen debut in 1947 and was soon appearing in such major productions as *Quo Vadis*. She is remembered fondly by genre fans for her wonderful role as the sinister housekeeper in *The Haunting* and for parts in two Hammer films: a bit as a hag in *Creatures the World Forgot* and a larger supporting role in *Blood from the Mummy's Tomb*. In *Tomb* she plays a member of the expedition that uncovers and plunders Queen Tara's tomb; as always in horror movies, a cruel and violent death shall be their fate. And so it goes with Ms. Crutchley; she has returned to her seemingly primary occupation as a fortune teller, sequestered away with her relics from the tomb and a young male who has long, painted fingernails. But before long, she's visited by Valerie Leon and all Hell breaks loose, with Crutchley torn to shreds by the statue of a cat. Her career and life lasted for another 26 years, including a role in *Smiley's People*, which also featured Ingrid Pitt.
Other genre credits: FILMS: *The Gamma People*, Warwick Film Productions, 1956 (Frau Bikstein); *The Haunting*, Argyle Enterprises, 1963 (Mrs. Dudley); *...And Now the Screaming Starts!* Amicus Productions, 1973 (Mrs. Luke); *The House in Nightmare Park*, Anglo-EMI Film Distributors, 1977 (Jessica Henderson) TELEVISION: *Hallmark Hall of Fame*: "The Hunchback of Notre Dame," 1982 (Simone); *Worlds Beyond*: "The Black Tomb," 1987; *Dark Season*: Episodes 1, 2, and 3, 1991 (Mrs. Polzinski)

Cuka, Frances (1936–)

BIRTHPLACE: London, England.
TELEVISION: *Hammer House of Horror*: "Charlie Boy," 1980 (Gwen Williams)
BIOGRAPHY — The daughter of a tailor (Mother) and process engraver (Dad), Frances

Cuka (pronounced "Chewka") is a British character actress with a fifty-year career, primarily in television but including such feature films as *Scrooge* and *The Watcher in the Woods*. Her lone effort for Hammer was "Charlie Boy," an episode of *Hammer House of Horror* in which she plays the wife of the man who owns the titular African fetish; his death (caused by "Charlie Boy") sets events in motion. She's tragic and eerie, spending most of the episode in an understandably shell-shocked condition until Charlie reunites her with her husband. She is still active and well and living in London.

Other genre credits: FILMS: *The Watcher in the Woods*, Walt Disney Productions, 1980 (Mary Fleming); *Afraid of the Dark*, Les Films Ariane, 1991 (Mrs. Dalton) TELEVISION: *Snow White: A Tale of Terror* (Movie), 1997 (Nannau)

Cunningham, Jane

FILM: *Moon Zero Two*, 1969 (Dancer)

Cunningham, Linda

FILM: *Captain Kronos, Vampire Hunter*, 1974 (Jane)
Other genre credits: TELEVISION: *Thriller*: "Spell of Evil," 1973 (Suzy)

Daine, Lois (1941–)

BIRTHPLACE: Bolton, Lancashire, England.
FILMS: *Hell Is a City*, 1960 (Cecily Wainwright); *Cash on Demand*, 1962 (Sally); *Captain Kronos, Vampire Hunter*, 1974 (Sara Durward)
BIOGRAPHY—A British character actress of stage, screen and television, she had roles in three Hammer films: a secretary who is kidnapped, robbed and killed in *Hell Is a City*, Peter Cushing's daughter in *Cash on Demand*, and the manly sister of fey Shane Briant in *Captain Kronos, Vampire Hunter* (her best of the three). Add to their sexual confusion a suggested incestuous relationship, and suspicions of being vampires, and you have two of the more intriguing Hammer supporting characters. She retired in 1994.

Dalby, Amy Mary (1888–1969)

BIRTHPLACE: Clerkenwell, London, England.
FILMS: *Further Up the Creek*, 1958 (Edie); *The Old Dark House*, 1963 (Gambler)
Other genre credits: TELEVISION: *The Avengers*: "The Rotters," 1968 (Mrs. Forsythe)

Dalton, Patty

FILM: *The Terror of the Tongs*, 1961 (Tong Room Girl)

Daniel, Jennifer (1939–)

REAL NAME: Jennifer Williams; BIRTHPLACE: Pontypool, South Wales.
FILMS: *The Kiss of the Vampire*, 1963 (Marianne Harcourt); *The Reptile*, 1966 (Valerie Spalding)
BIOGRAPHY—Jennifer Daniel will be forever remembered by Hammer fans for playing two of the strongest leading character in two of the company's greatest films, *The Kiss of the Vampire* and *The Reptile*. Born in 1939, she showed an early aptitude for music and was a clarinetist in the Welsh National Youth Orchestra. She attended the Central School of Speech and Drama and spent time in a repertory company before getting her first break in television (the medium in which she spent virtually her whole career), as the First Fairy in *BBC Sunday*

There's no end to the horrors that Jennifer Daniel has to face up to on this Mexican lobby card from *The Reptile*.

Night Theatre's presentation of "A Midsummer Night's Dream." The Hammer films were her first feature film work, although not her last: In 1992, she appeared as Mrs. Linton in *Wuthering Heights*, and in 1996 as a singer in Paramount's *Love Is All There Is*, which was, to date, her last role of any kind.

In both of her Hammer films, she plays a newlywed, and in both she faces off against Noel Willman. A case could be made that Hammer's non–Dracula films featured some of their most inventive and lasting contributions to vampire cinema; without being able to rely on the commanding presence of Christopher Lee to carry a movie, they had to rely on creativity, and nowhere is this better illustrated than in *The Kiss of the Vampire*. Daniel plays, what would seem on the surface, a typical Hammer heroine: the wife or girlfriend of the Young Leading Man, or the daughter or niece of the Wiser Older Man, and she gets victimized in some manner by the monster and is then saved by either one of the leading men or some combination thereof. And indeed, this is precisely what happens to Daniel in *The Kiss of the Vampire*. But *Kiss* isn't the typical Hammer vampire film. Her musical seduction by Willman's son is reminiscent of similar scenes from other classic horrors, but a different kind of frisson is added when it becomes apparent that Willman's daughter Jacquie Wallis is also getting a visible charge out of it. Daniel is bitten by Willman's vampire, but rather than turning into a sexually charged animal, her demeanor remains much the same (although tradition is not completely out the window; her necklines take the usual agreeable plunge). But then there's the moment when she is brought before her trussed-up husband and spits in his face. Then, in an inversion of the earlier scene, it is her turn to watch, as Isobel Black prepares to initiate her hubby into the fold by sashaying up to him slowly and then stripping away his shirt. The look on Daniel's face is one of both bemusement and anticipation. After hubby and Clifford Evans, as this film's Van Helsing figure, have snatched her from the clutches of the castle's cult, and Willman wills her to return, even her obligatory "walk through the woods in a nightie" scene is not the usual dazed wafting through the trees, but rather more determined, with a sense of purpose and look of determination.

She displays the same sense of purpose, and just plain sense, in *The Reptile*. Her character isn't the focus of events that it was in the previous film; this time it is more in the standard vein of Hammer heroine. But she still manages to give something a little more than the script asks for, especially in the scene where she has to cut open and tend to her husband's wound after he has been attacked by the fanged fiend. She keeps herself on an even keel, and her "Soccer Mom" type of beauty helps to cement the illusion. She showed the same stability in her personal life: She married fellow actor Dinsdale Landen in 1959, and it was a happy union until his death in 2003.

Other genre credits: TELEVISION: *Beauty and the Beast*: Episodes 1 and 2, 1961 (Beauty); *One Step Beyond*: "Signal Received," 1961 (Sheilah); *Doomwatch*: "Red Sky," 1970 (Dana Colley); *Suspense*: "Virus X," 1962 (Jane Callon); *Thriller*: "Spell of Evil," 1973 (Liz); *The Boy Merlin*: "Red Dragon, White Dragon," 1979 (Ismena)

Danielle, Suzanne (1957–)

REAL NAME: Suzanne Morris; BIRTHPLACE: London, England.

TELEVISION: *Hammer House of Horror*: "Carpathian Eagle," 1980 (Natalie Bell)

BIOGRAPHY—Beautiful Suzanne Danielle was born in London and trained as a dancer at the Bush Davies School of Theatre Arts. She made her first stage appearance in a musical, and joined a dancing troupe. Her first TV role was in the show *The Professionals* and she also appeared in big-budget films like *The Wild Geese* and *Flash Gordon*. She also played a featured role in a *Doctor Who* story arc. Her long, gorgeous dancer's legs are front and center in her starring role for *Hammer House of Horror*, as a writer who takes her research to the extreme. By day, she wears glasses and plain dresses, but by night she slips into a wig and microminiskirt, attracting men who she then stabs to death. She's deliciously evil and devastatingly sexy. She had a seven-year relationship with fellow Hammer alum Patrick Mower (*The Devil Rides Out*), and one of her last roles was in *The Stud* with another former Hammer Heroine, Joan Collins. She retired from the business in 1987, shortly after meeting and marrying golfer Sam Torrance, with whom she has four children.

Other genre credits: FILMS: *Flash Gordon*, Starling Films, 1980 (Serving Girl) TELEVISION: *Doctor Who*: "Destiny of the Daleks," 1979 (Agella); *Tales of the Unexpected*: "Hijack," 1981 (Milly); "Pattern of Guilt," 1982 (Elaine)

Darby, Jane

FILM: *Vampire Circus*, 1972 (Jenny Schilt)

Das Gupta, Bandana

FILMS: *The Two Faces of Dr. Jekyll*, 1960 (Sphinx Girl); *The Terror of the Tongs*, 1961 (Anna Chang)

Other genre credits: FILM: *The Brain*, Central Cinema Company Film, 1962 (Miss Soong) TELEVISION: *The Avengers*: "Crescent Moon," 1961 (Carmelita Mendoza) NOTE: *The Brain* is an adaptation of *Donovan's Brain*.

Davies, Rachel

TELEVISION: *Hammer House of Horror*: "The House That Bled to Death," 1980 (Emma)

BIOGRAPHY—A staple on British television since 1971, the lovely Rachel Davies has only appeared in two feature films. One of her early appearances was for *Hammer House of Horror* in the episode "The House That Bled to Death." She plays a single mother who hooks up with a sleazebag who subjects her and her daughter to untold horrors in a "murder house" (including killing their cat) so that he can sell the movie rights to their story for a cool million. Davies forgives him, but the little girl doesn't. She's smashing, whether she's strutting her stuff in a pink bikini or being drenched in Kensington Gore. At the time of this writing, she shows no signs of slowing down.

Other genre credits: FILM: *Police 2020*, 1997 (DCI Marsha Beagley) TELEVISION: *Thriller*: "The Next Voice You See," 1975 (Nancy): *Tales of the Unexpected*: "The Man at the Top," 1980 (Diane); *Doctor Who*: "State of Decay," 1980 (Camilla)

Davis, Bette (1908–1989)

REAL NAME: Ruth Elizabeth Davis; BIRTHPLACE: Lowell, Massachusetts, USA.

FILMS: *The Nanny*, 1965 (The Nanny); *The Anniversary*, 1968 (Mrs. Taggart)

BIOGRAPHY—So much has already been written about the legendary Oscar winner Bette Davis that it seems fairly futile to recount the details of her life, so this biographical section will instead simply cover her two films for Hammer, which tend to get glossed in discussions of her career. Without a doubt, she's the top dog in Hammer's "Avenging Grannies" series,

Bette Davis (left) and Jill Bennett in *The Nanny*.

achieving that status with two wonderfully intense performances that, like the films themselves, are as different as night and day. There was trouble between Davis and, well, practically everyone else connected with the movies, but no co-worker could deny her professionalism and talent. Inspired by her success in *What Ever Happened to Baby Jane?* and *Hush ... Hush, Sweet Charlotte*, Hammer first cast her in *The Nanny*, an atmospheric B&W thriller that still retains the power to unsettle. At the root of both of her Hammer films are dysfunctional families that Davis, whether she's a nanny or a mother, dominates. Her performance in *The Nanny* is subtly evil and manipulative, yet ultimately touching; the audience knows from the moment that she appears on screen that she's so unctuous that there has to be something amiss, but the little boy she attends to, William Dix is so obnoxious that our sympathies lie with Davis. In fact, most of the family members are such idiots that even when the tragic events begin to unfold, she still seems like the only sane one in the house. Of course, it can be argued that those tragic events have made the little Dix what he is, but when the flashbacks begin to flash, he shows himself to be a sullen, self-involved brat who cares little about his sweet little sister, whose accidental death at Davis's hands would unhinge the most stable of us. True, she didn't have to blame it on him, but given his actions prior to the death, it's certainly easy to see how he could be blamed. Jill Bennett's Pen is the only sympathetic character in the movie, which is why her death scene continues to have the impact it does, and is masterfully played by both her and Davis: Bennett grasping for the life-saving medicine that Davis holds so close and yet so far away, even as she tries to make Bennett as comfortable as possible.

The contrast between this role and that of Mrs. Taggart in *The Anniversary* could not be greater; of course, the tone of the two films is different to begin with, but she could have played the nanny in much broader fashion. She is under no restraints in *The Anniversary*, a black comedy so black that at times it seems closer to reality than the more serious *The Nanny*. Her performance is so deliciously and absurdly cruel that it has to be a case of, as the British say, "taking the piss," a fact confirmed by Davis in the film's final scene, where she plays with one of those old toys that squirts water when it drops its pants and laughs hysterically. But the whole point is that the toy is the only man in the film, figuratively, with a penis (and, by extension, balls). One son is henpecked, one will be, and the other is a transvestite. So it's not just Davis who wields the "girl power" in this film, it's the other women as well, although they're mere amateurs when trying to compete with a professional who is both the irresistible force *and* the immovable object — in both real and reel life.

Other genre credits: FILMS: *What Ever Happened to Baby Jane?* Associates and Aldrich Company, 1962 (Baby Jane Hudson); *Hush ... Hush, Sweet Charlotte*, Associates and Aldrich Company, 1964 (Charlotte Hollis); *Madame Sin*, 2X Productions/ITC, 1972 (Madame Sin); *Burnt Offerings*, Produzioni Europee Associati, 1976; *Return to Witch Mountain*, Walt Disney Pictures, 1978 (Letha); *The Watcher in the Woods*, Walt Disney Pictures, 1980 (Mrs. Aylwood); *Wicked Stepmother*, Larco Productions, 1989 (Miranda Pierpoint) TELEVISION: *Suspicion*: "Fraction of a Second," 1958 (Mrs. Wilfred Ellis); *Alfred Hitchcock Presents*: "Out There — Darkness," 1959 (Miss Fox); *Scream, Pretty Peggy* (Movie), 1973 (Mrs. Elliott); *The Dark Secret of Harvest Home* (Mini-Series): 1978 (Widow Fortune)

Day, Vera (1935–)

BIRTHPLACE: London, England.
FILMS: *Quatermass 2*, 1957 (Sheila); *Up the Creek*, 1958 (Lily); *A Clean Sweep*, 1958 (Daphne Watson); *Watch it, Sailor!* 1961 (Shirley Hornett)
BIOGRAPHY — Blonde bombshell Vera Day was a model and chorus girl in the early days of her career. While she was in the chorus line, she was spotted by director Val Guest, who

cast her in her first film, *Dance Little Lady*, and then in her first film for Hammer, *Quatermass 2*, in which she plays a woman scarred by an alien meteorite—not, as most of the victims, on the face, but below her neck. As with all the Quatermass films, any female involvement is purely coincidental, and so she does what she can with the role and does look great doing it. She did three more films for Hammer, all comedies, but her lack of formal training, coupled with her easily exploitable physical assets, conspired to keep her out of the big time. (She came close in films like Marilyn Monroe's *The Prince and the Showgirl*, which also featured fellow Hammer Heroines Daphne Anderson and Maxine Audley.) In 1963, she married celebrity photographer Terry O'Neill, and retired until her comeback appearance in the award-winning *Lock, Stock, and Two Smoking Barrels*.

   Other genre credits: FILMS: *Grip of the Strangler*, Amalgamated Productions, 1958 (Pearl); *The Woman Eater*, Fortress Film Productions, 1958 (Sally Norton)

De la Tour, Frances (1944–)

BIRTHPLACE: Bovingdon, Hertfordshire, England.
FILM: *To the Devil a Daughter*, 1976 (Salvation Army Major)
Other genre credits: FILMS: *Harry Potter and the Goblet of Fire*, Warner Brothers, 2005 (Madame Olympe Maxine); *The Book of Eli*, Alcon Entertainment, 2010 (Martha); *Alice in Wonderland*, Walt Disney Pictures, 2010 (Aunt Imogene); *Harry Potter and the Deathly Hallows, Part 1*, Warner Brothers, 2010 (Madame Olympe Maxine); *Hugo*, Paramount, 2011 (Madame Emilie)

De Rauch, Micky

FILM: *One Million Years B.C.*, 1966 (Shell Girl)

De Sain, Monique

TELEVISION: *Hammer House of Mystery and Suspense*: "The Late Nancy Irving," 1985 (Anne)

Dean, Margia (1922–)

REAL NAME: Marguerite Louise Skliris; BIRTHPLACE: Chicago, Illinois, USA.
FILM: *The Quatermass Xperiment*, 1955 (Judith Caroon)
BIOGRAPHY—Strikingly beautiful brunette Margia Dean was born in the town that Billy Sunday couldn't shut down, and began acting at the age of seven. She also quite naturally gravitated towards modeling and in 1939 won both the Miss San Francisco and Miss California titles. Her first film appearance was in *Casanova in Burlesque* (1944) for the greatest-ever studio for movie serials, Republic Pictures. Although her beauty and talent merited more, she spent the majority of her 20-year career in low-budget films and television. She got a bit of a lift with her starring role in the historic first *Quatermass* film (which, admittedly, was of a low budget itself, just of higher quality): As the wife of tragic astronaut Richard Wordsworth, she can do nothing to stop her husband's transformation into a hideous monster that is no longer even human. The *Quatermass* movies didn't exactly offer a mass of opportunities for its female characters, but Dean is convincing in her anguish and her suspicions of Doc Quatermass. She has been happily married since 1965, and her widely varied talents have seen her as the vice-president of a top real estate company, restaurateur, and dress shop owner.

   Other genre credits: FILMS: *Superman and the Mole-Men*, Lippert Pictures, 1951 (Mrs. Benson); *Mesa of Lost Women*, Ron Ormond Productions, 1953 (Lost Brunette) TELEVISION: *The Adventures of Superman*: "The Secret of Superman," 1952 (Agency Woman)

Dear, Elizabeth

FILMS: *Nightmare*, 1963 (Janet as a Child); *Captain Kronos, Vampire Hunter*, 1974 (Ann Sorell)

Dearman, Jennifer

FILM: *Four-Sided Triangle*, 1953 (Lena as a Child)

Delany, Pauline (1925–2007)

BIRTHPLACE: Dublin, Ireland.
TELEVISION: *Hammer House of Horror*: "The Two Faces of Evil," 1980 (Ward Sister)
BIOGRAPHY — Pauline Delany trained in Dublin's Brendan Smith Academy of Acting. She began her career on the stage and then graduated to mostly television work, although she did make the odd appearance in feature films such as the dumb penis transplant "comedy" *Percy* and John Wayne's dumber *Brannigan* ("Knock, knock!"). She's wonderfully sinister in the *Hammer House of Horror* episode "The Two Faces of Evil," radiating malevolence as a ward sister in the hospital where Everything Is Not What It Seems — and nobody who works there seems very concerned who knows. She had a 40-year career which lasted into the 1990s, and she passed away from natural causes in 2007.

Other genre credits: TELEVISION: *The Avengers*: "The Golden Eggs," 1963 (Elizabeth Bayle); "The £50,000 Breakfast," 1967 (Mrs. Rhodes)

Denberg, Susan (1944–)

REAL NAME: Dietlinde Zechner; BIRTHPLACE: Bad Polzin, Germany.
FILM: *Frankenstein Created Woman*, 1967 (Christina)
BIOGRAPHY — The rumors of the death of Susan Denberg have been exaggerated. Although it has been reported in a number of books and fan journals that she was a suicide stemming from her well-publicized battles with drugs, alcohol and mental illness, the happy fact is that she is still with us. She doesn't do interviews or appear at fan conventions, but it is enough for her fans to know that she is alive and well.

Denberg came to Las Vegas as a member of a chorus line, which she soon quit to marry her first husband; the marriage broke up after six months, and she had an affair with the star of her first movie, Stuart Whitman. When the movie shoot ended, so did the affair, and she began another with an actor who introduced her into the world of drugs, kinky sex and physical abuse. She took acting lessons, appeared in an episode of *Star Trek*, and then was *Playboy*'s playmate of the month (August 1966). This directly led to her getting the role in Hammer's classic *Frankenstein Created Woman*.

Denberg's voice was dubbed, but her performance as Christina is one of the most iconic in the history of Hammer. Her acting lessons had paid off; she conveys great sympathy as the disfigured Christina, is properly incredulous when confronted with her new form, and beautifully evil (and evilly beautiful) when she is possessed by the soul of Hans when she kills the upper-class twits who framed him for a crime they committed (murdering her father). Her tears before her first suicide seem very real, her eyes a mirror of her tormented soul. The movie's posters, photos and lobby cards are iconic: Denberg in a cloth bikini on the upright operating table, a sexy takeoff on Elsa Lanchester's similar (but completely wrapped) poses as the Bride of Frankenstein (just as the film's title was a takeoff on the Brigitte Bardot movie *...And God Created Woman*); Denberg in the same bikini carried in the arms of Peter Cushing, and especially Denberg with that meat cleaver.

With her appearance in *Playboy* and a leading role in an internationally seen, quality

Susan Denberg and Barry Warren get "tits up" in this lobby card from *Frankenstein Created Woman* (courtesy Mel Bridgeman).

movie, her future appeared bright, but her life continued to unravel with a series of high-profile affairs and harder drug use. Because of this, she was soon gone from the business completely, her mental condition severely deteriorated. She underwent shock treatment and endured an agonizing stay in a mental hospital. With the help of her parents, she began the long road to recovery. She now lives in Austria. Although she remains elusive, she has certainly earned her right to privacy, the right to live a life, which is far more important than any film.

Other genre credits: *Star Trek*: "Mudd's Women," 1966 (Magda)

Dennis, Winifred

FILM: *Fanatic*, 1965 (Shopkeeper)

Desni, Tamara (1910–2008)

REAL NAME: Tamara Brodsky; BIRTHPLACE: Berlin, Germany.
FILM: *Dick Barton at Bay*, 1950 (Anna)

Devereux, Marie (1941–)

REAL NAME: Patricia Sutcliffe; BIRTHPLACE: Edmonton, London, England.
FILMS: *I Only Arsked!* 1958 (Harem Girl); *The Stranglers of Bombay*, 1959 (Karim); *The*

Brides of Dracula, 1960 (Village Girl); *A Weekend with Lulu*, 1961 (Girl); *The Pirates of Blood River*, 1962 (Maggie Mason)

BIOGRAPHY—Always a bridesmaid, never a bride (except of Dracula), gorgeous Marie Devereux reportedly had the largest bust of any Hammer Heroine. This attribute kept her very busy for a number of years as both a pin-up model and an actress and ultimately, like other actresses in this book, kept her from realizing her ambition to be cast for her talent instead of her figure. Her first role for the company was as a harem girl in the gormless comedy *I Only Arsked!*; her second in *The Stranglers of Bombay* was essentially the same, only with a name and a bit more to do. Her most memorable was as one of the Brides of Dracula—or at least David Peel's Baron Meinster. She's first glimpsed as a fresh corpse, but is soon rising from the grave in one of the film's best scenes, where she is coaxed out of the ground to the cackling sounds of Freda Jackson. She returns later, teamed up with Andree Melly, to corner Peter Cushing and Yvonne Monlaur. The fate of Devereux and Melly is never revealed, unless they just drop dead when Meinster does and go up in flames along with the rest of the windmill. Her next Hammer was more eye candy in a jocular vein, in *A Weekend with Lulu*, which starred the "Golden Girl" of *Goldfinger*, Shirley Eaton. Devereux's last Hammer was the swashbuckling *The Pirates of Blood River*, which starred Kerwin Mathews (*The 7th Voyage of Sinbad*). She doubled for Elizabeth Taylor in *Cleopatra*, and then went to Hollywood where she scored roles in Sam Fuller's *Shock Corridor* and *The Naked Kiss*; the latter proved to be her last.

Marie Devereux is looking to catch anything other than haddock in these fishnets, in a glamor shot from the set of *The Brides of Dracula* (courtesy Mel Bridgeman).

Other genre credits: FILMS: *Grip of the Strangler*, Amalgamated Productions, 1958 (Girl); *The Woman Eater*, Fortress Film Productions, 1958 (Girl)

Di Leo, Serafina (1912–2007)

BIRTHPLACE: New York City, New York, USA.
FILM: *The Curse of the Werewolf*, 1961 (Senora Zumara)
Other genre credits: TELEVISION: *Out of the Unknown*: "The Fox and the Forest," 1965 (Mexican Woman)

Dickie, Olga (1900–1992)

BIRTHPLACE: India
FILMS: *Dracula*, 1958 (Gerda); *The Kiss of the Vampire*, 1963 (Woman at Graveyard); *The Curse of the Mummy's Tomb*, 1964 (Housekeeper)
BIOGRAPHY—Indian-born of Scottish parents, Olga Dickie was a character actress and radio announcer, active in both fields for almost 40 years. She is memorable in *Dracula* (as is the entire cast) as the housekeeper Gerda, who manages to keep her job despite letting Dracula vampirize both Lucy and Mina and letting her young child wander alone in the woods at night with vampires. She was in two other Hammer Horrors: a bit part in the classic *The Kiss of the Vampire* and another housekeeper role in *The Curse of the Mummy's Tomb*. In the latter, she lets the Mummy carry off the lady of the house, so this was understandably her last role as a domestic. She passed away from natural causes in 1992.

Dickson, Louise

FILM: *The Terror of the Tongs*, 1961 (Tong Room Girl)

Dignam, Rebecca

FILM: *The Damned*, 1963 (Anne)

Doherty, Aoife

FILM: *The Woman in Black*, 2012 (Lucy Jerome)

Don, Maggie

FILM: *Journey to Midnight*, 1971 (Barbara)
TELEVISION: *Journey to the Unknown*: "Poor Butterfly," 1969 (Barbara)

Donnelly, Elaine (1948–)

BIRTHPLACE: Cheltenham, England.
TELEVISION: *Hammer House of Horror*: "The Silent Scream," 1980 (Annie Spillers)
BIOGRAPHY—A staple of British television since her first appearance in 1969, Elaine Donnelly was in the "Silent Scream" episode of *Hammer House of Horror*, in which she plays the wife of a convict who gets involved with Peter Cushing's experiments with animals, and then both become test cases themselves. She's quite convincing going postal. The episode is notable for Cushing's role, but dog lovers are nonetheless advised to steer clear. She hasn't appeared in a film or television show since 2006.
Other genre credits: TELEVISION: *Thriller*: "Sleepwalker," 1976 (Esme)

Donovan, Erin

TELEVISION: *Hammer House of Mystery and Suspense*: "The Sweet Scent of Death," 1986 (Young Girl)
Other genre credits: FILM: *E.T.—The Extra-Terrestrial*, Universal Pictures, 1982 (Additional Voices, 2002 Special DVD Edition) TELEVISION: *Lois & Clark: The New Adventures of Superman*: "Just Say Noah," 1995 (Betty)

Dors, Diana (1931–1984)

REAL NAME: Diana Mary Fluck; BIRTHPLACE: Swindon, Wiltshire, England.
FILMS: *The Last Page* (a.k.a. *Man Bait*), 1952 (Ruby Bruce); *The Saint's Return* (a.k.a. *The Saint's Girl Friday*), 1953 (The Blonde)

TELEVISION: *Hammer House of Horror*: Mrs. Ardoy, "Children of the Full Moon," 1980 (Mrs. Ardoy)

BIOGRAPHY—Despite the plethora of incredibly beautiful women chronicled in this book, for many Britons (especially those of a particular generation), there is only one, true British sex symbol, and that is Diana Dors. She is known as "the British Marilyn Monroe," and there is a large dose of Jayne Mansfield as well. Like Monroe, she proved to be much more than just another pretty face, with talent as ample as their "assets," and like Mansfield, she also had an ample talent for self-promotion and later, self-parody—whether intentional or not. And like both of them, Dors lived out her life through the tabloids and died much too young, although Dors managed to survive long enough to prove her talent as an actress long after her fabled looks had faded.

Dors had just begun to trade on the blonde bombshell image when she made Hammer's *The Last Page* in 1952, and was well-immersed in it (and already close to self-parody) by the next year's *The Saint's Return*. But it was well after her glory days (and Hammer's) that she gave her best performance for the studio, in the superior "Children of the Full Moon" episode of *Hammer House of Horror*, as a foster mother to a brood of werewolves. This was the first time Hammer had dealt with lycanthropes since their classic *The Curse of the Werewolf*, and the opening scenes of this episode echo the film with its dead sheep and child with blood-stained lips (as well as the closing ones, in which a woman dies giving birth to a werewolf). The episode not only recalls the studio's formative years with Dors, but also Hammer's Golden Age of Horror with the welcome inclusion of Robert Urquhart from *The Curse of Frankenstein*. But it is Dors' show all the way; she is eminently charming and sweet, with a twinkle in her eyes masking the foul intentions in her heart, showing genuine care and motherly love towards her murderous brood. It was a completely delightful performance that promised many more to come, but ovarian cancer took its final toll just a few short years later.

Other genre credits: FILMS: *Berserk*, Herman Cohen Productions, 1967 (Matilda); *The Amazing Mr. Blunden*, Hemdale Film, 1972 (Mrs. Wickens); *Theater of Blood*, Cineman Productions, 1973 (Maisie); *From Beyond the Grave*, Amicus Productions, 1974 (Mabel Lowe) TELEVISION: *Alfred Hitchcock Presents*: "The Sorcerer's Apprentice," 1962 (Irene); *The Alfred Hitchcock Hour*: "Run for Doom," 1963 (Nicki Carole); *Thriller*: "The Devil's Web," 1975 (Bessie); *Doctor Jekyll and Mister Hyde* (Movie), 1980 (Kate Winterton)

Dotrice, Michele (1948–)

BIRTHPLACE: Cleethorpes, Lincolnshire, England.
FILM: *The Witches*, 1966 (Valerie Creek)
Other genre credits: FILM: *The Blood on Satan's Claw*, Tigon British Film Productions, 1971 (Margaret) TELEVISION: *Late Night Horror*: "The Bells of Hell," 1968 (Phrynne Banstead)

Douglas, Katya (1938–)

BIRTHPLACE: Gdynia, Pomorskie, Poland.
FILM: *Stop Me Before I Kill!* 1960 (Connie)
Other genre credits: FILM: *The Day of the Triffids*, Security Pictures, 1962 (Mary)

Down, Lesley-Anne (1954–)

BIRTHPLACE: Wandsworth, London, England.
FILM: *Countess Dracula*, 1971 (Ilona)
BIOGRAPHY—Lesley-Anne Down began modeling at an early age; in 1969 at 15 she was voted "Britain's Most Beautiful Teenager." She made her film debut the same year in *The*

Smashing Bird I Used to Know, and the next year she was at work on her only role for Hammer, as Ingrid Pitt's daughter in *Countess Dracula*. Since Ingrid is trying to pass herself off as her own daughter, Lesley-Anne's presence is distinctly unwelcome; Lesley-Anne spends the majority of her screen time either kidnapped, and locked away in a remote house in the woods, or rescued but locked in a room of her mother's castle. She later went on to much bigger things in television (*Upstairs, Downstairs* and *Dallas*) and films (*The Pink Panther Strikes Again* with Hammer Opera Phantom Herbert Lom). She is still active; as of this writing, she has been in the cast of the daytime soap *The Bold and the Beautiful* since 2003 and still does film work as well. She resides in Malibu with her husband.

Other genre credits: FILMS: *From Beyond the Grave*, Amicus Productions, 1974 (Rosemary Seaton); *Night Trap*, West Side Studios, 1993 (Christine Turner); *Haunted*, Greenway Entertainment, 2012 (Haunted Woman) TELEVISION: *Out of the Unknown*: "To Lay a Ghost," 1971 (Diana Carver); *Supernatural*: "Mr. Nightingale," 1977 (Felizitas); *Hallmark Hall of Fame*: "The Hunchback of Notre Dame," 1982 (Esmeralda); *Beastmaster: The Eye of Braxus* (Movie), 1996 (Morgana)

Drake, Gabrielle (1940–)

BIRTHPLACE: Lahore, Punjab, British India (Pakistan).
TELEVISION: *Journey to the Unknown*: "The Beckoning Fair One," 1968 (Kit Beaumont)
BIOGRAPHY—This beautiful British character actress trained at RADA; played her first television role in *Intrigue* (1966), but really got noticed when she played Lt. Gaye Ellis in the Gerry Anderson series *UFO* (with purple hair and a sparkly mini-skirt, it would have been hard *not* to notice her). She found further success in a number of British sex comedies, and also lent her gorgeous legs to a lead role in the *Journey to the Unknown* episode "The Beckoning Fair One" as the girlfriend of an artist (the spectacularly uncharismatic and far older Robert Lansing) who becomes obsessed with (and possessed by?) a dead beauty's painting. At first, it's reminiscent of Otto Preminger's *Laura*, but then it becomes much more complex. Unfortunately, it spends much more time concerned with Lansing's mad ramblings than it does developing a character for Ms. Drake, so she doesn't have much to do other than look increasingly concerned. She keeps returning after each serious "accident" and ever-escalating abuse from Lansing—but perhaps that's the point, and like many such real-life victims, she pays for her misplaced devotion. At this writing, she is still active.

Other genre credits: FILM: *UFO... Annientare S.H.A.D.O. Stop. Uccidete Straker...* [a compilation of *UFO* TV episodes], Italian, 1974 (Lt. Gaye Ellis) TELEVISION: *The Avengers*: "The Hidden Tiger," 1967 (Angora); *Haunted*: "The Chinese Butterfly," 1967 (Virginia Land); *UFO*: "Identified," "A Question of Priorities," "E.S.P.," "Kill Straker!" "Destruction," "The Square Triangle," "Close Up," 1970; "Flight Path," "Ordeal," "Computer Affair," 1971; "Responsibility Seat," 1973 (Lt. Gaye Ellis); *Thriller*: "Kill Two Birds," 1976 (Tracy); *The New Avengers*: "Dead Men Are Dangerous," 1977 (Penny Redfern)

Du Sautoy, Carmen (1950–)

BIRTHPLACE: London, England.
TELEVISION: *Hammer House of Mystery and Suspense*: "The Sweet Scent of Death," 1986 (Suzy Kendrick)
BIOGRAPHY—Leggy Carmen Du Sautoy is a still-active British character actress of stage, screen and television. Her first television role came in 1970 in the *Play for Today* series, and in her first feature she was a Bond Girl, playing the belly dancer in the memorable scene in *The Man with the Golden Gun* where Roger Moore extracts a golden shell casing from her

navel with his teeth. She provides solid support in an episode of *Hammer House of Mystery and Suspense*, "The Sweet Scent of Death," in which she plays Dean Stockwell's secretary and co-conspirator in his plot to murder his wife.

Other genre credits: FILM: *The Man with the Golden Gun*, Eon Productions, 1974 (Saida) TELEVISION: *Highlander*: "Duende," 1997 (Anna Hidalgo)

Duffell, Bee (1914–1974)

BIRTHPLACE: Belfast, Ireland.
FILM: *Quatermass and the Pit*, 1968 (Miss Dobson)
Other genre credits: FILMS: *Fahrenheit 451*, Anglo Enterprises, 1966 (Book Woman); *Battle Beneath the Earth*, Reynolds-Vetter Productions, 1967 (Matron's Friend)

Duke, Patty (1946–)

REAL NAME: Anna Marie Duke; BIRTHPLACE: Elmhurst, New York, USA.
FILM: *Journey to the Unknown*, 1969 (Barbara King)
TELEVISION: *Journey to the Unknown*: "The Last Visitor," 1969 (Barbara King)

BIOGRAPHY—A name not normally associated with Hammer Films, beautiful Patty Duke is the very definition of a Hammer Heroine. She was the daughter of an alcoholic father and clinically depressed, abusive mother; at the age of eight she was turned over to a couple named Ross for the management of her career. This they did, but they also got her hooked on drugs and alcohol, sexually abused her and stole her money. She took refuge in her career, and won an Oscar at the age of 16 for *The Miracle Worker* (1962); she has also won a Golden Globe and two Emmys. She is best known to baby boomers for *The Patty Duke Show*, but by the end of the show's run, she was weary of her all–American image and began to branch out into more adult roles, like *Valley of the Dolls* and an episode of *Journey to the Unknown*, "The Last Visitor," in which she plays a young woman who needs a rest as a result of overwork and a failed affair, but instead finds herself menaced by a perverted, murderous maniac. The part itself is clichéd, but Duke manages to invest it with a certain edginess and tension that was partly due to her thespian skills and partly due to her unfortunate real-life struggle with bipolar disorder (undiagnosed at the time). The plot, too, is clichéd; it's *Psycho* with a gender switch, but we don't mind because of the quality of the performances of Duke and co-star Kay Walsh. She had a short recording career in the mid–1960s, and is also an author. On top of everything else, she has also survived cardiac bypass surgery. She is still active as an actress, and especially as an activist for mental health causes.

Other genre credits: FILMS: *4D Man*, Fairview Productions, 1959 (Marjorie Sutherland); *You'll Like My Mother*, Bing Crosby Productions–Universal Pictures, 1972 (Francesca Kinsolving); *The Swarm*, Warner Brothers Pictures, 1978 (Rita) TELEVISION: *Rod Serling's Night Gallery*: "The Diary," 1971 (Holly Schaeffer); *She Waits* (Movie), 1972 (Laura Wilson); *The Sixth Sense*: "With Affection, Jack the Ripper," 1972 (Elizabeth); *Circle of Fear*: "Graveyard Shift," 1973 (Linda Colby); *Look What's Happened to Rosemary's Baby* (Movie), 1976 (Rosemary Woodhouse); *Curse of the Black Widow* (Movie), 1977 (Laura Lockwood); *Amityville: The Evil Escapes* (Movie), 1989 (Nancy Evans); *Grave Secrets: The Legend of Hilltop Drive* (Movie), 1992 (Jean Williams)

Dukes, Pauline

FILMS: *The Two Faces of Dr. Jekyll*, 1960 (Sphinx Girl); *The Terror of the Tongs*, 1961 (Tong Room Girl)

Duncan, Fiona

FILM: *The Damned*, 1963 (Control Room Guard)

Dunion, Sheila

FILM: *Frankenstein and the Monster from Hell*, 1974 (Gerda)

Dunlop, Lesley (1956–)

BIRTHPLACE: Newcastle, England.
TELEVISION: *Hammer House of Mystery and Suspense*: "A Distant Scream," 1986 (Sarah Kimble)

Other genre credits: FILM: *The Monster Club*, Amicus Productions, 1981 (Luna) TELEVISION: *Haunted: The Ferryman* (Movie), 1974 (Jill Attingham); *Leap in the Dark*: "The Living Grave," 1980 (Pauline); *Doctor Who*: "Frontios," 1984 (Norna); "The Happiness Patrol," 1988 (Susan Q)

Dyson, Anne "Annie" (1908–1996)

BIRTHPLACE: Manchester, England.
TELEVISION: *Hammer House of Horror*: "The Mark of Satan," 1980 (Mrs. Rord)

BIOGRAPHY—This veteran British character actress does a delightful turn in "The Mark of Satan" as a vitriolic mother reminiscent of Tallulah Bankhead's religious nut in *Fanatic*. She directs lines like "We used to have a name for things like *her*!" at Georgina Hale's single mother and harangues her son until he sticks a knife in her gut—which, of course, he's not responsible for, since the Devil made him do it.

East, Susanna

FILM: *Captain Kronos, Vampire Hunter*, 1974 (Isabella Sorell)

Easter, Jill

FILM: *The Vampire Lovers*, 1970 (Woodsman's Wife)

Edwards, Jeillo (1942–2004)

BIRTHPLACE: Freetown, Sierra Leone.
TELEVISION: *Hammer House of Mystery and Suspense*: "Paint Me a Murder," 1985 (Landlady)

BIOGRAPHY—Jeillo Edwards attended the Guildhall School of Music and Drama. She has a nice bit in *Hammer House of Mystery and Suspense* as a landlady who can't figure out what some man is ranting about, especially when he tells her he's dead. She was also a school governor and the owner of Auntie J's restaurant in Brixton, where the Clash wrote their classic "Guns of Brixton."

Other genre credits: TELEVISION: *The League of Gentleman*: "Royston Vasey and the Monster from Hell," 2000 (Yvonne)

Ege, Julie (1943–2008)

REAL NAME: Julie Dzuli; BIRTHPLACE: Sandnes, Norway.
FILMS: *Creatures the World Forgot*, 1971 (Nala); *The Legend of the 7 Golden Vampires* (a.k.a. *The 7 Brothers Meet Dracula*) 1974 (Mrs. Vanessa Buren)

BIOGRAPHY—Gorgeous blonde bombshell Julie Ege left school at 15 and won the Miss

Norway contest two years later; she also competed for the Miss Universe title. A modeling career led to a shoot for *Penthouse*, and she was the *Penthouse* Pet of the Month for May 1967. She was crowned "The New Sex Symbol of the 1970s" after a competition in which over 1,500 hopefuls took part, when Hammer was in search of said sex symbol, but the fix was in, and it was later revealed that the "contest" had been a clever publicity campaign concocted by Sir James Carreras, Columbia, and Ms. Ege's agent to publicize their newest prehistoric epic, *Creatures the World Forgot*. As it turns out, the title was quite accurate, and the creatures that the world forgot were the dinosaurs! And without the expertly animated saurians of Ray Harryhausen or Jim Danforth, that left nothing but a bunch of grunting half-naked men and women battling the elements and snakes, bears, and mud people. Ege wears her fur bikini (or doesn't) well, and her character comes off as actually having the goods to cut it in the prehistoric times, as opposed to the too-demure Victoria Vetri. But the Powers of the Fur Bikini failed to work their magic, and soon Ege was relegated to smarmy sex comedies and other minor films. When *Creatures the World Forgot* wrapped, Ege had a brief affair with Hammer's Jimmy Sangster, and then took up with Beatles associate Tony Bramwell, whom she was with for a number of years. It was during that time that Ege made her other appearance for Hammer, as wealthy adventuress Vanessa Buren in the cult classic *The Legend of the Seven Golden Vampires*. Opinion is sharply divided on this film; some consider it to be the literal last nail in Hammer's Dracula coffin, others marveling at the sheer audacity of the concept and its execution. True, there are plot holes big enough to drive a funeral carriage through — for instance, Kah tells Dracula that the Seven Golden Vampires no longer have any power in their village and that the people "go their own way," but when we check in at the village, the vampires are still holding the village in a grip of deadly fear. And since when does Dracula need someone else's "mortal coil" to leave his castle? But there are pleasures for those willing to look: Peter Cushing's last, meaty performance as Van Helsing, a return to period, chopsocky, and the sense of fun that had been missing from *Satanic Rites*. At least Ege gets a chance to show her chops, which she vividly does in her climactic scene after she is bitten by one of the Seven Golden Vampires. She then tries to put the bite on her lover, who impales her, and then impales himself on the very same stake, expiring on top of her in a scene that's as overflowing with symbolism as it is with blood. As she herself admitted, she wasn't the world's greatest actress, but she

Julie Ege models the Clothes the World Forgot in this publicity still from *Creatures the World Forgot*.

plays the part of the jaded roué with more game than the situation demands. It was only a few years later that Ege retired from the business altogether (having spent a good deal of her career in the altogether), went back to school, and in 1998 became a registered nurse, working in a hospital until her death from breast cancer in 2008.

Other genre credits: FILMS: *On Her Majesty's Secret Service*, Danjaq/Eon Productions, 1969 (Scandinavian Girl); *The Mutations*, Cyclone/Getty Pictures Corporation, 1974 (Hedi)

Ellis, Aunjanue L. (1969–)

BIRTHPLACE: San Francisco, California, USA.
FILM: *The Resident*, 2011 (Sydney)
Other genre credits: TELEVISION: *True Blood*: "Burning House of Love," "Mine," "The First Taste," 2008 (Diane)

Ellis, June

FILM: *Quatermass and the Pit*, 1968 (Blonde)
Other genre credits: FILM: *Frenzy*, Universal Pictures, 1971 (Maisie the Barmaid) TELEVISION: *Out of the Unknown*: "Something in the Cellar," 1969 (Brenda); "The Uninvited," 1971 (Millicent Pattison)

Elvin, Elizabeth

FILM: *Beyond the Rave*, 2008 (Bea)

Evans, Jessie (1918–1993)

BIRTHPLACE: Mountain Ash, Wales.
FILM: *Countess Dracula*, 1971 (Rosa)
Other genre credits: TELEVISION: *Thriller*: "Lady Killer," 1973

Everest, Barbara (1890–1968)

BIRTHPLACE: Southfields, London, England.
FILM: *The Damned*, 1963 (Miss Lamont)
Other genre credits: FILMS: *Phantom of the Opera*, Universal Pictures, 1943 (The Aunt); *The Uninvited*, Paramount Pictures, 1944 (Lizzie Flynn)

Ewing, Barbara (1944–)

BIRTHPLACE: New Zealand
FILM: *Dracula Has Risen from the Grave*, 1968 (Zena the Barmaid)
TELEVISION: *Hammer House of Horror*: "Guardian of the Abyss," 1980 (Laura Stephens)
BIOGRAPHY—Barbara Ewing is a woman whose support status in *Dracula Has Risen from the Grave* belies her standing as an actress and author, the career to which she almost now exclusively devotes her time. RADA-trained, she made her film debut in a genre movie, Amicus' *Torture Garden*. Shortly afterward (and despite her disclaimer; see below), she was unforgettable as Zena, the brassy, busty barmaid who becomes Dracula's slave, imploring, "What do you want her for when you got *me*?" and we all know how that's going to go over. The night she is vampirized, she is nursing her neck wounds while in lingerie and stockings and is happened upon by Barry Andrews as Paul; it is amusing that she is brusque and goes out of her way to cover the wounds on her neck—as if he could look at her neck! She went on to much bigger things on television and stage, and has been particularly successful as an

Barbara Ewing (right) and Veronica Carlson in *Dracula Has Risen from the Grave*.

author, having published eight entertaining novels through 2011. Like many celebrities, she has her own website, but those looking for a treasure trove of Hammer memories will be disappointed (except for a photo of her as Zena in her stockings): "I have this nightmare of being remembered most for my performance as Zena the barmaid in one of the films I have been in, *Dracula Has Risen from the Grave*, about which people still write me *today*, forty years later." She goes on to say that she wasn't really that brassy or busty, either, but one red wig and one stuffed bra later, she created a character the fans will never forget, apparently whether she likes it or not. Twelve years after her signature role for the company, she returned to guest-star in one of the better episodes of *Hammer House of Horror*, "Guardian of the Abyss," which doubled up on the nostalgic appeal by also featuring former Hammer mainstay John Carson from *The Plague of the Zombies*, playing much the same role as in that film. The part is a far cry from Zena; Ewing plays Laura Stephens, an antique dealer who sets the events in motion, fancies the hero to no avail, and gets bloodied by one of her antiques in the hands of the heroine.

Other genre credits: FILMS: *Torture Garden*, Amicus Productions, 1967 (Dorothy Endicott); *Haunters of the Deep*, Children's Film and Television Foundation, 1984 (Mrs. Holman) TELEVISION: *Chiller*: "Number Six," 1995 (Mrs. Keegan)

Farmer, Suzan (1942–)

BIRTHPLACE: Kent, England.
FILMS: *The Crimson Blade*, 1964 (Constance Beverly); *The Devil-Ship Pirates*, 1964 (Angela

Smeeton); *Dracula, Prince of Darkness*, 1966 (Diana Kent); *Rasputin, the Mad Monk*, 1966 (Vanessa)

BIOGRAPHY—Lovely blonde Suzan Farmer left school at 15 to become an actress, and made her very first film appearance the next year; even so, she felt compelled to attend the Central School of Speech and Drama. She then divided her time between television and films. She made two back-to-back sets of features for Hammer, with a featured role as Boris Karloff's daughter in *Die, Monster, Die!* wedged in between them. Her first Hammer job was a double dose of "aargh, matey" in the swashbuckling adventures *The Crimson Blade* and *The Devil-Ship Pirates*, in which she is given little to do except act as a plot device that could have easily been filled by any young, pretty girl. Her most substantial role was in *Dracula, Prince of Darkness* as a young bride. This is a pretty standard part as well, but at least she has more to do and is involved in a scene that was the physical realization of the kind of scene that was only talked about in the 1931 *Dracula*, when Mina tells David Manners that "he opened his vein — and made me drink!"

Suzan Farmer sets all flags at full mast in this glamor shot from the set of *Devil-Ship Pirates*.

Thirty-five years later, Christopher Lee bares his chest, draws his own blood, and then draws Farmer to him, and makes her drink. Farmer is rather caught between a rock and a hard place in *Prince*; she must be virginal, but not virginal enough to simply be a younger version of Barbara Shelley, who, like Melissa Stribling before her, has never been properly sexually satisfied. When the film begins, the contrast is much sharper; Farmer is lively and takes things as they come (and even sneaks a peek at Father Shandor's bum while Shelley pointedly averts her gaze), while all Shelley can rightly feel is foreboding. Farmer grows up very quickly after being had by Dracula, which perhaps could lead to Shelley's situation in reverse. But at least for the present, she rebounds enough from her ordeal in the film's climax, where she has the presence of mind to grab Father Shandor's rifle and in firing, inadvertently discovers the method of Dracula's destruction (at least for this film). Her part in *Rasputin, the Mad Monk* brought her full circle back to *The Crimson Blade*, where she was used as "bait," only this time it's Christopher Lee who lets his "sword" do his thinking for him and suffers mightily for it. She lasted in films until her last appearance in 1980.

Other genre credits: FILM: *Die, Monster, Die!* Alta Vista Productions, 1965 (Susan Witley) TELEVISION: *Out of the Unknown*: "Target Generation," 1969 (Mary Hoff); *UFO*: "Survival,"

1971 (Tina Duval); *Thriller*: "Death in Deep Water," 1975 (Gilly); *Blake's 7*: "Deliverance," 1978 (Meegat); *Leap in the Dark*: "Jack be Nimble," 1980 (Grace)

Faye, Janina (1948–)

REAL NAME: Janina Smigelski; BIRTHPLACE: London, England.

FILMS: *Dracula*, 1958 (Tania); *Never Take Sweets from a Stranger*, 1960 (Jean); *The Two Faces of Dr. Jekyll*, 1960 (Jane)

BIOGRAPHY—It has to be troubling for any actress or actor to have played their best-remembered roles between the ages of 10 and 14, but elfin Janina Faye never let that impede the rest of her career, and takes great pride and satisfaction that she is remembered for them. She had her first part in 1956, and in a portent of things to come, soon played future Hammer Heroine Heather Sears as a child in *The Story of Esther Costello*. But soon she was acting in *Dracula* at Bray, in her signature role as Tania in the child who nearly becomes a victim of the vampires. She is unforgettable in the scene where she is brought to the Holmwoods' house, trembling, crying and frightened because of the experience she has just had alone in the woods with a woman; when Melissa Stribling asks who the woman was, Faye tearfully replies, "Aunt Lucy!" a response that still has the power to chill the spine. Faye never saw the completed film until she was an adult (when she made it, she was too young to see it); and as an adult, she played Lucy in a stage production of *Dracula*. She evoked sympathy as the deaf-mute child in *The Two Faces of Dr. Jekyll*, and appeared as Jean in *Never Take Sweets from a Stranger*, which involves one of the ultimate horrors, child rape. Understandably intense and never exploitative (for which Hammer is to be commended), the film takes on an even more chilling cast in the light of (and with parallels to) the Penn State scandal, where a respected football coach was found guilty of raping young boys but whose heinous crimes were covered up by a university administration more concerned with football than child welfare. The child rapist in *Sweets* is likewise protected—protected by the fear of the populace, since he is also the richest, most powerful man in town. Both of the sexual predators got what was coming to them, but as reel and real life so graphically demonstrated, the crimes are neither new nor limited in their scope. Janina made a welcome return to the genre in 2000, as Nurse Foley in the short film *Green Fingers*, which starred another Hammer Heroine, her pal Ingrid Pitt; it was a semi-remake of the 1972 episode of *Rod Serling's Night Gallery* which starred Elsa Lanchester. In 2000 she also became Patron of the Kingston Junior Drama Company. She is still active on stage, at Hammer revivals, and fan conventions.

Other genre credits: FILMS: *The Hands of Orlac*, Pendennis Films, 1960 (Girl); *The Day of the Triffids*, Security Pictures, 1962 (Susan); *Green Fingers*, Big H Productions, 2000 (Nurse Foley) TELEVISION: *Thriller*: "Good Salary, Prospects, Free Coffin," 1975 (Wendy Phillips)

Feller, Catherine

FILM: *The Curse of the Werewolf*, 1961 (Christina Fernando)

BIOGRAPHY—Although she enjoyed a 32-year career, Catherine Feller kept a low profile. Her first screen role was in *The Belles of St. Trinians* in 1954, and she played various bit roles in films and television before being cast as Oliver Reed's love interest in *The Curse of the Werewolf*. And although she plays a featured role, it is almost as if she is the "Invisible Woman" of the film; all of the most prominent and iconic promotional shots of the film feature Reed and Yvonne Romain, presumably because of Ms. Romain's much larger bust line. While her part is nowhere as showy as Romain's, it is as integral to the plot as hers; she can save Leon from the horrors of the full moon with her love; because he is denied her love and presence near him in his jail cell, he undergoes his final and ultimately tragic transformation. Although she didn't possess Romain's oomph, she is very pretty, brave, and independent-minded, defying her father's wishes for her to marry into the money of the upper-class twit to whom she's engaged. Her last screen appearance was as a chambermaid in the television series *Fresh Fields* in 1986; since then she has worked as an educator, and is also a translator for the magazine *Vogue Gioiello*.

Other genre credits: TELEVISION: *One Step Beyond*: "The Prisoner," 1961 (Ruth Goldman)

Ffrangcon-Davies, Gwen (1891–1992)

REAL NAME: (Dame) Gwen Lucy Ffrangcon-Davies; BIRTHPLACE: London, England.

FILMS: *The Witches*, 1966 (Granny Rigg); *The Devil Rides Out*, 1968 (Countess)

BIOGRAPHY—Dame Ffrangcon-Davies made her stage debut in 1911, and it was on stage that she spent the best part of her career until she retired from the boards in 1970; she continued to do movies and television, which she had done only sporadically since 1938. Her

Catherine Feller in a rare portrait from *The Curse of the Werewolf*.

first Hammer film, *The Witches*, is her best, as the strange, domineering Granny Rigg, but she barely has anything to do in *The Devil Rides Out* except to act regal and participate in Hammer's idea of a Satanic orgy, which means lots of people spinning around like they're dancing to the Grateful Dead and looking just as silly. The oldest person to ever receive the DBE, she made her last appearance in *The Casebook of Sherlock Holmes*, the year that she died.

Other genre credits: TELEVISION: *BBC Play of the Month*: "The Picture of Dorian Grey," 1976 (Lady Agatha)

Field, Shirley Anne (1938–)

REAL NAME: Shirley Broomfield; BIRTHPLACE: Bolton, Lancashire, England.

FILM: *The Damned* (a.k.a. *These are the Damned*), 1963 (Joan)

BIOGRAPHY—After being shuttled back and forth between children's homes because her parents could not afford to care for her, beautiful Shirley Anne Field attended the Lucie Clayton School. She initially became famous as a pin-up model; her first film role was in 1955. Frustrated at her lack of success and the parts she was offered, she nearly quit the business. Her role in *Saturday Night and Sunday Morning* changed all that, and soon she was playing parts commensurate with her talent, a talent vividly on display in her first and only Hammer, the classic *The Damned* (which inspired the pioneering horror-punk band of the same name). *The Damned* is the most different of all the classic Hammer horrors: no monsters, no bulging breasts and no happy ending. Field certainly looks as though she will be just another dolly bird, drawing in men with her ample charms so that her brother (Oliver Reed) and his Teddy

Boys can rob them, but this is all just foreplay, as it were; not only does the movie actually take time to develop a believable romance between Field and Macdonald Carey, but her gradual transformation from callow youth to utter helplessness and hopelessness is delineated in similarly credible fashion. Her career stalled again in the mid-1970s, but lightning struck twice and she became part of another decade-defining film, *My Beautiful Launderette* (1985). She has not looked back since.

Other genre credits: FILMS: *Horrors of the Black Museum*, Carmel Productions, 1959 (Angela Banks); *Peeping Tom*, Michael Powell Theatre, 1960 (Pauline Shields); *Curse of the Dead*, Associated Film Productions, 1976 (Mary Anne Carew); *U.F.O.*, George Forster, 1993 (Supreme Commander)

Fielding, Fenella (1927–)

REAL NAME: Fenella Feldman; BIRTHPLACE: London, England.

FILM: *The Old Dark House*, 1963 (Morgana Femm)

BIOGRAPHY—"The British Queen of the Double Entendre" (delivered in her trademark deep, sonorous voice) is one of that country's most respected actresses, and as of 2012, still one of its most active. She only did one film for Hammer, *The Old Dark House*, but her performance as the sex-starved Morgana Femm is a gem. Although Janette Scott is the nominal lead, Fielding steals the show—not an easy task, considering the (sometimes literally) heavyweight cast, including Robert Morley and Peter Bull.

Shirley Anne Field and Oliver Reed in *The Damned*.

Other genre credits: FILMS: *Carry on Screaming*, Peter Rogers Productions, 1966 (Valeria Watt) TELEVISION: *The Avengers*: "The Charmers," 1964 (Kim Lawrence); *Uncle Jack and the Loch Ness Monster*: six episodes, 1991 (The Vixen); *Uncle Jack and the Dark Side of the Moon*: six episodes, 1992 (The Vixen); *Uncle Jack and Cleopatra's Mummy*: six episodes, 1993 (The Vixen)

Fielding, Janet (1957–)

REAL NAME: Janet Claire Mahoney; BIRTHPLACE: Brisbane, Queensland, Australia.
TELEVISION: *Hammer House of Horror*: "Charlie Boy," 1980 (Mandy)

BIOGRAPHY—The daughter of a doctor, leggy Janet Fielding graduated from Queensland University, where she took up acting as well. She appeared in stage plays before scoring her first television role with a bit part in the *Hammer House of Horror* series as a secretary. The next year, she went from this inauspicious debut to cult stardom as Tegan Jovanka, one of the most popular companions in the *Doctor Who* series; her tenure stretched over two Doctors.

But just ten years later, she gave up acting and took an administrative position with Women in Film and Television UK. She was with them for three and a half years, then became the head of finance for a charity and a theatrical agent. Although she has not returned to the screen, she has reprised the role of Tegan for a number of *Doctor Who* audio stories, and attended her first fan convention in 2012.

Other genre credits: TELEVISION: *Doctor Who*: Tegan Jovanka, "Logopolis," 1981; "Castrovalva," "Four to Doomsday," "Kinda," "The Visitation," "Black Orchid," "Earthshock," "Time-Flight," 1982; "Arc of Infinity," "Snakedance," "Mawdryn Undead," "Terminus," "Enlightenment," "The King's Demons," "The Five Doctors," 1983; "Warriors of the Deep," "The Awakening," "Frontios," "Resurrection of the Daleks," "The Caves of Androzani," 1984 (Tegan Jovanka)

Finlay, Marilyn

TELEVISION: *Hammer House of Horror*: "The House That Bled to Death," 1980 (Sister)

Finn, Catherine (1915–1980)

BIRTHPLACE: Dublin, Ireland.
FILMS: *The Witches*, 1966 (Nurse); *Journey into Darkness*, 1969 (Elsie Cole)
TELEVISION: *Journey to the Unknown*: "Paper Dolls," 1968 (Elsie Cole)
Other genre credits: FILMS: *The Deadly Bees*, Amicus Productions, 1967 (Mary Hargrove); *Torture Garden*, Amicus Productions, 1967 (Nurse Parker); *The Creeping Flesh*, Tigon Pictures, 1972 (Emily)

Fitzgerald, Maggie

FILM: *The Satanic Rites of Dracula*, 1973 (Vampire Girl)

Flanagan, Maureen (1941–)

BIRTHPLACE: London, England.
FILM: *Dracula A.D. 1972*, 1972 (Go-Go Girl)
BIOGRAPHY—Sexy Maureen Flanagan (who is known professionally as "Flanagan") was famous for nude pictorials in the kind of magazines men like, as well as exotic dancing, and enjoyed a short screen career that capitalized on that notoriety with appearances in *Monty Python's Flying Circus*, *Benny Hill*, and big-screen sex comedies. She has a brief but very visible part in *Dracula A.D 1972*, dancing on the tables to the pseudo-rock played by Stoneground. She became even more notorious with her very vocal defense of former employers and notorious gangsters the Kray Twins (the parodic object of the Piranha Brothers sketch on *Monty Python*), which didn't exactly help to further her career.

Fleming, Eve Lucinda "Lucy" (1947–)

BIRTHPLACE: Nettlebed, Oxfordshire, England.
FILM: *Rasputin, the Mad Monk*, 1966 (Wide Eyes)
BIOGRAPHY—She is the niece of Ian Fleming and the daughter of Peter Fleming (who was actually a more famous author than his brother at one point). She is an occasional character actress and, along with her sister, controls Ian Fleming Publications. Her first movie role was a bit part in *Rasputin, the Mad Monk* with Christopher Lee, who had been considered for a role in *Dr. No*.

Other genre credits: TELEVISION: *Haunted*: "The Girl on a Swing," 1967 (Helen); *The*

Avengers: "Invasion of the Earthmen," 1968 (Emily Wade); *Mystery and Imagination*: "Uncle Silas," 1968 (Maud Ruthyn)

Fontaine, Joan (1917–)

REAL NAME: Joan de Beauvoir de Havilland; BIRTHPLACE: Tokyo, Japan.
FILM: *The Witches*, 1966 (Gwen Mayfield)

BIOGRAPHY — Born to Walter Augustine de Havilland and actress Lillian Fontaine (the inspiration for Joan's stage name), Joan Fontaine is the sister of equally legendary actress Olivia de Havilland, from whom she has been estranged for decades. Nineteen thirty-five was a big year for Ms. Fontaine; she graduated from the American School in Japan, and made both her stage and film debuts as well. Nineteen forty-two was even bigger; she won the Academy Award for Hitchcock's *Suspicion* (1941), as the timid girl swept off her feet by Cary Grant and becomes increasingly, er, suspicious that he's a murderer. She appeared in a number of A-list films after that, but by the 1960s, quality parts became harder to find. Enamored of Norah Lofts' novel *The Devil's Own*, she bought the screen rights and brought the project to Seven Arts, who brought it to the attention of Hammer. Esteemed Hammer scholar Dr. Wayne Kinsey calls the resulting film "a cross between *Taste of Fear* and *The Plague of the Zombies*" — a fair cop, and there is also much that anticipates *The Wicker Man* from seven years later, with Ms. Fontaine slowly discovering that the whole small village is in on the scheme. There are also echoes of her character in *Suspicion*, although here she's not a timid, innocent girl swept

Joan Fontaine gets lessons in film cutting from Kay Walsh in *The Witches*.

off her feet, she's a woman who suffers two nervous breakdowns during the course of the film after being swept away by events beyond her control; both characters become increasingly distraught during the course of the respective films. Even though Fontaine is rather upstaged by Kay Walsh in *The Witches*, she still displays the consummate acting skill that only an actress of her caliber could bring to Hammer's "Avenging Grannies" series (and with none of the problems experienced with other actresses of her stature like Bette Davis or Tallulah Bankhead). But despite these two cracking performances and the genuinely uneasy atmosphere, the film (released in the U.S. as *The Devil's Own*) was not a critical or financial success, which was a great blow to Fontaine. It was her last theatrically released film, although she continued playing roles on stage and television into the mid–1990s. She was married four times; one of the marriages, to producer William Dozier, the father of her only child. She now lives in seclusion with her garden, her dogs, and her memories.

Other genre credits: FILMS: *Voyage to the Bottom of the Sea*, 20th Century–Fox, 1961 (Dr. Susan Hiller) TELEVISION: *One Step Beyond*: "The Visitor," 1960 (Ellen Grayson); *The Alfred Hitchcock Hour*: "The Paragon," 1963 (Alice Pemberton); *Dark Mansions* (Movie), 1986 (Margaret Drake)

Forde, Leila

FILM: *The Phantom of the Opera*, 1962 (Teresa)

Foster, Julia (1943–)

BIRTHPLACE: Lewes, Sussex, England.
TELEVISION: *Hammer House of Horror*: "The Thirteenth Reunion," 1980 (Ruth Cairns)

Julia Foster is about to find out what (or who) is on the menu in this publicity still from Hammer's second television series, *Hammer House of Horror*.

BIOGRAPHY—Foster is a long-standing British actress in films and television. Her first television appearance came in 1960, and she made her film debut the following year. Her most high-profile film was *Alfie* with Michael Caine, and one of her TV jobs was a starring role as a female reporter in the *Hammer House of Horror* series. She brings a mature sensibility to a role that needs it, a healthy cynicism fit for a veteran beat writer but enough sense to believe her eyes when confronted by the cold, hard facts (such as a meat cleaver). She is still sporadically active in the business, dividing her time between that and being Britain's leading expert on 18th and 19th century Scandinavian painted furniture (as well as being a seller of these rare antiquities).

Fox, Marcia

FILM: *Creatures the World Forgot*, 1971 (The Mute Girl)

BIOGRAPHY—Foxy Marcia Fox was raised in Kenya and was an air hostess for BOAC before being bitten by the acting bug. Her career only lasted five years and ten credits, the first of which was *Doctor in Trouble*, which also featured fellow Hammer Heroines Yutte Stensgaard and Marianne Stone. The last was *Old Dracula*, which has more Hammer Heroines in it than some Hammer films: Linda Hayden, Veronica Carlson, Jennie Linden, Carol Cleveland, and Luan Peters. Along the way were stops at *Jason King* and her only Hammer feature, *Creatures the World Forgot*. As a mute cave girl, she is fought over by cavemen and almost raped by the winner, but she escapes. After other prehistoric perils, she gets her revenge by stabbing her attacker, who falls to his deserved doom. She disappeared from show business after her appearance in *Old Dracula*.

Other genre credits: FILMS: *Old Dracula*, World Film Services, 1975 (Air Hostess); *The Exorcism of Hugh*, LMG Film Productions, 1972 (Love Scene Girl) TELEVISION: *Thriller*: "A Coffin for the Bride," 1974 (Connie)

Fox, Sonia

FILM: *Never Take Sweets from a Stranger*, 1960 (Receptionist)
Other genre credits: TELEVISION: *UFO*: "Flight Path," 1971 (Carol Roper)

Francis, Jan (1947–)

REAL NAME: Janet Stephanie Francis; BIRTHPLACE: Westminster, London, England.

TELEVISION: *Hammer House of Mystery and Suspense*: "The Corvini Inheritance," 1985 (Eva Bailey)

BIOGRAPHY—Jan Francis attended the Lady Eldridge Grammar School and later the Royal Ballet School. After graduation, she toured with the Royal Ballet Company, which she left to pursue acting on stage, screen and television. She played Mina in the 1979 version of *Dracula* with Frank Langella, which led to a double-edged sword of an in-joke for her appearance in the "The Corvini Inheritance." She plays a working girl pursued by a stalker; she lets professional security man David McCallum install cameras to catch the ski-masked man in black, and after he's secured her windows, she remarks that "not even Dracula could get in." Her performance is solid; and although she doesn't get too much of a chance to show off her dancer's legs (unlike *Hammer House of Horror*, *House of Mystery and Suspense* almost seemed to have an aversion to suggestiveness), she more than compensates by showing palpable fear and frustration. Unfortunately, this fine performance, as well as others, and some genuinely creepy atmosphere are ruined by a totally illogical and telegraphed ending that transfers the palpable frustration to the viewer. As of 2012, she is still active.

Other genre credits: FILM: *Dracula*, Universal Pictures, 1979 (Mina) TELEVISION: *Thriller*:

"File It Under Fear," 1973 (Gillie Randall); *Tales of the Unexpected*: "Death Can Add," 1982 (Leila); *Ghostbusters of East Finchley*: Episodes 1 & 2, 1995 (Grace); *Twisted Tales*: "Fruitcake of the Living Dead," 2005 (Penny Marchant)

Francis, Nina

FILM: *Vampire Circus*, 1972 (Schoolgirl)

Franklin, Gretchen (1911–2005)

BIRTHPLACE: Convent Garden, West London, England.
TELEVISION: *Journey to the Unknown*: "The Beckoning Fair One," 1968 (Mrs. Barrett)
BIOGRAPHY—This British character actress was beloved, particularly by animals and senior citizens, to whom she donated all of the rerun royalties from the perennial *EastEnders* television series. Active for over 50 years, she applied her skills to everything from genre films to *Help!* and *How I Won the War*. She has a supporting role in *Journey to the Unknown* as Robert Lansing's increasingly put-upon landlady.
Other genre credits: FILMS: *Die, Monster, Die!* Alta Vista Productions, 1965 (Miss Bailey); *Twisted Nerve*, Charter Film Productions, 1968 (Clarkie); *The Night Visitor*, Glazier/Hemisphere Pictures, 1971 (Mrs. Hanson); *The Quatermass Conclusion*, Euston Films, 1979 (Edna) TELEVISION: *Quatermass*: "An Endangered Species," "What Lies Beneath," 1979 (Edna); *Dr. Jekyll and Mister Hyde* (Movie), 1980 (Cook)

Franklin, Pamela (1950–)

BIRTHPLACE: Yokohama, Japan.
FILM: *The Nanny*, 1965 (Bobbie Medman)
BIOGRAPHY—Beautiful genre stalwart Pamela Franklin attended the Elmhurst School of Ballet and made her film debut at age 11 in *The Innocents*. Her career took off from there, and in 1965 she was cast in *The Nanny* as the teenager that little William Dix confides in. She's wise, and a borderline "bad girl"—not just messing about with the lads, but smokin' Lucky Strikes and wearin' nylons, too. She retired in 1981.
Other genre credits: FILMS: *The Innocents*, Achilles–20th Century–Fox, 1961 (Flora); *And Soon the Darkness*, Associated British Pictures Corporation, 1970 (Jane); *Necromancy*, Compass/Zenith International, 1972 (Lori Brandon); *The Legend of Hell House*, Academy Pictures Corporation, 1973 (Florence Tanner); *The Food of the Gods*, American International Pictures, 1976 (Lorna) TELEVISION: *The Sixth Sense*: "I Did Not Mean to Slay Thee," 1972 (Bonnie); *Satan's School for Girls* (Movie), 1973 (Elizabeth Sayers); *The Six Million Dollar Man*: "Operation Firefly," 1974 (Susan Abbott); *Thriller*: "Screamer," 1974 (Nicola Stevens); "Won't Write Home, Mum, I'm Dead," 1975 (Abby Stevens); *Gemini Man*: "Escape Hatch," 1976 (Daphne); *Project U.F.O.*: "Sighting 4013: The St. Hilary Incident," 1978 (Sister Lucy Ryker)

Fraser, Shelagh (1920–2000)

REAL NAME: Sheila Mary Fraser; BIRTHPLACE: Purley, Surrey, England.
FILM: *The Witches*, 1966 (Mrs. Creek)
Other genre credits: FILMS: *Doomwatch*, Tigon British Film Productions, 1972 (Mrs. Betty Straker); *Star Wars*, Lucasfilm/20th Century–Fox, 1977 (Aunt Beru) TELEVISION: *Doomwatch*: "The Islanders," 1971 (Joan Prentice); *Beasts*: "Baby," 1976 (Dorothy Plummery)

Frederick, Lynne (1954–1994)

BIRTHPLACE: Hillingdon, Middlesex, England.
FILM: *Vampire Circus*, 1972 (Dora Mueller)
BIOGRAPHY—Lynne Frederick attended an all-girl school and originally wanted to teach math and physics. She opted for a screen career instead and made her first film at the age of 16. She acted in a number of genre films, the best being *Vampire Circus*, in which she plays the willing young daughter of a professor who has helped bring a vampire's curse down upon their village, and now becomes one of the instruments of the vampire's revenge. Unfortunately she is better known for her personal life than her acting achievements; her marriage to Peter Sellers was widely condemned by both his family and friends as fortune-hunting. His subsequent death left her exceedingly well off, but also left her genuinely depressed. Despite other high-profile marriages, she sank ever deeper into substance abuse, and died when she was only 39.

Other genre credits: FILMS: *The Amazing Mr. Blunden*, Hemdale Film, 1972 (Lucy Allen); *Phase IV*, Alced Productions, 1974 (Kendra Eldridge); *Schizo*, Heritage, 1976 (Samantha) TELEVISION: *The Canterville Ghost* (Movie), 1975 (Virginia Otis); *Space: 1999*: "A Matter of Balance," 1976 (Shermeen Williams)

Frere, Dorothy (1910–1989)

BIRTHPLACE: Blyth, Northumberland, England.
FILM: *Vampire Circus*, 1972 (Grandma Schilt)
Other genre credits: FILMS: *The Snake Woman*, Caralan Productions, 1961 (Martha Adderson); *It!* Gold Star Films Limited, 1967 (Miss Swanson)

Frost, Sadie (1965–)

REAL NAME: Sadie Liza Vaughan; BIRTHPLACE: London, England.
FILM: *Beyond the Rave*, 2008 (Fallen Angel)
Other genre credits: FILM: *Dracula*, American Zoetrope, 1992 (Lucy Westerna) TELEVISION: *The Fear*: 2001 (Storyteller)

Fuller, Toria

TELEVISION: *Hammer House of Mystery and Suspense*: "The Sweet Scent of Death," 1986 (Paula)
BIOGRAPHY—Toria Fuller was a very pretty British character actress who worked mostly in television from 1976 through 1988, although she managed a few feature films, one (*The Bitch*) with fellow Hammer Heroine Joan Collins. She also appeared in *Poor Little Rich Girl* with Carmen du Sautoy, her co-star from the "Sweet Scent of Death" episode of *Hammer House of Mystery and Suspense*. Fuller has a marvelous bit as a red herring in this murder mystery; even though the solution is apparent about five minutes into the show, it still manages to throw the viewer off the, er, scent with odd behavior, furtive glances and mysterious actions.

Furneaux, Yvonne (1928–)

REAL NAME: Elisabeth Yvonne Scarcherd; BIRTHPLACE: Roubaix, Nord-Pas-De-Calais, France.
FILM: *The Mummy*, 1959 (Isobel Banning/Princess Ananka)
BIOGRAPHY—Born in France, gorgeous Yvonne Furneaux studied Modern Language at Oxford, where she easily earned a degree in French, and then trained at RADA. She did her first film in 1952, and seven years later, she was on the lot at Bray filming Hammer's newest

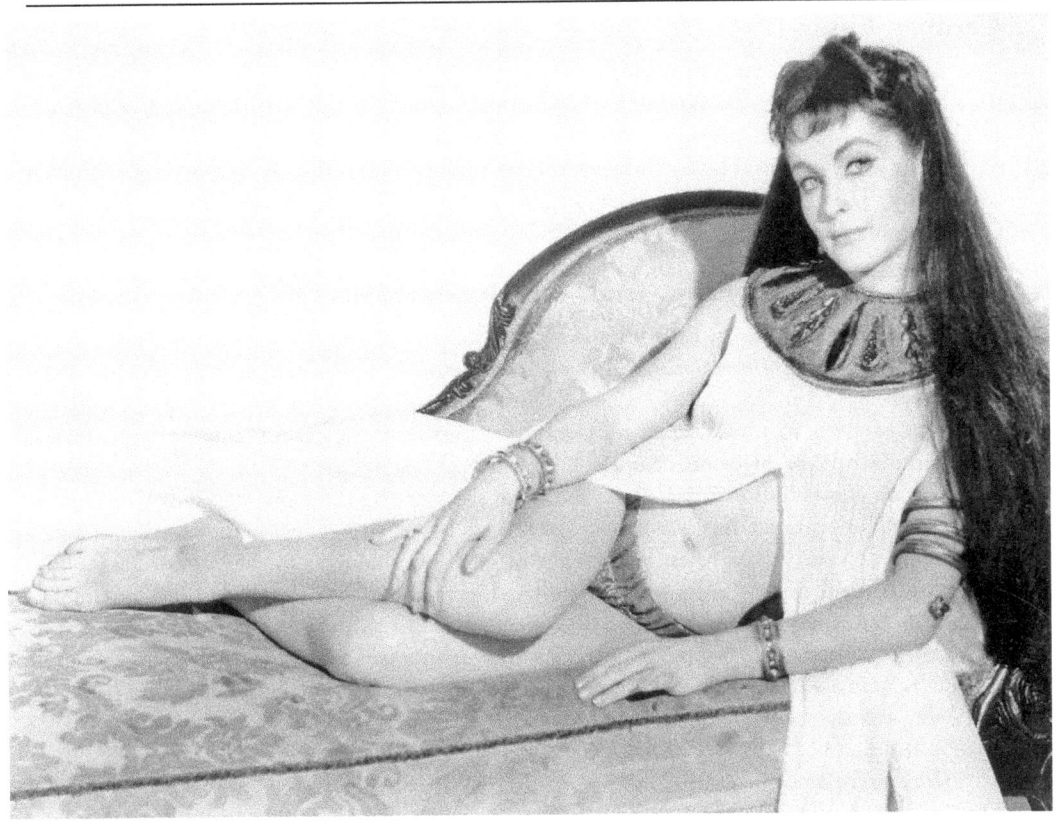

Regrettably Yvonne Furneaux's costume in *The Mummy* wasn't nearly this revealing.

addition to their classic horror character roster, *The Mummy*. At first, she was hesitant about her starring role(s) in *The Mummy*; she thought the film merely foolish, and that her character(s) were too passive to be interesting. She changed her tune after witnessing the rarely better team of Cushing and Lee at work, but really, her initial reservations about her role(s) proved to be correct. *The Mummy* is a certified Hammer classic, but unlike *The Curse of Frankenstein* and *Horror of Dracula*, it brought no new elements to the table (i.e., respectively, gore and sex), and subsequently, no new dimensions to the character of Isobel; the moviemakers were content to feature her as simply the latest in a long line of reincarnations of mummies' lost loves. Still, she is elegant and stunningly beautiful, stopping us and the Mummy in our respective tracks. She went on to do such classics as *La Dolce Vita* and *Repulsion*, working steadily until 1972; she then took a break until 1984, when she made the rather unwise decision to star in *Frankenstein's Great Aunt Tillie*, which would have driven a stake through anybody's career, and so it did for her. She is now happily retired and lives in Switzerland.

Other genre credits: FILMS: *The Secret of Dr. Mabuse*, Central Cinema Company, 1964 (Gilda Larsen); *Repulsion*, Compton Films, 1965 (Helen); *Frankenstein's Great Aunt Tillie*, Tillie Productions, 1984 (Matilda "Tillie" Frankenstein)

Fussey, Sharon

TELEVISION: *Hammer House of Horror*: "Guardian of the Abyss," 1980 (Second Girl)

Gardner, Caron (1941–)

BIRTHPLACE: London, England.

FILMS: *The Evil of Frankenstein*, 1964 (Burgomaster's Wife); *The Brigand of Kandahar*, 1965 (Serving Maid); *Frankenstein Must Be Destroyed*, 1969 (Passer-by)

Other genre credits: FILMS: *Goldfinger*, 1963 (Flying Circus Pilot); *Queen Kong*, Cine-Art Munchen, 1976 (Prostitute) TELEVISION: *The Avengers*: "Quick-Quick Slow Death," 1966 (Lucille Banks)

Gardner, Geraldine a.k.a. Trudi Van Doorn (1950–1987)

BIRTHPLACE: Windsor, Berkshire, England.

TELEVISION: *Hammer House of Mystery and Suspense*: "Last Video and Testament," 1984 (Secretary)

BIOGRAPHY — Strikingly beautiful Geraldine Gardner made her first film in 1968, and she soon became a prime piece of "crumpet" in British sex comedies such as *Up the Workers* and on television shows like *Benny Hill*. At the time, she went by the name of Trudi Van Doorn, but after her appearance in *Queen Kong* she reverted back to her real name to try and avoid being identified with those roles. She was the original Bombalurina in the London stage show of *Cats*, and one of her last roles was a bit part as a secretary in the "Last Video and Testament" episode of *Hammer House of Mystery and Suspense*. But just three years later, she gave birth to a pair of twins and then began to suffer from severe post-natal depression. She committed suicide by going to the beach, taking off her clothes, walking into the sea, walking back out and lying on the beach, where she froze to death.

Other genre credits: FILM: *Queen Kong*, Cine-Art Munchen, 1976 (Crew Girl) TELEVISION: *The New Avengers*: "The Eagle's Nest," 1976 (Gerda)

Gardner, Hazel

FILM: *The Terror of the Tongs*, 1961 (Tong Room Girl)

Gaunt, Valerie (1932–)

BIRTHPLACE: Stratford-on-Avon, Warwickshire, England.

FILMS: *The Curse of Frankenstein*, 1957 (Justine); *Dracula*, 1958 (Vampire Girl)

BIOGRAPHY — She only two films and two TV appearances, and then left the business, but her two films were the iconic one-two punch of *The Curse of Frankenstein* and *Dracula*. In *Dracula*, she was Hammer's first screen vampire to bare fangs (Christopher Lee does so a bit more spectacularly a moment later), and in *Curse*,

Valerie Gaunt in *Horror of Dracula*.

she's Victor's maid and mistress who finds that he has made her pregnant, and threatens to spill the beans unless he marries her. This earns her a blind date with Lee's Creature; her death scream is the lead-in to Cushing's classic "Pass the marmalade" line.

Gayson, Eunice (1928–)

REAL NAME: Eunice Sargaison; BIRTHPLACE: Croydon, London, England.

FILMS: *To Have and to Hold*, 1951 (Peggy); *The Revenge of Frankenstein*, 1958 (Margaret Conrad)

BIOGRAPHY—She began acting in 1948, and played her first part for Hammer three years later in the turgid *To Have and to Hold*. She returned in 1958 for the sequel to *The Curse of Frankenstein*, but her character, like Hazel Court in the previous entry, has little to do but exist as the dedicated, stalwart love interest for Francis Matthews and the elegant, beautiful lust interest for the latest Creature. She became the first "official" Bond Girl with her appearance as Sylvia Trench in *Dr. No*; it is to her line "I admire your luck, Mister..." that Sean Connery first recites his immortal "Bond, James Bond." She played the same character in the sequel *From Russia with Love*, but plans for her to continue as Trench were dropped with *Goldfinger*. *From Russia with Love* was her last feature film appearance, although she continued to appear steadily on stage and television throughout the remainder of the decade, retiring at the beginning of the next.

Other genre credits: FILMS: *Dr. No*, Eon Productions, 1962 (Sylvia Trench); *From Russia with Love*, Eon Productions/Danjaq, 1963 (Sylvia Trench) TELEVISION: *The Avengers*: "Quick-Quick Slow Death," 1966 (Lucille Banks)

Eunice Gayson doesn't look unduly worried at the fact that Michael Gwynn is only a couple of feet behind her in *The Revenge of Frankenstein*.

Gee, Prunella (1950–)

BIRTHPLACE: London, England.

TELEVISION: *Hammer House of Horror*: "Witching Time," 1980 (Mary Winter)

BIOGRAPHY—The lovely Prunella Gee was trained at the London Academy of Music and

Gee whiz! Prunella Gee wonders just what a woman's gotta do to get rid of a witch in *Hammer House of Horror*.

Dramatic Art, and appeared in both her first film and first television show in 1974; the latter (*Shabby Tiger*) gave her instant notoriety due to her nude scenes. She became a virtual staple of British television thereafter, and was chosen to guest-star in the inaugural episode of the *Hammer House of Horror*, Hammer's second television series and one that displays a very distressing tendency towards cruelty to animals. She plays the unfaithful wife of a composer who happens upon a witch who, naturally, makes life extremely difficult for the couple. Gee doesn't get her kit off in this one, although she does cavort for a bit in a sexy bra and panties, but she runs the gamut of characterizations. It's a part very nicely played, although she was overshadowed by flamboyant Patricia Quinn. Gee's biggest feature film was the James Bond adventure *Never Say Never Again*, and she's most familiar to British television viewers for her role in the long-running *Coronation Street*. Since 2006, she has worked as a counselor and therapist in Camden, London, and still takes on an occasional movie or TV part.

Other genre credits: FILM: *Never Say Never Again*, PSO International, 1983 (Patricia)

Geeson, Judy (1948–)

REAL NAME: Judith Amanda Geeson; BIRTHPLACE: Arundel, Sussex, England.
FILM: *Fear in the Night*, 1972 (Peggy Heller)
BIOGRAPHY—The daughter of the editor of the National Coal Board magazine, pretty, pouty-lipped Judy Geeson graduated from the Corona Stage Academy. She made her television debut in 1962 and her film debut the following year. Her greatest fame (or infamy) came during the 1960s, when she appeared in a number of controversial films and got her kit off; this and her individualistic lifestyle kept her in the movies and her name in the tabloids. Her lone effort for Hammer came in the form of a starring role in their seemingly 100th "psycho-

Judy Geeson has a big gun, and she knows how to use it in *Fear in the Night*.

logical thriller" *Fear in the Night*, in which (sigh) someone is trying to drive someone mad. She is very effective in a role that is essentially bleak and hopeless, a role in which she is put upon from the beginning and is never really given, metaphorically, a chance to see the sun, except at the climax, but even then she's in a daze and simply wanders off in shock caused by the preceding events. Like Joan Fontaine in *The Witches*, she begins the film recovering from a nervous breakdown, and is put through the wringer physically and emotionally. The role is custom-built to be sympathetic, and she certainly is, but the premise and that type of role were so overly familiar by this time. Fortunately for her and the film, she has Peter Cushing, Ralph Bates and Joan Collins to back her up (not to mention the underrated James Cossins), so even if the movie itself was thematically standard, the performances make it well worth the effort. She is still active in the business, although she briefly took a hiatus to open her own antique shop, Blanche and Co., which closed in 2009. Her extensive stage, screen and television work has included a fair number of genre efforts, and she ended her hiatus with a role in Rob Zombie's *The Lords of Salem*.

Other genre credits: FILMS: *Berserk*, Herman Cohen Productions, 1967 (Angela Rivers); *Doomwatch*, Tigon British Film Productions, 1972 (Victoria Brown); *It Happened at Nightmare Inn*, Vega Films, 1973 (Laura); *Inseminoid* (a.k.a. *Horror Planet*), Jupiter Film Productions, 1981 (Sandy); *The Lords of Salem*, Alliance Films, 2012 (Lacy Doyle) TELEVISION: *Thriller*: "Night Is the Right Time for Killing," 1975 (Helen Marlow); *Space: 1999*: "Another Time, Another Place," 1976 (Regina Kesslann); *Star Maidens*: "Escape to Paradise," "Nemesis," "Nightmare Cannon," "The Proton Storm," "Kidnap," "The Perfect Couple," "Hideout,"

"The Enemy," 1976 (Fulvia); *Tales of the Unexpected*: "Poison," 1980 (Sandra); "The Memory Man," 1983 (Mary); *Monsters*: "Refugee," 1990 (Anna); *Star Trek: Voyager*: "Twisted," "The Cloud," 1995 (Sandrine); *Alien Fury: Countdown to Invasion* (Movie), 2000 (Alien Voice)

George, Susan (1950–)

BIRTHPLACE: London, England.
TELEVISION: *Hammer House of Mystery and Suspense*: "Czech Mate," 1985 (Vicky Duncan)

BIOGRAPHY—Susan George trained at the Corona Theatre School and made her first television appearance at the age of twelve. She's appeared in a goodly number of horror films and genre pieces, although she's probably best known for her roles in *Straw Dogs* and *Dirty Mary, Crazy Larry* (she was the dirty one). She would have been quite a catch for Hammer in their prime, but at least they got around to her for an episode of *Hammer House of Mystery and Suspense*, in which she plays a television researcher caught up in an international espionage affair. She's brought into it by her ex-husband, who himself is a pawn in a much larger game, and gives a harrowing performance as a tough, smart, and resilient woman ultimately rendered powerless by forces beyond her control. Her final scene conveys an abject desolation and hopelessness that proves her a bit more than just the average, garden-variety sexpot. She is still active, not only as an actress, but as a producer and renowned horse breeder.

Other genre credits: FILMS: *The Sorcerers*, Curtwel Productions/Tigon, 1967 (Audrey Woods); *Die Screaming, Marianne!* Pete Walker Film Productions, 1971 (Marianne); *Fright*, Fantale Films, 1972 (Amanda); *Tintorera: Killer Shark*, Conacite Uno, 1977 (Gabriella); *Venom*, Morison Film Group, 1981 (Louise Andrews); *The House Where Evil Dwells*, Cohen, 1982 (Laura Fletcher) TELEVISION: *Mystery and Imagination*: "Dracula," 1968 (Lucy); *Tales of Unease*: "Ride, Ride," 1970 (Sarah Stone); *Dr. Jekyll and Mr. Hyde* (Movie), 1973 (Anne); *Tales of the Unexpected*: "Lamb to the Slaughter," 1979 (Mary Marney); "Royal Jelly," 1980 (Mabel Taylor); *Jack the Ripper*: 1988 (Catherine Eddowes); *Tales of Mystery and Imagination*: "The Black Cat," 1995

Gilan, Yvonne

TELEVISION: *Journey to the Unknown*: "Jane Brown's Body," 1968 (Mrs. Brown)

Gillespie, Dana (1949–)

REAL NAME: Richenda Antoinette de Winterstein Gillespie; BIRTHPLACE: Woking, Surrey, England.
FILMS: *The Vengeance of She*, 1967 (Girl at Party); *The Lost Continent*, 1968 (Sarah)

BIOGRAPHY—Dana Gillespie, the daughter of a prominent radiologist, is one of a number of actresses in this volume whose output for Hammer represents but a minuscule aspect of their career. But the same could be said for her film career in general, which is more of a sideline to her real source of fame, as an internationally renowned recording artist, with over 60 albums to her credit. Too bad she couldn't have performed some of this magic for the soundtrack of the deliriously deranged *The Lost Continent*, which features a theme song that achieves the level of kitsch of a "Green Slime" (the theme song for the movie of the same name). But it's just the first instance of said kitsch, which reaches cosmic (or is it comic?), er, proportions in Gillespie's first scene: Dana, who freely admits that she was cast for her role solely due to her cleavage, is walking across this carnivorous seaweed, but since it's carnivorous seaweed, one has to walk across it with the aid of puffy footwear that look life tiny life rafts, and balloons attached to her shoulders. And so, though she's actually running for her life, the

Dana Gillespie looks pretty bugged in *The Lost Continent* (courtesy Mel Bridgeman).

scene becomes unintentionally hilarious, and achieves the same level of inspired vulgarity achieved by Jayne Mansfield's scene with the milk bottles clutched against her own wondrous breasts in *The Girl Can't Help It*. The battle scene that follows is almost as funny, with Gillespie's similarly balloon-festooned pursuers attacking the stranded ship, their attire making them appear to be somewhat less than fearsome; it's as though the boat is being besieged by an out-of-work circus. But Ms. Gillespie, all of 17 at the time, impresses as much with her developing acting skills as her bust line, and more than holds her own alongside the more experienced actresses in the cast. It's been over twenty years now since her last film appearance, as she now devotes her full attention to her spiritual studies and her musical career, which is still very much a going proposition.

Other genre credits: FILM: *The People That Time Forgot*, AIP/Amicus Productions, 1977 (Ajor); *The Hound of the Baskervilles*, Michael White Productions, 1978 (Mary Frankland)

Gillespie, Vicky

FILM: *Taste the Blood of Dracula*, 1970 (Bordello Girl)

Gilmore, Lianne

FILM: *Frankenstein and the Monster from Hell*, 1974 (Inmate)

Gilpin, Toni

FILMS: *The Gorgon*, 1964 (Sascha Cass); *The Mummy's Shroud*, 1967 (Pharaoh's Wife)
BIOGRAPHY — This short-tenured British character actress appeared in both films and tel-

evision in a ten-year career that ended in 1970. For Hammer, she was memorable as the doomed Sascha Cass in *The Gorgon*, and only briefly glimpsed as the Pharaoh's dying wife in *The Mummy's Shroud*.

Other genre credits: TELEVISION: *The Avengers*: "Death on the Rocks," 1962 (Jackie Ross); "The Rotters," 1968 (Sonia)

Ginders, Angela

FILM: *Blood from the Mummy's Tomb*, 1971 (Nurse)

Glessing, Mollie (1891–1971)

BIRTHPLACE: Leon, Iowa, USA
FILM: *The Quatermass Xperiment*, 1955 (Mother at Zoo)
Other genre credits: FILMS: *Journey to the Center of the Earth*, 20th Century–Fox, 1959 (News Vendor); *The Time Travelers*, American International Pictures, 1964 (Android) TELEVISION: *One Step Beyond*: "The Secret," 1959 (Essie); *Thriller*: "The Cheaters," 1960 (Mrs. Ames); "Well of Doom," 1961 (Miss Price); "The Closed Cabinet," 1961 (Agnes); *Alfred Hitchcock Presents*: "Back for Christmas," 1956 (Maid); "The Orderly World of Mister Appleby," 1956 (Elly the Maid); "The Three Dreams of Mister Findlater," 1957 (Bridget); "The Impromptu Murder," 1958 (Marjorie Daw); "Relative Value," 1959 (Mrs. Simpson); "The Silk Petticoat," 1962 (Parlor Maid); "Most Likely to Succeed," 1962 (Maid)

Goddard, Daphne

TELEVISION: *Hammer House of Mystery and Suspense*: "Black Carrion," 1986 (Miss Elsie Barrett)

Godley, Anne

FILM: *The Devil Rides Out*, 1968 (Satanist)
Other genre credits: TELEVISION: *The Avengers*: "The Sell-Out," 1962 (Lillian Harvey)

Godsell, Vanda (1922–1990)

BIRTHPLACE: Bognor Regis, Sussex, England.
FILMS: *Hell Is a City*, 1960 (Lucy Lusk); *Sword of Sherwood Forest*, 1960 (The Prioress); *The Shadow of the Cat*, 1961 (Louise Venable)

BIOGRAPHY—This popular British character actress was born to a naval officer and a mother who was the sister of novelist and actress Naomi Jacobs. She joined the Bristol repertoire at the age of 14, then made her first film in 1953 and her last 30 years later. In between, she found work in three Hammer films, as well as some second-tier genre gems. Her most high-profile appearances came in two "Pink Panther" films which found her cast in two different roles of the matronly type she generally essayed.

Other genre credits: FILMS: *The Atomic Man*, Merton Park Studios, 1955 (Stenographer); *Horrors of the Black Museum*, Carmel Productions, 1959 (Miss Ashton); *Konga*, Merton Park Studios, 1961 (Bob's Mother); *The Earth Dies Screaming*, Lippert Films, 1964 (Violet Courtland)

Gold, Lauren

FILM: *Beyond the Rave*, 2008 (Lucretia)

Goldoni, Lelia (1936–)

BIRTHPLACE: New York City, New York, USA.

FILM: *Hysteria*, 1965 (Denise James)

BIOGRAPHY—Lelia Goldoni made her first screen appearances in 1949, and then waited ten years before her next (and most acclaimed role) in *Shadows*. Her casting in *Hysteria* represented a rare double-dip for Hammer, in that both of the leads were American. Unfortunately for her, the other American was dreary jobbing actor Robert Webber, who from all accounts made life on the set Hell for Ms. Goldoni, bullying and harassing her at every opportunity. She did not let the behind-the-scenes rancor affect her performance, playing her devil-in-disguise role as cool as the other side of the pillow. *Hysteria* was Hammer and Jimmy Sangster's fifth, and mercifully last, black & white psychological thriller; the plot is the all-too-familiar "Let's drive (fill in the blank) mad" for our own nefarious purposes, and the only mystery is why on Earth they want to do it to Webber's character, a man with no fixed moral compass, a drifter who's bluff, rude, macho and overbearing—in short, the "Ugly American." Goldoni did not let her experience on the film discourage her from her chosen profession; her career stretched well into the new millennium, and along the way has included high-profile appearances in *Alice Doesn't Live Here Anymore* and the 1978 remake of *Invasion of the Body Snatchers*.

Other genre credits: FILMS: *Blood Fiend*, Pennea Productions Limited, 1967 (Dani Gireaux); *Invasion of the Body Snatchers*, Solofilm, 1978 (Katherine Hendley)

Gordon, Hannah Campbell Grant (1941–)

BIRTHPLACE: Edinburgh, Scotland.

TELEVISION: *Hammer House of Mystery and Suspense*: "Tennis Court," 1985 (Maggie Dowd)

BIOGRAPHY—Scottish rose Hannah Gordon was orphaned at age 11, but she overcame this tragedy to become an accomplished actress of stage, screen and television. This wasn't her original ambition; she attended RADA with the intention of becoming an acting coach, but decided to hit the boards instead with the Dundee Repertory Theatre. She did her first television work in 1965, and has appeared in such classic films as *The Elephant Man*. She turned in a superior performance on *Hammer House of Mystery and Suspense* as a woman whose tennis court is possessed by the spirit of her mother's former lover. It sounds fairly silly on paper but it plays very well, given the one-two punch of Gordon and Isla Blair. Gordon, like most of the series' heroines, is a mature beauty (she looks simply smashing in a tennis skirt), and strong, even performing her own home-brewed exorcism. She suffered another tragedy with the death of her husband, and as of 2012 she is still active.

Other genre credits: TELEVISION: *Out of the Unknown*: "No Place Like Earth," 1965 (Zeyla); *Doctor Who*: "The Highlanders," 1966–67 (Kitty McLaren); *Menace*: "Something Cries Out," 1970 (Francesca)

Gordon, Nora (1893–1970)

BIRTHPLACE: West Hartlepool, England.

FILMS: *Blackout*, 1954 (Casey's Mother); *The Glass Tomb*, 1955 (Marie); *A Day of Grace*, 1956 (Mrs. Kemp); *The Curse of the Mummy's Tomb*, 1964 (Sir Giles' Housekeeper); *The Nanny*, 1965 (Mrs. Griggs)

Other genre credits: FILM: *Horrors of the Black Museum*, Carmel Productions, 1959 (Woman in Hall)

Gorst, Irene

FILM: *Moon Zero Two*, 1969 (Dancer)

Goss, Helen Margaret (1903–1985)

BIRTHPLACE: London, England.

FILMS: *The Hound of the Baskervilles*, 1959 (Mrs. Barrymore); *The Two Faces of Dr. Jekyll*, 1960 (The Nanny)

BIOGRAPHY—This long-serving British character actress made two appearances for Hammer. She was solid, mysterious and sympathetic as the long-suffering Mrs. Barrymore in their classic *The Hound of the Baskervilles*.

Gott, Elizabeth

FILM: *The Hound of the Baskervilles*, 1959 (Mrs. Goodlippe)

Graeme, Hazel

FILM: *The Two Faces of Dr. Jekyll*, 1960 (Sphinx Girl)

Other genre credits: TELEVISION: *The Avengers*: "Toy Trap," 1961 (Mary Murton)

Graham, Sally (1947–)

FILM: *Moon Zero Two*, 1969 (Dancer)

NOTE: Graham was a singer with New Seekers.

Grant, Angela

TELEVISION: *Hammer House of Mystery and Suspense*: "And the Wall Came Tumbling Down," 1985 (Jill)

Other genre credits: FILMS: *Zeta One*, Tigon British Film Productions, 1969 (Angvisa Girl); *Tales from the Crypt*, Amicus Productions, 1972 (Susan Blake) TELEVISION: *Spectre* (Movie), 1977 (Butler)

Gray, Nadia (1923–1994)

REAL NAME: Nadia Kujnir-Herescu; BIRTHPLACE: Bucharest, Romania.

FILM: *Maniac*, 1963 (Eve Beynat)

BIOGRAPHY—Many actresses act like a princess; like Grace Kelly, Nadia Gray actually was one, and like Kelly, by marriage, to Romania's top fighter ace of World War II. They were married until his death in 1958. Her most famous role came in *La Dolce Vita*, as a jaded socialite who celebrates her divorce with a steamy striptease. She brings the same worldly qualities to her role as the scheming Eve Beynat in Hammer's *Maniac*, wielding her seductive power over men to manipulate them in ways they never suspect. Gray reportedly was an expert linguist, cook, and skin diver. She settled permanently in America after marrying her second husband, retiring from films in the '70s. She suffered a stroke and passed away in 1994. See photograph on page 91.

Greco, Mary

TELEVISION: *Hammer House of Mystery and Suspense*: "The Sweet Scent of Death," 1986 (Girl in Park)

Kerwin Mathews (literally and figuratively) stands between Nadia Gray and Lillian Brousse in *Maniac*.

Greek, Beatrice

FILM: *Frankenstein and the Monster from Hell*, 1974 (Inmate)
Other genre credits: TELEVISION: *Detective*: "The Murders in the Rue Morgue," 1968 (Madame Douterc)

Green, Frances

FILM: *Never Take Sweets from a Stranger*, 1960 (Lucille)

Green, Libertad

FILM: *The Woman in Black*, 2012 (Theater Patron)
Other genre credits: FILMS: *Take-Away Spirit*, One Shot Productions, 2009 (Ethel Hampton); *Dawn of the Redneck Samurai*, Good as A Mugg Productions, 2012 (Wing) TELEVISION: *Exorcism: Driving Out the Devil* (Movie), 2006 (Possessed Girl); *Zombie Apocalypse* (Movie), 2011 (Zombie)

Green, Wilhelmina

TELEVISION: *Hammer House of Horror*: "Children of the Full Moon," 1980 (Young Girl)
Other genre credits: FILM: *The Godsend*, Cannon Films, 1980 (Bonnie)

Gregg, Virginia (1916–1986)

REAL NAME: Virginia Greg Burkett; BIRTHPLACE: Harrisburg, Illinois, USA.

FILM: *The Kiss of the Vampire*, 1963 (Rosa in U.S. television version)

BIOGRAPHY—A ubiquitous American character actress, Gregg appeared in well over 200 films and television shows, not to mention radio. You may not recognize the name, but you know the face; and if you don't know the face, you definitely recognize the voice, because arguably her most famous genre role is one in which she is heard, not seen: Tony Perkins's mother in the *Psycho* franchise. She's included in this book on a technicality: When *The Kiss of the Vampire* was shown on American television, some scenes were cut and other scenes, filmed in Hollywood with American actors, including Gregg, replaced them, with unsatisfactory results.

Other genre credits: FILMS: *The Amazing Mr. X*, Ben Stoloff Productions, 1948 (Emily); *Psycho*, Shamley Productions, 1960 (Voice of Norma Bates); *Two on a Guillotine*, Warner Brothers, 1965 (Dolly Bast); *Psycho II*, Universal Pictures, 1983 (Voice of Norma Bates); *Psycho III*, Universal Pictures, 1986 (Voice of Norma Bates) TELEVISION: *The Addams Family*: "Feud in the Addams Family," 1965 (Eleanor Courtney); *Alfred Hitchcock Hour*: "A Home Away from Home," 1963 (Miss Gibson); "Consider Her Ways," 1964 (The Third Doctor); "Thou Still Unravished Bride," 1965 (Mrs. Essie Setlin); *Alfred Hitchcock Presents*: "Don't Come Back Alive," 1955 (Mildred Partridge); "Santa Claus and the Tenth Avenue Kid," 1955 (Miss Clementine Webster); "And So Died Riabouchinska," 1956 (Voice of Riabouchinska); "Nightmare in 4-D," 1957 (Norma Parker); *Thriller*: "Mr. George," 1961 (Edna Leggett); *Twilight Zone*: "Jess-Belle," 1963 (Ossie Stone); "The Masks," 1964 (Emily Harper); *My Favorite Martian*: "How Are Things in Glocca, Martian?," 1965 (Eileen McGinty); *The Girl from U.N.C.L.E.*: "The Danish Blue Affair," 1966 (Granny); *The Herculoids*: All episodes, 1967–69 (Voice of Tarra); *Bewitched*: "Samantha's Super Maid," 1969 (Leslie Otis); *The Night Stalker* (Movie), 1972 (Mrs. Brandon); *The Sixth Sense*: "Gallows in the Wind," 1972 (Thelma Young); *Kolchak, the Night Stalker*: "The Spanish Moss Murders," 1974 (Dr. Hollenbeck); *The Six Million Dollar Man*: "Population: Zero," 1974 (Mrs. Nelson); "The Pal-Mir Escort," 1974 (Sarah); "The Return of the Bionic Woman" (Part Two), 1975 (Mrs. Raymond); *Man from Atlantis*: "Man from Atlantis," 1977 (Whale Scientist); *Project U.F.O.*: "Sighting 4004: The Howard Crossing Incident," 1978 (Greta Marshall); "Sighting 4013: The St. Hilary Incident," 1978 (Sister Superior)

Gregory, Celia Christine (1949–2008)

BIRTHPLACE: England.

TELEVISION: *Hammer House of Horror*: "Children of the Full Moon," 1980 (Sarah Martin)

BIOGRAPHY—Darkly beautiful Celia Christine Gregory spent her childhood abroad after her parents divorced. She grew up to become a star of British stage, screen and television. She played her first television role in 1972 and was feted as one of the decade's most promising actresses. She plays heroine Sarah Martin in the best episode of *Hammer House of Horror*, "Children of the Full Moon," which boasted above-average performances from everyone in the strong cast. She begins the episode as a slightly neglected, prim and proper wife, complete with high starched collar. Along with her husband, she is trapped in an old estate that houses a family of werewolves. When her husband is knocked unconscious, she is attacked by a werewolf. When he wakes up in a hospital, she tells him it was all a dream. But then she tells him she's pregnant, and needless to say, he's not the father. Gregory plays both personality sides with skill, and has fun being bad, becoming more sexually aggressive and devouring strips of raw meat with relish. She went on to even greater heights, but began to question her role in the grand scheme of things and retired in 1993 to become a faith healer. She died in 2008.

Other genre credits: TELEVISION: *Tales of the Unexpected*: "Kindly Dig Your Own Grave," 1981 (Fatima); "The Last of the Midnight Gardeners," 1984 (Edna)

Grenfell, Joyce (1910–1979)

REAL NAME: Joyce Irene Phipps; BIRTHPLACE: Montpelier Square, London, England.
FILM: *The Old Dark House*, 1963 (Agatha Femm)
BIOGRAPHY—Joyce Grenfell was the daughter of Nora Langhorne, the sister of Nancy Astor, who was the first woman to sit in the House of Commons. As a child she showed a flair for imitations and creating her own characters, but had to be persuaded to attend RADA by her father. Still, she found the formal structure of stage plays too restrictive, with no room for spontaneity, and began a career as a writer. She began to alternate this work with reviews and one-woman shows, which she supplanted with film work, only one of which was for Hammer: she gave a brilliant comic performance in their underrated remake of *The Old Dark House*. Her every blissfully-unconnected-from-reality line is delivered with consummate skill and her death scene contains the never-to-be-forgotten, wonderfully twisted image of her gaily-smiling corpse's neck skewered with knitting needles. She was forced to retire from the stage in 1973 after she lost sight in one eye from an infection. Six years later, the blind eye became cancerous, she had it removed with surgery and died a month later at home.

Other genre credits: FILM: *Alice in Wonderland*, Lou Bunin Productions, 1949 (Ugly Duchess/Dormouse)

Gresley, Marjorie (1909–1988)

BIRTHPLACE: Doncaster, South Yorkshire, England.
FILM: *The Revenge of Frankenstein*, 1958 (Countess Barscynska)

Grey, Shirley (1902–1981)

REAL NAME: Agnes Zetterstrand; BIRTHPLACE: Naugatuck, Connecticut, USA.
FILM: *The Mystery of the Mary Celeste* (a.k.a. *Phantom Ship*), 1935 (Sarah Briggs)
BIOGRAPHY—Pretty blonde Shirley Grey began her short career with Sylvester Poli's theater company The Poli Players. She made an amazing 46 Hollywood films from 1930 to 1935, many of them mysteries or B-Westerns, such as the John Wayne serial *The Hurricane Express*, and became the very first Hammer Heroine with her appearance in *Mary Celeste*, where she eventually falls prey to an unhinged Bela Lugosi in a fanciful depiction of the tragic events of the real-life mystery which inspired the film. She married her *Mary Celeste* co-star Arthur Margetson the year after the film was released, and had a son. But the roles dried up, she and Margetson divorced, and the final blow was administered when their son was killed in action in World War II. She spent the remainder of her life as a recluse and passed away in a rest home in 1981.

Griffiths, Lucy (1919–1982)

BIRTHPLACE: Birley, Hertfordshire, England.
FILMS: *The Ugly Duckling*, 1959 (Cellist); *The Two Faces of Dr. Jekyll*, 1960 (Tavern Woman); *Frankenstein and the Monster from Hell*, 1974 (Old Hag)
BIOGRAPHY—A popular British character actress, Griffiths was a staple of films and television for nearly 50 years, including many of the *Carry On* entries, and three for Hammer.

She parlayed her gift for comedy into a hilariously memorable bit in *Frankenstein and the Monster from Hell*, spitting out her medicine all over a nonplussed Shane Briant.

Other genre credits: FILMS: *Jack the Ripper*, Mid Century Film Productions, 1959 (Salvation Army Woman); *The Flesh and the Fiends*, Triad Productions, 1960 (Old Crone); *The Hound of the Baskervilles*, Michael White Productions, 1978 (Iris) TELEVISION: *Dead of Night*: "Death Cancels All Debts," 1972 (Florence)

Gurpinar, Gigi

FILM: *Captain Kronos, Vampire Hunter*, 1974 (Blind Girl)
Other genre credits: TELEVISION: *Thriller*: "The Colour of Blood," 1973 (Woman on Train)

Gutteridge, Lucy Karima (1956–)

BIRTHPLACE: London, England.
TELEVISION: *Hammer House of Horror*: "Rude Awakening," 1980 (Lolly Fellows)
BIOGRAPHY—A distant cousin of the late King Farouk of Egypt, beautiful Lucy Karima Gutteridge had a fifteen-year career on British stages, television screens and in film. In 1980 she had an amazing turn in the third episode of *Hammer House of Horror*, a series that gave its many actresses better opportunities and much better roles as women than they had ever been given in Hammer's films. "Rude Awakening," at root, was one of those annoying "dream in a dream inside a riddle wrapped in enigma" scenarios, but it afforded Gutteridge the opportunity to change her wardrobe (and personality) in literally every new scene. She opens the show as a ditzy blonde in a tight red suit, then she's a spiky-haired, spiky-tongued punk, then mysterious in fashionable posh leather, a schoolgirl after that, followed by big hair and red spandex, finishing up as the prim and proper secretary who she really is — or is she? Whatever the answer, she has a field day with the part, virtually writing a textbook on versatility in 60 minutes, and plays well off of the always reliable Denholm Elliott. That versatility eventually got her nominated for a Golden Globe (for the TV miniseries *Little Gloria: Happy at Last*), but she hasn't appeared in a film or on television since her role in the film *Grief* (1993). She lives on the Isle of Wight.

Other genre credits: TELEVISION: *Tales of the Unexpected*: "Skin," 1980 (Josie); "The Wrong 'Un," 1983 (Molly); "The Finger of Suspicion," 1988 (Soroya)

Hale, Georgina (1943–)

BIRTHPLACE: Ilford, Essex, England.
TELEVISION: *Hammer House of Horror*: "The Mark of Satan," 1980 (Stella)
BIOGRAPHY—Georgina Hale was trained at RADA, and in 2010 was voted by Britain's *Guardian* newspaper as third in a list of 10 Great Character Actors. Hale is known not only for her stage work, but for her many roles in Ken Russell films. She won a BAFTA Award for *Mahler*, and played the younger version of Bette Davis in *The Watcher in the Woods*. In 1980 she played the female lead in the *Hammer House of Horror* episode "The Mark of Satan": a single mother who may or may not be an emissary of the Devil (although the scene where she gnaws on a priest is a pretty good indicator). It's a convoluted variation on the "everyone is trying to drive the heroine mad" scenario, except that this time it's a repressed, working-class hero who's convinced that Satan is out to get him. Hale is wonderful, whether she's bemusedly listening to the hero rant, or casually helping him stuff his mother's body in the freezer after he's killed her (not to mention that priest-gnawing part).

Other genre credits: FILMS: *The Watcher in the Woods*, Walt Disney Productions, 1980 (Young Mrs. Aylwood); *Cockneys vs. Zombies*, Tea Shop & Film Company, 2011 TELEVISION: *Doctor Who*: "The Happiness Patrol," 1988 (Daisy K); *T-Bag and the Pearls of Wisdom*: 10 episodes, 1990 (Tabatha Bag); *T-Bag's Christmas Ding Dong*: Movie, 1990 (Tabatha Bag); *T-Bag's Christmas Turkey*: Movie, 1991 (Tabatha Bag); *T-Bag and the Sunstones of Montezuma*: 10 episodes, 1992 (Tabatha Bag); *Take Off with T-Bag*: 10 episodes, 1992 (Tabatha Bag)

Hamilton, Gay (1943–)

BIRTHPLACE: Hamilton, Scotland.

FILMS: *A Challenge for Robin Hood*, 1967 (Lady Marian Fitzwarren); *Journey to the Unknown*, 1969 (Sylvia Ann Hahlen)

TELEVISION: *Journey to the Unknown*: "Matakitas Is Coming," 1968 (Sylvia Ann Hahlen)

BIOGRAPHY— Pixie-like Gay Hamilton is a Scottish character actress who made two appearances for Hammer. One was in a lead role, as Lady Marian in *A Challenge for Robin Hood*, and the other as the devil's librarian in the "Matakitas Is Coming" episode of *Journey to the Unknown*. Her first role was on television in 1963, and she is still active.

Other genre credits: TELEVISION: *The Hunchback of Notre Dame*: "Abduction," "Torture," "Seduction," "Interrogation," "Accusation," "Repentance," "Retribution," 1966 (Esmeralda); *Out of the Unknown*: "Tunnel Under the World," 1966 (April Dorn); *Space: 1999*: "Force of Life," 1975 (Eva Zoref)

Hamilton, Wendy

FILM: *Scars of Dracula*, 1970 (Julie)

BIOGRAPHY— Buxom Wendy Hamilton, the first wife of actor-musician Michael Des Barres, had a two-year career in movies and television, and one of her bit parts was in *Scars of Dracula* as yet another brassy barmaid (in Hammer films, "brassy" seems to be something of a job requirement). She doesn't have much to do other than fall victim to Christopher Lee, but she sure does it pretty.

Hammer, Sue

FILMS: *The Horror of Frankenstein*, 1970 (Maid); *Nearest and Dearest*, 1972 (Scarlet O'Hara)

BIOGRAPHY— A busty British character actress, Hammer appeared in only two films in her radar blip of a career, and both were for the company whose name she shared.

Hancock, Sheila Cameron (1933–)

BIRTHPLACE: Blackgang, Isle of Wight, England.

FILM: *The Anniversary*, 1968 (Karen Taggart)

BIOGRAPHY— The daughter of Ivy Louise and Enrico Cameron Hancock, she attended Dartford County Grammar School and RADA. One of England's most versatile actresses, she is equally at home on the stage, screen, television or radio. She was a member of the Actor's Company at the Royal Theatre and the Royal Shakespeare Company, and won a Laurence Olivier Award for Best Performance in a Supporting Role in a Musical in 2006. One of her stage performances was in "The Anniversary," which led to her being cast in the same role in the 1968 Hammer film (much to the displeasure of star Bette Davis). Working in the movie reunited her with two other actors from the stage production, Jack Hedley and James Cossins. She's wonderful as a strong, defiant woman in a film that's full of them. Neither she nor Elaine Taylor can stand up to the iron-willed, shameless and completely unscrupulous Davis, although she does put up a marvelous fight. In fact, she's so strong that you wonder what she ever saw in her weak-willed husband in the first place, and why she even puts up with the whole situation (we discover the reasons for that later). A breast cancer survivor who has outlived two husbands, she is heavily involved in charity work and is a member of the Religious Society of Friends. She was awarded an OBE in 1974 and a CBE in 2011.

Other genre credits: TELEVISION: *Doctor Who*: "The Happiness Patrol," 1988 (Helen A)

Hanley, Jenny (1947–)

BIRTHPLACE: Gerrards Cross, Buckinghamshire, England.

FILM: *Scars of Dracula*, 1970 (Sarah Framsen)

BIOGRAPHY—Jenny Hanley was born with performance in her blood: Her mother was actress Dinah Sheridan and her father was Jimmy Hanley, one of the stars of Hammer's *The Lost Continent*. After serving time as a nanny and model, she made her first film appearance in *Joanna*, which also featured fellow Hammer Heroine Caroline Munro. Around that same time, she made a commercial for movie theaters; it was seen by the talent scout for producer Harry Saltzman, and she became a Bond Girl with her appearance in *On Her Majesty's Secret Service*. This led to her role as the heroine Sarah in *Scars of Dracula*, her only appearance for Hammer—with the word "appearance" stressed, since her voice was dubbed by another actress. (Hanley's was considered too low and grown-up for the sweet young thing she played.) She was not best pleased by this fact, but otherwise had a grand time making the film, and credits director Roy Ward Baker with helping her develop greatly as an actress. Despite this grounding, her best-known role was as a hostess for the ITV program *Magpie*. She is retired now, her last film coming in 1976 and her last television spot in 1983.

Jenny Hanley manages to look both terrifyingly beautiful and beautifully terrified in *Scars of Dracula* (courtesy Mel Bridgeman).

Other genre credits: FILMS: *On Her Majesty's Secret Service*, Danjaq/Eon Productions, 1969 (Irish Girl); *The Devil's Widow*, Commonwealth United Entertainment, 1970 (Caroline); *The Flesh & Blood Show*, Peter Walker (Heritage), 1972 (Julia Dawson)

Hargreaves, Janet (1937–)

FILM: *Frankenstein and the Monster from Hell*, 1974 (Chatter)

Other genre credits: TELEVISION: *The Avengers*: "Dead on Course," 1962 (Sister Isobel); *Doctor Who*: "The Greatest Show in the Galaxy," 1988/89 (Mother)

Harmon, Molly

FILM: *The Woman in Black*, 2012 (Fisher Girl)

Harris, Julie (1925–)

REAL NAME: Julia Ann Harris; BIRTHPLACE: Grosse Pointe, Michigan, USA.
FILM: *Journey to Midnight*, 1971 (Leona Gillings)
TELEVISION: *Journey to the Unknown*: "The Indian Spirit Guide," 1969 (Leona Gillings)
BIOGRAPHY— One of America's most respected actresses, Julie Harris has received five Tony and three Emmy Awards, a Grammy, a National Medal of the Arts, an Oscar nomination and more. She attended the Hewitt School, made her first film appearance in 1952 and went on to first-rank pictures like *East of Eden* and *Requiem for a Heavyweight* and the genre classic for which she is best remembered, *The Haunting*. She brings much the same character traits displayed in that film to her role in "The Indian Spirit Guide," an episode of Hammer's first television series *Journey to the Unknown*. She plays the lonely, vulnerable and insecure Leona Gillings, whose condition makes her vulnerable to the schemes and charms of a low-rent private investigator. She wants to contact her dead husband, and wants the dick's help sorting through all the phony mystics and shysters, unaware that her secretary and he are in cahoots as well as bed, and that all the frauds he exposes have been set up by her. She brings a whopping amount of talent and class to the show, which was later edited into the feature *Journey to Midnight*. Harris is still active of this writing, in her chosen profession as well as in her position on the board of directors of the Wellfleet Harbor Actors Theatre. She is a cancer and stroke survivor and, in the United Sates, a national treasure.

Other genre credits: FILM: *The Haunting*, Argyle Enterprises, 1963 (Eleanor Lance) TELEVISION: *Tarzan*: "The Perils of Charity Jones," 1967; "The Four O'Clock Army," 1968 (Charity Jones); *Tales of the Unexpected*: "Mrs. Bixby and the Colonel's Coat" (Mrs. Bixby); "The Way Up to Heaven," 1979 (Mrs. Foster); *Annihilator* (Movie), 1986 (Girl); *The Outer Limits*: "Lithia," 1998 (Hera)

Harris, Toni

FILM: *Frankenstein and the Monster from Hell*, 1974 (Inmate)

Hartford, Fiona

FILM: *Rasputin, the Mad Monk*, 1966 (Tania)
Other genre credits: TELEVISION: *The Avengers*: "You'll Catch Your Death," 1968 (Janice); *Mystery and Imagination*: "Feet Foremost," 1968 (Maggie)

Harvey, Vivienne (1982–)

BIRTHPLACE: Glasgow, Scotland.
FILM: *Beyond the Rave*, 2008 (Tess)
Other genre credits: FILMS: *Nine Lives*, A&A Films Limited, 2002 (Lucy); *The Dead Outside*, Mothcatcher Films, 2008 (Eleanor)

Hassall, Imogen (1942–1980)

BIRTHPLACE: Woking, Surrey, England.
FILM: *When Dinosaurs Ruled the Earth*, 1970 (Ayak)
BIOGRAPHY— The light that was Imogen Hassall burned out before it really had the chance to shine. She came from an artistic family; her grandfather and aunt were illustrators,

and her father was a poet and lyricist for her godfather, Ivor Novello, who coincidentally happened to be her father's lover. She attended the Royal Ballet School and the London Academy of Music and Dramatic Art, made her first television appearance in 1963, and made her first headline when she spilled tea on Princess Margaret during a school visit. She found steady work in television, and soon thereafter films; she became known as the "Countess of Cleavage" and "Queen of the Premieres" due to her often-revealing wardrobe, her propensity for the spotlight and her lurid, gift-to-the-tabloids lifestyle. She cuts a sexy and memorable figure in her lone Hammer *When Dinosaurs Ruled the Earth* with seemingly similarly cursed co-star Victoria Vetri and Jim Danforth's Oscar-nominated animation. It seemed like she was always merely eye candy and always second fiddle, and though she seemed to revel in her B-movie career and celebrity, there was an undercurrent of sadness and frustration just below the surface. In 1980 she ended that sadness and frustration with an overdose of Tuinals. She was found by police summoned by her friend Suzanna Leigh, whom she was due to go with on a holiday. The tickets were still clutched in her hand.

Other genre credits: FILM: *Incense for the Damned*, Lucinda Films, 1972 (Chriseis) TELEVISION: *The Avengers*: "Escape in Time," 1967 (Anjali)

Hawkins, Carol (1949–)

BIRTHPLACE: Barnet, Hertfordshire, England.
FILM: *When Dinosaurs Ruled the Earth*, 1970 (Yani)
Other genre credits: TELEVISION: *Blake's 7*: "City at the Edge of the World," 1980 (Kerril); *Leap in the Dark*: "Room for an Inward Light," 1980 (Yvonne Thompson)

Hayden, Linda (1953–)

REAL NAME: Linda M. Higginson; BIRTHPLACE: Stanmore, Middlesex, England.
FILM: *Taste the Blood of Dracula*, 1970 (Alice Hargood)
TELEVISION: *Hammer House of Mystery and Suspense*: "Black Carrion," 1986 (Ellen Jarvis)
BIOGRAPHY— The sister of actress Jane Hayden, the mesmerizingly beautiful and alluring Linda Hayden specialized in good little girls gone bad; Marsha Brady turning tricks at the Devil's Whorehouse. While attending the posh Aida Foster Stage School, she made her film debut at the age of 15 in the notorious *Baby Love*, in which she plays a girl whose mother (Diana Dors) commits suicide, and then seduces the family who takes her in (yes, the whole family). In her first appearance for Hammer, as Alice in *Taste the Blood of Dracula*, she again brought to the screen a blend of innocence and evil. In the beginning, she is virginal yet headstrong and quite aware of her budding sexuality. But her desires are suppressed by her brutal bastard of a father, whose puritanical tyranny masks a liar and hypocrite who frequents brothels. After he and his friends have unleashed Dracula, the vampire king uses her and her friend Lucy (Isla Blair) as pawns in his scheme of revenge against her father and the others. Alice is the first to be taken; fleeing from her drunken, violent father, she runs straight into the arms of Christopher Lee. In far and away her best scene in the picture, she immediately and very convincingly falls under his spell and turns to face her enraged father, whom she quickly terminates with extreme prejudice, with a shovel to the head, her face radiating an evil glow. But just because she's under Dracula's spell doesn't mean she's not still headstrong, and quite jealous, too, when he chooses to vampirize Lucy instead of her (and after she hooked them up!). When he tells her he has no more use for her, she shows him that Hell hath no fury like a nymphet scorned, and helps her boyfriend destroy him, making her a bit more than the generally helpless Hammer heroine. She shares another great scene with Blair when they ambush Blair's dad and Hayden holds him down while Blair stakes her claim.

Whether it's Linda Hayden or Isla Blair, you can bet Christopher Lee will soon be rubbin' up a daughter in *Taste the Blood of Dracula*.

She made her greatest contribution to the genre in her next film, the grossly underrated *The Blood on Satan's Claw*, and seemed to be on the verge of a major breakthrough, but her career faltered with the '70s collapse of the British film industry, and she was soon appearing in sex comedies and similar low-budget fare. But she rebounded with a role in *The Boys from Brazil* and continued to work steadily in television throughout the 1980s, including a return to Hammer in the "Black Carrion" episode of *Hammer House of Mystery and Suspense*: In a series of flashbacks, she plays the mother of the little girl who grows up to be Season Hubley. Married to theatre producer Paul Elliot, she is semi-retired, returning to the screen in 2010 for a remake of her 1976 thriller *Exposé*.

Other genre credits: FILMS: *The Blood on Satan's Claw*, Tigon British Film Productions, 1971 (Angel Blake); *Madhouse*, American International Pictures, 1974 (Elizabeth Peters); *Old Dracula*, World Film Services, 1975 (Helga); *Exposé* (a.k.a. *Trauma*), Norfolk International Pictures, 1976 (Linda); *Queen Kong*, Cine-Art Munchen, 1976 (The Singing Nun); *The Boys from Brazil*, Lew Grade, 1978 (Nancy); *Stalker* (a.k.a. *Exposé*), Black & Blue Films, 2010 (Mrs. Brown)

Hayes, Patricia (1909–1998)

REAL NAME: Patricia Lawlor Hayes; BIRTHPLACE: Wandsworth, London, England.
FILMS: *Love Thy Neighbour*, 1973 (Annie Booth)

TELEVISION: *Hammer House of Mystery and Suspense*: "And the Wall Came Tumbling Down," 1985 (Gran Waters)

BIOGRAPHY—A venerated character actress of stage, screen and television, she attended the Sacred Heart School and grew up to be an accomplished comedienne, winning a BAFTA Award for her role in the *Play for Today* episode "Edna, the Inebriate Woman" and appearing in such "A" fare as *A Fish Called Wanda*. She did one film and one television episode for Hammer, the film being the comedy *Love Thy Neighbour*. She has a delightful bit in *Hammer House of Mystery and Suspense* as the grandmother of a lad who's a reincarnation of a lad who's part of Peter Wyngarde's Satanic Plan to Destroy the World. Her career lasted for sixty years, and she performed until only two years before she passed away in 1998.

Other genre credits: FILMS: *The Terrornauts*, Amicus Productions, 1967 (Mrs. Jones); *Willow*, Imagine Films Entertainment, 1988 (Fin Raziel) TELEVISION: *The Witches and the Grinnygog* (Mini-Series), 1983 (Miss Bendybones)

Haynes, Carol

FILM: *The Two Faces of Dr. Jekyll*, 1960 (Sphinx Girl)

Haythorne, Joan (1915–1987)

REAL NAME: Joan Haythornewaite; BIRTHPLACE: Ealing, London, England.
FILM: *Countess Dracula*, 1971 (Second Cook)
Other genre credits: TELEVISION: *Thriller*: "Death to Sister Mary," 1974 (Mother Superior)

Hearne, Biddy

FILM: *Countess Dracula*, 1971 (Gypsy Dancer)

Hempel, Anouska (1941–)

REAL NAME: Anne Geissler; BIRTHPLACE: Wellington, New Zealand.
FILM: *Scars of Dracula*, 1970 (Tania)

BIOGRAPHY—World-famous interior designer and architect Anouska Hempel (aka Lady Weinberg) was once a Bond Girl and a Hammer vampire girl in *Scars of Dracula*, a fact that she would much rather forget, and that this book will once again remind her of. She was also a trash cinema presence, another part of her past that she would just as soon obliterate; she's bought the rights to a couple of those films to prevent them from ever being shown again, a fact that bootleggers could care less about. Wikipedia reports that her first film role was also for Hammer, a bit part in *The Kiss of the Vampire*, but no other sources confirm this information.

Anouska Hempel is ready to sink her teeth into her work with this classic portrait from *Scars of Dracula.*

Other genre credits: FILM: *On Her Majesty's Secret Service*, Danjaq/Eon Productions, 1969 (The Australian Girl) TELEVISION: *UFO*: "Mindbender," "The Man Who Came Back," 1971; "The Long Sleep," 1973 (S.H.A.D.O. Operative Tamara Paulson); "Reflections in the Water," 1971 (Skydiver Operative); *Space: 1999*: "The Metamorph," 1976 (Annette Fraser); *Tales from the Crypt*: "Loved to Death," 1991 (Larry)

Hemson, Joyce (1905–1978)

BIRTHPLACE: London, England.
FILMS: *The Gorgon*, 1964 (Martha); *Dracula, Prince of Darkness*, 1965 (Mother)
BIOGRAPHY— Hemson was a long-serving British character actress primarily known for stage work who also found time for a twenty-year career in films and (mostly) television.
Other genre credits: FILMS: *Island of Terror*, Planet Film Productions, 1966 (Mrs. Bellows) TELEVISION: *Menace*: "Pick Up," 1973 (Cashier)

Hendry, Zoe

FILM: *To the Devil a Daughter*, 1976 (First Girl)
Other genre credits: FILMS: *Queen Kong*, Cine-Art Munchen, 1976 (Native Dancer) TELEVISION: *The Hitch Hiker's Guide to the Galaxy*: Episode 3, 1981 (Co-Pilot)

Henriques, Sylvana

FILM: *The Lost Continent*, 1968 (Traveler)
Other genre credits: FILMS: *Deadlier Than the Male*, Greater Films Limited, 1967 (Masseuse); *You Only Live Twice*, Eon Productions, 1967 (Silhouette of Japanese Fan Dancer in Title Sequence); *On Her Majesty's Secret Service*, Eon Productions, 1969 (Jamaican Girl)

Heywood, Patricia "Pat" (1931–)

BIRTHPLACE: Gretna Green, Scotland.
TELEVISION: *Hammer House of Horror*: "Rude Awakening," 1980 (Emily Shenley)
BIOGRAPHY— One of five children, Heywood was educated at the Bristol Old Vic Theatre School, and spent the first part of her career on the stage. She film-debuted at the age of 36 in *Romeo and Juliet*, for which she was nominated for a BAFTA Award. A reliable character actress, Heywood appeared in such films as *Young Winston*, which starred Simon Ward from *Frankenstein Must Be Destroyed*, and worked for Hammer in their *Hammer House of Horror* episode "Rude Awakening," in which she plays Denholm Elliott's much put-upon (in more ways than one) wife. She retired after her role as Sister Teresa in *Sparrow* (1993).
Other genre credits: FILMS: *10 Rillington Place*, Filmways, 1971 (Ethel Christie); *Whoever Slew Auntie Roo?* American International Productions, 1972 (Dr. Mason)

Hignett, Mary (1915–1980)

BIRTHPLACE: England.
FILMS: *Prehistoric Women*, 1967 (Mrs. Hammond); *Demons of the Mind*, 1972 (Matronly Woman)
BIOGRAPHY— Born into a Britain that was then in the midst of World War I, Mary Hignett grew up to become one of the most familiar character faces on British television for three decades. Her only three feature film appearances were in genre movies, two Hammer films and the cult classic *The Corpse*. Her co-star in *Demons of the Mind*, Robert Hardy, also co-starred with her when she played her most fondly remembered role, as the cook and housekeeper in *All Creatures Great and Small*.

Other genre credits: FILM: *The Corpse* (a.k.a. *Crucible of Horror*), Abacus Productions, 1971 (Servant) TELEVISION: *Doomwatch*: "The Battery People," 1970 (Mrs. Adams)

Hilary, Jennifer Mary (1942–2008)

BIRTHPLACE: Frimley, Surrey, England.
FILM: *Journey into Darkness*, 1969 (Anne Prentiss)
TELEVISION: *Journey to the Unknown*: "The New People"; 1968 (Anne Prentiss)
BIOGRAPHY—Born in the U.K. before moving to Miami Beach, beautiful Jennifer Mary Hilary attended Elmhurst Ballet School and RADA, first plying her trade in Liverpool rep. Her first film appearance was in *Becket* (1964), and four years later she played the female lead, Anne Prentiss, in *Journey to the Unknown* as one of the recent arrivals in a neighborhood chock full of swinging Satanists. There are unmistakable parallels to *Rosemary's Baby*, except there's no baby and the plot is much more straightforward; she knows Patrick Allen fancies her, she just doesn't know what for, and he doesn't want Anne to have the Devil's child, he just wants to sacrifice her and new hubby Robert (*Brady Bunch*) Reed to ol' Scratch for kicks. She plays it well, especially her scenes with Allen and Adrienne Corri, but her character's resolution is disappointing; not so much because she dies, but because she meets her fate without being allowed to figure out what's going on—she simply goes from a teasing after-party scene to the sacrificial slab. Hilary stayed active until the year before her death, and also operated her own specialist flower arranging business.

Other genre credits: TELEVISION: *Out of the Unknown*: "Welcome Home," 1971 (Penny Bowers); *Tales of the Unexpected*: "The Umbrella Man," 1980 (Wendy)

Hills, Gillian (1944–)

BIRTHPLACE: Cairo, Egypt.
FILM: *Demons of the Mind*, 1972 (Elizabeth)
BIOGRAPHY—Daughter of the famous Denis Hills, Gillian Hills was discovered by Roger Vadim, who had visions of her becoming the next Brigitte Bardot. She did nude scenes for *Demons of the Mind*, but she was no stranger to getting her kit off; she had done it previously in the classic *Blow-Up* as well as in her most well-remembered bit in *A Clockwork Orange*, where she and a friend do a hilariously high-speed horizontal bop with Malcolm McDowell to the tune of the William Tell Overture. Her role in *Demons of the Mind*, unfortunately, is not nearly as lively: She plays another in the long line of that old Hammer standby, the woman who begins the film in a state of mental disarray, which tends to happen when one witnesses one's mother commit suicide, and spends the rest of it in a (forcibly) drug-induced stupor. Her condition is exacerbated by her father, who is trying to "cure" her of *his* own madness by "bleeding the evil out of her" and the fact that she is in love with her brother. She inherited the role from Marianne Faithfull, who could not take the job due to her own drug-induced stupor. Hills left the business just three years later, became a successful magazine illustrator, and married the manager of AC/DC, ELP, Cyndi Lauper, Foreigner, Billy Squier and the Scorpions—different kinds of horrors entirely.

Other genre credits: FILMS: *Lana, Queen of the Amazons*, Arca Studio, Berlin, 1964 (Amazon); *A Clockwork Orange*, Warner Brothers, 1971 (Sonietta); *The Killer Wore Gloves*, Producciones Cinematograficas Cine XX, 1974 (Peggy Foster)

Hird, Dame Thora (1911–2003)

BIRTHPLACE: Morecambe, Lancashire, England.
FILMS: *The Quatermass Xperiment*, 1955 (Rosemary); *Women Without Men*, 1956 (Granny Rafferty); *A Clean Sweep*, 1958 (Vera Watson); *Further Up the Creek*, 1958 (Mrs. Galloway)

BIOGRAPHY— Dame Thora Hird's career spanned an incredible eight decades, making her first appearance at the age of two ... months! A deeply religious woman with a gift for comedy, she made over 100 films and television appearances, and lent her considerable talents to four Hammer features, including the classic *The Quatermass Xperiment*. She was the mother of Janette Scott, who would herself star twice for Hammer, and in 1993 was made a Dame Commander of the British Empire for her contributions to the arts. She passed away ten years later, a month after she suffered a stroke.

Holden, Jan (1931–2005)

REAL NAME: Valerie Jeanne Wilkinson; BIRTHPLACE: Southport, England.

FILMS: *Quatermass 2*, 1957 (Young Girl); *Man with a Dog*, 1957 (Nurse); *The Camp on Blood Island*, 1958 (Nurse); *The Stranglers of Bombay*, 1959 (Mary Lewis)

TELEVISION: *Journey to the Unknown*: "Girl of My Dreams," 1968 (Mrs. Wheeler)

BIOGRAPHY— Jan Holden's father was a senior manager at the Swadeshi cotton mills, and she spent most of her childhood in India. He disapproved of the stage, and she had to turn down an invitation to RADA, but he finally agreed to let her take director's courses at the Old Vic. Holden was always a Hammer bridesmaid but never a bride; her most substantial part was as Guy Rolfe's stoic wife in *The Stranglers of Bombay*, where her elegant beauty but status quo role relegated her playing second fiddle to the more "exotic" charms of Marie Devereux. One could say she grew up during the course of those films; in her first, she played a young girl, in the next two, a young, single nurse, and in the fourth, a married woman. And not only was she a significant player in their supporting ranks, she is the very definition of a real-life Hammer Heroine: Her twin brother drowned in the early '60s, and her marriage broke down in 1973, leaving her to raise three daughters, one of whom died from a brain tumor. And she herself was in ill health the last 20 years of her life, but she never let the weight of the accumulated tragedies dampen her spirit for it.

Other genre credits: FILMS: *Fire Maidens of Outer Space*, Criterion Films, 1956 (Fire Maiden); *Horror House*, Tigon British Film Productions/American International Pictures, 1969 (Peggy) TELEVISION: *The Avengers*: "The Undertakers," 1963 (Paula Madden); "Dial a Deadly Number," 1969 (Ruth Boardman)

Holland, Sophie

FILM: *Beyond the Rave*, 2008 (Lydia)

Other genre credits: FILMS: *Forest of the Damned*, Gatlin Pictures, 2005 (Ally); *Worms* (short), Andris Films Limited, 2007 (Carla); *Cold Earth*, Bridgeway Productions, 2008 (Stacey Smith)

Holman, Valerie

FILM: *The Terror of the Tongs*, 1961 (Tong Room Girl)

Holt, Penelope

FILM: *Blood from the Mummy's Tomb*, 1971 (Nurse)

Hood, Noel (1909–1979)

BIRTHPLACE: Bristol, England.

FILM: *The Curse of Frankenstein*, 1957 (Aunt)

Hool, Veronica
FILM: *The Resident*, 2011 (Nurse)

Horner, Yvonne
FILMS: *One Million Years B.C.*, 1966 (Ullah); *Slave Girls*, 1967 (First Amazon)

Horton, Helen
BIRTHPLACE: Chicago, Illinois, USA.
FILM: *Never Take Sweets from a Stranger*, 1960 (Sylvia Kingsley)
Other genre credits: FILMS: *Phase IV*, Alced Productions, 1974 (Mildred Eldridge); *Alien*, Brandywine Productions/20th Century–Fox, 1979 (Voice of Mother); *Superman III*, Cantharaus Productions N.V. 1983 (Miss Henderson) TELEVISION: *Out of the Unknown*: "Satisfaction Guaranteed," 1966 (Brenda Claffern); *Tales of the Unexpected*: "Kindly Dig Your Own Grave," 1981 (Martha); "Hijack," 1981 (American Lady Passenger)

Houston, Renee (1902–1980)
REAL NAME: Katherina Houston Gibbin; BIRTHPLACE: Johnstone, Renfrewshire, Scotland.
FILMS: *Watch It, Sailor!* 1961 (Mrs. Mottram); *The Phantom of the Opera*, 1962 (Mrs. Tucker)
Other genre credits: FILMS: *The Flesh and the Fiends*, Triad Productions, 1960 (Martha Burke); *Repulsion*, Compton Films, 1965 (Miss Balch); *Legend of the Werewolf*, Tyburn Film Productions, 1975 (Chou-Chou)

Howard, Cathy
FILM: *Twins of Evil*, 1971 (Girl on Tomb)
Other genre credits: FILM: *Bizarre*, Balch/Noteworthy Films, 1970 (The Cat Burglar)

Hroncich, Rachel
FILM: *Let Me In*, 2010 (Admitting Nurse)

Hubley, Season (1951–)
REAL NAME: Susan Hubley; BIRTHPLACE: New York City, New York, USA.
TELEVISION: *Hammer House of Mystery and Suspense*: "Black Carrion," 1986 (Cora Berlaine)
BIOGRAPHY—Coolly beautiful Season Hubley is an American character actress whose career began in 1972. She is best known for her roles in *Hardcore* and the TV movie *Elvis*. She's excellent in the "Black Carrion" episode of *Hammer House of Mystery and Suspense* as a no-nonsense researcher haunted by unconnected visions of her mother's death (the mother may or may not have been killed by '60s rock stars who have seemingly vanished from the face of the earth). The no-nonsense demeanor is revealed to be a psychological mask that falls away when the gaps in those visions are filled in, but she remains in control. Hubley has apparently retired, her last appearance coming in 1998.
Other genre credits: FILMS: *Tomorrow's a Killer*, Dax Avant Productions, 1987 (Heather Todd); *Children of the Corn V: Fields of Terror*, Blue Rider Pictures, 1998 (Lilly's Mother) TELEVISION: *The Twilight Zone*: "Little Boy Lost," 1985 (Carol Shelton); *Alfred Hitchcock Presents*: "Final Escape," 1985 (Lena Trent); *Stepfather III* (Movie), 1992 (Jennifer Ashley); *Humanoids from the Deep* (Movie), 1996 (Timmy's Mother)

Hudson, Christine

FILM: *Creatures the World Forgot*, 1971 (Prehistoric Woman)

Hughes, Beulah

FILM: *Hands of the Ripper*, 1971 (Second Pub Whore)
Other genre credits: FILMS: *The Hands of Orlac*, Pendennis Films, 1960 (Whore); *Supergirl*, Artistry Limited, 1984 (Argonian Citizen) TELEVISION: *Space: 1999*: "Devil's Planet," 1977 (Guard)

Hughes, Hazel (1913–1974)

BIRTHPLACE: Transvaal, South Africa.
FILM: *Journey into Darkness*, 1969 (Mrs. Biddle)
TELEVISION: *Journey to the Unknown*: "Paper Dolls," 1968 (Mrs. Biddle)

Hughes, Lynne

FILM: *Dracula A.D. 1972*, 1972 (Member of Stoneground)

Hume, Marjorie (1900–1976)

BIRTHPLACE: Great Yarmouth, Norfolk, England.
FILM: *The Curse of Frankenstein*, 1957 (Mother)

Hunt, Marsha (1946–)

BIRTHPLACE: Philadelphia, Pennsylvania, USA.
FILM: *Dracula A.D. 1972*, 1972 (Gaynor)
BIOGRAPHY—Marsha Hunt was raised by her mother, aunt and grandmother after her father committed suicide. She attended Berkeley, moved to England in 1966, and married Mike Ratledge of Soft Machine; she fronted her own band at the Isle of Wight and performed in *Hair*. Just prior to making her one film for Hammer, *Dracula A.D. 1972*, she met and had a child with Mick Jagger, and she brought the little girl to the Hammer set. Hunt plays Gaynor, one of a group of swinging London hipsters who participate in a black mass to revive Dracula. They succeed. Hunt becomes Dracula's first black victim and participates in an interracial love scene with Christopher Neame (daring stuff for the time). She had just a handful of movie–TV credits over the course of 21 years, with her last coming in 1990. Now an author, she has always been an activist, and is a cancer survivor. She has lived in Ireland since 1995.
Other genre credits: FILM: *Howling II*, Hemdale Film, 1985 (Mariana)

Hunt, Martita (1899–1969)

BIRTHPLACE: Buenos Aires, Argentina.
FILM: *The Brides of Dracula*, 1960 (Baroness Meinster)
BIOGRAPHY—One of Britain's most distinguished character actresses, Martita Hunt was born in Argentina and moved to England ten years later. After conquering the stage, she moved on to motion pictures and later television. She won a 1949 Tony Award as Best Actress for her performance in *The Madwoman of Chaillot*; her last stage role was in 1956. She made her first film in 1920 and didn't make another for 12 years; her most famous was *Great Expectations*, and she is most fondly remembered by genre fans for her wonderful performance as Baroness Meinster in *The Brides of Dracula*. Beneath her stately demeanor, the baroness is a monster, in two ways. First, she procures victims for her son, the vampire, but then he is set

free and vampirizes her, turning her into an actual monster. But she knows what she has become and accepts the consequences, literally with open arms. Hunt's voice and her performance drip with class, and her scenes with Peter Cushing take the production to a whole other level. Genre fans also remember her fondly for her role in the "Lizard's Leg and Owlet's Wing" episode of *Route 66*, which teamed up Peter Lorre, Boris Karloff and Lon Chaney Jr. for one last go-around as the characters they had made famous (Lorre simply played Lorre, which was more than good enough).

Other genre credits: FILM: *The Wonderful World of the Brothers Grimm*, Cinerama/MGM, 1962 (Anna Richter) TELEVISION: *Thriller*: "The Last of the Sommervilles," 1961 (Celia Sommerville); *Route 66*: "Lizard's Leg and Owlet's Wing," 1962 (Mrs. Baxter)

Hylton, Jane (1927–1979)

REAL NAME: Audrey Gwendolene Clark; BIRTHPLACE: London, England.

TELEVISION: *Journey to the Unknown*: "Stranger in the Family," 1969 (Margaret Wilson)

BIOGRAPHY— Blond British character actress and B-movie leading lady Jane Hylton was a graduate of the Rank "Charm School" who rose above that institution's reputation for turning out eye candy rather than actresses. She had a solid if unspectacular career, mostly in television. In her episode of *Journey to the Unknown*, she plays the long-suffering mother of a mutant son who has the power to force others to do whatever he wants them to, which leads to some tense moments for his mother when she tosses the keys to their apartment to the pavement far below.

Other genre credits: FILMS: *The Manster*, Lopert Pictures, 1959 (Linda Stanford); *Circus of Horrors*, Lynx Films, 1960 (Angela); *House of Mystery*, Independent Artists, 1961 (Stella Lemming) TELEVISION: *One Step Beyond*: "The Room Upstairs," 1961 (Joan Morrison); *Kraft Mystery Theater*: "Deadly Record," 1959 (Ann Garfield); "House of Mystery," 1961 (Stella Lemming); *Doctor Who*: "Doctor Who and the Silurians" (Part 6), 1970 (Extra)

Hyman, Prudence (1914–1995)

BIRTHPLACE: London, England.

FILMS: *The Two Faces of Dr. Jekyll*, 1960 (Tavern Woman); *The Gorgon*, 1964 (The Gorgon); *Rasputin the Mad Monk*, 1966 (Chatty Woman); *The Witches*, 1966 (Stephanie's Maid)

BIOGRAPHY— Some actresses, you just don't know about — literally. Although she lived to a ripe old age and portrayed one of Hammer's most

Barbara Shelley was the star, but Prudence Hyman was *The Gorgon* (courtesy Paul C. Riggie).

visually iconic monsters, there is very little information about Prudence Hyman, either before her career or after it. She had bit parts in four Hammer films (a full quarter of her entire output), including the iconic Gorgon. There have been pages and pages, even whole chapters of books, devoted to the Gorgon makeup and the attendant battles over how to make everything work properly, interviews with actors and technicians on the various troubles encountered and obstacles surmounted — but apparently, nobody at the time (or since) bothered to ask Hyman about any of these things. And a note about that makeup: In this book's section on Barbara Shelley, the Gorgon's makeup is referred to as "risible," and above, it's referred to as "iconic"; so which is it? Well, it's both — the facial makeup is appropriately hideous and mesmerizing, and, seen in still photographs, the snakes in the hair look fantastic. It's only when the Gorgon and the snakes move that the illusion is shattered — and then only in close-up. Seen in long or medium shot, or in shadows or reflections, the Gorgon is a perfectly adequate monster. Her last film for Hammer, *The Witches*, was also the last film of her career.

Impey, Betty

FILMS: *The Quatermass Xperiment*, 1955 (Central Clinic Nurse); *Quatermass 2*, 1957 (Kelly)

Inns, Trudy

FILM: *Creatures the World Forgot*, 1971 (Prehistoric Woman)

Ismail, Doreen

FILM: *The Two Faces of Dr. Jekyll*, 1960 (Second Sphinx Girl)

Jackson, Freda (1907–1990)

BIRTHPLACE: Nottingham, England.
FILMS: *The Brides of Dracula*, 1960 (Greta); *The Shadow of the Cat*, 1961 (Clara)
BIOGRAPHY— Freda Jackson was a distinguished British stage actress who also appeared in two Hammer films and had parts in other noted genre productions. She is one of the best things about the great *The Brides of Dracula*; as the mad, cackling housekeeper Greta, she comes close to stealing the whole picture (no easy task with the talent involved). She unquestionably owns the screen in one of Hammer's most memorable scene ever, when Peter Cushing's Van Helsing comes upon her in the cemetery, caressing the cold ground out of which Marie Devereux is about to rise, rasping, "Yes, I know it's dark but you've got to push! Come, come, my little precious; the master's waiting for you!" and "Ah, there she comes, my little beauty!" (when Devereux's hand breaks the soil). And her full-throttle performance doesn't stop until she takes a flying leap from the windmill, trying to attack Van Helsing. She falls to her death again, albeit in a different manner, in *The Shadow of the Cat*, in which she plays a housekeeper who not only knows where they hide the bodies, but helps to bury them as well. This time the exit isn't nearly as spectacular, taking a tumble down a flight of stairs after being clawed by the titular kitty. She went on to play the invalid Letitia Witley opposite Boris Karloff and Suzan Farmer in *Die, Monster, Die!*, and an old gypsy woman in Ray Harryhausen's *The Valley of Gwangi*, where she gets folded, spindled and mutilated by Gwangi. *Clash of the Titans* was her last film.

Other genre credits: FILMS: *Die, Monster, Die!* Alta Vista Productions, 1965 (Letitia Witley); *The Valley of Gwangi*, Warner Brothers/Seven Arts, 1969 (Tia Zorina); *Clash of the Titans*, MGM, 1981 (Stygian Witch) TELEVISION: *My Partner the Ghost*: "The Smile Behind the Veil," 1970 (Mrs. Evans); *Blake's 7*: "The Keeper," 1979 (Tara)

Jacobs, Paula

TELEVISION: *Hammer House of Horror*: "The Thirteenth Reunion," 1980 (Joyce)
Other genre credits: FILM: *An American Werewolf in London*, PolyGram Filmed Entertainment, 1981 (Mrs. Kessler)

Jaffe, Shirley

FILM: *Taste the Blood of Dracula*, 1970 (Betty)
Other genre credits: FILM: *A Clockwork Orange*, Warner Brothers, 1971 (Gang Victim)

Jago, June (1926–2010)

BIRTHPLACE: Australia.
FILM: *Journey into Darkness*, 1969 (Emily Blake)
TELEVISION: *Journey to the Unknown*: "Paper Dolls," 1968 (Emily Blake)

James, Olga

FILM: *The Vampire Lovers*, 1970 (Village Girl)
Other genre credits: TELEVISION: *Sealab 2020*: 1972 (Voice of Mrs. Thomas)

James, Sally (1950–)

BIRTHPLACE: Chiswick, London, England.
FILM: *Journey to the Unknown*, 1969 (Peggy)
TELEVISION: *Journey to the Unknown*: "The Last Visitor," 1969 (Peggy)
BIOGRAPHY—The very pretty Sally James is a British character actress best known for her role as a presenter for the classic Saturday morning kids' show *Tiswas*, a favorite of rock acts such as The Clash and Motorhead. One of her first roles was as a sweet, short-skirted maid in *Journey to the Unknown*. She now sells school uniforms and is a presenter for *Film24*.

Jay, Josephine

FILM: *The Two Faces of Dr. Jekyll*, 1960 (Sphinx Girl)

Jayne, Jennifer (1931–2006)

REAL NAME: Jennifer Jones; BIRTHPLACE: Yorkshire, England.
FILMS: *The Black Widow*, 1951 (Sheila Kemp); *Hysteria*, 1965 (Gina McConnell)
Other genre credits: FILMS: *The Crawling Eye*, Tempean Films, 1958 (Sarah Pilgrim); *Dr. Terror's House of Horrors*, Amicus Productions, 1965 (Nicole Carroll); *They Came from Beyond Space*, Amicus Productions, 1967 (Lee Mason); *The Medusa Touch*, Coatesgold/ITC, 1978 (Mother); *The Doctor and the Devils*, Brooksfilms/20th Century–Fox, 1985 (Barmaid) TELEVISION: *Invisible Man*: "Shadow Bomb," 1959 (Betty)

Jeayes, Carol

FILM: *The Horror of Frankenstein*, 1970 (Woodsman's Daughter)

Jefford, Barbara (1930–)

REAL NAME: Mary Barbara Jefford; BIRTHPLACE: Plymstock, Devon, England.
FILM: *Lust for a Vampire*, 1971 (Countess Herritzen/Karnstein)
TELEVISION: *Journey to the Unknown*: "Miss Belle," 1968 (Miss Belle Weston)

BIOGRAPHY— Barbara Jefford trained at RADA, and has become one of Britain's most distinguished stage actresses, receiving her OBE in 1965. She made her debut on radio in 1946, her stage debut three years later, and her first television movie (*Tess of the D'Urbervilles*) three years after that. Her most famous *visible* role was that of Molly Bloom in the 1967 film of James Joyce's *Ulysses*, and she dubbed the voices of three different Bond Girls, Daniela Bianchi, Molly Peters, and Caroline Munro. Her first Hammer credit was the "Miss Belle" episode of *Journey to the Unknown*, where she plays the title character, a woman so cruel and creepy that she easily rivals Bette Davis in *The Anniversary* or Joan Crawford in *Mommy Dearest* for sheer twisted heartlessness. She hates men with much more than a passion; her young nephew Bobby is a boy but Miss Belle won't admit it, and if he says he is, he gets punished (killing his pets and more). Of course, the best-laid plans often go awry, and so they do when George Maharis comes to town, playing basically the same character he played in *Route 66*, only without a car. She is so completely (and realistically) evil that she makes her Countess Karnstein in *Lust for a Vampire* seem like a pussycat in comparison. She's still active and still waiting for her CBE.

Other genre credits: FILMS: *From Russia with Love*, Danjaq/Eon Productions, 1963 (Voice of Tatiana Romanova); *Thunderball*, Eon Productions, 1965 (Voice of Molly Peters); *The Spy Who Loved Me*, Danjaq/Eon Productions, 1977 (Voice of Caroline Munro); *The Ninth Gate*, Artisan Entertainment, 1999 (Baroness Kessler).

Jennings, Hazel

FILM: *Never Take Sweets from a Stranger*, 1960 (Mrs. Olderberry)

Jessop, Clytie

FILM: *Nightmare*, 1963 (Woman in White/Mrs. Baxter)

BIOGRAPHY— British character actress Clytie Jessop made her screen debut (and an impression) in *The Innocents*. She also made an impression on that film's cinematographer, Freddie Francis, who subsequently cast her in his *Nightmare*, drawing on her role in *The Innocents*, where she is seen only in long shot. She's just as unforgettable and spooky in *Nightmare*, playing the spectral Woman in White who haunts Jennie Linden. She only made one other film for Francis, Amicus's *Torture Garden*. Jessop went on to direct and produce *Flamingo Park*, *Conrad Martens*, and *Emma's War*, which she also wrote.

Other genre credits: FILMS: *The Innocents*, Achilles/20th Century–Fox, 1961 (Miss Jessel); *Torture Garden*, Amicus Productions, 1967 (Atropos, Goddess of Destiny).

Johnston, Mildred

FILM: *Creatures the World Forgot*, 1971 (Prehistoric Woman)

Joseph, Joanna

TELEVISION: *Hammer House of Mystery and Suspense*: "Child's Play," 1986 (Space Child)
Other genre credits: TELEVISION: *Quatermass*: "Lovely Lightning," "Ringstone Round," 1979 (Debbie Kapp)

Joshi, Indira

TELEVISION: *Hammer House of Mystery and Suspense*: "Paint Me a Murder," 1985 (Mrs. Patel)
BIOGRAPHY— A British character actress of Indian extraction, Indira Joshi made her first

television appearance in 1979. She has a charming bit in *Hammer House of Mystery and Suspense* as a druggist who sells Michelle Phillips some arsenic (Phillips claims she has a rat problem) with no idea what she's really planning on using the poison for. Joshi is still active.

Other genre credits: FILMS: *Superman IV: The Quest for Peace*, Cannon Films, 1987 (U.N. Secretary General) TELEVISION: *Worlds Beyond*: 1987 (Captain Randolph)

Joslin, Annis

TELEVISION: *Hammer House of Mystery and Suspense*: "Tennis Court," 1985 (Innes Bray)

Joyce, Yootha (1927–1980)

BIRTHPLACE: Wandsworth, London, England.

FILMS: *Fanatic*, 1965 (Anna); *Nearest and Dearest*, 1972 (Mrs. Rhoda Rowbottom); *Man About the House*, 1974 (Mildred Roper)

BIOGRAPHY— The wonderfully named Yootha Joyce was trained at RADA (Roger Moore was a classmate) and, like most of its graduates, plied her trade first on stage and then in films and television. Two of her roles for Hammer were feature films that had originally been Britcoms: In *Man About the House* (both the show and the film), she starred as Mildred Roper, her most beloved character. Mildred was the wife of landlord George, whose upstairs tenants are two girls and a man living together in the same apartment. Obviously this was the inspiration for the insipid American comedy *Three's Company*. In *Fanatic*, she's the housekeeper who, along with her husband, works for (and with) Tallulah Bankhead to terrorize Stefanie Powers, and she applies herself quite enthusiastically and utterly creepily to the task until Miss Tallulah fills hubby's face with buckshot; then, like all self-respecting monsters, she turns on her employer. Her last role was as Mildred Roper in 1980s *George and Mildred*; years of alcoholism took their toll, and she died that same year of liver failure.

Other genre credits: FILM: *The Night Digger*, MGM, 1971 (Mrs. Palafox) TELEVISION: *The Avengers*: "Something Nasty in the Nursery," 1967 (Miss Lister); *Frankenstein, the True Story* (Movie), 1973 (Hospital Matron)

Kane, Beatrice

FILMS: *Dick Barton—Detective*, 1948 (Betsy Horrock); *Dick Barton at Bay*, 1950 (Betsy Horrock)

Other genre credits: *Out of the Unknown*: "Random Quest," 1969 (Mrs. Kane)

Karlin, Miriam (1925–2011)

REAL NAME: Miriam Samuels; BIRTHPLACE: Hampstead, London, England.

FILMS: *Watch It, Sailor!* 1961 (Mrs. Lack); *The Phantom of the Opera*, 1962 (Charwoman)

Other genre credits: FILMS: *A Clockwork Orange*, Warner Brothers, 1971 (Cat Lady) TELEVISION: *Suspense*: "Wormwood," 1963 (Catherine); *Jekyll & Hyde* (Movie), 1990 (Mrs. Hackett); *So Haunt Me*: 1992–1994 (Yetta Feldman)

Kay, Sibylla

FILM: *Vampire Circus*, 1972 (Mrs. Schilt)

Other genre credits: FILM: *The Night Digger*, MGM, 1971 (Whore) TELEVISION: *Out of the Unknown*: "Second Childhood," 1966 (Maid)

Keats, Viola (1911–1998)

BIRTHPLACE: Doune, Perthshire, England.
FILM: *The Witches*, 1966 (Mrs. Curd)
Other genre credits: FILM: *Witchcraft*, Lippert Films, 1964 (Helen Lanier) TELEVISION: *One Step Beyond*: "Signal Received," 1961 (Mrs. Breed); *Suspense*: "The Troubled Heart," 1963 (Dr. Connie Woodbridge); *Mystery and Imagination*: "A Place of One's Own," 1968 (Mrs. Bogarde)

Keller, Sarah

TELEVISION: *Hammer House of Horror*: "The House That Bled to Death," 1980 (Second Mother)
Other genre credits: FILM: *Terror*, Bowergange Productions, 1978 (Suzy)

Kellerman, Barbara (1949–)

REAL NAME: Barbara R. Kellermann; BIRTHPLACE: Manchester, England.
TELEVISION: *Hammer House of Horror*: "Growing Pains," 1980 (Laurie Morton)
BIOGRAPHY— Born in Manchester after her Jewish parents fled Nazi Germany, elegant Barbara Kellerman trained at Rose Bruford College. Her first appearance was in 1969 in the television series *How We Used to Live*. In addition to her genre credits in film and television, she has also portrayed Modesty Blaise on radio. She starred in the fourth episode of *Hammer House of Horror* as Laurie Morton, a career woman whose son dies after ingesting experimental chemicals in her husband's lab, and tries to cope with strange and gruesome events after they adopt a new boy — who exhibits some rather strange tendencies of his own. She is still active, although her appearances have become less frequent since 2000.
Other genre credits: FILMS: *Satan's Slave*, Monumental Films, 1976 (Frances); *The Quatermass Conclusion*, Euston Films, 1979 (Clare Kapp); *The Monster Club*, Amicus Productions, 1981 (Angela) TELEVISION: *Space: 1999*: "Dragon's Domain," 1975 (Dr. Monique Bouchere); *Quatermass*: "Lovely Lightning," "Ringstone Round," 1979 (Clare Kapp); *The Lion, the Witch and the Wardrobe*: Episodes 1–6, 1988 (The White Witch); *Prince Caspian and the Voyage of the Dawn Treader*: "Prince Caspian," Part 2, 1989 (Old Hag)

Kelly, Claire (1934–1998)

REAL NAME: Claire Ann Green; BIRTHPLACE: San Francisco, California, USA.
FILM: *Straight on Till Morning*, 1972 (Margo Thompson)
Other genre credits: FILM: *Whatever Happened to Aunt Alice?* American Broadcasting Company, 1969 (Elva)

Kemball, Stella (Died 2002)

FILM: *X: The Unknown*, 1956 (Willie's Room Nurse)

Kent, Lizbeth

FILMS: *The Witches*, 1966 (First Villager); *Frankenstein Created Woman*, 1967 (First Woman)

Keogh, Barbara (1929–2005)

BIRTHPLACE: Cheshire, England.
TELEVISION: *Hammer House of Horror*: "The Thirteenth Reunion," 1980 (Joan Hubbard); *Hammer House of Mystery and Suspense*: "Last Video and Testament," 1984 (Mrs. Villiers)

BIOGRAPHY—One of the most versatile character actresses in British film history, Barbara Keogh attended the Birmingham School of Speech and Drama and the London Academy of Music and Dramatic Art. She made her film debut in the 1956 version of George Orwell's *1984*; she is best remembered by fans as Mrs. Frawley in *The Abominable Dr. Phibes*. She found time for Hammer in the form of two television episodes, one for each of their second and third series. She's particularly delightful in "The Thirteenth Reunion," in a bit part as one of the survivors of an airplane crash who convene once a month to mourn their dead, celebrate their good fortune, and indulge in their ... specialized appetites; Keogh licks her lips at the thought of some sautéed Julia Foster. She's also delightful in her *Hammer House of Mystery and Suspense* appearance as a housekeeper who wears what appears to be a school crossing guard's sash at all times, inside the house or out. In 2005, she died with her boots on, while working in the British television comedy show *Little Britain*.

Other genre credits: FILMS: *1984*, Holiday Film Productions, 1956 (Special Woman); *The Abominable Dr. Phibes*, American International Pictures, 1971 (Mrs. Frawley); *Dark Corners*, Matador Pictures, 2006 (Old Woman) TELEVISION: *The Haunted House*: Episodes 1 & 2, 1960 (Delphium); *Quatermass*: "Ringstone Round," 1979 (Makeup Lady); *Ghostbusters of East Finchley*: Episodes 4 & 6, 1995 (Thelma Thane); *Highlander*: "Forgive Us Our Trespasses," 1997 (Grandmother)

Key, Janet (1945–1992)

BIRTHPLACE: Bath, Somerset, England.
FILMS: *The Vampire Lovers*, 1970 (Gretchen); *Dracula A.D. 1972* (Anna)
Other genre credits: FILMS: *...And Now the Screaming Starts!* Amicus Productions, 1973 (Bridget); *The Devil Within Her*, The Rank Organization, 1975 (Jill Fletcher) TELEVISION: *Thriller*: "Ring Once for Death," 1973 (Lisa); *Worlds Beyond*: "Oliver's Ghost," 1988 (Lady Lucinda Beresford)

Khazanova, Alisa (1974–)

REAL NAME: Alisa Gennadyevna Khazanova; BIRTHPLACE: the U.S.S.R.
FILM: *The Woman in Black*, 2012 (Mrs. Drablow)

Kiesouw, Josje

FILM: *Creatures the World Forgot*, 1971 (The Young Dumb Girl)

Kimberly, Maggie (1942–)

REAL NAME: Margaret Simons; BIRTHPLACE: South Africa.
FILM: *The Mummy's Shroud*, 1967 (Claire De Sangre)
Biography—Stunningly beautiful Maggie Kimberly, with cheekbones stronger than Hercules, was a model and actress whose parents owned a café. Her last name derives from her short-lived marriage to the 4th Earl of Kimberley. The marriage ended in 1965, and only then did she begin acting in films, among them *The Mummy's Shroud*. Still photos show the Mummy Prem hovering over a frightened-looking Kimberly who wears a cleavage-emphasizing low-cut blouse, but in fact she stays quite conservatively attired for the whole film, which is fine because it emphasizes those killer cheekbones and an equally arresting pair of eyes. She is not a typical Hammer Heroine; whereas most of their female leads' life stories are pretty much all there on screen, the wonderfully named Claire De Sangre has an air of mystery that makes the viewer want to know her backstory. In the first part of the film, she appears to be psychic, but this aspect of the character is downplayed once we get in the presence of major-league

Maggie Kimberly bewares the beat of the cloth-wrapped feet in *The Mummy's Shroud* (courtesy Mel Bridgeman).

clairvoyant Haiti (Catherine Lacey). Kimberly's sultry beauty was also on display in Vincent Price's *Witchfinder General*, but then after that, there was only an episode of *Department S* (the show that spawned *Jason King*), in which she plays Jason's "companion." At last report, she was living in Florida.

Other genre credits: FILM: *Witchfinder General*, Tigon British, 1968 (Elizabeth Clark)

Kind, Sophie

TELEVISION: *Hammer House of Horror*: "Children of the Full Moon," 1980 (Eloise)
Other genre credits: TELEVISION: *Quatermass*: "Lovely Lightning," "Ringstone Round," 1979 (Sara Kapp)

King, Ann

TELEVISION: *Journey to the Unknown*: "Somewhere in a Crowd," 1968 (The Watcher)

King, Diana (1918–1986)

BIRTHPLACE: Buckinghamshire, England.
FILM: *Fanatic*, 1965 (Woman Shopper)
TELEVISION: *Hammer House of Mystery and Suspense*: "Black Carrion," 1986 (Madge Bircher)

BIOGRAPHY—Busy British character actress King had a forty-year career in television and feature films, including Pink Floyd's *The Wall*; she was best known for situation comedies. She did two turns for Hammer, twenty years apart; one a bit part in *Fanatic* and then a much showier role in *Hammer House of Mystery and Suspense* as a high-strung, nagging wife who, along with her stuffy husband, is forced off the road by a truck and then stop in a village of the damned. It was one of her final roles before she passed away in 1986.

Other genre credits: FILMS: *They Came from Beyond Space*, Amicus Productions, 1967 (Mrs. Trethowan) TELEVISION: *The Avengers*: "Dance with Death," 1961 (Mrs. Marnell); *Tales of the Unexpected*: "The Absence of Emily," 1982 (Ruth)

Kinski, Nastassja (1961–)

REAL NAME: Nastassja Aglaia Nakszynski; BIRTHPLACE: West Berlin, West Germany.
FILM: *To the Devil a Daughter*, 1976 (Catherine)

BIOGRAPHY—The daughter of dreary, jobbing German actor Klaus (*Nosferatu*) Kinski, Kinski was raised by her mother in a Munich commune after her parents' divorce. Like many of this book's actresses, she was a model, which led to her first film appearance in Wim Wenders' *The Wrong Move*. Kinski made a pit stop at Hammer on her way to international stardom: In *To the Devil a Daughter*, she gets naked, even though she was not yet of legal age to do so on film. She's nude and spread-eagled on an altar with some kind of red, slimy demon-baby crawling here and there atop her. She continued to do nude scenes; a Richard Avedon photo of her nude self, covered only by a python, became a teen-bedroom staple in 1981. She was romantically linked to Roman Polanski at the age of 15, and later appeared in Polanski's *Tess*, for which she won a Golden Globe. Her only other significant genre film was the pallid 1982 remake of *Cat People*, which doubled (or quadrupled) the skin and sex part of the recipe but forgot to add even a dash of the atmosphere which made Val Lewton's original a classic.

Other genre credits: FILM: *Cat People*, Universal Pictures, 1982 (Irena Gallier) TELEVISION: *The Day the World Ended* (Movie), 1981 (Dr. Jennifer Stillman)

Kirkwood, Roberta

FILM: *The Two Faces of Dr. Jekyll*, 1960 (Second Brass)

Knef, Hildegard (1925–2002)

REAL NAME: Hildegard Frieda Albertine Knef; BIRTHPLACE: Ulm, Germany.
FILM: *The Lost Continent*, 1968 (Eva Peters)

BIOGRAPHY—Like Ingrid Pitt, whom she resembles both physically and vocally, Hildegard Knef spent time in a concentration camp and was a breast cancer survivor. Her screen career began in 1940, but most of the films she made at this time weren't released until after the War. Her deep, sonorous voice also earned her a career as a chanteuse, and like her *Lost Continent* co-star Dana Gillespie, she enjoyed as much if not more popularity in that area of her career as movies; she pursued both with great success until nearly the end of her life. She brings real gravitas to her *Lost Continent* role as a dictator's ex-mistress, an excellent performance that rises above the material, inviting sympathy for a character that doesn't deserve that much. She is both wise and weary of the world, and brings undeserved shading to her role as Eva Peters. Her best scene is the one where, in the lifeboat, she shoots the guy in the gut with a flare gun, which is just so cool!

Other genre credits: FILM: *Witchery*, Filmirage, 1988 (Woman in Black)

Knight, Shirley (1936–)

BIRTHPLACE: Goessel, Kansas, USA.

TELEVISION: *Hammer House of Mystery and Suspense*: "The Sweet Scent of Death," 1986 (Ann Fairfax Denver)

BIOGRAPHY—The daughter of an oil company executive, Shirley Knight trained at the HB Studio in Greenwich Village. It would almost be easier to list the films and television shows that she *hasn't* done, having appeared in nearly 200 of them, beginning in 1955 with *Picnic* starring William Holden. She's been nominated for two Academy Awards, won two Emmys (and been nominated for six more), won a Golden Globe, the Susan B. Anthony Award, and a Volpi Cup from the Venice Film Festival. She is often above the level of the material she's given to work with (see—or don't—*Paul Blart, Mall Cop*) and unfortunately, this was the case with her episode of *Hammer House of Mystery and Suspense*, "The Sweet Scent of Death." She plays the loving, trusting wife of Dean Stockwell in a murder mystery that's so old-fashioned that the culprits are as transparent as glass. Still and all, she turns in an exceptional, emotional performance, and at least that, if not the rest of the story, holds up under closer examination. Although the series as a whole runs hot and cold, one thing that can be said about it is that it didn't rely on young, busty, and inexperienced vixens to carry the load of the leads, which were played by mature actresses of standing (perhaps this is why their kit didn't come off as often) and beauty. Knight shows no signs of slowing down, even after 50-plus years; a very good Knight indeed.

Other genre credits: TELEVISION: *The Outer Limits*: "The Man Who Was Never Born," 1963 (Noelle Anderson); *The Invaders*: "The Watchers," 1967 (Margaret Cook); *Circle of Fear*: "Legion of Demons," 1973 (Beth); *Tales of the Unexpected*: "A Woman's Help," 1981 (Elizabeth Bourdon); *The Uninvited* (Movie), 1996 (Delia)

Konopka, Magda (1943–)

BIRTHPLACE: Warsaw, Poland.

FILM: *When Dinosaurs Ruled the Earth*, 1970 (Ulido)

Other genre credits: FILMS: *Satanik*, Rodiacines, 1968 (Dr. Marny Bannister); *Super Stooges vs. the Wonder Women*, A Erre Cinematografica/Shaw Brothers, 1975 (Beghira, Amazon Queen)

Krippen, Brenda

FILM: *Moon Zero Two*, 1969 (Dancer)

La Porte, Deirdre

FILM: *Dracula A.D. 1972*, 1972 (Member of Stoneground)

Lacak, Irene

FILM: *Beyond the Rave*, 2008 (Vampire Sword Girl)

Lacey, Catherine (1904–1979)

BIRTHPLACE: London, England.

FILMS: *The Shadow of the Cat*, 1961 (Ella Venable); *The Mummy's Shroud*, 1967 (Haiti); *Journey to Midnight*, 1971 (Miss Sarah Prinn)

TELEVISION: *Journey to the Unknown*: "The Indian Spirit Guide," 1969 (Miss Sarah Prinn)

BIOGRAPHY—A delightful British character actress, Lacey began her career on the stage, and made an impression in her film debut as the high heel–wearing nun in Alfred Hitchcock's *The Lady Vanishes*. Her first of three Hammers was *The Shadow of the Cat* (1961), in which she plays the old lady who gets bumped off for her dough. The second was by far the best: She played the evil clairvoyant Haiti in *The Mummy's Shroud* and gives a wonderful performance, hamming it up for dear life, such as in the scene where she tells Andre Morell that his death will be coming "in a few minutes now! Hee, hee, hee, hee!" right before the Mummy pops his skull like an egg. She plays much the same character, minus the finely glazed ham of Haiti, in her episode of *Journey to the Unknown*, "The Indian Spirit Guide," which was one of the installments that were re-edited into the feature film *Journey to Midnight*. She's the one psychic that Julie Harris's would-be boyfriend hasn't set up to expose as a fake, and she turns out to be the real deal. Her last acting credit was in 1973.

Other genre credits: FILMS: *The Sorcerers*, Curtwel Productions/Tigon, 1967 (Estelle Monserrat), *The Private Life of Sherlock Holmes*, Compton Films, 1970 (Woman in Wheelchair)

Laird, Jenny (1917–2001)

REAL NAME: Phyllis Edith M. Laird; BIRTHPLACE: London, England.
TELEVISION: *Hammer House of Horror*: "The Two Faces of Evil," 1980 (Mrs. Roberts)
BIOGRAPHY—British character actress Laird attended Maidstone High and London University. She made her first film in 1935 and her stage debut two years later; her last role was in the *Inspector Morse* television series in 1991. Along the way she appeared in Peter Cushing's return to the role of Sherlock Holmes, *Sherlock Holmes and the Masks of Death*, and an episode of *Hammer House of Horror* in which she plays a housekeeper.

Other genre credits: FILMS: *Village of the Damned*, MGM, 1960 (Mrs. Harrington); *Sherlock Holmes and the Masks of Death*, Tyburn Film Productions, 1984 (Mrs. Hudson) TELEVISION: *Thriller*: "A Place to Die," 1973 (Nan); *Doctor Who*: "Planet of the Spiders," Parts 3, 4, and 5, 1974 (Neska)

Lancaster, Ann (1920–1970)

BIRTHPLACE: London, England.
FILM: *Journey to Midnight*, 1971 (Red Queen)
TELEVISION: *Journey to the Unknown*: "Poor Butterfly," 1969 (Red Queen)
Other genre credits: FILMS: *The Flesh and the Fiends*, Triad Productions, 1960 (Dancer) TELEVISION: *Out of the Unknown*: "Come Buttercup, Come Daisy, Come...?" 1965 (Mrs. Bryant)

Landi, Marla (1933–)

REAL NAME: Marcella Teresa Scarafina; BIRTHPLACE: Turin, Italy.
FILMS: *The Hound of the Baskervilles*, 1959 (Cecile Stapleton); *The Pirates of Blood River*, 1962 (Bess Standing)
BIOGRAPHY—Saucy Marla Landi garnered great fame as a model for many leading fashion magazines of the day, and later became an editor for *Harper's Bazaar*. She played the female lead in two classic Hammer films. The first was the best Sherlock Holmes movie ever, the 1959 *The Hound of the Baskervilles*. Her character is named Cecile here; the name was Beryl in the novel and 1939 film, and she is very different from those two interpretations. In the novel, Beryl is Stapleton's wife, and she is in on the plot to kill Sir Henry until she falls in love with him and refuses to go through with the plan, for which she is beaten and tied to a bedpost by her husband. In the 1939 film, she is Stapleton's sweet sister and completely

ignorant of her brother's scheme. But in the Hammer version, she undergoes a name change and now she is Stapleton's hot daughter. She's again in on the plot, and this time there's no getting cold feet — just wet, when she gets sucked into the bog. And she's a hellion, too, only softening in the moments when Christopher Lee romances her. But it's all part of the show — she displays a ton of class animus when railing at Lee that he and his kind have looked down on her and hers, and that he's not the only Baskerville that wanted her. She gloats that Sir Charles "died *screaming*! I know ... I *watched*!" spitting out the words like she's whipping a galley slave. Her other turn at Bray, *The Pirates of Blood River*, was less satisfying because she had very little to do except be Kerwin Mathews's sister and watch Oliver Reed fight over her. Her fashion career was always more important than her acting chores (although she remembers them fondly). She quit the business a few years later and began a successful international wig business. She is a Knight of the Italian Republic.

Other genre credits: FILMS: *First Man into Space*, Amalgamated Productions, 1959 (Tia Francesca) TELEVISION: *Invisible Man*: "The White Rabbit," 1959 (Suzanne Dumasse); *One Step Beyond*: "The Villa," 1961 (Stella)

Landor, Rosalyn (1958–)

BIRTHPLACE: London, England.
FILM: *The Devil Rides Out*, 1968 (Peggy Eaton)
TELEVISION: *Hammer House of Horror*: "Guardian of the Abyss," 1980 (Allison Lussan)
BIOGRAPHY— Lovely Rosalyn Landor was an in-demand child actress who made her film debut for Hammer in *The Devil Rides Out*. She attended the Royal Ballet School and the Tolworth Girls' School and supplemented her acting income by working retail. By 1980, she had grown into a beautiful young woman and returned to the place where she'd gotten her start, in the "Guardians of the Abyss" episode of *Hammer House of Horror*, in which she is under the control of Satanic cult leader John Carson. She fights valiantly, but ultimately, and gladly, becomes the bride of the demon that Carson summons; perhaps she was a pawn all along, even her resistance being part of a larger, grander scheme. The last time she actually appeared on screen was in 1990, in the film *Bad Influence*. Since then, she has lent her sonorous voice to a number of Disney productions and products, such as the Incredibles video game and many others. She is also an award-winning audiobook reader. She currently lives in Los Angeles.

Other genre credits: FILM: *The Amazing Mr. Blunden*, Hemdale Film, 1972 (Sara Latimer) TELEVISION: *Star Trek: The Next Generation*: "Up the Long Ladder," 1989 (Brenna O'Dell); *The Real Ghostbusters*: "Jenny, You've Changed," 1990 (Voice of Makeoveris Lotsabucks)

Langrishe, Caroline (1958–)

BIRTHPLACE: London, England.
TELEVISION: *Hammer House of Horror*: "Guardian of the Abyss," 1980 (Tina)
Other genre credits: FILMS: *Holocaust 2000*, Aston Film, 1977 (Carol); *Death Watch*, Films A2, 1980 (Girl in the Bar) TELEVISION: *Tales of the Unexpected*: "Shatterproof," 1981 (Ellen)

Lapotaire, Jane (1944–)

BIRTHPLACE: Ipswich, Suffolk, England.
FILM: *Crescendo*, 1970 (Lillianne)
BIOGRAPHY— Jane Lapotaire attended the Bristol Old Vic Theatre School. She has done as much stage as film work and in 1981 won a Tony Award for *Piaf*. Her first screen appearance

was somewhat of a harbinger of the near future: She played the part of Anna Harrison in "The Naval Treaty," an episode of the classic Peter Cushing *Sherlock Holmes* television series, and the very next year, she was at Hammer for her first feature film, *Crescendo*. She gives a deliciously sleazy performance as the evil French maid Lillianne, who likes to feed James Olson heroin and sex him up, removing her clothes at the drop of a chapeau. Of course, morality and the storyline demand that a woman this wanton must pay for her sins, and so she does, in an exceedingly well-handled murder scene in a swimming pool (for which she has to get her kit off). She is still active and has authored two books, *Everybody's Daughter, Nobody's Child* and *Time Out of Mind*, which chronicled her recovery from a cerebral hemorrhage in 2000.

Other genre credits: FILMS: *The Asphyx*, Glendale, 1973 (Christina Cunningham); *One of Our Dinosaurs Is Missing*, Walt Disney Productions, 1975 (Miss Prescott) TELEVISION: *Uncle Silas*: Episodes 1, 2, and 3, 1989 (Madame de la Rougierre); *Chillers*: "A Curious Suicide," 1990; *Johnny and the Dead*: 1995 (Mrs. Sylvia Liberty); *Arabian Nights* (Movie), 2000 (Miriam)

Larman, Cherry

FILM: *She*, 1965 (Handmaiden)

Larsen, Gerda

FILM: *The Man Who Could Cheat Death*, 1959 (Street Girl)

Lawrence, Andrea

FILMS: *On the Buses*, 1971 (Betty); *Countess Dracula*, 1971 (Ziza); *Love Thy Neighbour*, 1973 (Norma); *Frankenstein and the Monster from Hell*, 1974 (Brassy Girl); *Man About the House*, 1974 (Miss Bird)

BIOGRAPHY— Buxom British character actress Andrea Lawrence had a 20-year career, mostly on television, and in films, mostly for Hammer, splitting her time between humor and horror. Her best bit is as the brassy barmaid and whore Ziza in *Countess Dracula*. She is used as a pawn to make Ingrid Pitt jealous of her young lover, but when that ploy fails, Ingrid simply decides to use her as her next meal. That ploy is doomed to failure too, though, as only the blood of virgins will work the rejuvenating magic, and obviously Ziza passed the point of no return long ago. She's back (and still brassy, even being billed as such) in *Frankenstein and the Monster from Hell*, still not particular about those she dispenses her sexual favors to, although at least this time she gets out alive. Her last role was in 1981.

Lawrence, Delphi (1926–2002)

REAL NAME: Delphi Enaver; BIRTHPLACE: Hertfordshire, England.

FILMS: *Blood Orange* (a.k.a. *Three Stops to Murder*), 1953 (Chelsea); *Murder by Proxy* (a.k.a. *Blackout*), 1954 (Linda); *The Man Who Could Cheat Death*, 1959 (Margo Philippe)

BIOGRAPHY— A striking British leading lady and character actress, Lawrence had roles in three Hammer films: two from Hammer's noir period that are undistinguished, and one from their Golden Age of horror, *The Man Who Could Cheat Death*, which is quite the opposite. In the latter she gives a wonderful account of herself as the woman scorned by Anton Diffring. She decides to confront him over it; big mistake. She lets out a great, ear-piercing scream when he sears her face with his hand, and we assume she is dead. But she's not, she's being kept in a filthy cell in his workshop, and the laugh she gives when Hazel Court discovers her is haunting. She keeps on laughing as she sets the now rapidly aging madman ablaze, and continues to do so until she too is consumed by the flames, and screams again for the last time. She moved to the U.S. in 1966, retired in 1973, and stayed in her adopted country until her death in 2002.

Other genre credits: FILMS: *Frozen Alive*, Alfa Film, 1964 (Joan Overton) TELEVISION: *The Avengers*: "Square Root of Evil," 1961 (Lisa); *Voyage to the Bottom of the Sea*: "Escape from Venice," 1965 (Julietta); *The Man from U.N.C.L.E.*: "The 'J' for Judas Affair," 1967 (Olivia Willis)

Lawrence, Marjie (1935–)

BIRTHPLACE: London, England.
FILM: *Hands of the Ripper*, 1971 (Dolly)
BIOGRAPHY— The wife of Harry Greene and mother of Sarah Greene, veteran British character actress Marjie Lawrence was already 16 years into her career when she made her only appearance for Hammer, as the ill-fated maid Dolly in *Hands of the Ripper*. Despite the brevity of the role, she cuts a memorable figure — or rather, she makes a memorable figure when she's cut by star Angharad Rees, who slices her neck from ear to ear in another of the film's memorable murder set pieces. She's still active, primarily in British television.

Other genre credits: FILM: *I, Monster*, Amicus Productions, 1971 (Annie)

Lawson, Sarah (1928–)

BIRTHPLACE: Wandsworth, London, England.
FILMS: *Man with a Dog*, 1957 (Vicky); *The Devil Rides Out*, 1968 (Marie Eaton)
TELEVISION: *Journey to the Unknown*: "Jane Brown's Body," 1968 (Pamela Denholt)
BIOGRAPHY— Lovely Sarah Lawson was trained at the Webber Douglas Academy of Dramatic Art, and plied her craft on the stage before making her debut in a 1951 TV movie. She appeared in three Hammer releases, each one of varying length and quality. In the tearjerker- "feel good" short *Man with the Dog*, she convinces a lonely man, whose only companions are his dog and his pet fish Eric, to have a life-saving operation, assuring him that his pets will be taken care of. She lent solid support to Stefanie Powers in an episode of *Journey to the Unknown*, but her real showcase came with *The Devil Rides Out* (known as *The Devil's Bride* in America because the distributors thought it sounded like a Western). In it she plays Marie Eaton, a wife and mother who plays just as critical a role as lead Nike Arrighi: Her association with Christopher Lee and Leon Greene pulls her into a world that she can neither explain nor understand but she has the courage to see through to the end. She has a number of standout scenes: falling under Charles Gray's power, inside the holy circle when she thinks her daughter is about to fall victim to a huge spider, and when she becomes a vessel for the temporarily dead Tanith, speaking with her voice and boldly retrieving her daughter from the sacrificial altar, bringing about the destruction of Gray's coven. All in all, she gave one of the best supporting performances in Hammer history, in one of their best films. She had a happy and lasting (until his death) marriage to actor Patrick Allen, who dubbed Leon Greene in *The Devil Rides Out*. She retired in 1989.

Other genre credits: FILM: *Island of the Burning Doomed*, Planet Film Productions, 1967 (Frankie Callum) TELEVISION: *The Trollenberg Terror*: "The Mind of Ann Pilgrim," "First Blood," "The Giggle of Madness," 1956; "The Power of the Ixodes," "The Trap," "The Trollenberg Terror," 1957 (Sarah Pilgrim); *Invisible Man*: "The Vanishing Evidence," 1959 (Jenny Reyden); *The Avengers*: "How to Succeed ... at Murder," 1966 (Mary Merryweather)

Leapman, Jackie

FILMS: *Lust for a Vampire*, 1971 (Schoolgirl); *Twins of Evil*, 1971 (Schoolgirl)

Leggatt, Alison (1904–1990)

REAL NAME: Alison Joy Leggatt; BIRTHPLACE: Kensington, London, England.
FILM: *Never Take Sweets from a Stranger*, 1960 (Martha)
Other genre credits: FILM: *The Day of the Triffids*, Security Pictures, 1962 (Miss Coker)

Leigh, Laurie

FILM: *Paranoiac*, 1963 (Woman #1)
Other genre credits: FILMS: *Dr. Terror's House of Horrors*, Amicus Productions, 1965 (Nurse)
TELEVISION: *The Avengers*: "Bullseye," 1962 (Dorothy Young)

Leigh, Suzanna (1946–)

REAL NAME: Suzanna Smyth; BIRTHPLACE: Belgrave, Leicester, England.
FILMS: *The Lost Continent*, 1968 (Unity Webster); *Lust for a Vampire*, 1971 (Janet Playfair)
TELEVISION: *Journey to the Unknown*: "One on an Island," 1968 (Vicki)

BIOGRAPHY— Although not the only actress in this volume to make a film with Elvis (*Paradise, Hawaiian Style*), blond, beautiful Suzanna Leigh is the only one who has capitalized on her association with "The King" in order to earn an existence (she even titled her autobiography *Paradise, Suzanna Style*). To be fair, though, capitalizing on one's association with Elvis has been a thriving business for decades; a time-honored American tradition. She and her daughter Natalia, now settled in Memphis, operate the Suzanna Leigh Experience which offers acting classes and organizes events for the fans who still flock to Graceland. But, obviously, it wasn't intended to turn out this way.

The daughter of a professional gambler (he died when she was six), she attended the Webber Douglas drama school but grew impatient and left after completing just two terms, beginning her career soon after. She looked as though she was on her way to big things, armed with a Hollywood contract and appearances in Jerry Lewis and Elvis movies, but a ruling by the SAG forced her to return to England.

Her first role for Hammer was in a disaster movie, *The Lost Continent*— oh, sorry, the film is really science fiction; it just turned out to *be* a disaster. Leigh plays Unity Webster, a character who is most often described as "over-sexed" (and true, she's doing the horizontal bop in her first extended scene), but really, she's no more over-sexed than Hildegard Knef, who is equally willing to jump in the sack with the nearest available Tom, Dick, or Ricaldi. Leigh gives some depth to a patently uninteresting and unlikable character; in fact, most of the characters are so unlikable that one really doesn't care whether they survive or not. Unity certainly gets put through her paces; she's nearly washed off a ship by a hurricane, nearly blown to smithereenies by the ship's illegal cargo, sees her right bastard of a father eaten by a shark, gets groped by a giant octopus, and gets groped by descendants of conquistadors wearing balloons. None of it makes any sense, but with the surreal title song and equally surreal atmosphere, ultra-cheesy monsters, and three gorgeous women, it doesn't have to.

She was all at sea again shortly there afterwards, in an episode of the now-rare first Hammer television series *Journey to the Unknown*, "One on an Island," which features Brandon De Wilde as a poor little rich boy who decides to sail around the world so that he can meet a girl. And meet one he does: Suzanna, rising out of the ocean in an evening gown in a scene obviously designed to bring back memories of Ursula Andress's entrance in *Dr. No* (the lovemaking scenes on the beach similarly recall *From Here to Eternity*). But after surviving *The Lost Continent*, here she's deep-sixed by simple drowning — or is she?

Leigh was not originally part of the cast of her next, and last, Hammer film, *Lust for a*

Vampire, but facing a personal emergency, she prevailed on her good friend Sir James Carreras, who gave her the role of the gym mistress, Janet Playfair. And with a character name like that, you just know she's not going to get her kit off, but she's still beautiful and one of the few sensible heads in the picture as the standard Good Girl who loves the hero who only has eyes for the Bad Girl. Although the movie is generally derided and even disowned by both fans and participants as a naff sequel to *The Vampire Lovers*, there are still plenty of great bits to be enjoyed, like when Suzanna is attacked by Yutte Stensgaard, or by the absolutely fabulous Ralph Bates in a film he absolutely could not stand. They were, after all, professionals.

But the profession was not kind to her, and neither was life — she even died on the operating table at one point during an operation after she'd crashed a Rolls. Her film career finished, she encountered one obstacle after another, but through it all, she stood tall, and never gave up or in, which brings us back to the point we started. So it may not have worked out the way she intended, but it worked.

Other genre credits: FILMS: *Deadlier Than the Male*, Greater Films Limited, 1967 (Grace); *The Deadly Bees*, Amicus Productions, 1967 (Vicki Robbins); *Son of Dracula*, Apple Corps, 1974 (Amber)

Lemoine, Joy (1954–)

BIRTHPLACE: Lagos, Nigeria.
TELEVISION: *Hammer House of Mystery and Suspense*: "The Late Nancy Irving," 1985 (Nurse Julie)

Leon, Valerie (1945–)

BIRTHPLACE: London, England.
FILM: *Blood from the Mummy's Tomb*, 1971 (Margaret Fuchs/Queen Tara)
BIOGRAPHY— The daughter of a textile designer (her father) and a RADA–trained mother who forsook her career to raise a family, Valerie Leon was nearly consigned to the workaday life as a fashion buyer for Harrods. In 1965, she became a chorus girl, and in 1966 appeared in Barbra Streisand's West End production *Funny Girl*. Her first television role was in an episode of *The Saint*, starring future James Bond Roger Moore, with whom she would reunite in *The Spy Who Loved Me*. She soon appeared in the first of seven films in the *Carry On...* series, as well as the first of a series of famous commercials for Hai Karate aftershave.

Her iconic role for Hammer, as Margaret/Tara in *Blood from the Mummy's Tomb*, almost wasn't. Despite having previously worked with ill-fated director Seth Holt, she was not a shoo-in, and in fact he chose actress Amy Grant for the part. But Sir James Carreras, who had become acquainted with her through Variety Club events, intervened and insisted she play the role. His faith in her did not go unrewarded: Instead of just another pretty face and figure (and she does rock a black negligee like few other actresses in film history), Hammer got a performance that was nuanced and powerful, and on the strength of that single performance, she would become one of the company's most lasting icons. But too often, that performance is ignored in favor of Valerie's obvious physical gifts. The movie had a troubled production history (Peter Cushing leaving the project due to his wife Helen's illness, which would claim her soon thereafter; the death of director Seth Holt five weeks into filming), and it's sometimes dismissed as simply another later-period Hammer with little to offer except more gore and sex. This is unfair to both her and the film, an adaptation of Bram Stoker's "Jewel of the Seven Stars" that is in every way superior to the later, very leaden *The Awakening*. Despite the tragedy that surrounded it, the film is not without humor, mostly in the form of nods to Universal; the young male lead is named Tod Browning, and Andrew Keir, once his left side is paralyzed, walks like the Mummy Kharis. As was their usual practice, Hammer surrounded its young female star with veteran character actors like Keir, Aubrey Morris and George Coulouris. Of course, their presence is more than welcome, especially Morris, but it is Valerie who carries the film, as she had to, and she proved herself more than equal to the task. For most, it's her body that does the talking, but if one can divert their attention from her breasts long enough, they will see that it is her eyes that speak volumes and her voice that conveys the dead queen's spirit slowly overtaking her own. One minute, both are innocent, frightened or confused; the next both are icy and commanding, delighting in their evil power and welcoming it. And her eyes are all of these in the final scene, when she is otherwise completely wrapped in bandages, like the traditional mummy — and it is also like the scene in *Bride of Frankenstein* when the Bride is brought to life. As in *Bride*, the bandages are removed from her eyes to reveal emotions that have no voice, and perfectly complement the ambiguous ending: Is it Margaret or Tara that has survived? But as if Hammer and the *Carry Ons* weren't enough to earn her spurs as a certifiable pop culture icon, she cemented that status by twice becoming one of the legendary Bond Girls, appearing with Roger Moore in the aforementioned *The Spy Who Loved Me* and with Sean Connery in *Never Say Never Again*. Still active, still vivacious, and gratefully astounded at the amount of attention she still receives, Valerie Leon has always been more than meets the eye — and considering what meets the eye, that is a great deal, indeed.

Valerie Leon in *Blood from the Mummy's Tomb*.

Other genre credits: FILMS: *Zeta One*, Tigon British Film Productions, 1969 (Atropos); *Queen Kong*, Cine-Art Munchen, 1976 (Queen of the Nabongas); *The Spy Who Loved Me*, 1977, Danjaq/Eon Productions, 1977 (Hotel Receptionist); *Never Say Never Again*, PSO International, 1983 (Lady in Bahamas) TELEVISION: *The Avengers*: "Whoever Shot Poor George Oblique Stroke XR40?" 1968 (Betty); *Space: 1999*: "Death's Other Dominion," 1975 (Thule Girl)

Leslie, Avril

FILM: *The Revenge of Frankenstein*, 1958 (Girl Gerda)

Lind, Gillian (1904–1983)

REAL NAME: Gillian Pratt; BIRTHPLACE: India.
FILM: *Fear in the Night*, 1972 (Mrs. Beamish)

Other genre credits: FILM: *...And Now the Screaming Starts!* Amicus Productions, 1973 (Aunt Edith)

Linden, Jennie (1939–)

REAL NAME: Jennifer Caroline Fletcher; BIRTHPLACE: Worthing, Sussex, England.
FILM: *Nightmare*, 1963 (Janet)

BIOGRAPHY—When Jennie Linden auditioned for Hammer's *Nightmare* (which started filming only two weeks later), it was her first time inside a film studio, period. This occurred because the already-signed original lead, Linden's former Central School of Art and Drama classmate Julie Christie, got a better opportunity (*Billy Liar*), and literally begged Hammer to tear up her contract. Then Linden was spotted in a stage version of *Under the Yum-Yum Tree*, in which she plays a zany teen; she auditioned, and the rest is history. Her "innocent" quality makes her performance affecting; she has witnessed her mother kill her father, she suffers horrible nightmares (and somebody is trying to drive her crazy on top of that), she is used as a tool in a murder plot, and she is sent to the asylum for the murder until the truth is discovered. But a funny thing happens to Linden on the way to the asylum: she disappears from the movie itself. In a departure from the normal Hammer psycho thriller, which would, as a rule, follow the heroine's trials and travails through to a conclusion, *Nightmare* drops its central protagonist halfway through, and instead embarks on a extended retribution cruise (for more, see the entry on Moira Redmond). The last we see of Linden is in a padded cell, and at the end of the film, we are told by a voice on the phone that she should be back to normal in a couple of months. *Nightmare* led to a long career for Linden; she went on to appear with Peter Cushing in *Dr. Who and the Daleks* and was nominated for a BAFTA award (Most Promising Newcomer) for *Women in Love*. She continued in films until she decided that she would rather raise her son in England than in Hollywood, and so back to England they went. She was active well into the 1990s, primarily on television.

Could David Knight be the cause of Jennie Linden's *Nightmare*?

Other genre credits: FILMS: *Doctor Who and the Daleks*, Amicus Productions, 1965 (Barbara); *Old Dracula*, World Film Services, 1975 (Angela) TELEVISION: *The Avengers*: "Lobster Quadrille," 1964 (Katie Miles); *Thriller*: "Death to Sister Mary," 1974 (Penny Stacey/Sister Mary); *Tales of the Unexpected*: "Pattern of Guilt," 1982 (Faye)

Linden, Joyce

FILM: *Dick Barton at Bay*, 1950 (Mary Mitchell)

Lindfors, Viveca (1920–1995)

REAL NAME: Elsa Viveca Torstensdotter Lindfors; BIRTHPLACE: Uppsala, Sweden.
FILM: *The Damned*, 1963 (Freya Neilson)
Other genre credits: FILMS: *Creepshow*, Creepshow Films, 1982 (Aunt Bedelia); *The Exorcist III*, Morgan Creek Productions, 1990 (Nurse X); *Stargate*, Canal +, 1994 (Catherine Langford)
TELEVISION: *Suspense*: "The Riddle of Mayerling," 1953 (Woman); *Voyage to the Bottom of the Sea*: "Hail to the Chief," 1964 (Laura)

Lindsay, Delia

FILM: *Scars of Dracula*, 1970 (Alice)
BIOGRAPHY—Delia Lindsay is a British character actress, primarily on television. Her movies include *Scars of Dracula*, her first feature film. She plays Alice, the burgomaster's daughter, who is in the process of getting randy with the film's hero when they are caught red-cheeked by the burgomaster. Lindsay turns the other cheek as she bounds up the stairs, bare butt bouncing, with the burgomaster close, er, behind. She is still active as of 2012.
Other genre credits: FILM: *The Devil's Widow*, Commonwealth United Entertainment, 1970 (Second Coven)

Ling, Barbara Yu (19??–1997)

FILM: *The Satanic Rites of Dracula*, 1973 (Chin Yang)
Other genre credits: FILM: *Hardware*, Palace Pictures, 1990 (Chinese Mother) TELEVISION: *The Avengers*: "The Golden Fleece," 1963 (Mrs. Kwan)

Ling, Lai

FILM: *Taste the Blood of Dracula*, 1970 (Chinese Girl)

Lister, Renny

FILM: *The Curse of the Werewolf*, 1961 (Yvonne)

Little, Caryl

FILM: *Lust for a Vampire*, 1971 (Isabel)

Liu, Hui-Ling (1951–)

BIRTHPLACE: Hanyang, Hebei, China.
FILM: *Legend of the 7 Golden Vampires*, 1974 (Hsi Hong)

Llewellyn, Josephine

FILM: *The Curse of the Werewolf*, 1961 (Marquesa)

Lloyd, Sue (1939–2011)

REAL NAME: Susan Margery Jeaffreson Lloyd; BIRTHPLACE: Aldeburgh, Suffolk, England.
FILM: *Hysteria*, 1965 (French Girl); *That's Your Funeral*, 1972 (Miss Peach)
TELEVISION: *Journey to the Unknown*: "The Madison Equation," 1969 (Barbara Rossiter)
BIOGRAPHY—Leggy Sue Lloyd originally wanted to be a ballet dancer, and attended

Wells Ballet School with that ambition, only to be judged too tall by the high sheriffs of ballet. Ballet's loss was acting's gain. She did dance in a chorus line and also modeled before her first TV role in 1963. She got good notices for *The Ipcress File* (1965); Hammer took note and cast her in a bit part in the same year's *Hysteria*. She also had a part in their comedy *That's Your Funeral*, but her biggest and best part for them was in *Journey to the Unknown*, as a red-herring computer expert assisting Barbara Bel Geddes in the creation of a super-computer that can even feel emotions — and boy, does it ever. She also appeared in *The Stud* and *The Bitch* with fellow Hammer Heroine Joan Collins, and with Caroline Munro in *Where's Jack?* She retired in 2001, and died of cancer ten years after.

Other genre credits: FILM: *U.F.O.*, George Forster, 1993 (Judge) TELEVISION: *The Avengers*: "A Surfeit of H2O," 1965 (Joyce Jason)

Lobegue, Madame

FILM: *Scream of Fear*, 1961 (Swiss Air Hostess)

Lodge, Jean (1927–)

BIRTHPLACE: Hull, Yorkshire, England.

FILMS: *Dick Barton Strikes Back*, 1949 (Tina); *Dr. Morelle: The Case of the Missing Heiress*, 1949 (Cynthia Mason); *Death of an Angel*, 1952 (Ann Marlow)

BIOGRAPHY — Beautiful Jean Lodge was a British leading lady and later character actress whose very first feature film was for Hammer. Then she was in two more of their early "Quota Quickies" (so named because their sole purpose was to be double-feature filler). Special Agent Dick Barton was a popular radio character, and can certainly be considered a type of proto-Bond, especially in the pulpy adventure *Dick Barton Strikes Back*, about a potentially London-destroying death ray. Lodge plays a secretary who is at first in league with the villains, but she can't resist the allure of Dick and is soon pulling his fat from the fire, aided by her faithful pooch Flash. She makes the most of a fairly standard role in an otherwise "boys' night out" thriller; she is appealing whether she's bad or good, and no wilting flower. Dr. Morelle was a radio sleuth transferred to film, and in *Dr. Morelle: The Case of the Missing Heiress*, Lodge plays the heiress. In her last Hammer, *Death of an Angel*, she plays a supporting role as a caregiver. She married producer Alfred Shaughnessy and retired in 1965 to concentrate on raising her sons David and Charles.

Other genre credits: FILMS: *The Masque of the Red Death*, Alta Vista Productions, 1964 (Scarlatti's Wife); *Curse of the Voodoo*, Futurama Entertainment, 1965 (Mrs. Lomas); *Invasion*, Merton Park Studios, 1965 (Barbara Gough)

Loe, Judy (1947–)

BIRTHPLACE: Urmston, Lancashire, England.

TELEVISION: *Hammer House of Mystery and Suspense*: "In Possession," 1985 (Betty Mervyn)

BIOGRAPHY — Lovely Judy Loe attended the University of Birmingham and began her acting career in a repertory company. She was in the original British cast of *Hair*, and carved out a substantial career as a character actress on British television. She had a supporting role in *Hammer House of Mystery and Suspense* as David Healy's wife; she doesn't have much to do, but she exhibits a nice strength of character. Still active, she is the mother of Kate Beckinsale.

Other genre credits: TELEVISION: *Sunday Night Thriller*: "The Business of Murder," 1981 (Dee); *Space Island One*: "Message from Keeler," "Quarantine," "Crew Test," "Sarcophagus," "Nemesis," "Mayfly," "Abandoned," "Anniversary," "Lost in Space," "Money Makes the World

Go 'Round," 1998 (Commander Kathryn McTiernan); *Doomwatch: Winter Angel* (Movie), 1999, (Angel)

Long, Jean

FILM: *The Two Faces of Dr. Jekyll*, 1960 (Sphinx Girl)

Longhurst, Sue (1943–)

BIRTHPLACE: Bognor Regis, England.
FILM: *Lust for a Vampire*, 1971 (Schoolgirl)

Lopez, Juliet

FILM: *Let Me In*, 2010 (Paramedic #3)
Other genre credits: FILMS: *Dead Beat*, 2010 (Victim); *Thor*, Paramount Pictures, 2011 (Admitting Nurse)

Lord, Justine (1938–)

REAL NAME: Justine Schooling; BIRTHPLACE: Sevenoaks, Kent, England.
FILM: *Maniac*, 1963 (Grace)
TELEVISION: *Journey to the Unknown*: "Girl of My Dreams," 1968 (Sue Tarleton)
BIOGRAPHY— British character actress Lord began her career in rep and then worked steadily in films and television in the 1960s until the mid–1970s, when she more or less retired; she did return in 1982 for a classic episode of *The Young Ones*. She had two bit parts for Hammer, one in *Maniac*, the other in the opening scene of *Journey to the Unknown*'s "Girl of My Dreams," where she plays an actress to whom Zena Walker describes her dream in which the actress dies.
Other genre credits: FILMS: *Deadlier Than the Male*, Greater Films, 1967 (Miss Peggy Ashenten) TELEVISION: *The Avengers*: "Propellant 23," 1962 (Jeanette); *Out of the Unknown*: "Stranger in the Family," 1965 (Paula); *The Young Ones*: "Flood," 1982 (The White Witch)

Lord, Rosemary (1947–)

BIRTHPLACE: Taunton, Somerset, England.
FILM: *Dr. Jekyll and Sister Hyde*, 1971 (Marie)
Other genre credits: FILM: *Return from Witch Mountain*, Walt Disney Productions, 1978 (Woman in Museum) TELEVISION: *Doctor Who*: "The Return," "The Bomb," 1966 (Guardian)

Lorraine, Nita

FILM: *The Viking Queen*, 1967 (Nubian Girl Slave)
Other genre credits: FILMS: *Curse of the Crimson Altar*, Tigon British, 1968 (Woman with Whip); *Zeta One*, Tigon British, 1969 (Angvisa Girl); *Son of Dracula*, Apple Corps, 1974 (Gorgon Woman) TELEVISION: *The Avengers*: "Who Was That Man I Saw You With?" 1969 (Kate)

Lovell, Angela

TELEVISION: *Journey to the Unknown*: "Eve," 1968 (Jennifer)
Other genre credits: FILM: *Beast of Morocco*, Associated British-Pathe, 1968 (Air Hostess)

Lumley, Joanna (1946–)

BIRTHPLACE: Srinagar, Kashmir and Jammu, British India.

FILM: *The Satanic Rites of Dracula*, 1973 (Jessica Van Helsing)

BIOGRAPHY— Elegant Joanna Lumley, an "army brat" with no formal acting training, has become a well-respected and well-loved actress, activist and author. She attended the Lucie Clayton Finishing School after being turned down by RADA, and worked as a model before finding her way into television and films. Her first role was as a patient in *Emergency Ward 10*, but she didn't make another appearance on any screen until 12 years later, with her part in *Some Girls Do* in 1969. That same year she joined the esteemed ranks of the Bond Girls in *On Her Majesty's Secret Service*, and a few years after that she became a Hammer Heroine with a starring role in their last Dracula. The part that she plays in *The Satanic Rites of Dracula* is interesting not in and of itself but because it's a character carried over from the previous film *Dracula A.D. 1972*, Jessica Van Helsing. Before, she had been a part of a swinging "scene," young and callow and dubious of her grandfather's theories; here (no doubt due to her experience in the previous movie), her demeanor is sober and she has become Van Helsing's "right hand." Since she is played by a different actress, it's difficult for the audience and the actor playing the inspector (Michael Coles repeating his role from *A.D.1972*) to suppress a smile as he tells her that it's nice to see her again; a nice in-joke. She went on to greater fame as Purdey in *The New Avengers*, and then scaled even greater heights of fame and popularity as the hilarious Patsy in the classic comedy *Absolutely Fabulous* (for which she won two BAFTA and one British Comedy awards and was nominated for three others). Lumley is still a working actress; a tireless human and animal rights activist and advocate of many charities; a Green Party supporter; the public face of the Gurkha Justice Campaign UK (her father was a decorated Gurkha officer), Survival International, and the Pastoral and Environmental Network in the Horn of Africa. Made an Officer of the Order of the British Empire in 1995, she lives with her second husband in London.

Other genre credits: FILMS: *On Her Majesty's Secret Service*, Danjaq/Eon Productions, 1969 (British Girl); *The Devil's Widow*, Commonwealth United Entertainment, 1970 (Georgia); *The House That Dripped Blood*, Amicus Productions, 1971 (Film

Joanna Lumley, star of *The Satanic Rites of Dracula*.

Crew Girl); *James and the Giant Peach*, Allied Filmmakers, 1996 (Aunt Spiker); *Corpse Bride*, Warner Brothers, 2005 (Voice of Maudeline Everglot) TELEVISION: *The New Avengers*: "House of Cards," "The Midas Touch," "The Eagle's Nest," "The Last of the Cybernauts...?," "Cat Amongst the Pigeons," "To Catch a Rat," "Target," "The Tale of the Big Why," "Three-Handed Game," "Faces," "Sleeper," "Dirtier by the Dozen," "Gnaws," 1976; "Dead Men are Dangerous," "Angels of Death," "Medium Rare," "Trap," "The Lion and the Unicorn," "Hostage," "Obsession," "K Is for Kill" "Complex," "The Gladiators," "Forward Base," "Emily," 1977 (Purdey); *The Tale of Sweeney Todd* (Movie), 1997 (Mrs. Lovett); *Alice in Wonderland* (Movie), 1999 (Voice of Tiger Lily); *Comic Relief: Doctor Who—The Curse of Fatal Death* (Movie), 1999 (The Doctor)

Luttrell, Constance

FILM: *Dracula A.D. 1972*, 1972 (Mrs. Donnelly)

Lynley, Carol (1942–)

REAL NAME: Carole Ann Jones; BIRTHPLACE: New York City, New York, USA.

TELEVISION: *Journey to the Unknown*: "Eve," 1968 (Eve); *Hammer House of Mystery and Suspense*: "In Possession," 1985 (Sylvia Daley)

BIOGRAPHY—As gorgeous Carol Lynley has said, she's never had a scandal, never been caught running naked down the street, shot anyone or been shot, her child is legitimate, she's never done porn or had any drug addictions, so anyone who wants to write a juicy book about her is going to have a problem. Fair enough, then; what she *has* had is a 50-year career that began as a child model and has included many classic genre efforts such as the original TV movie *The Night Stalker*. She appeared in *Playboy* in 1965, and one would think this would have been her Hammer screen test, but she never appeared in any of their films. She did appear in episodes of two of their television series; in the first, the "Eve" episode of *Journey to the Unknown*, she plays a dummy that comes to life, in a Hammer version of the comedy *One Touch of Venus*, which starred Ava Gardner and Robert Walker. Like Walker, the "hero" is a young window dresser, and like Gardner, Lynley is the dummy who comes to life (only to him, of course). The original is a comedy, and this being Hammer, the consequences are a bit more 'orrible—which doesn't at all keep it from still being 'ilarious. The soft-focus dreams of consumerist seduction are side-splitting as Lynley plays the almost wordless, compliant and accepting Eve, as are the scenes of the hero frantically avoiding the police, dashing about the countryside clutching his fur-coated shop dummy. No such relief is to be found in her second role as a Hammer Heroine, in the "In Possession" episode of *Hammer House of Mystery and Suspense*; directed by Hammer vet Val Guest. It is one of the scariest installments in the series. She is still active and still not doing anything she shouldn't be.

Other genre credits: FILMS: *The Shuttered Room*, Seven Arts Productions, 1967 (Susannah/Sarah); *The Maltese Bippy*, MGM, 1969 (Robin Sherwood); *Beware! The Blob*, Jack H. Harris Enterprises, 1972 (Leslie); *Cotter*, Producers Studio, 1973 (Leah); *The Cat and the Canary*, Grenadier Films, 1978 (Annabelle West); *The Shape of Things to Come*, CFI Investments, 1979 (Nikki); *Dark Tower*, Sandy Howard, 1989 (Tilly Ambrose); *Spirits*, American Independent Productions, 1990 (Sister Jillian); *Howling VI: The Freaks*, Allied Entertainments Group PLC, 1991 (Miss Eddington) TELEVISION: *Alfred Hitchcock Presents*: "The Young One," 1957 (Janice); *The Alfred Hitchcock Hour*: "Final Vow," 1962 (Sister Pamela Wiley); *The Man from U.N.C.L.E.*: "The Prince of Darkness Affair," 1967 (Annie Justin); *The Invaders*: "The Believers," 1967 (Elyse Reynolds); *The Night Stalker* (Movie), 1972 (Gail Foster); *Rod Serling's Night Gallery*: "The Waiting Room/Last Rites for a Dead Druid," 1972 (Jenny Tarraday); *The

Sixth Sense: "The House That Cried Murder," 1972 (Gail Sumner); *The Evil Touch*: "Dear Cora, I'm Going to Kill You," (Cora); "Dream by Dreaming," 1974; *Thriller*: "If It's a Man, Hang Up," 1974 (Suzy Martin); *Tales of the Unexpected*: "The Gift of Beauty," 1984 (Elizabeth); *Monsters*: "Stressed Environment," 1990 (Dr. Elizabeth Porter)

Lynn, Janet

FILM: *Twins of Evil*, 1971 (Schoolgirl)
Other genre credits: FILMS: *Brain Robbers from Outer Space*, Sub Atomic Productions, 2004 (Janet Lynn); *Behold the Raven*, Batwolf Films, 2004 (Aunt Paula)

Lynton, Maggie

FILM: *When Dinosaurs Ruled the Earth*, 1970 (Rock Mother)

MacLennan, Elizabeth

BIRTHPLACE: Glasgow, Scotland.
FILM: *Hands of the Ripper*, 1971 (Mrs. Wilson)
BIOGRAPHY—A British character actress and radical popular theater practitioner, she founded the 7:84 Theatre Company and 7:84 Scotland, and authored *The Moon Belongs to Everyone*.
Other genre credits: FILM: *The House in Nightmare Park*, Anglo-EMI Film Distributors, 1977 (Verity Henderson)

Malin, Diana (1957–)

TELEVISION: *Hammer House of Mystery and Suspense*: "Black Carrion," 1986 (Secretary)

Manahan, Anna Maria (1924–2009)

BIRTHPLACE: County Waterford, Irish Free State.
FILM: *The Viking Queen*, 1967 (Shopkeeper's Wife)
Other genre credits: FILMS: *Clash of the Titans*, MGM, 1981 (Stygian Witch) TELEVISION: *The Young Indiana Jones Chronicles*: "Ireland, April 1916," 1993 (Old Woman at GPO)

Mareno, Lydia

FILM: *Dracula A.D. 1972*, 1972 (Member of Stoneground)

Marks, Patricia

FILM: *Never Take Sweets from a Stranger*, 1960 (Nurse)

Marla, Norma

FILMS: *The Ugly Duckling*, 1959 (First Girl); *The Two Faces of Dr. Jekyll*, 1960 (Maria)
BIOGRAPHY—Norma Marla made two films, both of them for Hammer. She has a bit part in the pre–*Nutty Professor* take on Jekyll and Hyde, *The Ugly Duckling*, and a role a bit more substantial in *The Two Faces of Dr. Jekyll*, in which she is a wonderful example of the strange British obsession with dancing girls who stick snakes' heads in their mouths. She is later strangled by the handsome Hyde. (See photograph on page 130.)

Marsh, Carol (1926–2010)

REAL NAME: Norma Lilian Simpson; BIRTHPLACE: Barton, Preston, Lancashire; England.
FILM: *Dracula*, 1958 (Lucy Holmwood)

Besides star Dawn Addams, this Mexican lobby card for *The Two Faces of Dr. Jekyll* features Norma Marla (reaching in basket; being strangled by Jekyll) and (inset photograph left to right) Pauline Shepherd, Lucy Griffiths and Prudence Hyman sans Gorgon makeup.

BIOGRAPHY— The daughter of an architect and surveyor, beautiful Carol Marsh trained with the J. Arthur Rank Company; her first film was the coveted lead in the classic *Brighton Rock* (1947). Two years later, she appeared in her first fantasy classic, as the voice of Alice in Disney's perennial *Alice in Wonderland*, and in 1958, she made her second, as Lucy Holmwood in Hammer's *Dracula*. And although she's billed underneath Melissa Stribling, she rather steals the show. Her first scene is a joy; she has been vampirized by Dracula but Mina and Arthur think she is merely anemic, and she plays the part. But when they leave the room, her eyes light up and an evil smile creeps across her face as she takes off her cross and lies back on the bed to await her vampire lover. She also shines in the scene where she takes Janina Faye to the graveyard and is confronted by Arthur, whom she approaches with apparently much more than familial love. She and we are then shocked by Van Helsing's dramatic entrance brandishing a cross, which he uses to "brand" her, sending her fleeing into a crypt. Her last screen appearance was in 1974, and she passed away in 2010, but her Lucy will never be forgotten.

Other genre credits: FILMS: *Alice in Wonderland*, Walt Disney, 1949 (Voice of Alice); *Scrooge*, George Minter Productions, 1951 (Fan Scrooge)

Marshall-Gardiner, Jessica (1978–)

TELEVISION: *Hammer House of Mystery and Suspense*: "Black Carrion," 1986 (Little Girl)

Martin, Malaika

FILM: *Taste the Blood of Dracula*, 1970 (Snake Girl)

Martin, Mia

FILM: *The Satanic Rites of Dracula*, 1973 (Vampire Girl)

Martinez, Deborah

FILM: *The Resident*, 2011 (Mrs. Portes)
Other genre credits: TELEVISION: *Terminator: The Sarah Connor Chronicles*: pilot episode, 2008 (News Anchor)

Matheson, Judy

FILMS: *Lust for a Vampire*, 1971 (Amanda McBride); *Twins of Evil*, 1971 (Woodsman's Daughter)
BIOGRAPHY—Judy Matheson got her start with the Bristol Old Vic Theatre Company and her first (small) screen appearance was in 1968. She dies in two Hammer films; in *Lust for a Vampire*, she's the student at an all-girl school who deduces that Yutte Stensgaard is more than just a classmate. Stensgaard's Mircalla-Carmilla then seduces and kills her in the accepted cinematic lesbian vampire fashion. She doesn't fare any better in *Twins of Evil*, where she plays an innocent woodsman's daughter burned at the stake by the Witch-Happy Joes of Puritan Company. Her last appearance was in a TV episode of *Blake's 7*, and the following year she became the continuity announcer for ITV.
Other genre credits: FILMS: *Crucible of Terror*, Glendale, 1971 (Marcia); *The Flesh and Blood Show*, Peter Walker (Heritage), 1972 (Jane); *The House That Vanished*, Blackwater Film Productions Limited, 1974 (Lorna Collins) TELEVISION: *Dead of Night*: "Two in the Morning," 1972 (Tessa); *Blake's 7*: "Volcano," 1980 (Mutoid)

Mathie, Marion D. (1925–2012)

BIRTHPLACE: Kingston upon Thames, Surrey, England.
FILM: *Dracula Has Risen from the Grave*, 1968 (Anna Mueller)

Maureen, Mollie (1904–1987)

REAL NAME: Elizabeth Mary Campfield; BIRTHPLACE: Dublin, Ireland.
TELEVISION: *Hammer House of Mystery and Suspense*: "The Corvini Inheritance," 1985 (Mrs. Courtney)
BIOGRAPHY—A delightful Irish character actress, Maureen made her first film in 1939, and kept on working right up to 1987, the year she passed away (her last movie was released posthumously). Most of her roles were on TV, and one of those was a nice bit for *Hammer House of Mystery and Suspense* as an old woman who distracts an auctioneer so her husband can extract some rare pieces. She gets quite indignant when they're accused, but their skullduggery is exposed by the unblinking eye of a security camera.
Other genre credits: FILMS: *Twisted Nerve*, Charter Film Productions, 1968 (Patient); *The Private Life of Sherlock Holmes*, Compton Films, 1970 (Queen Victoria); *Jabberwocky*, Python Films, 1977 (Head Nun); *The Hound of the Baskervilles*, Michael White Productions,

1978 (Mrs. Oviatt) TELEVISION: *The Haunted House*: Episode 1, 1960 (Scapha); *The Avengers*: "Dead on Course," 1962 (Kiosk Woman)

May, Dinah (1954–)

BIRTHPLACE: Heswall, Cheshire, England.
TELEVISION: *Hammer House of Mystery and Suspense*: "Mark of the Devil," 1984 (Sexy Blonde)
Other genre credits: TELEVISION: *Blake's 7*: "Gold," 1981 (Passenger)

Maynard, Patricia (1942–)

BIRTHPLACE: Beighton, West Riding of Yorkshire, England.
TELEVISION: *Hammer House of Horror*: "The House That Bled to Death," 1980 (Jean Evans)
BIOGRAPHY— The mother of actress Hannah Waterman (from her marriage to actor Dennis Waterman), Maynard had a forty-year career, the first five of which were spent on stage. Her first film, *Night Train to Paris* (1964), was also her last, but she continued to appear on stage and television until her retirement in 2005. She plays the neighbor of Rachel Davies in the *Hammer House of Horror* episode "House That Bled to Death."
Other genre credits: TELEVISION: *Doomwatch*: "Train and De-Train," 1970 (Miss Sephton); *Doctor Who*: "Robot," 1975 (Miss Winters)

Mazor, Deborah L.

FILMS: *Let Me In*, 2010 (Day Nurse); *The Resident*, 2011 (Stunt Double for Hilary Swank)

McCabe, Ruth

FILM: *Wake Wood*, 2011 (Peggy O'Shea)

McConnell, Bridget

FILM: *Rasputin, the Mad Monk*, 1966 (Gossip)
Other genre credits: TELEVISION: *Out of the Unknown*: "Some Lapse of Time," 1965 (Sister); *Tales of the Unexpected*: "Shatterproof," 1981 (Mrs. Emerson); *The Young Indiana Jones Chronicles*: "Prague, August, 1917," 1993 (Lady with Buns)

McCrea, Alice

FILM: *Wake Wood*, 2011 (Female Customer)

McSharry, Carmel (1930–)

BIRTHPLACE: Dublin, Ireland.
FILM: *The Witches*, 1966 (Mrs. Dowsett)
Other genre credits: FILM: *The Day the Earth Caught Fire*, Pax Films, 1961 (Woman Lost in Fog) TELEVISION: *One Step Beyond*: "The Confession," 1961 (Martha)

McTeer, Janet (1961–)

BIRTHPLACE: Newcastle, Tyne and Wear, England.
FILM: *The Woman in Black*, 2012 (Mrs. Daily)
BIOGRAPHY— Lovely Janet McTeer trained at RADA, after which she began a stage career that has brought her as much acclaim as her films. She's been nominated for an Academy

Award twice so far, and has won a Tony, Golden Globe and numerous other critics' awards. She ostensibly plays a supporting role in *The Woman in Black*, but her gripping performance as the slightly mad (because she knows the truth) Mrs. Daily nearly steals the movie away from Daniel "Harry Potter" Radcliffe, in his first role since the boy wizard. She is especially creepy when her voice is double-tracked with that of her dead child. Although the film had a fair-to-middling box office and critical reception, it is one of the best so far from the reincarnated Hammer; a good, old-fashioned period ghost story that doesn't rely on extreme gore or torture porn to tell that story. At the time of this writing she is reportedly due to star in a remake of Dario Argento's *Suspiria*.

Other genre credits: FILMS: *Tideland*, Recorded Picture Company, 2005 (Dell) TELEVISION: *Psychoville*: "Jelly," "Blackmail," 2009 (Cheryl)

Meagher, Aoife

FILM: *Wake Wood*, 2011 (Deirdre)

Meineke, Eva Maria (1923–)

BIRTHPLACE: Berlin, Germany.
FILM: *To the Devil a Daughter*, 1976 (Eveline De Grass)

Melford, Jill (1934–)

BIRTHPLACE: London, England.
FILMS: *Blackout*, 1954 (Miss Nardis); *The Vengeance of She*, 1968 (Sheila)
Other genre credits: TELEVISION: *Out of This World*: "Immigrant," 1962 (Employment Officer); *The New Avengers*: "Faces," 1976 (Sheila Rainor)

Melly, Andree (1932–)

BIRTHPLACE: Liverpool, England.
FILM: *The Brides of Dracula*, 1960 (Gina)
BIOGRAPHY— Even if you don't know the name, you know the face, for the various shots of Andree Melly have not only become a kind of shorthand for *The Brides of Dracula* but for Hammer vampire girls and Hammer films in general. The sister of famous jazz singer, author and critic George Melly (*Revolt into Style*), Melly made her first screen appearance in 1952, and eight years later, she was signed to her signature role of Gina in *The Brides of Dracula*, which in some ways can be seen to carry a hint of the more overt lesbianism of *The Vampire Lovers* (1970): "My darling, you haven't forgotten your little Gina, have you? Put your arms around me, please ... hug me ... I want to kiss you ... say you'll forgive me for letting *him* love me." But it's not her sexual proclivities that entrance, it's her face, looking like a fanged Mona Lisa, her smile hinting at a thousand unnamed evils, the very picture of corruption. Her career lasted for another 30 years; her last role was in *T-Bag and the Pearls of Wisdom* (1990). She now lives in Ibiza with her husband.

Other genre credits: FILM: *The Horror of it All*, Lippert Pictures, 1964 (Natalia Marley) TELEVISION: *Turn On to T-Bag*: "The Two Musketeers," 1988 (The Queen); *T-Bag and the Pearls of Wisdom*: "Tut-Tut," 1990 (Osiris) (See photograph on page 134.)

Mendez, Julie

FILMS: *The Two Faces of Dr. Jekyll*, 1960 (Crew: Choreographer); *She*, 1965 (Night Club Dancer)
Other genre credits: FILMS: *From Russia with Love*, Danjaq & Eon Productions, 1963

Andree Melly invites Yvonne Monlaur out for a bite in *The Brides of Dracula* (courtesy Mel Bridgeman).

(Dancing Girl in Titles Sequence); *Devils of Darkness*, Planet Film Productions, 1965 (Snake Dancer); *Theatre of Death*, Pennea Productions, 1967 (Belly Dancer)

Meredith, Jill Mai

BIRTHPLACE: Colchester, England.
FILM: *The Curse of the Mummy's Tomb*, 1964 (Jenny)
Other genre credits: TELEVISION: *Mystery and Imagination*: "The Open Door," 1966 (Jeanie Mortimer)

Merrow, Jane (1941–)

REAL NAME: Jane Meirowsky; BIRTHPLACE: Hertfordshire, England.
FILMS: *The Phantom of the Opera*, 1962 (Chorus Girl); *Hands of the Ripper*, 1971 (Laura)
BIOGRAPHY— Lovely Jane Merrow was born to a British mother and German dad, and educated at RADA. Her first role was in 1961, and she soon became quite active and well-regarded. Like fellow Hammer Heroine Tracy Reed, she was considered for the *Avengers* role vacated by Diana Rigg (it eventually went to Linda Thorson). She did two turns for Hammer, although her first could be more accurately termed a half-turn, as she was a chorus girl among many in *The Phantom of the Opera*. Her second was much more substantial (and sympathetic); in *Hands of the Ripper*, she plays the blind fiancée of the Young Male Lead and nearly meets

her maker at the hands of Angharad Rees. In the 1970s she moved to America, where she landed the bulk of her genre television roles, and then moved back to England some 20 years later to run a family business and continue her career.

Other genre credits: FILMS: *The Woman Who Wouldn't Die*, John Parsons–Neil McCallum Productions, 1965 (Alice Taylor); *Island of the Burning Damned*, Planet Film Productions, 1967 (Angela Roberts) TELEVISION: *Mystery and Imagination*: "Carmilla," 1966 (Carmilla); *The Avengers*: "Mission... Highly Improbable," 1967 (Susan Rushton); *The Hound of the Baskervilles* (Movie), 1972 (Beryl Stapleton); *The Horror at 37,000 Feet* (Movie), 1973 (Sheila O'Neill); *UFO*: "The Responsibility Seat," 1973 (Josephine Fraser); *The Six Million Dollar Man*: "Doomsday and Counting," 1974 (Irina Leonova); "Death Probe," 1977 (Woman); *The Incredible Hulk*: "Bring Me the Head of the Hulk," 1981 (Dr. Jane Cabot)

Merton, Zienia (1945–)

BIRTHPLACE: Burma.

TELEVISION: *Hammer House of Mystery and Suspense*: "The Late Nancy Irving," 1985 (Nurse Lee Parquet)

Other genre credits: FILMS: *Masters of Venus*, Wallace Productions, 1962 (Marla); *Message from Moonbase Alpha* (short), Kindred Productions, 1999 (Sandra Benes) TELEVISION: *Doctor Who*: "Assassin at Peking," "Mighty Kublai Khan," "Rider from Shang-Tu," "The Wall of Lies," "Five Hundred Eyes," "The Singing Sands," "The Roof of the World," 1964 (Ping Cho); *Space: 1999*: "Breakaway," "Force of Life," "Collision Course," "War Games," "Death's Other Dominion," "Voyager's Return," "Alpha Child," "Earthbound," "Dragon's Domain," "Mission of the Darians," "Black Sun," "The Guardian of Piri," 1975; "The End of Eternity," "Matter of Life and Death," "The Full Circle," "Another Time, Another Place," "The Infernal Machine," "Ring Around the Moon," "Missing Link," "The Last Sunset," "Space Brain," "The Troubled Spirit," "The Testament of Arkadia," "The Last Enemy," "The Metamorph," "The Exiles," "One Moment of Humanity," "Seed of Destruction," "Catacombs of the Moon," "Space Warp," "The Beta Cloud," "The Lambda Factor," 1976; "The Bringers of Wonder," "The Séance Spectre," 1977 (Sandra Benes); *Journey Through the Black Sun* (Movie), 1976 (Sandra Benes); *Alien Attack* (Movie), 1976 (Sandra Benes); *Destination: Moonbase Alpha* (Movie), 1978 (Sandra Benes); *Chiller*: "Prophecy," 1995 (Maria Monsanto); *Dinotopia*: 2002 (Teacher)

Miles, Vera (1929–)

REAL NAME: Vera June Ralston; BIRTHPLACE: Boise City, Oklahoma, USA.

FILM: *Journey to the Unknown*, 1969 (June Wiley)

TELEVISION: *Journey to the Unknown*: "Matakitas Is Coming," 1968 (June Wiley)

BIOGRAPHY— American leading lady Vera Miles was Miss Kansas of 1948, and after moving to Los Angeles, she began to play small movie and television roles, her first coming in 1950. Her stellar talent was soon on display in such classics as John Ford's *The Searchers* and Hitchcock's *The Wrong Man*. She had first worked for Hitchcock in 1955, signed a personal contract with him, and was slated for the lead in *Vertigo* until production delays and her pregnancy caused Hitchcock to go with Kim Novak. He next cast her in her most famous role, Janet Leigh's sister in *Psycho*. Hammer managed to snag her for an episode of *Journey to the Unknown*, "Matakitas Is Coming," in which she plays a magazine writer who somehow stumbles into a time warp—and is menaced by a psycho. She gives an assured performance even though, as is usually the norm in this type of story, some of the details about the mix-up in the time-space continuum don't hold water; for instance, it seems to be 1927 everywhere except the room she's in, because she's still about to use the microfilm viewing machine. Like Hammer's other "Journey" films, "Matakitas" was mashed up with another to create a feature that was only released to TV. (Somewhat similarly, *The Unknown* (no relation) was a pilot film that was never bought, and so became an episode of *The Outer Limits* and was also released as a TV movie.) She has been married four times, once to actor Gordon Scott, with whom she starred in *Tarzan's Hidden Jungle*. She retired in 1995, currently resides in sunny California, and refuses all interviewers and requests for public appearances.

Other genre credits: FILMS: *Tarzan's Hidden Jungle*, Sol Lesser Productions, 1955 (Jill Hardy); *Psycho*, Shamley Productions, 1960 (Lila Crane); *Psycho II*, Universal Pictures, 1983 (Lila Loomis) TELEVISION: *Science Fiction Theatre*: "No Food for Thought," 1955 (Dr. Jan Corey); *Alfred Hitchcock Presents*: "Revenge," 1955 (Elsa Spann); *Twilight Zone*: "Mirror Image," 1960 (Millicent Barnes); *The Outer Limits*: "The Forms of Things Unknown," 1964 (Kasha Paine); *The Unknown* (Movie), 1964 (Kasha Paine); *The Alfred Hitchcock Hour*: "Don't Look Behind You," 1962 (Daphne); "Death Scene," 1965 (Nicky Revere); *The Man from U.N.C.L.E.*: "The Bridge of Lions Affair," 1966 (Madame Raine de Sala); *Live Again, Die Again* (Movie), 1974 (Marcia Carmichael); *Mazes and Monsters* (Movie), 1982 (Cat); *Alfred Hitchcock Presents*: "Revenge," 1985

Miley, Peggy

FILM: *The Resident*, 2011 (Mrs. Rosenbaum)

Other genre credits: FILMS: *Star Trek: Insurrection*, Paramount Pictures, 1998 (Regent Cuzar); *The Irish Vampire Goes West*, Raven Productions, 2007 (Aunt Mary) TELEVISION: *The Others*: "Mora," 2000; *Sabrina, The Teenage Witch*: "Sabrina the Activist," 2001 (Mrs. Smiley)

Millard, Tamsin

FILM: *Creatures the World Forgot*, 1971 (Prehistoric Woman)

Miller, Magda (1935–)

BIRTHPLACE: Strathblane, Scotland.
FILM: *The Two Faces of Dr. Jekyll*, 1960 (Sphinx Girl)

Miller, Tallulah

FILM: *Hands of the Ripper*, 1971 (Third Pub Whore)
Other genre credits: FILM: *The Hands of Orlac*, Pendennis Films, 1960 (Pub Whore)

Mitchell, Yvonne (1915–1979)

REAL NAME: Yvonne Frances Joseph; BIRTHPLACE: London, England.
FILM: *Demons of the Mind*, 1972 (Hilda)
Other genre credits: FILMS: *The Corpse* (a.k.a. *Crucible of Horror*), Abacus Productions, 1971 (Edith Eastwood) TELEVISION: *BBC Sunday Night Theatre*: "1984," 1954 (Julia); *Out of the Unknown*: "The Machine Stops," 1966 (Vashti)

Mockler, Suzanne (1944–)

FILM: *Journey into Darkness*, 1969 (Susan Redford)
TELEVISION: *Journey to the Unknown*: "The New People," 1968 (Susan Redford)
BIOGRAPHY—During the short career of this cute British character actress, she plays a bit part in *Journey to the Unknown* as a zany, perky Satanist who's married to Damien Thomas (*Twins of Evil*).

Monlaur, Yvonne (1939–)

REAL NAME: Yvonne Bedat de Monlaur; BIRTHPLACE: Pau, France.

FILMS: *The Brides of Dracula*, 1960 (Marianne Danielle); *The Terror of the Tongs*, 1961 (Lee)

BIOGRAPHY— Strikingly beautiful Yvonne Monlaur began her short screen career as a model, which led to her working in numerous Italian films before making her visit to England, where she made *Circus of Horrors*. This brought her to the attentions of Hammer, who signed her to star in *The Brides of Dracula* with nary a screen test, and billed her as "France's Latest Sex Kitten." Marianne Danielle seems at first the standard Hammer Heroine, but there are subtle differences between her and the usual standard-issue naïve virgin. For one thing, she's a teacher, which immediately gives her a professional standing, unlike the *de rigueur* newly minted housewife or silly young niece. Not only that, but she's traveling alone and unattached, which was generally regarded in those days with more than a bit of suspicion. She's also fairly

Could Yvonne Monlaur be about to get a pain in the neck from David Peel in *Brides of Dracula*? (courtesy Paul C. Riggie).

resourceful and resilient; of course, she suffers a huge lapse in judgment by falling for the baron, and seems a bit slow to grasp the unfolding events—but of course, love is blind, not to mention there wouldn't be a story if she didn't. But all in all, she is one of the most memorable and beautiful Hammer Heroines in the best Dracula sequel, one of the company's all-time classics. Her other effort at Bray, *The Terror of the Tongs*, was a historical costume adventure in the vein of *The Stranglers of Bombay*; Yvonne plays the unwilling wife of a Tong who helps Geoffrey Toone get his revenge against the Tongs who killed his daughter. She continued to work for another few years, but began to question the quality of her roles and her place in the film industry, and took a break that turned into a permanent vacation. She is happy in retirement, and occasionally makes appearances at fan conventions such as Monster Bash, where in 2011 she, Veronica Carlson and Caroline Munro participated in a reading of *Dracula's Guest* by actor Zach Zito.

Other genre credits: FILM: *Circus of Horrors*, Lynx Films, 1960 (Nicole Vanet)

Monteros, Rosenda (1935–)

BIRTHPLACE: Veracruz, Veracruz, Mexico.
FILM: *She*, 1965 (Ustane)

BIOGRAPHY— Pert Rosenda Monteros honed her craft on the stage for years before her first movie role in 1954. She then worked in Mexican films exclusively until her big break in the classic *The Magnificent Seven*, which brought her to the attention of European distributors and then Hammer, for whom she played the handmaiden Ustane in *She*. Like Shirley Anne Field in *The Damned*, she is at first simply used to lure the hero into a very compromising position, but finds herself falling in love with him — with tragic results (she is lowered into a pit of fire, literally a "bird" in a gilded cage). But during her brief celluloid life, she provides a warm, human contrast to the coldly evil Ayesha of Ursula Andress. Monteros is still active, although she retired from 1983 to 2000.

Other genre credits: The Skeleton of Mrs. Morales, Alfa Film S.A., 1960

Moretz, Chloe Grace (1997–)

BIRTHPLACE: Atlanta, Georgia, USA.
FILM: *Let Me In*, 2010 (Abby)
BIOGRAPHY—Lovely and talented beyond her years, Chloe Moretz looks to be the next big thing who made a stop at Hammer on her way up. She began modeling at age five, and acting at age six, and already has over 40 credits, including a number of impressive genre roles. So far, the best of those has been in Hammer's *Let Me In*, easily one of the best vampire films, not only in a long time, but in Hammer history. Moretz showcases a rare maturity and sensitivity in her portrayal of a 12-year-old vampire who has "been 12 for a long time." She is evil by deed but not by nature, unencumbered by metaphysical musings on the nature of her plight, with a simple acceptance of that's just "how it is." She achieves a great chemistry with Owen (Cody Smit-McPhee), a bullied boy who befriends her and accepts her for what she is, even though he has seen what the last boy she grew old with had to do and how he ended up. The fact that all they have is each other is reinforced by the way Owen's mother is portrayed and photographed: She is overly religious, rarely there and never clearly in shot when she is, almost faceless. His parents are divorced, and his dad is only heard as a voice over the phone, equally faceless. The only time the film really falters is when Moretz gets her full vampire on and becomes cookie-cutter CGI, which makes for some cookie-cutter jump scares. But her scenes immediately before and after are exceedingly well-done, especially the one where Owen discovers her true self when he tries to make a blood pact with her. Let's hope that she doesn't fritter away real talent and end up a casualty like so many other young actresses both in and out of this book.

Chloe Grace Moretz knows their snow vampire like a Hammer vampire in *Let Me In*.

Other genre credits: FILMS: *The Amityville Horror*, MGM, 2005 (Chelsea Lutz); *Room 6*, CFQ Films, 2006 (Melissa); *Wicked Little Things*, Millennium Films, 2006 (Emma); *The Eye*, Lionsgate, 2008 (Alicia); *Hugo*, Paramount Pictures, 2011 (Isabelle); *Dark Shadows*, Dan Curtis Productions, 2012 (Carolyn Stoddard); *Carrie*, MGM, 2013 (Carrie White)

Morgan, Elizabeth

FILM: *Frankenstein Must Be Destroyed*, 1969 (Christina)
Other genre credits: TELEVISION: *Captain Scarlet and the Mysterons*: "The Mysterons,"

"Winged Assassin," "Big Ben Strikes Again," "Avalanche," "White as Snow," "Operation Time," "Spectrum Strikes Back," "Point 783," "Model Spy," 1967; "Seek and Destroy," "Renegade Rocket," "Treble Cross," "Flight 104," "Place of Angels," "Expo 2068," "The Launching," "Codename Europa," "Inferno," "Attack on Cloudbase," 1968 (Voices of Destiny Angel, Rhapsody Angel, Harmony Angel, Nurse, Helga, Airport Tannoy)

Morgan, Taylor

FILM: *Beyond the Rave*, 2008 (Girl 1)

Morrow, Alexandria

FILM: *The Resident*, 2011 (Art Model)
Other genre credits: FILM: *Cowboys and Aliens*, Paramount Pictures, 2011 (Lady of the Night)

Mort, Patricia

TELEVISION: *Hammer House of Horror*: "Rude Awakening," 1980 (Mabel)
Other genre credits: TELEVISION: *Out of this World*: "The Tycoons," 1962 (Miss Cook); *Tales of the Unexpected*: "I'll Be Seeing You," 1980 (Olive Parsons)

Moulan, Rosita

FILM: *Creatures the World Forgot*, 1971 (The Dancer)

Moyens, Judi

FILM: *The Hound of the Baskervilles*, 1959 (Servant Girl)
BIOGRAPHY— In her only film, pretty Judi Moyens makes a striking impression as the servant girl for whom Sir Hugo Baskerville plans a fate worse than death for. She escapes and meets actual death at his hands.

Munro, Caroline (1949–)

BIRTHPLACE: Windsor, Berkshire, England.
FILMS: *Dracula A.D. 1972*, 1972 (Laura Bellows); *Captain Kronos, Vampire Hunter*, 1974 (Carla)
BIOGRAPHY— One of the most naturally beautiful, and genuinely sweet, women ever to grace the genre with her presence, Caroline Munro is known as "The First Lady of Fantasy." She is the unassuming daughter of unassuming parents (and not, as is sometimes erroneously reported, of actress Janet Munro); her life changed when her mother entered Caroline's photo in a "Face of the Year" competition, which she won. This led to her first modeling assignments, one of which was for Lamb's Navy Rum; in ad campaigns, she was their "face" for many years. This led to her contract with Hammer: Sir James Carreras spotted her on one of the many billboards bearing her image, and, she was soon signed to a contract.

Her first role for the company was Laura Bellows, Christopher Lee's first victim in the cult favorite *Dracula A.D. 1972*, which could be retitled "Dracula Meets Hammer's Idea of Hippies" (which is precisely why it's a cult favorite). As the first of Dracula's snacks, her screen time is limited, but in her hot pants and thigh-high boots, every eye in the audience is on her, and she makes a sizable impact in a role which requires her to do little but party and scream, which she does quite convincingly. She played the non-speaking but pivotal role of Victoria Regina Phibes in *The Abominable Dr. Phibes* and its sequel *Dr. Phibes Rises Again*, then graduated to leading-lady status with her appearance as the gypsy girl Carla in *Captain Kronos, Vampire Hunter*. In her first scene she is far from glamorous: chained up in stocks for the crime of having danced on a Saturday, her hair dripping with eggs and tomatoes after the villagers have pelted her with them. At first rather reluctant, she soon proves herself to be an able and (in more ways than one) quite willing accomplice unflinchingly following Kronos into battle and even acting as bait for the vampires in the swashbuckling climax. It was her *Kronos* performance which secured her the part of Margiana in *The Golden Voyage of Sinbad*, which cemented her status as a fan favorite. And yet another Lamb's Navy Rum billboard caught the eye of "Cubby" Broccoli, who subsequently cast her in *The Spy Who Loved Me* as the beautiful but deadly Naomi (she had previously appeared in a bit part in the original *Casino Royale*). Her moment of true big-screen immortality comes when she winks at Bond from her helicopter — right before he blows both of them to smithereens. She gained a whole new generation of fans with her appearances in slasher movies in the '80s, is still beautiful and still active in the business, and remains one of the most popular guests on the fan convention circuit.

Other genre credits: FILMS: *Casino Royale*, Columbia Pictures, 1967 (Guard Girl); *The Abominable Dr. Phibes*, American International Pictures, 1971 (Victoria Regina Phibes); *Dr. Phibes Rises Again*, American International Pictures, 1972 (Victoria Regina Phibes); *The Golden Voyage of Sinbad*, Columbia Pictures, 1973 (Margiana); *The Devil Within Her*, The Rank Organization, 1975 (Mandy Gregory); *At the Earth's Core*, Amicus Productions, 1976 (Dia); *The Spy Who Loved Me*, Danjaq/Eon Productions, 1977 (Naomi); *Starcrash*, New World Pictures, 1978 (Stella Star); *Maniac*, Magnum Motion Pictures, 1980 (Anna D'Antoni); *The Last Horror Film*, Shere Productions/Winters Hollywood Entertainment Holdings Corporation, 1982 (Jana Bates); *Slaughter High*, Spectacular Trading International/Vestron Pictures, 1986 (Carol Manning); *El Aullido Del Diablo*, Freemont-Nasch International, 1987 (Carmen); *Faceless*, ATC 3000, 1987 (Barbara Hallen); *Demons 6: De Profundis*, 21st Century Film, 1989 (Nora McJudge); *Flesh for the Beast*, Fever Dreams, 2003 (Carla the Gypsy); *The Absence of Light*, New Illusions Pictures, 2006 (Abbey Church)

TELEVISION: *The New Avengers*: "Angels of Death," 1977 (Tammy)

Myers, Cynthia (1950–2011)

REAL NAME: Cynthia Jeanette Myers; BIRTHPLACE: Toledo, Ohio, USA.
FILM: *The Lost Continent*, 1968 (Native Girl)

Nadasi, Mia

REAL NAME: Mia Nardi
FILM: *Countess Dracula*, 1971 (Crew: Choreographer)
TELEVISION: *Hammer House of Horror*: "Visitor from the Grave," 1980 (Margaret Tabori)
Other genre credits: FILM: *The Devil Within Her*, The Rank Organization, 1975 (Crew: Choreographer) TELEVISION: *Supernatural*: "Viktoria," 1977 (Elizabeth/Viktoria)

Nappi, Malya

FILM: *One Million Years B.C.*, 1966 (Tohana)

Neilson, Catherine (1957–)

BIRTHPLACE: England.
TELEVISION: *Hammer House of Mystery and Suspense*: "Czech Mate," 1985 (Marie Vladekova)

BIOGRAPHY—A British character actress who was active on stage, films and television from 1970 through 1994, she has a small featured role in the "Czech Mate" episode of *Hammer House of Mystery and Suspense* as a mysterious foreign agent whose alleged resemblance to star Susan George makes her a key plot device in this Cold War thriller.

Other genre credits: FILMS: *Biggles: Adventures in Time*, Compact Yellowbill, 1986 (Young Nun) TELEVISION: *Doomwatch*: "Hear No Evil," 1970 (Woman)

Nelmes, Judith

FILM: *Dracula*, 1958 (Woman in Coach; scenes deleted)
Other genre credits: TELEVISION: *The Quatermass Experiment*: 1953 (Cinemagoer's Friend)

Nelson, Julia

FILM: *The Revenge of Frankenstein*, 1958 (Inga)

Nesbitt, Sally (1938–)

REAL NAME: Sally Hunt; BIRTHPLACE: Darjeeling, West Bengal, British India.
FILM: *The Gorgon*, 1964 (Nurse)
Other genre credits: TELEVISION: *The Avengers*: "The Joker," 1967 (Ola Monsey-Chamberlain); "Bizarre," 1969 (Helen Pritchard)

Newell, Joan Megan (1921–)

BIRTHPLACE: Hove, Sussex, England.
FILM: *Journey to the Unknown*, 1969 (Mrs. Plimmer)
TELEVISION: *Journey to the Unknown*: "The Last Visitor," 1969 (Mrs. Plimmer)

Newman, Nanette (1934–)

BIRTHPLACE: Northampton, England.
FILMS: *Journey into Darkness*, 1969 (Jill Collins); *Man at the Top*, 1973 (Lady Alex Ackerman)
TELEVISION: *Journey to the Unknown*: "Paper Dolls," 1968 (Jill Collins)
Other genre credits: FILMS: *House of Mystery*, Independent Artists, 1961 (Joan Trevor); *Captain Nemo and the Underwater City*, Omnia Pictures, 1969 (Helena Beckett); *The Stepford Wives*, Fadsin Cinema Associates, 1975 (Carol Van Sant)

Nicholson, Veronica

FILM: *Rasputin, the Mad Monk*, 1966 (Young Girl)

Noel, Danielle

FILM: *The Vengeance of She*, 1968 (Sharna)
Other genre credits: FILM: *Bedazzled*, Stanley Donen Films/20th Century–Fox, 1967 (Avarice)

Noone, Nora-Jane (1984–)

BIRTHPLACE: Newcastle, Galway, Ireland.
FILM: *Beyond the Rave*, 2008 (Jen)
BIOGRAPHY—A beautiful Irish actress, Noone trained at the Performing Arts School and is best known for her award-winning first role in *The Magdalene Sisters* (2002). She has also

appeared in a number of genre films, including the first production from the newly reincarnated Hammer, *Beyond the Rave*, which was not actually a film *per se* but released in "webisodes" of an online serial intended to "recalibrate the DNA of Hammer Films for a new audience." This it did, basically by recalibrating *Dracula A.D. 1972*'s vampire(s) vs. hipsters storyline. Noone does well in portraying the inherent shallowness of the "rave culture" (which was simply another name for getting blotto), and recalibrating the role of the Hammer Heroine as well; she's stronger-minded and more independent, decapitating vampires as easily as she is seduced by them (no recalibration there, then).

Other genre credits: FILMS: *The Descent*, Celador Films, 2005 (Holly); *Doomsday*, Rogue Pictures, 2008 (Read); *Insatiable*, Kirbyfilms, 2008 (Ellie); *Legend of the Bog*, Bog Body Films, 2009 (Saiorse Reilly); *The Descent Part 2*, Celador Films, 2009 (Holly) TELEVISION: *Afterlife*: "Roadside Bouquets," 2006 (Tessa); *The Day of the Triffids*: Episodes 1 & 2, 2009 (Lucy)

Nowag, Lilian M.

FILM: *Creatures the World Forgot*, 1971 (Prehistoric Woman)

O'Brien, Glenys

FILM: *The Horror of Frankenstein*, 1970 (Maggie)
Other genre credits: FILM: *Thirst*, F.G. Film Productions, 1979 (Guide)

O'Brien, Maria

FILM: *When Dinosaurs Ruled the Earth*, 1970 (Omah)
Other genre credits: TELEVISION: *Doomwatch*: "Say Knife, Fat Man," "Cause of Death," 1972 (Susan Proud)

O'Brien, Siobhan

FILM: *Wake Wood*, 2011 (Pharmacy Customer)

O'Mara, Kate (1939–)

REAL NAME: Frances M. Carroll; BIRTHPLACE: Leicester, England.
FILMS: *The Vampire Lovers*, 1970 (Madame Perrodon); *The Horror of Frankenstein*, 1970 (Alys)

BIOGRAPHY—Like her co-star in *The Horror of Frankenstein*, Veronica Carlson, Kate O'Mara's father was in the RAF (as flying instructor); her mother was actress Hazel (*London's Burning*) Bainbridge. From boarding school, she went to art school and then on to acting, securing roles in movies, plays and television. Her smoldering, raven-haired beauty got her noticed by Hammer, where she made her first appearance as the governess, Mme. Perrodon, in *The Vampire Lovers*. Although a supporting role, it is apparently written so that at times Mme. Perrodon seems as mysterious as Carmilla (Ingrid Pitt) and her seduction by that character is one of the film's most highly charged, erotic moments. Her death scene is equally charged, her dark eyes begging for Carmilla's love, only to receive death for her devotion. The scene, belied by how it plays on screen, was also apparently charged with something else — laughter, as Ingrid's fangs kept falling into O'Mara's cleavage. Of course, many stagehands volunteered to remove them from said cleavage, but of course the ladies had the situation well in hand — if not in mouth.

Her success in the role prompted Hammer to offer her a contract, which she turned down, for fear of being typecast (a not uncommon phobia among actors); but it was nothing

Kate O'Mara, Kirsten Betts, Pippa Steel and Madeline Smith pay their respects to Ingrid Pitt in *The Vampire Lovers*.

personal, and she went on to make *The Horror of Frankenstein* for them, and was almost Sister Hyde (Martine Beswicke got the role, because of her stronger facial resemblance to co-star Ralph Bates). It was opposite Bates as Frankenstein that O'Mara played one of her most indelible roles, as Alys in the parodic "remake" of *The Curse of Frankenstein*. She is essentially playing the Justine character, but much expanded: instead of keeping a low profile and engaging in the occasional discreet nuzzling with Herr Baron, Alys is the star of the picture, a cunning, conniving, bold and brassy sexual animal who meets the same fate as Justine, but in much more spectacular and lurid fashion.

Her role as Alys was a virtual blueprint for her most famous role (at least to Americans) in later years, that of fellow former Hammer Films alum Joan Collins' sister in *Dynasty*. She also made her mark as the Rani in *Doctor Who*, and is still active on television and stage, founding her own touring company and even finding time to write two books. A strict vegetarian and animal rights activist, she is still a striking woman who says she would not hesitate in the least to pose for *Playboy*.

Other genre credits: FILMS: *Beauty and the Beast*, Bevanfield Films, 1992 (Voice of Lucinda) TELEVISION: *The Avengers*: "Stay Tuned," 1969 (Lisa); *Doctor Who*: "The Mark of the Rani," 1985; "Time and the Rani," 1987 (The Rani); *Doctor Who: Dimensions in Time*: 1993 (The Rani)

O'Neil, Colette (1937–)

BIRTHPLACE: Glasgow, Scotland.
FILM: *Frankenstein Must Be Destroyed*, 1969 (Mad Woman)
Other genre credits: TELEVISION: *Mystery and Imagination*: "The Listener," 1968 (Emily); *Thriller*: "Come Out, Come Out, Wherever You Are," 1974 (Alice Lewis); *Doctor Who*: "Snakedance," 1983 (Tanha)

Oo-Bla-Da Dancers

FILM: *She*, 1965 (Native Dancers)

Osborne, Alexia

FILM: *The Woman in Black*, 2012 (Victoria Hardy)
Other genre credits: FILM: *Dark Shadows*, Dan Curtis Productions, 2012 (Young Victoria Winters)

O'Shannon, Finnuala

FILM: *The Satanic Rites of Dracula*, 1973 (Vampire Girl)

Oxenford, Daphne (1919–)

BIRTHPLACE: Barnet, London, England.
FILM: *Frankenstein Must Be Destroyed*, 1969 (Lady in Garden)
Other genre credits: TELEVISION: *Doctor Who*: "Dragonfire," Part 2, 1987 (Archivist)

Pagett, Nicola (1945–)

REAL NAME: Nicola Mary Scott; BIRTHPLACE: Cairo, Egypt.
FILM: *The Viking Queen*, 1967 (Talia)
BIOGRAPHY—British character actress Nicola Pagett studied for two years at RADA and made her first television appearance in 1964. In *The Viking Queen*, her first feature film, she plays Talia, a girl who is raped by a Roman, giving Carita the incentive she needs to lead her Britons in all-out revolution (as if Carita's being horsewhipped, nude, in public wasn't enough). Pagett went on to a substantial career, one that was almost derailed by manic depression; she chronicled her struggles with the disease in her book *Diamonds Behind My Eyes*.

Other genre credits: TELEVISION: *The Avengers*: "Have Guns—Will Haggle," 1968 (Lady Adriana Beardsley); *Frankenstein: The True Story* (Movie), 1973 (Elizabeth)

Palmer, June (1940–2004)

BIRTHPLACE: London, England.
FILM: *Taste the Blood of Dracula*, 1970 (Prostitute)
BIOGRAPHY— Stunningly beautiful and buxom June Palmer began modeling in her teens, and got her start in the adult entertainment industry as a topless dancer. She soon began appearing in pictorials in men's magazines and 8mm nudie films for George Harrison Marks (who stopped using the first name when you-know-who got famous). In the 1960s, Palmer became one of the most popular pin-up models on either side of the Atlantic. She and the man who would become her husband opened Strobe Studios for both professional and amateur photographers and also provided models for them. She has a small (but visually memorable) part in *Taste the Blood of Dracula* as a red-headed prostitute (she was employed strictly as human set decoration). She died suddenly in 2004.

Palmer, Maria (1917–1981)

REAL NAME: Maria Pichler; BIRTHPLACE: Vienna, Austria-Hungary.
FILM: *The Evil of Frankenstein*, 1964 (Rena's Mother in Additional U.S. Sequence)
Other genre credits: TELEVISION: *Rocky Jones, Space Ranger*: "Crash of the Moons" (Episodes 1, 2 and 3), 1954 (Cotanda/Colenda); *One Step Beyond*: "The Secret," 1959 (Sylvia Ackroyd); *World of Giants*: "Panic in 3-B," 1959 (Woman)

Parfitt, Judy (1935–)

BIRTHPLACE: Sheffield, West Riding of Yorkshire, England.
FILM: *Journey to Murder*, 1971 (Faith Wheeler)
TELEVISION: *Journey to the Unknown*: "Do Me a Favor and Kill Me," 1968 (Faith Wheeler)
BIOGRAPHY— A British leading lady and character actress, vivacious Judy Parfitt attended RADA, made her stage debut in 1954 and her first television show eight years later. In her episode of *Journey to the Unknown*, she plays the wife of has-been film star Joseph Cotten (*The Third Man*, *The Abominable Dr. Phibes*), who decides to end it all and hires a man to kill him. Things become complicated when he rethinks his decision, only to find out that he can't communicate that decision to his would-be killer. She is still active.
Other genre credits: TELEVISION: *Out of the Unknown*: "Time in Advance," 1965 (Marie); *The Avengers*: "Bullseye," 1962 (Doreen Ellis); "The White Elephant," 1964 (Brenda Paterson); "Escape in Time," 1967 (Vesta); "Whoever Shot Poor George Oblique Stroke XR40?" 1968 (Loris); *Alice Through the Looking Glass* (Movie), 1973 (The Red Queen)

Parsons, Alibe

TELEVISION: *Hammer House of Mystery and Suspense*: "Mark of the Devil," 1984 (Momma Rose)
Other genre credits: FILMS: *Biggles: Adventures in Time*, Compact Yellowbill, 1986 (Maxine Fine); *Aliens*, 20th Century–Fox, 1986 (Med Tech) TELEVISION: *Space: 1999*: "Devil's Planet," "The Immunity Syndrome," "The Dorcons," 1977 (Alibe); *Doctor Who*: "The Trial of a Time Lord" (Parts 5, 6, 7, 8), 1986 (Matrona Kani)

Paul-Podlasky, Christine (1948–)

REAL NAME: Krystyna Podleska; BIRTHPLACE: London, England.
FILM: *Vampire Circus*, 1972 (Rosa)
BIOGRAPHY— A lovely British character actress of Polish extraction, Paul-Podlasky made her debut in 1970. Soon thereafter she played Rosa, the burgomaster's daughter, in *Vampire*

Circus, where she gets rubbed up by Anthony Corlan and becomes his slave. In 1977, she reclaimed her heritage and moved back to Poland, and since then she has only appeared in Polish films.

Pavlovic, Drina (1953–)

BIRTHPLACE: Derby, England.
FILM: *Vampire Circus*, 1972 (Schoolgirl)

Payne, Natalie

TELEVISION: *Hammer House of Horror*: "Children of the Full Moon," 1980 (Irenya)

Payton, Barbara (1927–1967)

REAL NAME: Barbara Lee Redfield; BIRTHPLACE: Cloquet, Minnesota, USA
FILMS: *The Flanagan Boy* (a.k.a. *Bad Blonde*), 1953 (Lorna Vecchi); *Four Sided Triangle*, 1953 (Lena/Helen)
BIOGRAPHY—Blonde bombshell Barbara Payton's story is one of the saddest in this or any other book, even her own (defiantly titled *I Am Not Ashamed*). Born to unassuming, hardy Midwestern parents, she became aware of her sexuality early on, and married when she was 16. The marriage was soon annulled, but the next year she was married again, and began to cultivate not only a modeling career but a reputation in Hollywood as a girl who liked to have fun, fun, fun. She got her big break in *Kiss Tomorrow Goodbye* with James Cagney, and scored roles in a couple of other high-profile productions, but her ever-increasing excess and affairs with a goodly number of Hollywood stars led to a loss of credibility and torpedoed her career almost as quickly as it had begun. She was soon reduced to appearing in low-budget fare such as *Bride of the Gorilla* and the early Hammer films. They too took a seemingly somewhat sadistic pleasure in exploiting her "bad girl" image, such as the title of the noir *Bad Blonde*, or even the opening narration of *Four-Sided Triangle*, in which the description of her character is uncomfortably close to Payton's own life. Unfortunately, neither *Bad Blonde* nor *Four-Sided Triangle* would anything to reverse the downward slide of her career. Often cited as a pioneering science fiction–horror for Hammer, *Four-Sided Triangle* is that and little else. Payton does well in the role as Lena *and* as an exact clone created in a duplicating machine, giving one person two personalities that are still yet the same; this was an ample display of the talent going to waste. She slid into drugs and alcohol, even prostitution, and had many run-ins with the law. In 1967, she moved back in with her parents, and died in their home later that year.
Other genre credits: FILM: *Bride of the Gorilla*, Jack Broder Productions, 1951 (Dina Van Gelder)

Peake, Lisa (1935–2000)

FILM: *She*, 1965 (Night Club Dancer)
Other genre credits: TELEVISION: *The Avengers*: "Kill the King," 1961 (Mei Li); "The Golden Fleece," 1963 (Esther Jones)

Pearce, Jacqueline (1943–)

BIRTHPLACE: Woking, Surrey, England.
FILMS: *The Plague of the Zombies*, 1966 (Alice Mary Tompson); *The Reptile*, 1966 (Anna Franklyn, the Reptile)
BIOGRAPHY—A beautiful, haunting presence in Hammer's "Cornwall Classics" *The Reptile* and *The Plague of the Zombies*, Jacqueline Pearce was abandoned by her mother at a young

age. Her father sent her to be raised in a convent, where she says she learned little more than how to despise organized religion. After the convent she, in her own words, drifted into the decadent world of drama via RADA. Her first role was a bit part in the cult favorite television series *Dangerman* (*Secret Agent* in the U.S.), followed by several more bits before landing her first lead roles at Hammer. The first of those was her part as the doomed Alice Mary Tompson in *The Plague of the Zombies*. Although billed below Diane Clare, it is Jacqueline's picture all the way, from her very first appearance on screen: She is asleep, under the influence of the voodoo, when blood begins to flow from her bandaged wrist, whereupon she sits up and screams into the camera. She is consequently in many of the most striking compositions and integral shock moments: her midnight stroll through the forest, pausing long enough to be framed by one of the huge iron gear wheels; her murder at the hands of an unseen zombie; the subsequent dumping of her corpse at the feet of Clare, by the maniacally laughing zombie; her transformation into a zombie, eyes popping open in un-life (again, directly at the audience), and her subsequent beheading. The Laughing Zombie scene, as effective in its own way as the later "rising from the grave" nightmare, does feature two small inconsistencies: The zombie laughs, but at no other time do the zombies make any sort of sound, even when they're on fire (perhaps it could be argued that they don't feel it since they're dead, but then, they really couldn't "feel" any other emotions). The second is when the zombie dumps the dead Alice down the hill in front of Sylvia, and she understandably screams. But then when they find Alice's body after it has been moved, she screams as if it's the first time she's seen the corpse. It must be added that these in no way detract from the overall power of the film, one of Hammer's finest ever and, in its own way, as much of an influence on the modern zombie movie as *Night of the Living Dead*.

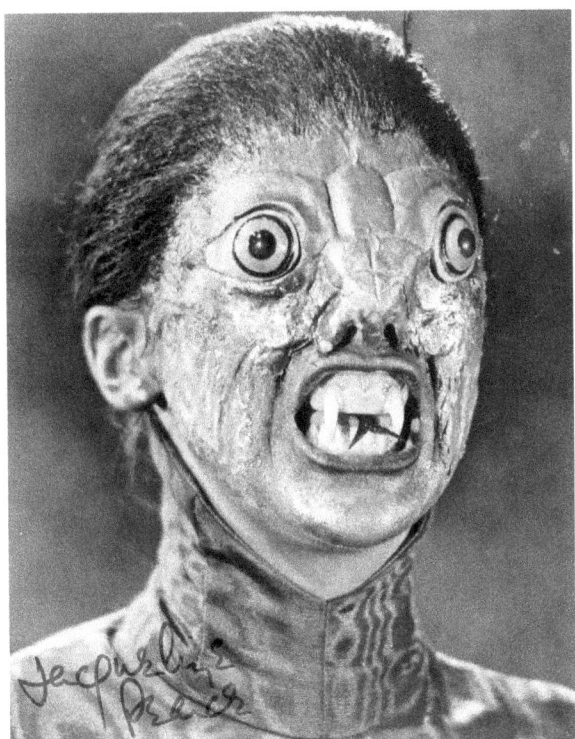

Jacqueline Pearce in *The Reptile*.

Jacqueline's character of Anna Franklyn in *The Reptile* is even more haunted and tragic than the one in *The Plague of the Zombies*. Unlike Barbara Shelley in *The Gorgon*, she is aware from the very first that she is the monster, and that knowledge is crushing her, just as her father is crushed by the knowledge that it is through his actions that she has become this creature. But instead of engendering sympathy (either from the audience or for himself for his daughter's plight), he is instead hateful and domineering; protective of his daughter to a degree but ultimately even more of a monster than she. This is acutely illustrated in the scene where he and Anna have the Spaldings as house guests, and Anna plays the sitar for them. She not only comes to life but, as her playing becomes more and more frantic, visibly erotically charged, at which point her father makes like Pete Townshend and obliterates the instrument. She is equally effective as the Reptile, striking at her victims like the snake she is, infecting them with the hideous "Black Death." Her makeup (by Roy Ashton) is unique, one of the most aesthetically satisfying in the history of Hammer. She even quickly and frequently flicks her tongue in and out like a snake, which is both very creepy and, in a perverse way, almost as erotically charged as her sitar playing. Hammer's most underrated film, *The Reptile* was an attempt to create a new, original monster, and at this it succeeded.

Eleven years after her two roles for Hammer, she scored another part for which she is fondly remembered, the cruel Servalan in the cult science-fiction television classic *Blake's 7*, about which she made her famous comment: "I'd been a masturbatory fantasy for an entire generation of young men. I mean, that made a girl feel good." But she ultimately felt unsatisfied by the business, and now spends most of her time at a preserve in the African Bush tending monkeys. She survived a bout with breast cancer, but at the time of this writing, the cancer has resurfaced, and she says she has decided to let nature take its course. Like fellow breast cancer sufferer Ingrid Pitt, Pearce has always been very much her own woman, and a brave one, and like Ingrid, should serve as an inspiration to us all.

Other genre credits: TELEVISION: *The Avengers*: "A Sense of History," 1966 (Marianne Gray); *Haunted*: "I Like It Here," 1967 (Jenny Brice); *Dead of Night*: "Bedtime," 1972 (Sarah Hopkirk); *Blake's 7*: "Seek — Locate — Destroy," "Project Avalon," "Deliverance," "Orac," 1978; "Weapon," "Pressure Point," "Trial," "Hostage," "Voice from the Past," "Gambit," "The Keeper," "Star One," 1979; "Aftermath," "Powerplay," "Volcano," "The Harvest of Kairos," "Children of Auron," "Rumors of Death," "Moloch," "Deathwatch," "Terminal," 1980; "Traitor," "Animals," "Assassins," "Games," "Sand," "Gold," "Orbit," "Warlord," 1981 (Servalan); *Leap in the Dark*: "The Ghost of Ardachie Lodge," 1977 (Dorothy McEwan); *Doctor Who*: "The Two Doctors" (Parts 1, 2 and 3), 1985 (Chessene); *Dark Season*: Episodes 4, 5 and 6, 1991 (Miss Pendragon); *The Young Indiana Jones Chronicles*: "Paris, October 1916," 1993 (Annabelle Levi)

Pearl, Elna

TELEVISION: *Journey to the Unknown*: "Eve," 1968 (Girl in Cinema)

Peart, Pauline (1951–)

FILMS: *The Satanic Rites of Dracula*, 1973 (Vampire Girl); *Man About the House*, 1974 (Secretary)

BIOGRAPHY — Exotically sexy Pauline Peart has a very flashy, thrilling part in *The Satanic Rites of Dracula* as one of the vampire girls in the basement of Dracula's disciples. They give Joanna Lumley a rough go of it before having their hissing, fiery performances cut short by the sprinkler system. She made a few other films, the bulk of them in the 1970s, including one other appearance for Hammer (the comedy *Man About the House*). Others included *Carry On, Girls*, *Nobody Ordered Love* with Ingrid Pitt, and *Cuba* with Ingrid's country club pal, Sean Connery. She appeared on television once in the 1980s and once in the 1990s.

Perry, Anna

TELEVISION: *Hammer House of Horror*: "The House That Bled to Death," 1980 (Journalist)

Other genre credits: TELEVISION: *Out of the Unknown*: "Liar," 1969 (Secretary)

Peters, Jo

FILM: *To the Devil a Daughter*, 1976 (Third Girl)

Peters, Luan; a.k.a. Karol Keyes (1946–)

REAL NAME: Carol Hirsch; BIRTHPLACE: Bethnal Green, London, England.

FILMS: *Lust for a Vampire*, 1971 (Trudi); *Twins of Evil*, 1971 (Gerta)

BIOGRAPHY—After winning a drama scholarship at age 16, beautiful Luan Peters began making records under the name Karol Keyes. Her earliest screen appearances were also under this name; the first was *Dixon of Dock Green* (1967). Her role as a serving wench in Hammer's *Lust for a Vampire* is so small as to barely rate a mention, and unlike a multitude of girls in the film who do so, she does not get her kit off. But oh, how that would change in her next, the third installment of the Karnstein Trilogy, *Twins of Evil*, when she played the willing participant in the count's debauchery, up to and including letting herself be chained to a wall for what she thinks will be some girl-girl action with Frieda, with the unexpected climax of Frieda sinking her fangs into her heaving, sweaty bosom. She also appeared in *Fawlty Towers* as well as two different *Doctor Who* serials, seven years apart. Her last film *Pacific Banana* was released in 1981, and her last TV appearance was in 1989.

Other genre credits: FILMS: *The Flesh and Blood Show*, Peter Walker (Heritage) Limited, 1972 (Carol Edwards); *Old Dracula*, World Film Services, 1975 (Secretary); *Land of the Minotaur*, Getty Pictures, 1976 (Laurie Gordon) TELEVISION: *Doctor Who*: "The Macra Terror" (Part 4), 1967 (Chicki Catchetorie); "Frontier in Space" (Part 3), 1973 (Sheila)

Peters, Petra (1925–2004)

BIRTHPLACE: Remscheid, Germany.

FILM: *To the Devil a Daughter*, 1976 (Sister Helle)

Phillips, Michelle (1944–)

REAL NAME: Holly Michelle Gilliam; BIRTHPLACE: Long Beach, California, USA.

TELEVISION: *Hammer House of Mystery and Suspense*: "Paint Me a Murder," 1985 (Sandra Lorenz)

BIOGRAPHY—The archetypal California girl, gorgeous Michelle Phillips was born to a merchant marine and an accountant. She married John Phillips at 18 and soon found worldwide fame as a member of the Mamas and the Papas. (She co-wrote their biggest hit, "California Dreamin'.") After divorcing Phillips, she married Dennis Hopper for eight days, and made her acting debut in his *The Last Movie*. In 1985, she starred in a very EC Comics–like episode of *Hammer House of Mystery and Suspense*, "Paint Me a Murder," in which she plays the wife of an artist. She decides that he will be more famous if he's dead, so they cook up a plot to keep him hidden and still producing "old" paintings. Things get complicated when she falls in love with an art dealer, and they cook up their own plot to make him *dead*-dead. She's calculating and tough, and suitably distraught when her plans go awry. Phillips has written her autobiography, is still active in both acting and music, and is a member of the Rock and Roll Hall of Fame and the Vocal Group Hall of Fame.

Other genre credits: TELEVISION: *Alfred Hitchcock Presents*: "If Looks Could Kill," 1988 (Katherine Clark); *Star Trek: The Next Generation*: "We'll Always Have Paris," 1988 (Janice Manheim); *Lois & Clark: The New Adventures of Superman*: "Target: Jimmy Olsen," 1995 (Claudette Wilder)

Phillips, Sian (1933–)

REAL NAME: Jane Elizabeth Ailwen Philips; BIRTHPLACE: Gwaun-Cae-Gurwen, Glamorgan, Wales.

TELEVISION: *Hammer House of Horror*: "The Carpathian Eagle," 1980 (Mrs. Henska)

BIOGRAPHY— Sian Phillips began her career at age 11 with BBC Radio Wales and trained at RADA. She appeared in such major productions as *Becket* and *Goodbye, Mr. Chips* and won a BAFTA Award for her work in *I, Claudius*. Her regal bearing served her well in her *Hammer House of Horror* episode, "The Carpathian Eagle," in which she plays the next-to-last relative of a notorious countess whose story is a thinly disguised version of the Elizabeth Bathory legend. (*Countess Dracula* did the same thing, and an allusion is made to the earlier film when one of the characters suggests that a "Lady Dracula" is responsible for a recent spate of bloody murders.) Two years after this, she appeared with the star of *Countess Dracula*, Ingrid Pitt, in the *Smiley's People* mini-series. Phillips, also an author, is still active in her profession as well as the posh seniors dating organization Social, Welsh and Sexy.

Other genre credits: FILMS: *Clash of the Titans*, MGM, 1981 (Cassiopeia); *Flash Gordon*, De Laurentiis, 1984 (The Reverend Mother Gaius Helen Mohiam); *The Doctor and the Devils*, Brooksfilms, 1985 (Annabelle Rock) TELEVISION: *Tales of the Unexpected*: "Back for Christmas," 1980 (Hermione); *Ewoks: The Battle for Endor* (Movie), 1985 (Charal); *The Snow Spider* (Movie), 1988 (Nain Griffiths); *Alice Through the Looking Glass* (Movie), 1998 (The Red Queen); *Cinderella* (Movie), 2000 (The Evil Baroness)

Pinkney, Lynn

TELEVISION: *Journey to the Unknown*: "Matakitas Is Coming," 1968 (Sylvia Ann Hahlen)

Pitt, Ingrid (1937–2010)

REAL NAME: Ingoushka Petrov; BIRTHPLACE: Warsaw, Poland.

FILMS: *The Vampire Lovers*, 1970 (Carmilla/Mircalla/Marcilla Karnstein); *Countess Dracula*, 1971 (Countess Elizabeth Nadasdy); *Beyond the Rave*, 2008 (Tooley's Mother)

BIOGRAPHY— Ingrid Pitt's real life was like a movie: comedy mixed with tragedy, happiness mixed with heartbreak and horror. Her career began in Spain, and she soon graduated to the ranks of "A" films with bit parts in *Doctor Zhivago* and *A Funny Thing Happened on the Way to the Forum*. With her featured role in the Clint Eastwood–Richard Burton action classic *Where Eagles Dare*, she seemed set for major-league stardom, but fate decreed otherwise. Had she attained that level of stardom, she likely never would have given horror movie fans two of the most indelible portraits in the annals of those movies.

She starred in *The Vampire Lovers*, the definitive screen adaptation of J. Sheridan LeFanu's classic "Carmilla." A number of films have tackled the story since, but the other films have taken the central themes and made them bloodier, or the lesbianism and/or nudity have been made more explicit than in *The Vampire Lovers*; none have been able to match the sheer class and beauty of Hammer's version. And they lack the central element that made it all work in the first place: Ingrid herself. She is haunting and haunted; at times, seemingly completely vulnerable; at others, commanding, cunning, a terrible force of nature.

She brought those same qualities to her performance in the title role of *Countess Dracula*, which had nothing to do with Hammer's Dracula series and everything to do with the "Blood Countess," Elizabeth Bathory. Pitt being an authority on Bathory, one of her major complaints was that the film wasn't nearly bloody enough—but once again, even though films that followed, up to the present day, certainly rectified that aspect (to mostly ridiculous extremes), they failed to find the balance between the gore and the gravitas that Hammer had perfected. They also failed to find any actress who could bring the kind of commanding presence to the role that Pitt did.

Pitt wasn't able to capitalize on her successes at Hammer. Despite more triumphs in *The House That Dripped Blood* and *The Wicker Man*, a failing marriage of convenience to an extremely powerful member of the British film industry got her blacklisted at the height of her career. More than anything else, though, Pitt was a survivor, and she survived the blacklisting, but breast cancer and ovarian cancer, and she made more movies, including a link-to-the-past, blink-and-miss-it cameo in Hammer's return to horror, *Beyond the Rave*. She also carved out a new career for herself as an accomplished author. She never stopped fighting for her family, herself, and what she thought was right, but then came the tragic day when she could fight no more, at least physically, and Ingrid left us, and left her family, her friends, and her countless fans with a void in our hearts that will never be filled. Besos, Ingrid.

Other genre credits: FILMS: *Sound of Horror*, Zurbano Films, 1966 (Sofia Minelli); *The Omegans*, W. Lee Wilder Productions, 1968 (Linda); *The House That Dripped Blood*, Amicus Productions, 1971 (Carla); *The Wicker Man*, British Lion Film Corporation, 1973 (The Librarian); *Octopussy*, United Artists/Eon Productions, 1983 (Voice of Galley Mistress); *Underworld* (a.k.a. *Transmutations*) Limehouse Productions, 1985 (Pepperdyne); *The Asylum*, Nunhead Films, 2000 (Isabella); *Greenfingers* (Short), Big H Productions, 2000 (Mrs. Bowen); *Dominator*, Renga Media, 2003 (Voice of Lady Violator); *Minotaur*, First Look International, 2006 (The Leper); *Sea of Dust*, 309 Productions, 2008 (Anna) TELEVISION: *Thriller*: "Where the Action Is," 1975 (Ilse); *Artemis 81* (Movie), 1981 (Hitchcock Blonde); *Doctor Who*: "The Time Monster" (Parts 5 & 6) 1972 (Queen Galleia of Atlantis); "Warriors of the Deep" (Parts 1, 2 and 3), 1984 (Dr. Solow); *Urban Gothic*: "Vampirology," 2000 (Herself)

Pockett, Christine

FILM: *The Vengeance of She*, 1968 (Dancing Girl)

Christine Pockett does the hippy-hippy shake in *The Vengeance of She*.

Poole, Jackie

FILM: *Dr. Jekyll and Sister Hyde*, 1971 (Margie)

Pooley, Kirstie

TELEVISION: *Hammer House of Mystery and Suspense*: "The Corvini Inheritance," 1985 (First Female Model)

BIOGRAPHY—Pretty British character actress Pooley was active from 1971 through 1989.

Other genre credits: TELEVISION: *Star Maidens*: "What Have They Done to the Rain?" 1976 (Guard); *Tales of the Unexpected*: "The Vorpal Blade," 1983 (Eva)

Portell, Petula

FILM: *Dr. Jekyll and Sister Hyde*, 1971 (Petra)

Porter, Sarah

TELEVISION: *Hammer House of Mystery and Suspense*: "In Possession," 1985 (Daughter)

Other genre credits: TELEVISION: *Thriller*: "Won't Write Home, Mum, I'm Dead," 1975 (Emma); *Worlds Beyond*: "Undying Love," 1987 (Woman)

Posta, Adrienne (1948–)

REAL NAME: Adrienne Poster; BIRTHPLACE: England.

TELEVISION: *Journey to the Unknown*: "Miss Belle," 1968 (Girl)

BIOGRAPHY—Sexy Adrienne Posta is a British character actress and singer who plays a small role in *Journey to the Unknown* as the girl who sleeps with George Maharis, thereby sending the insane Barbara Jefford into another rage. Posta is semi-retired now, splitting her time between acting and teaching, both at the Midlands and the Italia Conti Academy of Theatre Arts.

Other genre credits: TELEVISION: *The Witches' Brew*: Episodes 13 and 14, 1973 (The Pink Witch); *Red Dwarf*: "Ouroboros," 1979 (Voice of Flight Announcer)

Power, Sandra

FILM: *The Nanny*, 1965 (Sarah)

Powers, Stefanie (1942–)

REAL NAME: Stefania Zofia Federkiewicz; BIRTHPLACE: Hollywood, California, USA.

FILMS: *Fanatic* (a.k.a. *Die! Die! My Darling!*) 1965 (Patricia Carroll); *Crescendo*, 1970 (Susan Roberts)

TELEVISION: *Journey to the Unknown*: "Jane Brown's Body," 1968 (Jane Brown/Jane Glenville)

BIOGRAPHY—Vivacious American beauty Stefanie Powers graduated from Hollywood High to become one of the country's busiest and most popular television actresses. Her sporadic film career (she made none from 1979 through 2006) gave her two starring roles in Hammer productions, as well as in an episode of their first television series. Being an American, she is portrayed as naturally more self-assured and independent. She exhibits these quantities in spades in *Fanatic*, and survives in the climax, she *is* ultimately the victim — of fellow American Tallulah Bankhead, who leaves no piece of scenery unchewed. An Olympic swimmer, she also exhibits her prowess in an attempted escape scene, and the athleticism displayed was reportedly a major factor in securing her the role of April Dancer in TV's *The Girl from U.N.C.L.E.* the following year. Her role in *Journey to the Unknown* was decidedly different, in a Frankensteinian story about a girl who is raised from the dead. She gives an affecting performance as a woman trying to come to grips with a new life, after she has taken her own and can't remember why. Two years later saw the last of her Hammer performances, in the "*déjà vu* all over again" *Crescendo*, again at the mercy of Margaretta Scott, widow of a famous musician, who wants to continue the family line by mating Powers with her insane son (one of a pair of twins played by *Moon Zero Two*'s James Olson)! This being the dawn of the '70s, the sleazy angle of heroin addiction is introduced, as well as the by-now *de rigueur* nudity, and Powers shows she is not above the notion by getting her kit off. The film was not nearly as satisfying as the previous go-around, nor as successful, and Powers went on to find her greatest fame as Jennifer Hart in the mystery series *Hart to Hart*. She is still quite active, both artistically and personally; she is president of the William Holden Wildlife Foundation and director of the Mount Kenya Game Ranch in Kenya, as well as being involved with both the Cincinnati and Atlanta zoos, and has a star on the Hollywood Walk of Fame.

Other genre credits: FILM: *Experiment in Terror*, Columbia Pictures, 1962 (Toby Sherwood) TELEVISION: *The Girl from U.N.C.L.E.*: "The Dog-Gone Affair," "The Prisoner of Zalamar Affair," "The Mother Muffin Affair," "The Mata Hari Affair," "The Montori Device Affair," "The Horns of the Dilemma Affair," "The Danish Blue Affair," "The Garden of Evil Affair," "The Atlantis Affair," "The Paradise Lost Affair," "The Lethal Eagle Affair," "The Romany Lie Affair," "The Little John Doe Affair," "The Jewels of Topango Affair," "The Faustus Affair," 1966; "The U.F.O. Affair," "The Moulin Ruse Affair," "The Catacomb and Dogma Affair," "The Drublegratz Affair," "The Fountain of Youth Affair," "The Carpathian Killer Affair," "The Furnace Flats Affair," "The Low Blue C Affair," "The Petite Prix Affair," "The Phi Beta Killer Affair," "The Double-O-Nothing Affair," "The U.N.C.L.E. Samurai Affair," "The High and Deadly Affair," "The Kooky Spook Affair," 1967 (April Dancer); *The Sixth Sense*: "Echo of a Distant Scream," "If I Should Die Before I Wake," 1972 (Paula Norris); *Topper Returns* (Movie), 1973 (Marian Kerby); *The Six Million Dollar Man*: "The Secret of Bigfoot," 1976, "The Return of Bigfoot," 1976 (Shalon); *The Bionic Woman*: "The Return of Bigfoot," 1976 (Shalon)

Prador, Irene (1911–1996)

REAL NAME: Irene Peiser; BIRTHPLACE: Vienna, Austria.

FILMS: *The Snorkel*, 1958 (French Woman); *To the Devil a Daughter*, 1976 (German Matron)

TELEVISION: *Hammer House of Mystery and Suspense*: "Last Video and Testament," 1984 (Hotel Guest)

Other genre credits: TELEVISION: *Doomwatch*: "The Logicians," 1972 (Mrs. Wilhelmina Grantz); *So Haunt Me*: Episode 14, 1994 (Mrs. Goldfarb)

Pravda, Hana (1918–2008)

REAL NAME: Hana Beckova; BIRTHPLACE: Prague, Austria-Hungary.

FILM: *And Soon the Darkness*, Associated British Pictures Corporation, 1970 (Madame Lassal)

TELEVISION: *Hammer House of Mystery and Suspense*: "Czech Mate," 1985 (Mrs. Pircek)

BIOGRAPHY— She may have made only a small contribution to Hammer's legacy, but Hana Pravda is a true Hammer Heroine. The actress was trained in Leningrad and made her first film in 1933, and several after that. World War II intervened in the most tragic way when she and her activist husband were interred in first the Thereseinstadt and then Auschwitz concentration camps. Like Ingrid Pitt, she survived the camps and the 1945 Death March, but her husband did not. She later resumed her career, which lasted until 2003, and added an episode of *Hammer House of Mystery and Suspense* to her CV, playing the mysterious Mrs. Pircek.

Other genre credits: TELEVISION: *Bram Stoker's Dracula* (Movie), 1974 (Innkeeper's Wife)

Price, Penny

FILM: *Captain Kronos, Vampire Hunter*, 1974 (Whore)

Quinn, Mary

FILM: *Rasputin, the Mad Monk*, 1966 (Innkeeper's Wife)

Quinn, Patricia (1944–)

BIRTHPLACE: Belfast, Northern Ireland.

TELEVISION: *Hammer House of Horror*: "Witching Time," 1980 (Lucinda Jessop)

BIOGRAPHY— Uniquely beautiful Patricia Quinn was the daughter of a well-known bookie. She trained at the British Drama League in Belfast, did repertory and, like Kathryn Leigh Scott, did a stint as a Playboy Bunny. She was just beginning to break into films and television when she was offered her signature role, that of Magenta in "The Rocky Horror Show," and was part of the cast of its very first performance. She reprised the role for the cult-classic film *The Rocky Horror Picture Show*, and was as electrifying as her *Bride of Frankenstein*–inspired hairdo. She brings the same supercharged qualities to her role as a witch, Lucinda Jessop, in the first episode of *Hammer House of Horror*; alternately hilarious (screaming in fright at an operating shower nozzle), terribly sexy (she gets her flimsy kit off quite willingly and leaves scratch marks in a musician's back), very, very evil and altogether absolutely smashing. She's obviously having a wonderful time with the role, and steals the whole show out from under everyone else involved. She appeared in another certified cult classic, Monty Python's *The Meaning of Life*, as well as *I, Claudius* and *Doctor Who*. She's still very active, and in posh circles she's known as Lady Stephens, a title she acquired due to her marriage to the British actor Robert Stephens.

Other genre credits: FILMS: *The Rocky Horror Picture Show*, 20th Century–Fox, 1975 (Magenta); *Shock Treatment*, 20th Century–Fox, 1981 (Dr. Nation McKinley); *Hawk the Slayer*, Incorporated Television Company, 1981 (Sorceress); *Mary Horror*, Weber Pictures, 2011 (Madam Ruth); *The Lords of Salem*, Alliance Films, 2012 (Megan) TELEVISION: *Hallmark Hall of Fame*: "Beauty and the Beast," 1976 (Susan); *Tales of the Unexpected*: "The Stinker," 1980 (Phyl Tinker); *Doctor Who*: "Dragonfire," 1987 (Belazs)

Raffin, Deborah (1953–2012)

BIRTHPLACE: Los Angeles, California, USA.

TELEVISION: *Hammer House of Mystery and Suspense*: "Last Video and Testament," 1984 (Selena Frankham)

BIOGRAPHY— The daughter of actress Trudy Marshall (*Mark of the Gorilla*), and possessor of cheekbones to die for, Deborah Raffin is an American actress, director and producer. Her first role was a bit part in 1973; she didn't really make a splash until a few years later when she was featured, along with her mother, in the trashy *Once Is Not Enough*. She gives a solid performance in the "Last Video and Testament" episode of *Hammer House of Mystery and Suspense* as the cheating young wife of a much older, rich electronics genius; it's a very EC Comics–like tale of sex, lies and videotape. Her Southern accent is a bit shaky but otherwise she's spot on, whether she's slinking on the sly in a black slip or succumbing to her spurned spouse's wall of sound. Her last appearance was in the TV series *The Secret Life of an American Teenager* in 2010. She passed away in 2012.

Other genre credits: FILMS: *God Told Me To*, New World Pictures, 1976 (Casey Forster); *The Sentinel*, Universal Pictures, 1977 (Jennifer); *Dance of the Dwarfs*, Dove, 1984 (Dr. Evelyn Howard); *Grizzly II: The Concert*, 1987 (Samantha Owens); *Scanners II: The New Order*, Allegro Films, 1991 (Julie Vale) TELEVISION: *The Twilight Zone*: "Something in the Walls," 1989 (Sharon Miles)

Raines, Cristina (1952–)

REAL NAME: Tina Herazo; BIRTHPLACE: Manila, Philippines.

TELEVISION: *Hammer House of Mystery and Suspense*: "The Late Nancy Irving," 1985 (Nancy Irving)

BIOGRAPHY—Character actress Raines had a short but substantial career. In the lead role in the *Hammer House of Mystery and Suspense* episode "The Late Nancy Irving" she plays pro golfer Nancy Irving; reports of her death have been greatly exaggerated by a member of the one percent who is keeping her prisoner because she shares the same blood type. She's got game, but the episode doesn't; it's a rather disappointing effort from *Countess Dracula* director Peter Sasdy. She retired in 1991.

Other genre credits: FILMS: *Hex*, Max L. Raab Productions, 1973 (Oriole); *The Sentinel*, Universal Pictures, 1977 (Alison Parker); *Nightmares*, Universal Pictures, 1983 (Lisa) TELEVISION: *Alfred Hitchcock Presents*: "Prisoners," 1985 (Julie Randall)

Raines, Jessica

BIRTHPLACE: Powys, Wales.
FILM: *The Woman in Black*, 2012 (The Nanny)

Randall, Stephanie

FILM: *Slave Girls*, 1967 (Amyak)

BIOGRAPHY—Winsome Stephanie Randall was a British character actress active for only four years, primarily on television; *Slave Girls* was her only feature film. In it she plays the rebellious yet level-headed Amyak, the glue that holds the prehistoric women together until she is chosen as the next White Rhino sacrifice. When the film's "Devils" engage in the selection of a sacrifice, their leader (Martine Beswick) chooses Randall in order to try and kill the head and hope the body follows. (See photograph on page 156.)

Rawlings, Margaret (1906–1996)

BIRTHPLACE: Osaka, Japan.
FILM: *Hands of the Ripper*, 1971 (Madame Bullard)

BIOGRAPHY—Educated at Oxford High School, Margaret Rawlings was one of Britain's most acclaimed stage actresses. She made only 23 film and television appearances; one of those film roles was as Royal Medium Madame Bullard in *Hands of the Ripper*. Unlike the character that Dora Bryan plays, Rawlings's Madame is authentic, and she reveals to Eric Porter that Angharad Rees's daddy was Jack the Ripper. This does nothing to save her from becoming another one of Rees's victims.

Other genre credits: TELEVISION: *Jekyll & Hyde* (Movie), 1990 (Jekyll's Mother)

There's Martine Beswick, on the border of this Mexican lobby card for *Prehistoric Women*, which also features Stephanie Randall (atop the rhinoceros) and Carol White (being womanhandled by Martine).

Raynor, Sheila (1908–1998)

BIRTHPLACE: London, England.
FILMS: *Dead on Course*, 1952 (Nurse); *Demons of the Mind*, 1972 (Old Crone)
BIOGRAPHY— Busy British character actress Raynor had undistinguished bit parts in two Hammer films. She's best remembered by genre fans as the "better" half of Malcolm McDowell's clueless and spineless parents in *A Clockwork Orange*.
Other genre credits: FILMS: *Die, Monster, Die!*, Alta Vista Productions, 1965 (Miss Bailey); *A Clockwork Orange*, Warner Brothers Pictures, 1971 (Mother); *The Omen*, 20th Century–Fox Productions, 1976 (Mrs. Horton) TELEVISION: *Doomwatch*: "The Red Sky" (Mrs. Knott); "Invasion," 1970 (Mrs. Smith)

Read, Dolly (1944–)

REAL NAME: Margaret Reed; a.k.a. Dolly Martin; BIRTHPLACE: Bristol, England.
FILM: *The Kiss of the Vampire*, 1963 (First Disciple)
BIOGRAPHY— Busty British character actress Read was the wife of comedian Dick Martin (*Laugh-In*), and had a short career in movies and television (although, oddly enough, she was never on *Laugh-In*). Her first movie was a Hammer film that was made three years *before* she was a Playmate of the Month (May 1966), *The Kiss of the Vampire*, in which she is shunted into the background as one of the disciples. She was married to Martin twice.

Reardon, Corinna

TELEVISION: *Hammer House of Horror*: "Children of the Full Moon," 1980 (Young Girl)

Redmond, Moira (1928–2006)

BIRTHPLACE: Bognor Regis, Sussex, England.

FILM: *Nightmare*, 1963 (Grace Maddox)

BIOGRAPHY—A British leading lady and character actress of stage, screen and television, Redmond made her film debut alongside future Hammer players Jane Hylton and Rupert Davies in *Violent Moment* (1959). Her career lasted for almost another 40 years, the majority of it spent on stage and TV. Her last feature film was in 1968. Only one of those films was for Hammer, unfortunately; she gave a bravura performance in *Nightmare* that rather leaves its nominal heroine, Jennie Linden, somewhat in the dust. As mentioned in the Linden biographical sketch, *Nightmare* is an atypical example of Hammer's psychological thrillers; what seems to be the standard plot (drive the usually already slightly unbalanced heroine mad) is given a twist. Redmond would have normally been cast as the seemingly benign presence who is later revealed to be guilty as sin, and indeed she is; she and her lover succeed in having Linden murder the lover's wife and get her committed. This all happens in the first half of the film. After Linden gets committed, the picture belongs to Redmond, who is made to undergo what they have just put Linden through, including a spectral presence in the halls of the manor. Amazingly, she can't see through it, but what a show she puts on while being bamboozled; from her wicked little smile when removing the original "ghost's" makeup to (when she believes Linden has escaped from the asylum and is hiding in the house) screeching "I'll *find* her!" her voice going up an octave on the second word, to her maniacal laughter in the climax. The perpetrators of the crimes in Hammer psycho thrillers generally pay for them, but never has the process been so drawn out; it's almost another film in itself, and Redmond makes the most of every minute of it, her performance more than making up for any gaping plot holes. This lovely and most talented actress passed away from a heart attack in 2006.

Other genre credits: TELEVISION: *Suspense*: "Payment in Full," 1960 (Jeanne Forester); *The Avengers*: "Hot Snow," 1961 (Stella); "Kill the King," 1961 (Mrs. Zoe Carter); *Menace*: "Trespasser," 1970 (Laurie); *Thriller*: "Sign it Death," 1974 (Janice Main)

Reed, Tracy (1942–)

REAL NAME: Clare Tracy Compton Pelissier; BIRTHPLACE: London, England.

FILM: *Journey to Midnight*, 1971 (Joyce)

TELEVISION: *Journey to the Unknown*: "The Indian Spirit Guide," 1969 (Joyce)

BIOGRAPHY—The beautiful stepdaughter of Sir Carol Reed (*The Third Man*) and the step-cousin of Oliver Reed, Tracy Reed was destined for a screen career literally from the cradle, as she made her first film appearance as a two-year-old in the classic British film *The Way Ahead*. Her career proper began in 1960. She was considered as a replacement for Diana Rigg in *The Avengers* before Linda Thorson was chosen; her best-remembered roles are the mistress of George C. Scott in the brilliant *Dr. Strangelove* and a Bond Girl in the original *Casino Royale*. In her only effort for Hammer, the *Journey to the Unknown* episode "The Indian Spirit Guide," she plays the scheming secretary Joyce, who helps her sleazy detective boyfriend bilk Julie Harris, until he decides to go for the whole bundle and marry Julie. Tracy's not having that, so she dials up a real psychic, with pointed results for her ex. After some busy years in the 1960s and the early '70s, Reed retired in 1975.

Other genre credits: FILMS: *Devils of Darkness*, Planet Film Productions, 1965 (Karen Steele); *Casino Royale*, Columbia Pictures, 1967 (F.A.N.G. Leader) TELEVISION: *Suspense*:

"Souvenir," 1963 (Laureet); *The Avengers*: "The Curious Case of the Countless Clues," 1968 (Janice Flanders); *Out of the Unknown*: "Random Quest," 1969 (Ottilie); *UFO*: "The Dalotek Affair," 1971 (Jane Carson)

Rees, Angharad (1949–2012)

BIRTHPLACE: Cardiff, Wales

FILM: *Hands of the Ripper*, 1971 (Anna)

BIOGRAPHY— The daughter of a prominent doctor, delicately beautiful Angharad Rees attended the Sorbonne and Rose Bruford College. She began her career doing voice work for films (including *The Son of Captain Blood*) before making her on-camera debut in 1968. She was cast as the lead of *Hands of the Ripper* by producer Aida Young after Young saw her performance in the "But Now They Are Fled" episode of the *Thirty-Minute Theatre* TV series. Like Nike Arrighi and Gillian Hills, Rees is not the typical buxom Hammer Heroine and, like those two, she is served by a more quiet sex appeal; but unlike those two, she plays the monster of the film, and a mighty fine job she does of it, too. Like the tortured heroine of Val Lewton's *Cat People*, she is relatively fine until she becomes aroused, or sees a shiny or sharp object — and then she's possessed by the spirit of her late dad. It's a role that could have easily been overplayed in either direction, making the other side of the personality unbelievable, but Rees achieves an admirable balance that makes her performance (and the film) an underrated gem. Her career lasted until 1998. She also founded her own jewelry design company, "Angharad." She passed away from pancreatic cancer in July 2012.

Other genre credits: TELEVISION: *The Avengers*: "They Keep Killing Steed," 1968 (Redhead); *Thriller*: "Once the Killing Starts," 1974 (Stella Mason); *Wide World Mystery*: "Once the Killing Starts," 1975 (Stella Mason); *The Curse of King Tut's Tomb* (Movie), 1980 (Lady Evelyn Herbert)

Rennie, Maggie; a.k.a. Margaret McGrath

FILMS: *On the Buses*, 1971 (Gladys)

TELEVISION: *Hammer House of Mystery and Suspense*: "Mark of the Devil," 1984 (Ma Perkins)

BIOGRAPHY— British character actress Rennie has a nice bit as a cigar-chomping biddy who runs an illegal poker dive in *Hammer House of Mystery and Suspense*. Her last screen appearance was in 1988.

Other genre credits: TELEVISION: *Thriller*: "Death to Sister Mary," 1974 (Housekeeper)

Rhodes, Marjorie (1897–1979)

REAL NAME: Millicent Wise; BIRTHPLACE: Hull, East Riding of Yorkshire, England.

FILMS: *Watch It, Sailor!* 1961 (Emma Hornett); *Hands of the Ripper*, 1971 (Mrs. Bryant)

BIOGRAPHY— Marjorie Rhodes was a British character actress of stage and screen; her first film was in 1938. In 1965, she was nominated for a Tony Award for "All in Good Time" and she reprised the role for the film version, *The Family Way*, in 1966. She did two funny turns for Hammer a decade apart; the first was in the actual comedy *Watch It, Sailor*. Then in the far-from-comedy *Hands of the Ripper*, her part itself is delightful, as Eric Porter's parodically proper housekeeper. It was one of her last roles.

Rice, Joan (1930–1997)

BIRTHPLACE: Derby, Derbyshire, England.

FILMS: *Women Without Men*, 1956 (Cleo Thompson); *The Horror of Frankenstein*, 1970 (Graverobber's Wife)

Richards, Lee

TELEVISION: *Hammer House of Horror*: "Charlie Boy," 1980 (Actress)

BIOGRAPHY— Large-breasted British character actress Richards displays them in an episode of *Hammer House of Horror* and is on the receiving end of a bawdy joke about their size.

Other genre credits: FILMS: *Indiana Jones and the Last Crusade*, Paramount Pictures, 1989 (Passenger on Airship) TELEVISION: *Doctor Who*: "Destiny of the Daleks," 1979 (Exotic Romana)

Richards, Susan (1898–1988)

BIRTHPLACE: Blaenau Festiniog, North Wales.

FILM: *Journey to Midnight*, 1971 (Mrs. Loker)

TELEVISION: *Journey to the Unknown*: "Poor Butterfly," 1969 (Mrs. Loker)

Other genre credits: FILMS: *Village of the Damned*, MGM, 1960 (Mrs. Plympton); *The Haunting*, Argyle Productions, 1963 (Nurse); *The Devil Within Her*, The Rank Organization, 1975 (Old Lady) TELEVISION: *One Step Beyond*: "Signal Received," 1961 (Heather Seller); *Out of the Unknown*: "Walk's End," 1966 (Miss Claythorpe); *Supernatural*: "Viktoria," 1977 (Kati)

Richardson, Beryl

FILM: *Journey into Darkness*, 1969 (Rhoda)

TELEVISION: *Journey to the Unknown*: "The New People," 1968 (Rhoda)

Richardson, Jo (Died 1976)

FILM: *Dracula A.D. 1972*, 1972 (Crying Matron)

Richmond, Irene (1911–2009)

BIRTHPLACE: Gresford, Wrexham, Clwyd, Wales.

FILMS: *Women Without Men*, 1956 (Guard); *Nightmare*, 1963 (Mrs. Gibbs); *Hysteria*, 1965 (Mrs. Keller)

Other genre credits: FILMS: *The Brain*, Central Cinema Company Film, 1962 (Mrs. Gabler); *Dr. Terror's House of Horrors*, Amicus Productions, 1965 (Mrs. Ellis)

Ridge, Marilyn

FILM: *The Two Faces of Dr. Jekyll*, 1960 (Sphinx Girl)

Ridley, Emma (1972–)

BIRTHPLACE: Hampstead, London, England.

TELEVISION: *Hammer House of Horror*: "The House That Bled to Death," 1980 (Young Sophia)

Other genre credits: FILM: *Return to Oz*, BMI (#9) Limited, 1985 (Ozma)

Roberts, Annette

FILMS: *Twins of Evil*, 1971 (Schoolgirl)

Robillard, Elizabeth

TELEVISION: *Journey to the Unknown*: "Somewhere in a Crowd," 1968 (Watcher)

Other genre credits: TELEVISION: *The Avengers*: "Take Me to Your Leader," 1969 (Sally Graham)

Robins, Sheila

FILM: *Never Take Sweets from a Stranger*, 1960 (Miss Jackson)
Other genre credits: FILMS: *Village of the Damned*, MGM, 1960 (Nurse) TELEVISION: *The Avengers*: "Dead of Winter," 1961 (Inez)

Roland, Jeanne (1942–)

BIRTHPLACE: England.
FILM: *The Curse of the Mummy's Tomb*, 1964 (Annette Dubois)
BIOGRAPHY—The career of Jeanne Roland, like more than a few of the actresses in this book, was short and sweet, lasting only five years. Her first and only film for Hammer was also her first film role, in *The Curse of the Mummy's Tomb*, and although her inexperience shows through at times, she is still utterly charming as Ronald Howard's wife (and the *objet d'amour* of Terence Morgan). She is torn between two lovers; the modern woman who is the spitting image (or the actual reincarnation) of a long-dead princess. Even if she had never made a Hammer film, her place in cinema history would be assured by virtue of being a Bond Girl twice over. She also had parts on *The Saint* (featuring future Bond Roger Moore) and the cult favorites *Secret Agent* and *The Avengers*; she played her last role in 1969.

Other genre credits: FILMS: *Casino Royale*, 1967 (Captain of the Guard Girls); *You Only Live Twice*, 1967 (Masseuse) TELEVISION: *The Avengers*: "Room Without a View," 1968 (Anna Wadkin)

Whatever *The Curse of the Mummy's Tomb* was, it wasn't Jeanne Roland.

Romain, Yvonne (1938–)

REAL NAME: Yvonne Warren; BIRTHPLACE: London, England.
FILMS: *The Curse of the Werewolf*, 1961 (Servant Girl); *Captain Clegg* (a.k.a. *Night Creatures*), 1962 (Imogene); *The Brigand of Kandahar*, 1965 (Ratina)
BIOGRAPHY—Yvonne Romain was born to a British father and Maltese mother, which accounts for the exotic look which won her a short but very substantial genre career. She began appearing in children's programs on the BBC at the age of 12, and later graduated from the Italia Conti Academy stage school, after which she modeled. Her first film appearance was in *The Baby and the Battleship* (1953), and her first genre role was alongside giants Boris Karloff and Christopher Lee in *Corridors of Blood*. Another solid role in *Circus of Horrors* brought her to the attention of Hammer, and she went on to play in two of their greatest films.

Oliver Reed and Yvonne Romain in a publicity photograph from *The Curse of the Werewolf* (courtesy Mel Bridgeman).

She plays a pivotal role in *The Curse of the Werewolf*, as the mute servant girl who is first groped by Anthony Dawson's scabrous, evil marquis and then raped by Richard Wordsworth's bestial beggar. She is featured in the film's most iconic shots of Oliver Reed's werewolf, despite the fact that she is his mother, and she dies giving birth to him. The magnificently talented Reed was her most frequent co-star; he was in all three of Romain's Hammer films, and co-starred with her in an early episode of *The Saint*. (In *Curse* she plays his mother, in *Clegg* his fiancée, and in *Brigand* his sister.) Since she is mute in *Curse*, she must express her emotions through her eyes and gestures, and the horrors perpetrated upon her seem all the more horrible because she must endure her pain in silence.

Her position was upgraded from servant girl to serving wench in *Captain Clegg*, but at least she had lines this time. Though her screen time is limited (there's not much for any of the women to do in this picture), she still manages to play an important part in the resolution when it is discovered that she is not an orphan, but in reality the daughter of Clegg (Peter Cushing), who she believes dead. In the grand tradition of disgraced movie fathers who never reveal themselves to their daughters in order to save them, Clegg doesn't, and sends her away with Oliver Reed before the king's men put a bullet through him.

Romain and Reed were back together in *The Brigand of Kandahar* which, despite their best efforts, neither one could save. It wasn't really their fault; although Hammer had a well-deserved reputation for making movies that belied their low budgets, occasionally they would bite off more than they could chew and want to make epics, but on the same budgets, and unfortunately, most of the time, it showed. Romain plays the sister of Reed's tribal chieftain, who hates him, and even arranges to have him killed in a raid, but he survives—only to be run through by the hero, who then proceeds to die along with Romain and most of the other principals.

Her career only lasted for nine years after that, when she abandoned it to devote more time to her family. Her final screen appearance was in the murder mystery *The Last of Sheila*. She married Oscar-winning composer Leslie Bricusse in 1958; apparently they cannot live with or without each other, as they have separated, divorced and remarried more than once.

Other genre credits: FILMS: *Corridors of Blood*, Amalgamated Productions, 1958 (Rosa); *Circus of Horrors*, Lynx Films, 1960 (Melina); *The Devil Doll*, Galaworldfilm Productions, 1964 (Marianne Horn)

Romanoff, Liz

FILM: *Dr. Jekyll and Sister Hyde*, 1971 (Emma)

Ronay, Edina (1943–)

BIRTHPLACE: Budapest, Hungary
FILM: *Slave Girls*, 1967 (Saria)

Edina Ronay adds some lovely shell accessories to her basic fur bikini ensemble for a smart look in *Slave Girls* (courtesy Mel Bridgeman).

BIOGRAPHY—Edina Ronay, born in Budapest in 1943, was in England just two years later, courtesy of her father, the now-famous food critic Egon Ronay. She had a short but very busy career, beginning with *The Pure Hell of St. Trinian's* (1960) and ending with the *Shades of Greene* TV series in 1975. In between she appeared in such diverse productions as the classic Sherlock Holmes vs. Jack the Ripper film *A Study in Terror* and the Beatles' *A Hard Day's Night*. Her best-remembered contribution to the genre came with Hammer's deliciously deranged *Slave Girls*, in which she plays sexy Saria, the most rebellious of the blond tribe of slave girls who has been subjugated by Martine Beswick. Ronay also plays her modern incarnation, Sara, in the film's climax. Despite the impressive skills displayed in these and her other roles, she lost interest in the business and concentrated on other skills, becoming a world-famous fashion designer with her own label. Like Anouska Hempel, she apparently doesn't acknowledge her former career; her personal website makes no mention of it whatsoever.

Other genre credits: FILM: *A Study in*

Terror, Compton Films, 1966 (Mary Kelly) TELEVISION: *The Avengers*: "The Removal Men," 1962 (Nicole Cauvin); "The Nutshell," 1963 (Elin Strindberg)

Rosay, Francoise (1891–1974)

REAL NAME: Francoise Bandy de Naleche; BIRTHPLACE: Paris, France.
FILM: *Stop Me Before I Kill!* 1960 (Madame Prade)

Ross, Annie (1930–)

REAL NAME: Annabelle Allan Short; BIRTHPLACE: Mitcham, London, England.
FILM: *Straight on Till Morning*, 1972 (Liza)
Other genre credits: FILMS: *The Beast Must Die*, Amicus Productions, 1974 (Voice of Caroline); *Superman III*, Cantharaus Productions N.V., 1983 (Vera); *Witchery*, Filmirage, 1988 (Rose Brooks); *Basket Case 2*, Shapiro-Glickenhaus Entertainment, 1990 (Granny Ruth); *Basket Case 3*, Shapiro-Glickenhaus Entertainment, 1992 (Granny Ruth)

Ross, Joanna

FILM: *Captain Kronos, Vampire Hunter*, 1974 (Myra)
Other genre credits: TELEVISION: *Doctor Who*: "The Ambassadors of Death," 1970 (Control Room Assistant); *Out of the Unknown*: "The Last Witness," 1971 (Barbara); *Moonbase 3*: "Achilles Heel," 1973 (Jane)

Rossini, Jan

FILM: *When Dinosaurs Ruled the Earth*, 1970 (Rock Girl)
Other genre credits: FILMS: *The Oblong Box*, American International, 1969 (Prostitute); *Cry of the Banshee*, American International, 1970 (Bess)

Royle, Carol B. (1954–)

BIRTHPLACE: Blackpool, Lancashire, England.
TELEVISION: *Hammer House of Mystery and Suspense*: "And the Wall Came Tumbling Down," 1985 (Catherine Parks/Kim Osborn)
BIOGRAPHY— Carol B. Royle is the daughter of actor Derek Royle and Jane Royle, who was an actress turned makeup artist. She attended the Central School of Speech and Drama, and her TV-film career began in 1976. She has also performed extensively on stage. She had a strong supporting role in the "And the Wall Came Tumbling Down" episode of *Hammer House of Mystery and Suspense* as the girlfriend of the reincarnation of a very naughty boy who is haunted by visions of the past and his continuing part in the ghastly plot. As it turns out, she's a reincarnation, too. She is still active, and her website lists her interests as interior design, fashion, writing and teaching.
Other genre credits: TELEVISION: *Blake's 7*: "Duel," 1978 (Mutoid); *Shades of Darkness*: "Feet Foremost," 1983 (Maggie)

Rule, Janice (1931–2003)

BIRTHPLACE: Norwood, Ohio, USA.
TELEVISION: *Journey to the Unknown*: "Stranger in the Family," 1969 (Paula Wilde)
BIOGRAPHY— An American character actress of stage, screen, and television, Rule made her film debut in 1946 after studying ballet and dancing in nightclubs. She appeared on the cover of *Time* in 1951, and made her own way in Hollywood, defying the conventional beauty

standards of the time. Her one appearance for Hammer was in the "Stranger in the Family" episode of *Journey to the Unknown*, playing an actress managed by an abusive boyfriend. They encounter a mutant teenager who has the power to force people to do whatever he wants, in a story that plays like an *X-Men* comic. The mutant is a teenager, outwardly normal in appearance (except he has no fingernails), whose fearsome power has made his family and himself fugitives; there is a "Professor X"–type character who wants to put him in a special "school"; and pleas for tolerance. Rule gives a solid performance; she is both attracted to and afraid of the handsome young man. Rule earned a Ph.D. in psychoanalysis in 1983, and practiced while also maintaining her career. She passed away in 2003 due to a cerebral hemorrhage.

Other genre credits: FILMS: *Bell Book and Candle*, Julian Blaustein Productions, 1958 (Merle Kittridge); *The Ambushers*, Columbia Pictures, 1967 (Sheila Summers) TELEVISION: *The Devil and Miss Sarah* (Movie), 1971 (Sarah Turner); *The Ray Bradbury Theater*: "Some Live Like Lazarus," 1992 (Anna at 60)

Ryder, Celia

FILM: *Rasputin, the Mad Monk*, 1966 (Fat Lady)

Sabine, Winifred

FILM: *Frankenstein and the Monster from Hell*, 1974 (Mouse)
Other genre credits: FILMS: *The House That Dripped Blood*, Amicus Productions, 1971 (Rita); *A Clockwork Orange*, Warner Brothers Pictures, 1971 (Old Lady at Duke of York)

St. Clement, Pam (1942–)

REAL NAME: Pamela Ann Clement; BIRTHPLACE: Harrow on the Hill, Middlesex, England.
TELEVISION: *Hammer House of Mystery and Suspense*: "Czech Mate," 1985 (Doctor)
Other genre credits: FILMS: *Doomwatch*, Tigon British Film Productions, 1972 (Young Woman); *Biggles: Adventures in Time*, Compact Yellowbill, 1986 (Mother Superior) TELEVISION: *Hallmark Hall of Fame*: "The Hunchback of Notre Dame," 1982 (Woman in Cathedral); *Doctor Who: Dimensions in Time*: 1993 (Pat Butcher)

Sampson, Annie

FILM: *Dracula A.D. 1972*, 1972 (Member of Stoneground)

Samuel, Julie Olive Mary (1944–)

BIRTHPLACE: London, England.
FILM: *Nightmare*, 1963 (Maid)

Sara, Catherine (1972–)

BIRTHPLACE: England.
FILM: *The Woman in Black*, 2012 (Mrs. Jerome)

Sargent, Gundel

FILM: *The Two Faces of Dr. Jekyll*, 1960 (Sphinx Girl)

Saville, Edith

FILM: *Four Sided Triangle*, 1953 (Lady Grant)

Sawday, Diana

FILM: *Countess Dracula*, 1971 (Gypsy Dancer)

Sayers, Patricia

FILM: *The Two Faces of Dr. Jekyll*, 1960 (Sphinx Girl)

Scarf, Donna (1958–)

TELEVISION: *Hammer House of Mystery and Suspense*: "In Possession," 1985 (Hotel Receptionist)
Other genre credits: TELEVISION: *Blake's 7*: "Gambit," 1979 (Gambling Customer)

Schell, Catherine (1944–)

REAL NAME: Katherina Freiin Schell von Bauschlott; BIRTHPLACE: Budapest, Hungary.
FILM: *Moon Zero Two*, 1969 (Clementine Taplin)
BIOGRAPHY— Catherine Schell's father was the diplomat Baron Paul Schell von Bauschlott, and her mother was Countess Katharina Maria Etelka Georgina Elisabeth Teleki de Szek. The family fled Hungary after their estates were seized by the Nazis. They eventually found a home in the United States, where Catherine attended the Otto Falkenberg Academy of Performing Arts. Her first role was in a 1964 genre picture, *Lana, Queen of the Amazons*, and her big break came in 1969 with her role as a Bond Girl in *On Her Majesty's Secret Service*— which was not as big a break as hoped, since the picture was a flop. Nineteen sixty-nine was a double whammy for Schell, as this was also the year of her starring part as "darling" Clementine Taplin in Hammer's big-budget, bizarre "space Western" *Moon Zero Two*, which also flopped, due to the interest in actual real-life astronauts actually landing on the moon. Schell handles her role as a futuristic "damsel in distress" with intelligence, humor and beauty. Particularly delightful is the look she gives the larch-like James Olson when she walks in on him getting out of the shower; her expression of amused embarrassment is reminiscent of the "Mona Lisa," making one wonder whether she's more embarrassed or amused. But space was the place for Schell, who went on to gain her greatest fame as Maya in *Space: 1999*. She retired in the mid–1990s (she came out of it momentarily to reprise her role as Maya in the parody short *Space: 1899* in 2004) and opened a bed-and-breakfast in France, but closed it after the death of her second husband. She is not related to either Maximillian or Maria Schell.
Other genre credits: FILMS: *Lana, Queen of the Amazons*, Arca Studio, Berlin, 1964 (Lana); *On Her Majesty's Secret Service*, Danjaq/Eon Productions, 1969 (Nancy); *Madame Sin*, 2X Productions, 1972 (Barbara); *Space: 1899* (Short), 2004 (Maya) TELEVISION: *Thriller*: "The Next Voice You See," 1975 (Julie); *Supernatural*: "Viktoria," 1977 (Theresa); *Space: 1999*: "The Guardian of Piri," 1975; "The Metamorph," "The Exiles," "Journey to Where," "One Moment of Humanity," "Brian the Brain," "New Adam New Eve," "The Mark of Archanon," "The Rules of Luton," "All That Glistens," "The Taybor," "Seed of Destruction," "The AB Chrysalis," "Catacombs of the Moon," "Space Warp," "A Matter of Balance," "The Beta Cloud," "The Lambda Factor," 1976; "The Bringers of Wonder," "The Séance Spectre," "Dorzak," "Devil's Planet," "The Immunity Syndrome," "The Dorcons," 1977 (Servant of the Guardian/Maya); *Destination Moonbase—Alpha* (Movie), 1978 (Maya); *Doctor Who*: "City of Death," 1979 (Countess Scarlioni)

Schofield, Joan

FILM: *Quatermass 2*, 1957 (Woman Shopper)

Scott, Anna Simone (1957–)

BIRTHPLACE: Sydney, Australia.
TELEVISION: *Hammer House of Horror*: "Growing Pains," 1980 (Nurse Foster)

Scott, Anne

FILM: *The Terror of the Tongs*, 1961 (Girl)

Scott, Janette (1938–)

REAL NAME: Thora Janette Scott; BIRTHPLACE: Morecambe, England.
FILMS: *Paranoiac*, 1963 (Eleanor Ashby); *The Old Dark House*, 1963 (Cecily Femm)
BIOGRAPHY — Janette Scott is the daughter of Dame Thora Hird, making them the second mother-daughter to both make films for Hammer (Hazel Court and Sally Walsh are the others). She was a popular all-around leading actress in the 1950s and 1960s, and made several fine contributions to the genre, including the SF classic *The Day of the Triffids* and other star turns in *The Old Dark House* and *Paranoiac*, the light and dark sides of family madness and murder. The former is the remake of the 1932 James Whale classic of the same name, and while not nearly as well-regarded as its predecessor, it nonetheless has some wonderful bits and superb ensemble playing. Scott's part almost seems to be a send-up of her usual (self-described) "sugary-sweet" roles: a Marilyn Munster, the only seemingly "normal" person in a house full of madmen and women. But she's so abnormally normal that it's obvious that she's as cracked as the rest — and ultimately, even more so, taking great relish in her revelation as the killer. She explored the dark side in a big way in *Paranoiac*, with a role she could really sink her teeth into. Again, she's cracked, and even though she doesn't go completely off the rails, her ride is much more harrowing: She plays a woman who believes the man she is falling in love with is her own brother. Her confusion and self-loathing is palpable, as is her relief when the man is not her brother after all. She married Mel Torme in 1966 (they divorced in 1977), and more or less retired from movies and television, after her appearance in *Bikini Paradise* (1967). She has only made two screen appearances since, and has been happily married to her third husband, William Rademaekers, since 1981.

Janette Scott makes a cutting remark to Fenella Fielding in *The Old Dark House.*

Other genre credits: FILMS: *The Day of the Triffids*, Security Pictures, 1962 (Karen Goodwin); *Crack in the World*, Security Pictures, 1965 (Dr. Maggie Sorenson)

Scott, Kathryn Leigh (1945–)

REAL NAME: Marlene Kringstad; BIRTHPLACE: Robbinsdale, Minnesota, USA.

TELEVISION: *Hammer House of Horror*: "Visitor from the Grave," 1980 (Penny Van Brutten)

BIOGRAPHY— The beautiful Kathryn Leigh Scott was born to parents of Norwegian descent. Her ambition took her to New York, where she first worked as a Playboy bunny. Her first acting job brought her everlasting cult fame, as a member of the cast of the original TV soap opera *Dark Shadows*. Ten years after leaving that show, she did a nice turn for Hammer in an episode of their second television series, *Hammer House of Horror*. Stunning in a white silk and satin negligee, she plays that most-favored Hammer heroine, the woman first seen in an unstable mental condition, a woman whom everyone else is trying to drive over the edge, all for their own reasons. When her husband's business partner tries to rape her, she kills him — or at least, she thinks she does, and things become even more problematic when he insists on returning from beyond the pale for revenge. There's a final twist in the tale, and Scott plays the whole thing wonderfully. In 1986, she founded Pomegranate Press and continues to be active in all things *Dark Shadows* (her own books, audio books, fan conventions, a cameo in the 2012 Tim Burton film) and in her acting career as well, continuing her association with the genre that brung her.

Other genre credits: FILMS: *House of Dark Shadows*, MGM, 1970 (Maggie Evans); *Witches' Brew*, 1980 (Susan Carey); *Parasomnia*, Luminous Processes, 2008 (Nurse Evans); *Dark Shadows*, Dan Curtis Productions, 2012 (Guest); *Dr. Mabuse*, Hollinsworth Productions, 2013 (Madame Von Harbau) TELEVISION: *Dark Shadows*: 309 untitled episodes, 1966–1970 (Maggie Evans/Maggie Evans Collins/Josette DuPres/Ghost of Josette/Rachel Drummond/Lady Hampshire/Kitty Soames); *Space: 1999*: "Dorzak," 1977 (Yesta); *The Incredible Hulk*: "A Solitary Place," 1979 (Gail Collins); *Star Trek: The Next Generation*: "Who Watches the Watchers?" 1989 (Nuria)

Scott, Margaretta (1912–2005)

BIRTHPLACE: London, England.

FILM: *Crescendo*, 1970 (Danielle Ryman)

BIOGRAPHY— The daughter of a respected music critic, and trained at RADA, Margaretta Scott was one of Britain's most distinguished Shakespearean actresses, and had a seventy-year career on stage, screen and television. Her screen debut was in Alexander Korda's *The Private Life of Don Juan* (1934), and two years later she appeared in his seminal science-fiction film *Things to Come*. She brought all her classical training to bear in her Avenging Granny role for Hammer, the mad Danielle Ryman of *Crescendo*. The film itself isn't a patch on its earlier incarnation as *Fanatic*, but Scott's performance rises above it; she eschews the over-the-top theatrics of a Bette Davis or Tallulah Bankhead to create a much more believable (and ultimately more chilling) portrayal, particularly in the scene where she blackmails Stefanie Powers. Like Mary Hignett (*Demons of the Mind*), Scott would become even more beloved due to a role in *All Creatures Great and Small*. She was married to composer John Woolridge, and they were parents to actress Susan Woolridge and theatre director Hugh Woolridge. Her husband died in 1958, and she never remarried.

Other genre credits: FILM: *Things to Come*, London Film Productions, 1936 (Roxana/Rowena) TELEVISION: *Tales of the Unexpected*: "Georgy Porgy," 1980 (Lady Birdwell)

Scott, Michelle

FILM: *The Evil of Frankenstein*, 1964 (Little Girl)

Other genre credits: FILM: *Doctor Who and the Daleks*, Amicus Productions, 1965 (Thal Child)

Scott-James, Shirli

FILM: *The Two Faces of Dr. Jekyll*, 1960 (Sphinx Girl)

Seagrove, Jenny (1957–)

REAL NAME: Jennifer Ann Seagrove; BIRTHPLACE: Kuala Lumpur, Malaysia.

TELEVISION: *Hammer House of Mystery and Suspense*: "Mark of the Devil," 1984 (Sara Helston)

BIOGRAPHY—Lovely Jenny Seagrove originally had her sights set on a culinary career, but the smell of the greasepaint caught her nostrils. She attended the Bristol Old Vic Theatre School, first exercising her talents on stage, where she still performs. Her career has included Hammer; in the "Mark of the Devil" episode of *Hammer House of Mystery and Suspense* she played the lead role of Sara, a rich girl hooked up with a fortune hunter who's in hock. His "creditors" can't wait for their marriage, so he robs and kills a tattoo artist (Bert Kwouk, getting it only slightly worse than he did in the *Pink Panther* movies). But a prick from Bert's knife forms an ever-expanding tattoo, and Jenny can't get no satisfaction from her man who has suddenly started to discover more and more ways to keep himself covered. Seagrove doesn't have a whole lot to do except look puzzled and frustrated, and she does it well. She has done mostly television since then. She's also an animal rights activist and advocate for the deregulation of the herbal remedy industry in the U.K.

Other genre credits: FILM: *The Guardian*, Universal Pictures, 1990 (Camilla)

Seal, Elizabeth (1933–)

BIRTHPLACE: Genoa, Italy.

FILM: *Vampire Circus*, 1972 (Gerta Hauser)

Other genre credits: FILM: *Lara Croft, Tomb Raider: The Cradle of Life*, Paramount Pictures, 2003 (Buyer) TELEVISION: *Supernatural*: "Ghosts of Venice," 1977 (Stella/Regina)

Sears, Heather (1935–1994)

BIRTHPLACE: Kensington, London, England.

FILM: *The Phantom of the Opera*, 1962 (Christine Charles)

BIOGRAPHY—The daughter of a doctor, lovely Heather Sears began acting at the age of five. She attended the Central School of Speech and Drama, and even before she graduated received a contract that allowed her to act in both films and on stage. Her first film was in 1955, and the critics sat up and took notice just two years later when she played the title role of *The Story of Esther Costello*, a deaf, dumb and blind girl. For her standout performance, she was nominated for a Golden Globe and won a BAFTA Award. She brought the same expressive qualities to her role as Christine in *The Phantom of the Opera*, a Hammer film which had originally been planned for Cary Grant (a fact that is accompanied in most texts by a parenthesized exclamation point, but Grant's desire to go against type and play the villain should come as no surprise; he had petitioned heavily to let his character in *Suspicion* be the murderer, but was overruled by studio heads). Sears doesn't do her own singing, but she brings everything else to a role that requires a bit more than just a plunging neckline, and she's just as effective as Joan of Arc in the opera-within-a-movie as she is as Christine. She brings an understated but dignified presence to the film. One "problem," for many genre fans, is that Hammer's *The Phantom of the Opera* is a very good film; it's just a very bad monster movie. Actually, it's never been that much of a monster movie, but Lon Chaney's performance and horrific skull-like makeup elevated his character into the ranks of filmdom's classic fiends. The Phantoms of Claude Rains and Herbert Lom are decidedly less omnipotent and more sympathetic than Chaney, which is not a bad thing for a monster, but in both cases, a key element, the makeup, was mishandled; instead of Chaney's face-altering skull and cheekbones, both Rains and Lom look as if Oscar Madison has thrown a plate of linguine in their faces. This is obviously most apparent in the unmasking scenes, which brings up perhaps an even more serious dramatic flaw: the absence of the impact on both the audience and Christine, the high shock point of the Chaney version. Instead of trapping Christine in his lair and having her perform the unmasking, Hammer's version has the Phantom put her through the operatic mill underground but he doesn't reveal himself to her and the audience until the climax when he swings, Tarzan-like, down on a rope to save her from the famous falling chandelier, which only crushes the Phantom. This deprives both Sears and the audience of a prime dramatic confrontation. Even if the director cannot or doesn't want to duplicate the mechanics of the original, the moment should still be preserved in some fashion. And this flaw is due to the screenplay, not Sears, and she is surely not only the most beautiful between herself, Mary Philbin and Susanna Foster, but far and away the best actress. But after this film, she only made one other, in 1989. She faded from the stage and television as well. She passed away too young, from multiple organ failure, at age 58 in 1994.

Other genre credits: TELEVISION: *Tales of the Unexpected*: "There's One Born Every Minute," 1981 (Margaret Pearson)

Seely, Wendy

TELEVISION: *Hammer House of Mystery and Suspense*: "Last Video and Testament," 1984 (Linda)

Seghal, Zohra (1912–)

BIRTHPLACE: Saharanpur, Uttar Pradesh, India.
FILM: *The Vengeance of She*, 1968 (Putri)
Other genre credits: FILM: *Tales That Witness Madness*, World Film Services, 1973 (Malia) TELEVISION: *Doctor Who*: "The Roof of the World," 1964 (Attendant/Ping-Cho); "The Knight of Jaffa," 1965 (Sheyra)

Sellars, Elizabeth (1923–)

BIRTHPLACE: Glasgow, Scotland.
FILMS: *Cloudburst*, 1951 (Carol Graham); *The Mummy's Shroud*, 1967 (Barbara Preston)
BIOGRAPHY— Elizabeth Sellars took to the stage at age 15 and trained at RADA. Her first film was *Floodtide* (1949), and she went on to play supporting roles in the A-list films *The Barefoot Contessa* and *55 Days at Peking*. She has the distinction of being in the first and last movies filmed at Hammer's legendary Bray Studios. She was entirely sympathetic and in for a particularly rough go of it in that first one, *Cloudburst*: Not only is she an expectant mother run down by a robbery-fleeing car early on, but, to add insult to death, they drive back over her in reverse! She's the top-billed female lead in the last Hammer-Bray, *The Mummy's Shroud*, and she not only survives in it, but is arguably much better off after the Mummy disposes of her overbearing bastard of a husband. Sellars gives interesting shadings of depth to what would normally be a standard long-suffering wife role; she dutifully endures his arrogance, cruelty and hypocrisy, but she is strangely calm and serene, even when the expedition members start dropping like flies, pointing out to her husband that *she* didn't enter the tomb. And her expressions at all times let us know that she is much smarter and aware than her husband gives her credit for: a knowing smile here, an uplifting of eyes there. Her last role was in 1990, and she retired to a wee cottage in Scotland.

Other genre credits: TELEVISION: *One Step Beyond*: "The Villa," 1961 (Mary Low); *The Avengers*: "Take-Over," 1969 (Laura Bassett); *Beasts*: "During Barty's Party," 1976 (Angie Truscott)

Serena

FILM: *Vampire Circus*, 1972 (Female Dancer)

BIOGRAPHY—Lithe, leggy Serena was a former model who only made two other films, playing strippers in both. Her scenes with partner Milovan are one of the best-remembered things about *Vampire Circus*; she doesn't have to strip in this one, as she's already completely nude when she hits the ground dancing, and not just nude, but bald and painted with tiger stripes, in a kinky variation on French Apache dancing, with whip-wielding Milo "hunting" her down and "vanquishing" her, much to the delight of the crowd. She created not only an indelible celluloid image, she also may have provided the visual inspiration for Marvel Comics' "Tigra, the Were-Woman."

Sharwin, Moyna

FILM: *The Two Faces of Dr. Jekyll*, 1960 (Sphinx Girl)

Shearing, Julie

FILM: *The Terror of the Tongs*, 1961 (Tong Room Girl)

Shelby, Sandi K.

FILM: *The Resident*, 2011 (Emergency Room Doctor)

Other genre credits: FILM: *Fright Night*, Albuquerque Studios/DreamWorks SKG, 2011 (Teacher)

Sheldon, Caroline

FILM: *The Damned*, 1963 (Elizabeth)

Shelley, Barbara (1933–)

REAL NAME: Barbara Kowin; BIRTHPLACE: London, England.

FILMS: *Mantrap* (a.k.a. *Man in Hiding*), 1953 (Young Woman); *The Camp on Blood Island*, 1958 (Kate Keiller); *The Shadow of the Cat*, 1961 (Beth Venable); *The Gorgon*, 1964 (Carla Hoffman); *The Secret of Blood Island*, 1964 (Elaine); *Dracula, Prince of Darkness*, 1966 (Helen Kent); *Rasputin, the Mad Monk*, 1966 (Sonia); *Quatermass and the Pit* (a.k.a. *Five Million Years to Earth*), 1967 (Barbara Todd)

BIOGRAPHY—There are a number of legitimate contenders for the unofficial title of "The Queen of Horror" but if one should wonder as to whom "The Queen of Hammer" was, there can only be one real answer: Barbara Shelley. Though she didn't possess the oomph of a Raquel Welch, Ursula Andress, Ingrid Pitt or Caroline Munro, she made more films for Hammer than those four women combined, and her combination of acting skill and mature, refined beauty gave her the opportunity to play a wide variety of roles for the company. Like Munro, she worked as a model, which led to film work; her first genre effort was the *Cat People*–inspired *Cat Girl*, which turned out to be quite uninspiring, except for Shelley's performance which, along with the title and genre, would set the tone for the most celebrated portion of her career.

Her first horror outing for Hammer was the female lead in another feline feature, *The

Shadow of the Cat, a programmer that featured a first-rate cast in an all-too predictable thriller. Shelley, the niece of a murdered wealthy woman, stands to inherit her fortune, and spends most of the film defending the cat that the murderers are trying to kill. Why do they want to kill the cat? Because it's the only witness to the murder, as if it's going to go to the police and spill the beans! But this is no ordinary cat: She wields a terrible power over the guilty parties, causing their deaths one by one. Or are they driven to their fates by their guilt? Shelley acquits herself well in a role hardly designed to tax her thespian abilities; she would go on to much bigger and battier roles.

She gave a superlative performance in *The Gorgon*, the Hammer classic that features Christopher Lee as a good guy who bears a striking resemblance to Grandpa Joe from *Willy Wonka and the Chocolate Factory*. It is a classic with an asterisk; and two major elements keep it from being wholly a success: The "mystery" element completely falls on its face (Shelley is obviously the reincarnation of Megera), and the title creature itself, played by Prudence Hyman. Although she is effective in long shots and medium shots, once the Gorgon gets a close-up, the risible Woolworth's rubber snakes in her hair shatter any illusion of credible threat. Add to that the simple fact that the creature was played by Hyman in the first place; this is not meant to be a slight against Hyman, but the duality obviously would have been much better communicated had Shelley played the role (which she was reportedly willing to do with a wig of live snakes!). But it was much more economical to have another actress play the role instead of spending the time to make up Shelley. Had she been able to play the actual Gorgon, it may have been a role as well-regarded as her vampiress in *Dracula, Prince of Darkness*. Still, she is mightily effective as Carla: caring, strong, intelligent enough to eventually realize that she is the monster. Her final scene is one of excellently played desperation and then resignation — hoping against hope that her lover will take her away from all this when she knows full well that she cannot escape it, and when he will not do so that night, she turns away muttering, "It's too late ... it's too late."

There was no such hedging in her next genre role; she gives what is perhaps her most well-regarded performance in *Dracula, Prince of Darkness*. She is absolutely smashing as Helen Kent, an archetypal prim and proper British matron who is transformed into a sensual, fanged and furious vampiress by Dracula. At first seen as impossibly stuffy, she is soon shown to be the only one in her traveling party with enough sense to stay away from Castle Dracula — which of course, they don't, and thereby hangs the tale. It is a tale she more or less dominates until her gory demise. Of course, it is Christopher Lee's movie, and Dracula is the engine that makes it run, but with no dialogue and scant screen time, he is more of an invisible pilot, with Shelley stepping up to provide one of the most (maybe *the* most) fascinating characters in the Hammer Dracula series. Her high collar gives way to a low-cut gown, and she purrs "You don't *need* Charles" as she tries to vampirically seduce her own sister-in-law, in a scene which both foreshadows the older-younger seduction in *The Vampire Lovers* and brings out the incestuous implications inherent in the vampire mythos. Her gory demise is the dramatic highlight of the film. Shelley's staking scene, courtesy of Father Sandor and his band of monks, has been described as gang-rape but, perhaps unintentionally, it goes a bit deeper than that. If one accepts the argument that Hammer's films were indeed reactionary, then the scene can be viewed as upholding that philosophy, that evil cannot stand up to the power of good. But, as in a number of other Hammers, this view can have the opposite effect on the audience; the massing of monks to subdue a single woman, no matter how dangerous, can also be seen as a symbol of the way religions and society have suppressed women throughout the centuries, particularly in regards to their sexuality. She may be undead, but she is actually more alive than ever, especially sexually, and since this removes her completely from her accepted roles, this is completely unacceptable to them. This suppression suspicion would seem to be rein-

Despite her obvious efforts, Barbara Shelley can't get a leg up on Andrew Keir in *Five Million Years to Earth*.

forced by the fact that Sandor takes a small army to physically destroy Shelley, but he doesn't even touch Dracula in the climax: He uses his gun to shoot ice out from under him. That's another scene rife with symbolism — for those who look for such things.

Rasputin, the Mad Monk, which began shooting the day after *Dracula, Prince of Darkness* wrapped, also featured Lee, Francis Matthews, Suzan Farmer and Shelley, the latter in the more traditional role of the czarina's lady-in-waiting, whose taste for forbidden fruit brings her into contact with Rasputin and ultimately causes her death by suicide. Much like Universal's *Tower of London* (1939), it's a low-budget "historical drama" with an almost invisible connection to history (due to threat of lawsuits) and instead ladled with the kind of horrific touches each company had come to be known for. She plays the role of a woman in an abusive relationship quite effectively, although the effect of her tragic death is somewhat lessened by the fact that it occurs off-screen.

Hammer generally had about as much luck with science fiction as it did with historical subjects; the imagination was willing but the budget wasn't, limiting the most important element common to both genres—the scope. *Quatermass and the Pit* was an exception, an extremely intelligent story with scope to spare. Shelley plays her most authoritative role in this film: As anthropologist Barbara Judd, she is again quite intelligent, independent and very resourceful (she is instrumental in helping Quatermass prove his theories), a spiritual descendent of the strong-willed female scientists that began in the science fiction films of the '50s, for example, Faith Domergue in *It Came from Beneath the Sea*, though without the romantic subplot that these characters were usually faced with, that made sure they didn't stray *too* far from traditionally accepted notions of femininity.

Quatermass and the Pit was Shelley's final appearance for Hammer, marking an end to a relationship that had lasted for 15 years; her first had been in the film noir *Mantrap*, and she also appeared in the *Blood Island* war films. She wanted to broaden her horizons beyond the genre (although she never abandoned it), finding success on both television and the stage and completely outside the entertainment world, as an interior decorator. She's also appeared at fan conventions where, if she ever needed convincing, she was reminded of the place she holds not only in Hammer history but in those fans' hearts.

Other genre credits: FILMS: *Cat Girl*, Insignia Films, 1957 (Leonora Johnson); *Blood of the Vampire*, Artistes Alliance Limited, 1958 (Madeleine Duval); *Village of the Damned*, MGM, 1960 (Anthea Zellaby); *Ghost Story*, Steven Weeks Company, 1974 (Matron); *The Stranger: More Than a Messiah* (Short), Bill & Ben Video, 1992 (Charlotte Darton) TELEVISION: *Invisible Man*: "The Big Plot," 1959 (Helen Peversham); *Suspense*: "The Man in My Shoes," 1962 (Betty Blair); *The Man from U.N.C.L.E.*: "The Odd Man Affair," 1965 (Bryn Watson); *The Avengers*: "Dragonsfield," 1961 (Susan Summers); "From Venus with Love," 1967 (Venus Brown); *Blake's 7*: "Stardrive," 1981 (Dr. Plaxton); *Doctor Who*: "Planet of Fire," 1984 (Sorasta); *Uncle Silas*: Episodes 1, 2, and 3, 1989 (Cousin Monica)

Shelley, Joanna

FILM: *The Vampire Lovers*, 1970 (Woodsman's Daughter)

Shenstone, Clare

FILM: *Moon Zero Two*, 1969 (Female Hotel Clerk)
Other genre credits: TELEVISION: *Out of the Unknown*: "1 + 1 = 1.5," 1969 (Secretary)

Shepherd, Pauline (1938–)

BIRTHPLACE: London, England.
FILM: *The Two Faces of Dr. Jekyll*, 1960 (Girl in Gin Shop)
Other genre credits: TELEVISION: *The Avengers*: "Dance with Death," 1961 (Valerie Marnell)

Sheridan, Dinah (1920–)

REAL NAME: Dinah Nadyejda Ginsburg; BIRTHPLACE: Hampstead, London, England.
TELEVISION: *Hammer House of Horror*: "The Thirteenth Reunion," 1980 (Gwen Cox)

BIOGRAPHY—Elegant beauty Dinah Sheridan was born into a family of successful photographers, known for their portraits of the royal family. She made her first film in 1937 and became a fixture on the stage, screen and television, except for a period of fifteen years when she retired due to her second marriage. Her first marriage was to actor Jimmy Hanley (*The Lost Continent*), and one of their children was Jenny Hanley, the female lead of *Scars of Dracula*. Sheridan was a latecomer to the Hammer ranks, not coming aboard until 1980, but she lends her still-elegant beauty and quiet authority to her role in "The Thirteenth Reunion" as the senior magazine editor who sends Julia Foster on her last assignment for the magazine. Her last appearance was in 1999. After having lived in the United States for a time, she is back in England following the death of her fourth husband.

Other genre credits: TELEVISION: *Doctor Who*: "The Five Doctors," 1983 (Chancellor Flavia)

Sherman, Marianne

TELEVISION: *Hammer House of Mystery and Suspense*: "Mark of the Devil," 1984 (Butch Girl)

BIOGRAPHY—British character actress Sherman also did some stage work.

Shevaloff, Valerie

FILM: *The Terror of the Tongs*, 1961 (Tong Room Girl)

Shih, Szu (1953–)

REAL NAME: Lei Qui Si; BIRTHPLACE: Hunan Province, Taiwan.

FILM: *Legend of the 7 Golden Vampires*, 1974 (Mei Kwei)

BIOGRAPHY—Cute and kick-ass Chinese leading lady and character actress Shih studied ballet as a child and at 16 became the go-to girl for the Shaw Brothers, for whom she starred in a number of chopsocky films. In *Legend of the 7 Golden Vampires*, she plays Mei Kwei, sister of the karate man I Ching who becomes the lover of Julie Ege. Shih is also the subject of an interracial romance, hooking up with Van Helsing's son. She made her last appearance on Taiwanese television in 1987 and has since retired.

Shorey, Emma

FILM: *The Woman in Black*, 2012 (Fisher Girl)

Shrimpton, Chrissie (1945–)

BIRTHPLACE: London, England.

FILM: *Moon Zero Two*, 1969 (Boutique Attendant)

BIOGRAPHY—The younger sister of 1960s supermodel Jean Shrimpton was also a model (just not as super as her sis), and had a short film career, including *G.G. Passion* with future Hammer heroine Caroline Munro. Shrimpton had a future with Hammer as well, playing a bit part as a boutique attendant in their "space Western" *Moon Zero Two*. She is perhaps best remembered as one of Mick Jagger's legion of ex-girlfriends. Her last film was in 1971; she is happily retired.

Sierra, Kisha (1981–)

BIRTHPLACE: Belize.

FILM: *The Resident*, 2011 (Good-Looking Girl)

Other genre credits: FILM: *The Eye*, Lionsgate, 2008 (Kisha)

Silvera, Simone
FILM: *Moon Zero Two*, 1969 (Girlfriend)

Sinclair, Peggy
TELEVISION: *Hammer House of Mystery and Suspense*: "Tennis Court," 1985 (Matron)
Other genre credits: TELEVISION: *Haunted*: "Girl on a Swing," "Living Doll," 1967; *Thriller*: "Kiss Me and Die," 1974 (Miss Faversham); *Leap in the Dark*: "Parlour Games," 1977 (Mrs. Verrall)

Smith, Amber Dean
FILM: *Moon Zero Two*, 1969 (Girlfriend)
Note: First-ever *Penthouse* Pet of the Year

Smith, Barbara
FILM: *The Terror of the Tongs*, 1961 (Tong Room Girl)

Smith, Christine
FILM: *Lust for a Vampire*, 1971 (Schoolgirl)

Smith, Dorothy
FILM: *Frankenstein Must Be Destroyed*, 1969 (Anna's Neighbor)

Smith, Madeline (1949–)
BIRTHPLACE: Hartfield, Sussex, England.
FILMS: *Taste the Blood of Dracula*, 1970 (Dolly); *The Vampire Lovers*, 1970 (Emma Morton); *Frankenstein and the Monster from Hell*, 1974 (Sarah)
BIOGRAPHY— One of the most beautiful and beloved of all the Hammer Heroines, "Maddy" Smith was one of the silver screen's most lethal combinations of angelic innocence and unbridled (if unintentional) sexuality, along with a deft touch for comedy. She brought all of these qualities to bear in the roles that made her famous, "crumpet" in leery British sex comedies of the '60s and '70s like *Up Pompeii* and *Up the Front*, and ultimately a Bond Girl in *Live and Let Die*. Not formally trained (although she later took acting classes), she was working at the Biba boutique and had begun to model when she was spotted on the street by a talent agent, and she soon had a part in the film *Escalation*. After appearing with fellow Hammer siren Veronica Carlson in *Pussycat, Pussycat, I Love You*, she was working for Hammer proper, as the prostitute Dolly in *Taste the Blood of Dracula*. It was an auspicious debut, a non-speaking part, but still the most gorgeous girl in the room (although admittedly even Smith has a hard time competing with Malaika Martin simulating oral sex with a snake).

Her next part for Hammer was quite a bit more substantial, in what was to become her signature role for the company as the virginal Emma Morton in the classic *The Vampire Lovers*, a film that is, in its own way, as groundbreaking as *The Curse of Frankenstein*. Smith says it wasn't difficult to play either a virgin or an innocent, as she was both at the time; and although she wasn't over the moon about doing the nude scenes, she was placated somewhat by producer Michael Style, who told her that the scenes wouldn't be seen in England, that they were being filmed for the "Japanese version" (there *was* none). But that didn't stop her from having fun on the film, and she hugely enjoyed the chance to work with and learn from actors Peter Cushing and Jon Finch and director Roy Ward Baker. She's so almost impossibly virginal that it sometimes seems as the scripters might be having a bit of a laugh, but she pulls it off (sometimes literally) with aplomb. She claims that with a bustline like hers, there's a very thin line between being sexy and ridiculous, and she wasn't ridiculous.

In her last role for Hammer, as Sarah in *Frankenstein and the Monster from Hell*, she wasn't required to show any skin at all, just a great deal of sympathy for Dave Prowse's hairy brute of a monster whom Peter Cushing (in the grand tradition of movie mad scientists everywhere) wants to mate her with. She's actually back to a non-speaking role in this one, as her character is a mute, and she gives a moving performance in a role that focuses on her face instead of her breasts. This accomplished performance showed how far she'd come as an actress in just a few years. She was also in another classic genre effort, *Theater of Blood* (she's Rosemary, the blond secretary), and continued to appear in films and TV shows like *Jason King*, which seemed to cast its leading ladies almost exclusively from the Hammer ranks. In 1974, Smith met another Hammer actor, David Buck (*The Mummy's Shroud*), with whom she had a relationship (they married six months before his death in 1989) and a daughter. Buck's death and the subsequent responsibility of raising her daughter as a single mother more or less forced her retirement. She has appeared at fan conventions and performed on British television in 2000 and 2011, but if she never plays another part, she's satisfied with her lot. Although fans always want more, we can be more than satisfied with what her films will continue to give.

Other genre credits: FILMS: *The Devil's Widow*, Commonwealth United Entertainment, 1970 (Sue); *The Amazing Mr. Blunden*, Hemdale Film, 1972 (Bella); *Theater of Blood*, Cineman Productions, 1973 (Rosemary); *Live and Let Die*, Eon Productions, 1973 (Miss Caruso); *Bloodbath at the House of Death*, Wildwood Productions, 1984 TELEVISION: *Dark Knight*: "The Dragon Singer," 2000 (Singer)

Soraya, Princess (1932–2001)

REAL NAME: Soraya Esfandiary-Bakhtiari; BIRTHPLACE: Isfahan, Iran.
FILM: *She*, 1965 (Soraya)

BIOGRAPHY—Hammer had featured Hollywood royalty and British acting royalty in their films, but in this instance, they featured actual royalty: The beautiful Princess Soraya was a real princess, the second wife of the shah of Iran. After her divorce from the shah (due to infertility on her part), she embarked on a very short-lived motion picture career. After *She*, despite her great beauty and presence, she retired to move about in high social circles. She battled severe depression for years, until her death in 2001.

Sparrow, Bobby

FILM: *To the Devil a Daughter*, 1976 (Fourth Girl)

Spencer, Sally-Jane (1945–)

BIRTHPLACE: Buckinghamshire, England.
FILM: *The Anniversary*, 1968 (Florist)
Other genre credits: TELEVISION: *The New Avengers*: "To Catch a Rat," 1976 (Mother)

Stallybrass, Anne (1938–)

BIRTHPLACE: Westcliff-on-Sea, Essex, England.
FILM: *Countess Dracula*, 1971 (Pregnant Woman)

Starr, Zoe

FILM: *The Devil Rides Out*, 1968 (Indian Girl)

Steafel, Sheila (1935–)

REAL NAME: Same; BIRTHPLACE: Johannesburg, South Africa.
FILM: *Quatermass and the Pit*, 1968 (Journalist)
Other genre credits: FILMS: *Daleks Invasion Earth: 2150 A.D.*, Amicus Productions, 1966 (Young Woman); *Bloodbath at the House of Death*, Wildwood Productions, 1984 (Sheila Finch) TELEVISION: *The Ghosts of Motley Hall*: 20 Episodes, 1976–1978 (The White Lady)

Steel, Pippa (1948–1992)

BIRTHPLACE: Flensburg, Germany.
FILMS: *The Vampire Lovers*, 1970 (Laura); *Lust for a Vampire*, 1971 (Susan Pelley)
BIOGRAPHY— Beautiful German character actress Steel made her first appearance in 1962, and went on to play two memorable roles in Hammer's Karnstein trilogy as a victim of Carmilla. In *The Vampire Lovers*, she is the first girl seduced by Ingrid Pitt, and in *Lust for a Vampire*, she is the one doing the seducing; unfortunately, she has picked Yutte Stensgaard to seduce, and that ends about as well as her relationship with Ingrid, with her corpse dumped unceremoniously in a well. She died, much too young, from cancer, at the age of 44 in 1992.
Other genre credits: TELEVISION: *UFO*: "Court Martial," 1971 (Diane); *Blake's 7*: "The Way Back," 1978 (Maja Varon)

Stensgaard, Yutte (1946–)

REAL NAME: Jytte Stensgaard; BIRTHPLACE: Thisted, Jutland, Denmark.
FILM: *Lust for a Vampire*, 1971 (Carmilla/Mircalla Karnstein)
BIOGRAPHY— The career of lovely Yutte Stensgaard was short and far from sweet. She moved to England in 1963, modeled, and enrolled at Ronald Curtis' Studio Film Craft Drama School. She fell in love with and married his son, art director Anthony, and the senior Mr. Curtis became her manager. Her first movie was the Italian production *Girl with a Pistol*; she then appeared in great films (*Scream and Scream Again*) and awful films (*Zeta One*) and on television. She next got her first and only leading role, as Carmilla/Mircalla Karnstein in the sequel to *The Vampire Lovers*, Hammer's *Lust for a Vampire*. Routinely castigated as one of the worst films ever made, even by its own participants, it's everything that its predecessor is routinely accused of being (vulgar, gratuitous, and exploitative), true. But it isn't half-bad in spots, and contains a wonderfully perverse performance by Ralph Bates. The only problem was with

Mike Raven has Yutte Stensgaard looking dazed and confused, with Barbara Jefford as his fellow Karnstein conspirator in *Lust for a Vampire*.

the performance that counted the most, Stensgaard's, but through no fault of her own. She is certainly beautiful, and did her best with what she had to work from, but it all comes down to the fact that she was just no Ingrid Pitt. She almost achieves liftoff in the graveyard scene with Bates, when he begs her to be her undead slave and she drains him, but one never gets the sense that she is a force of nature in the way that Ingrid was. At the end of 1971, Stensgaard and her husband divorced, and without her father-in-law's connections and guidance, the parts began to dry up. By 1972, they became non-existent; she began the year working in a clothes shop. She met an NBC foreign correspondent and went to America with him in the hopes of starting a career in music, but it never materialized, and her second marriage ended in divorce as well. In the late 1980s, she became a born-again Christian and is now the national account director for a monolithic radio conglomerate. As former Pittsburgh Steelers coach Chuck Noll would have said, she's finally found her life's work.

Other genre credits: FILMS: *Zeta One*, Tigon British Film Productions, 1969 (Ann Olson); *Scream and Scream Again*, American International Pictures, 1970 (Erika); *Burke & Hare*, Armitage/Kenneth Shipman Productions, 1972 (Janet) TELEVISION: *Dead of Night*: "Bedtime," 1972 (Gertrude Wicket)

Stevenson, Alexandra

FILM: *Slave Girls*, 1967 (Luri)

Stewardson, Cheryl

FILM: *Creatures the World Forgot*, 1971 (Cave Girl)

Stockley, Mary

FILM: *The Woman in Black*, 2012 (Mrs. Fisher)
Other genre credits: FILMS: *V for Vendetta*, Warner Brothers Pictures, 2006 (Ruth); *Artifacts*, Title Films, 2007 (Kate); *7lives*, Starfish Films, 2011 (Michelle)

Stone, Marianne Haydon; a.k.a. Mary Stone and Marion Stone (1922–2009)

BIRTHPLACE: King's Cross, London, England.
FILMS: *Spaceways*, 1953 (Mrs. Rogers); *Terror Street*, 1953 (Pam Palmer); *The Quatermass Xperiment*, 1955 (Central Clinic Nurse); *Quatermass 2*, 1957 (Secretary); *Man with a Dog*, 1957 (Mrs. Stephens); *Hell Is a City*, 1960 (Woman); *Watch it, Sailor!* 1961 (Woman with Child); *Paranoiac*, 1963 (Woman #2); *The Curse of the Mummy's Tomb*, 1964 (Landlady); *Hysteria*, 1965 (Miss Grogan); *Countess Dracula*, 1971 (Kitchen Maid)
TELEVISION: *Hammer House of Mystery and Suspense*: "In Possession," 1984 (Woman Downstairs)
BIOGRAPHY—As Barbara Shelley is far and away the go-to Hammer Heroine, then the ubiquitous Marianne Stone is the female Michael Ripper, with even more Hammer titles than Shelley to her credit. In fact, she holds the record as the actress with the most screen credits (over 200). Many of her parts were without dialogue, and little more than walk-ons (she didn't have much time for more). She was born in London and attended RADA, beginning her stage career soon after. She married Peter Noble in 1947, with future *Phantom of the Opera* star Herbert Lom as the best man, and it was a happy union that lasted until his death in 1997. Her first film appearance was in 1943, and among her more prominent credits are *Lolita* and *A Hard Day's Night*; her last role came on television in 1989. She also appeared in nine *Carry On* comedies.

Other genre credits: FILMS: *Corridors of Blood*, Amalgamated Productions, 1958 (Woman Arrested at Black Ben's); *Horrors of the Black Museum*, Carmel Productions, 1959 (Neighbor); *Jack the Ripper*, Mid Century Film Productions Limited, 1959 (Drunken Woman); *The Day the Earth Caught Fire*, Pax Films, 1961 (Miss Evans); *Witchcraft*, Lippert Films, 1964 (Secretary); *Blood Beast from Outer Space*, Armitage Film Productions, 1965 (Madge Lilburn); *Carry On Screaming*, Peter Rogers Productions, 1966 (Mrs. Parker); *Bloodsuckers*, Lucinda Films, 1972 (Cheerful Party Lady); *Horror on Snape Island*, Grenadier Films, 1972 (Nurse); *The Creeping Flesh*, Tigon Pictures, 1973 (Female Assistant); *The Vault of Horror*, Amicus, 1973 (Jane) TELEVISION: *Dead of Night*: "Two in the Morning," 1972 (Mrs. Frith)

Strasberg, Susan (1938–1999)

BIRTHPLACE: New York City, New York, USA.
FILM: *Taste of Fear* (a.k.a. *Scream of Fear*), 1961 (Penny Appleby)

BIOGRAPHY— The daughter of legendary theater director and drama coach Lee Strasberg, beautiful Susan Strasberg was a true "star of stage, screen, and television," dividing her time equally (and equally well) between all three pursuits. She made a number of contributions to the genre, the most significant of which was *Taste of Fear*, the first of Jimmy Sangster's *Psycho*-inspired thrillers. *Psycho* apparently wasn't the only inspiration; the scene where the chauffeur "discovers" her "father's" corpse in the swimming pool is very reminiscent of Shelley Winters' corpse in the river scene in Charles Laughton's *The Night of the Hunter* (1955), and the opening

Susan Strasberg and Ronald Lewis in *Scream of Fear*.

scene, with Strasberg's corpse being hauled from a lake, bears more than a passing resemblance to William Holden's corpse being fished out of the swimming pool in the all-time classic *Sunset Blvd*. It's the best of the psychological thrillers but not so much because of the plot, which is a fairly standard "Drive (fill in the blank) mad so murderer(s) can collect their inheritance" trope, but because of the players themselves and the unnerving atmosphere built up by director Seth Holt, along with some novel twists. Strasberg more than holds her own against old pros like Ann Todd and Christopher Lee as Penny, the wheelchair-bound girl whom wicked stepmother Todd needs out of the way in order to collect her unjust reward for murdering the girl's dad. But didn't we see Penny being hauled out of the lake at the very beginning? Well, that's one of the plot's convoluted twists, with Strasberg proving she's as good an actress in "reel" life as she was in real life. Besides her genre roles, she's also fondly remembered by cult movie fans for her parts in the seminal psychedelic–rock 'n' roll movies *The Trip* and *Psych-Out*. The last few years of that life were spent battling breast cancer; she lost the battle in 1999.

Other genre credits: FILMS: *So Evil, My Sister*, 1974 (Brenda); *The Legend of Hillbilly John*, Two's Company, 1974 (Polly); *The Manitou*, Mid-America Pictures, 1978 (Karen Tandy); *Bloody Birthday*, Judica Productions, 1981 (Viola Davis); *The Returning*, 1983 (Sybil Ophir); *Sweet 16*, 1983 (Joanne Morgan) TELEVISION: *The Invaders*: "Quantity Unknown," 1967 (Diane Oberly); *The Sixth Sense*: "Once Upon a Chilling," 1972 (Laura Anders); *Wide World Mystery*: "Frankenstein, Part One," 1973 (Elizabeth Lavenza); *Rod Serling's Night Gallery*: "Midnight Never Ends/Brenda," 1971 (Ruth Asquith); "The Doll of Death," 1973 (Sheila Trent); *The Evil Touch*: "Marcie," 1973 (Elizabeth); *Mazes and Monsters* (Movie), 1982 (Meg); *Tales of the Unexpected*: "I Like It Here in Wilmington," 1984 (Roberta Elton); "In the Cards," 1985 (Madame Myra); *Tales from the Darkside*: "Effect and Cause," 1985 (Kate Collins)

Stratford, Tracy Allison (1955–)

BIRTHPLACE: Los Angeles, California, USA.
FILM: *The Evil of Frankenstein*, 1964 (Rena as Child in Additional U.S. Sequence)
Other genre credits: TELEVISION: *The Twilight Zone*: "Little Girl Lost," 1962 (Tina Miller); "Living Doll," 1963 (Christie Streator)
Note: She was the voice of Lucy in *A Boy Named Charlie Brown* and *A Charlie Brown Christmas*.

Stribling, Melissa (1927–1992)

BIRTHPLACE: Gourock, Scotland.
FILMS: *Dracula* (a.k.a. *Horror of Dracula*), 1958, (Mina Holmwood); *Journey into Darkness*, 1969 (Helen Ames)
TELEVISION: *Journey to the Unknown*: "The New People," 1968 (Helen Ames)
BIOGRAPHY— Beautiful Scottish character actress Melissa Stribling was active in films for over 30 years, but she will always be remembered for one role by genre fans, that of Mina in Hammer's legendary first Dracula film. She is at first every inch the proper wife, all high, starched collars and demeanor, but soon we see she has a mind of her own when she sneaks out to see Van Helsing, whom her husband has no use for. She is obviously sexually unfulfilled by that stuffy husband, and the satisfaction she feels after being rubbed up by Dracula is communicated quite successfully by her knowing smile the morning after, as are the confused emotions she feels in the moments leading up to it (communicated so well through her eyes). It is interesting to note that the vampire women of the film are in three stages of development: Valerie Gaunt is already a vampire when the film begins, Carol Marsh is well on the way, and

Stribling will become one if she doesn't watch it. Hence, she is the only one we get to see the process from scratch, and she becomes the model for all those who followed in her footsteps of Dracula's victims that suddenly find their repressed middle-class values turned into unspeakable desires. She returned to Hammer ten years later an episode of *Journey to the Unknown*, "The New People," still quite lovely and definitely not on the side of the angels this time as the swinging wife of fellow Hammer vet Patrick Allen, a Satanist whose kicks just keep getting harder to find. Her last screen appearance was in 1998. She and Christopher Lee are seen in *Dracula* clips in Tim Burton's *Frankenweenie* (2012).

Other genre credits: FILMS: *Ghost Ship*, Vernon Sewell Productions, 1952 (Party Girl Vera); *Crucible of Terror*, Glendale, 1971 (Joanna Brent) TELEVISION: *The Avengers*: "Hunt the Man Down," 1961 (Stella Preston); "School for Traitors," 1963 (Claire Summers); *The New Avengers*: "Angels of Death," 1977 (Sally Manderson)

Stuckey, Sophie (1991–)

BIRTHPLACE: Camden, London, England.

FILM: *The Woman in Black*, 2012 (Stella Kipps)

BIOGRAPHY—Attractive young British actress Stuckey made her screen debut at the age of 11; she has a brief bit in *The Woman in Black* as the ghost of Daniel Radcliffe's dead wife.

Other genre credits: FILMS: *Close Your Eyes* (a.k.a. *Doctor Sleep*), BBC Films, 2002 (Heather); *The Dark*, Constantin Film, 2005 (Sarah); *Comedown*, Serotonin Films, 2012 (Jemma) TELEVISION: *Summer in Transylvania*: "The Summer That Time Forgot," "Attack of the Psycho Dates," "Banned," "Kiss of the Wolfboy," 2010 (Summer)

Sui Lin

FILM: *The Terror of the Tongs*, 1961 (Chinese Girl)

Summerfield, Eleanor (1921–2001)

BIRTHPLACE: London, England.

FILMS: *Man Bait*, 1952 (Vi); *The Black Glove*, 1954 (Barbara Quigley); *Blackout*, 1954 (Maggie Doone)

TELEVISION: *Hammer House of Horror*: "Rude Awakening," 1980 (Lady Strudwick)

BIOGRAPHY—Trained at RADA, Eleanor Summerfield was one of Britain's busiest character actresses for over 50 years, appearing regularly on stage (in many musicals, at which she excelled), screen, television and radio. Her work for Hammer encompasses two different eras and genres; her efforts for them in the 1950s in their pre–*Curse of Frankenstein* film noir productions and the post–glory days television shows. She's delightful in the "Rude Awakening" episode of *Hammer House of Horror*, playing a wealthy, witty (and evil) ghost in one act of Denholm Elliott's fevered dream in a dream in a dream. The wife of Leonard Sachs, and the mother of Robin Sachs (who also became an actor), she made her last appearance on television in 1998.

Other genre credits: FILMS: *Scrooge*, George Minter Productions, 1951; *The Watcher in the Woods*, Walt Disney Productions, 1980 (Mrs. Thayer)

TELEVISION: *UFO*: "The Cat with Ten Lives," 1970 (Muriel Thompson)

Swank, Hilary (1974–)

BIRTHPLACE: Lincoln, Nebraska, USA.

FILM: *The Resident*, 2011 (Dr. Juliet Devereaux)

BIOGRAPHY—Add yet another Oscar-winner to Hammer Films' legacy. Hilary Swank made her first stage appearance at the age of nine, and was also a champion gymnast. Her parents separated when she was fifteen, and she moved to Los Angeles with her mother, where they lived out of their car until they could afford an apartment. Her first film role was a genre role, and it endeared her to the hearts of fantasy fans worldwide: Kimberly in *Buffy the Vampire Slayer*. Her Academy Awards were for *Boys Don't Cry* and *Million Dollar Baby*, and she has become an executive producer as well, as she is for *The Resident*.

The Resident is another new offering from the revived Hammer Films; it went straight to DVD in the United States, but received theatrical distribution in England and other European countries.

A throwback to Hammer's Golden Age, the film is a psychological thriller, a direct spiritual descendant of the company's previous efforts *Taste of Fear*, *Nightmare*, and *Fanatic*. Christopher Lee is on hand to lend a direct link to the past, playing a negligible part well. But there are also plenty of reminders that this is not your father's Hammer. For one thing, Lee is the only British person in the cast. Of course, Hammer films, especially in the early days, would often feature Americans in major roles to help sell them to that audience, but in *The Resident*, everybody except Lee is resolutely American, and on top of that, it takes place in New York City, so there's not even any familiar shots of the English countryside (let alone Black Park) to stamp it as distinctly British, an anomaly from a company so firmly identified with Queen and Country.

Swank is everything fans have come to expect from her: athletic, beautiful, strong of character and smart — except, seemingly, when it comes to her choice of landlords, but Jeffrey Dean Morgan's character is so personable at first, one can't blame her for being taken in. And since her character is a doctor, one would think she would be familiar with the Physicians' Desk Reference and realized that she's being drugged, but then, of course, there'd be no story. She sure does wield a mean nail gun, but unfortunately, she has to use it more than once, when the film gives in to the convention of the maniac who just won't stay dead (although the April 2012 news story about a man who shot a nail into his own heart and survived perhaps makes it not so implausible after all). *The Resident* didn't earn Swank a third Oscar, but she proved herself a worthy new addition to the pantheon of Hammer Horror Heroines, and she showed both a knowledge of that tradition and a sense of humor by channeling Raquel Welch from *One Million Years B.C.* and posing in a fur bikini for publicity shots.

Now the circle is complete: Hilary Swank, star of ***The Resident***, channels Raquel Welch in this publicity shot for the film.

Other genre credits: FILMS: *Buffy the Vampire Slayer*, 20th Century–Fox, 1992 (Kimberly); *Sometimes They Come Back ... Again*, Trimark Pictures, 1996 (Michelle Porter)

Talfrey, Hira

BIRTHPLACE: New Zealand.
FILM: *The Curse of the Werewolf,* 1961 (Teresa)
Other genre credits: FILMS: *Witchfinder General,* Tigon British International Productions–AIP, 1968 (Hanged Woman); *The Oblong Box,* AIP, 1969 (Martha) TELEVISION: *The Avengers:* Charlie Bonnay, "The Removal Men," 1962

Taylor, Elaine Regina (1943–)

BIRTHPLACE: Hemel Hempstead, Hertfordshire, England.
FILM: *The Anniversary,* 1968 (Shirley Blair)
BIOGRAPHY— Encouraged by her mother to follow her dream, beautiful Elaine Regina Taylor attended the Italia Conti Academy of Theatre Arts and was a member of the London Festival Ballet. She landed her first gig on *The Benny Hill Show,* soon followed by automatic cinematic immortality as a Bond Girl in her first feature film, *Casino Royale,* which also featured Caroline Munro. Her only Hammer was a great one, the film version of the play *The Anniversary,* as the latest fiancée of one of the sons that Bette Davis dominates with an iron eye patch. She's smart and spunky and very sexy, especially when she's cavorting in her bra and panties, which leads to two things: one, a continuity gaffe. When she's getting dressed, she makes an elaborate show out of adjusting her hosiery, but later, when she undresses for sex, she's wearing neither stockings nor pantyhose. It also leads to the film's best-remembered

Elaine Regina Taylor in *The Anniversary.*

scene: When Taylor finds Davis's eye in a dresser drawer. It's the price she pays for being spunky; so spunky that she quite reminds Davis of herself. And so she gets the only break that Davis gives anybody in the film, but done on Davis's cynical assumption that Taylor will turn out even *more* like Davis. Taylor took a break from 1974 through 1988, although she added only a few credits to her CV after that, and retired for good in 1992. She specializes in French gourmet cooking, which she feeds to her husband, actor Christopher Plummer, on their palatial New England estate.

Other genre credits: FILM: *Casino Royale*, Columbia Pictures Corporation, 1967 (Peg)

Taylor, Siobhan

FILM: *The Damned*, 1963 (Mary)

Telezynska, Izabella

FILM: *To the Devil a Daughter*, 1976 (Margaret)

Thater, Heinke

FILM: *Creatures the World Forgot*, 1971 (Prehistoric Woman)

Thomas, Lisa

FILM: *One Million Years B.C.*, 1966 (Sura)

Thompson, Sophie (1962–)

BIRTHPLACE: London, England.
TELEVISION: *Hammer House of Horror*: "Guardian of the Abyss," 1980 (First Girl)
Other genre credits: FILM: *Harry Potter and the Deathly Hallows: Part 1*, Warner Brothers Pictures, 2010 (Mafalda Hopkirk) TELEVISION: *A Traveler in Time*: Penelope, "The Door," "The Kitchen," "The Locket," "The Tunnel," "The Ribbon," 1979 (Penelope)

Tilton, Connie

FILM: *When Dinosaurs Ruled the Earth*, 1970 (Sand Mother)
Other genre credits: FILM: *Gorgo*, King Brothers Productions, 1961 (Crew: Stuntwoman)

Tirard, Anne (1917–2003)

BIRTHPLACE: London, England.
FILM: *Stop Me Before I Kill!* 1960 (Nicole)
Other genre credits: FILMS: *The Frozen Dead*, Gold Star Productions, 1966 (Mrs. Schmidt); *Witchfinder General*, Tigon British Film Productions/AIP, 1968 (Old Woman); *The Witches*, Jim Henson Company, 1990 (Lady One) TELEVISION: *The Avengers*: "Toy Trap," 1961 (Mrs. McCabe); *Doctor Who*: "Conspiracy," 1965 (Locusta); "The Ribos Operation" (Parts 3 & 4), 1978 (The Seeker); *The Young Indiana Jones Chronicles*: "Transylvania 1918," 1993 (Tarot Reader)

Todd, Ann (1909–1993)

REAL NAME: Dorothy Anne Todd; BIRTHPLACE: Hartford, Cheshire, England.
FILM: *Scream of Fear*, 1961 (Jane Appleby)
Other genre credits: TELEVISION: *Alfred Hitchcock Presents*: "Sylvia," 1958 (Sylvia Leeds Kent); *Thriller*: "Letter to a Lover," 1961 (Sylvia Lawrence)

Traister, Sheila Ivy (1958–)

FILM: *The Resident*, 2011 (E.R. Nurse)
Other genre credits: FILMS: *Strangeland*, 1998 (Reporter # 2) TELEVISION: *Asteroid* (Movie), 1997, (Red Cross Check-In Woman)

Tushingham, Rita (1942–)

BIRTHPLACE: Liverpool, England.
FILM: *Straight on Till Morning*, 1972 (Brenda Thompson)
BIOGRAPHY— Rita Tushingham began her career on stage, and struck gold with her very first movie role in *A Taste of Honey*, which earned her both a BAFTA and Golden Globe Award. She went on to appear in such epics as *Dr. Zhivago*. It was also her misfortune to appear in one of Hammer's most interminable and symbolically heavy-handed "psychological thrillers," *Straight on Till Morning*, which had most people heading Straight on Till the Exit sign. She plays a "plain Jane" who lives in a never-never land of finding the "perfect man" to fall in love with and bear his child, only to hook up with psycho killer Shane Briant. The Peter Pan parallels are turgid enough, although not the deal-breaker; the line to unbearable is crossed, however, with not only the killing of a dog, but the recording of its dying screams to be played back later along with the screams of Briant's other victims. A sad example of how far the mighty could fall, the film is deservedly little-seen today. But other actresses have survived worse films and lived long and prospered, and this is what Tushingham has done; she is still active in the business and is equally active on behalf of breast cancer health and support.
Other genre credits: FILM: *Puffball: The Devil's Eyeball*, Amerique Films, 2007 (Molly)

Twigge, Jenny (1950–)

BIRTHPLACE: England.
FILM: *Vampire Circus*, 1972 (Schoolgirl)
Other genre credits: TELEVISION: *Blake's 7*: "Star One," 1979 (Lurena)

Tyrell, Joan

FILM: *The Two Faces of Dr. Jekyll*, 1960 (Major Domo)

Ustinov, Tamara (1945–)

BIRTHPLACE: London, England.
FILM: *Blood from the Mummy's Tomb*, 1971 (Veronica)
BIOGRAPHY— The daughter of Peter Ustinov and the niece of Angela Lansbury, Tamara Ustinov has been active on stage since the '60s and on screen since 1970. Her first feature film was *The Blood on Satan's Claw*, and her second was *Blood from the Mummy's Tomb*, in which she has a small part as an archaeologist's assistant.
Other genre credits: FILMS: *The Blood on Satan's Claw*, Tigon British Film Productions, 1971 (Rosalind Barton); *The Last Horror Movie*, Prolific Films, 2003 (Bride's Mother) TELEVISION: *Tales of the Unexpected*: "Accidental Death," 1984 (Beryl); *Hex*: "Ellen Burns," 2005 (Tour Guide)

Valentine, Elizabeth (1877–1971)

BIRTHPLACE: New York City, New York, USA.
FILM: *The Kiss of the Vampire*, 1963 (Second Disciple)

Van der Zyl, Monica "Nikki" (1935–)

BIRTHPLACE: Berlin, Germany.

FILMS: *She*, 1965 (Voice of Ayesha); *One Million Years B.C.*, 1966 (Voice of Loana); *Scars of Dracula*, 1970 (Voice of Sarah Framsen)

BIOGRAPHY—The daughter of a rabbi, Nikki Van der Zyl is truly a contender for the title of the ultimate Bond Girl, and she has never even appeared in any of the movies. But the voices that fans think belong to Ursula Andress, Eunice Gayson, Shirley Eaton, Mie Hama and so many others have all been dubbed by Van der Zyl—in fact, in *Dr. No*, she provided every female voice except for Miss Moneypenny and one other. She was also a dialogue coach for Gert Frobe on *Goldfinger*, even though his voice, too, was ultimately dubbed over. And although it was Raquel Welch and her fur bikini that put *One Million Years B.C.* on the map, once again it was really Van der Zyl exclaiming "Archelon!" and "Tumak!" She retired after her voiceovers for *Moonraker* to practice law, and currently divides her time between art, poetry, and public speaking.

Other genre credits: FILMS: *Dr. No*, Eon Productions, 1962 (Voice of Honey Ryder and others); *From Russia with Love*, Eon Productions, 1963 (Voice of Sylvia Trench and Receptionist); *Goldfinger*, Eon Productions, 1964 (Voice of Jill Masterson and Bonita); *Thunderball*, Eon Productions, 1965 (Voice of Domino Derval); *Deadlier Than the Male*, Greater Films Limited, 1967 (Voice of Penelope); *Casino Royale*, Columbia Pictures Corporation, 1967 (Voice of Vesper Lind); *You Only Live Twice*, Eon Productions, 1967 (Voice of Kissy Suzuki); *On Her Majesty's Secret Service*, Eon Productions, 1969 (Olympe and various voices); *Live and Let Die*, Eon Productions, 1973 (partial voice of Solitaire); *The Man with the Golden Gun*, Eon Productions, 1974 (Chew Mee and various voices); *Moonraker*, Danjaq/Eon Productions, 1979 (various voices)

Van Ost, Valerie (1944–)

BIRTHPLACE: Berkhamsted, Hertfordshire, England.

FILM: *The Satanic Rites of Dracula*, 1973 (Jane)

BIOGRAPHY—British character actress Van Ost made her debut in 1962, and became most well-known for her roles in the *Carry On* films. She has a solid supporting part in *The Satanic Rites of Dracula* as a secretary who gets kidnapped by Dracula's satanic cult and is vampirized by Christopher Lee, later turning up chained in his cellar as one of the hissing vampire girls who nearly do in Joanna Lumley. She gets a stake run through her for her troubles. She was active until 1976, and retired to form a casting company with her husband.

Other genre credits: FILMS: *Bloodsuckers*, Lucinda Films, 1972 (Don's Wife) TELEVISION: *The Avengers*: "Dead Man's Treasure," 1967 (Penelope Blaine); *Space: 1999*: "Breakaway," 1975 (Main Mission Operative); *Alien Attack* (Movie), 1976 (Main Mission Operative)

Ventham, Wanda (1935–)

BIRTHPLACE: Brighton, East Sussex, England

FILM: *Captain Kronos, Vampire Hunter*, 1974 (Lady Durward)

BIOGRAPHY—Like quite a number of women in this book, Wanda Ventham attended the Central School of Speech and Drama; her film debut came in 1956 with *Teenage Bad Girl*. She became a fixture of British TV and is remembered fondly by genre fans for both her continuing role as Colonel Virginia Lake in *UFO* and her role in *Captain Kronos, Vampire Hunter*, as the last of the line of Hammer's cinematic Karnstein family tree. (Listen closely and you'll hear that Ventham pronounces it "Karstein.") Her role is actually more Countess Dracula than Carmilla; she begins the film as aged and bedridden, and although it's discovered in the climax that this was only literally a mask, it apparently was her real condition before her hot blood injections, and she reverts back to that condition when Kronos gives her a cold steel injection. They also cob a bit from Dracula and have her shed a tear of blood after her undead husband receives the same, but it's still effective, especially with the way she underplays her reaction to his death. She doesn't fly into a frenzy, but maintains the same cool manner, the change to icy fury signified by that tear of blood and the accompanying look in her eyes as she slowly advances on Kronos. The role itself might be somewhat derivative, but her performance of it can certainly stand by itself. Her last role to date was in 2007.

Other genre credits: FILMS: *The Blood Beast Terror*, Tigon British Film Productions, 1969 (Clare Mallinger); *Invasion UFO*: 1974 (Col. Virginia Lake) TELEVISION: *The Avengers*: "The Gravediggers," 1965 (Nurse Spray); *Out of the Unknown*: "The Eye," 1966 (Josephine); *UFO*: Col. Virginia Lake, "Identified," "The Cat with Ten Lives," "Destruction," The Psychobombs," 1970; "Mindbender," "The Man Who Came Back," "Timelash," "Reflections in the Water," 1971; "The Long Sleep," 1973 (Col. Virginia Lake); *Doctor Who*: "The Faceless Ones," 1967 (Jean Rock); "Image of the Fendahl," 1977 (Thea Ransome); "Time and the Rani," 1987 (Faroon)

Verdugo, Nicole

FILM: *Beyond the Rave*, 2008 (Iraqi Girl)

Vetri, Victoria; a.k.a. Angela Dorian (1944–)

REAL NAME: Victoria Cecilia Vetry; BIRTHPLACE: San Francisco, California, USA.
FILM: *When Dinosaurs Ruled the Earth*, 1970 (Sanna)
BIOGRAPHY— For every actress who has had a successful career, with rewards and honors earned, there are many more for whom celebrity has been a seeming curse, its bright lights concealing a dark, sordid underbelly. Victoria Vetri is a member of the latter group. Born to hard-working immigrant parents, she attended Hollywood High, and made her first film appearance (*The Pigeon That Took Rome*) before she graduated. She appeared in *Playboy* under the name Angela Dorian; in September, 1967, she was the Playmate of the Month, and in 1968 was voted the Playmate of the Year. This led to a number of roles in genre television shows and films, including the classic *Rosemary's Baby*, where she appeared as a character named Angela Dorian and even gets her own in-joke when Rosemary mistakes her for the actress Victoria Vetri. She inherited Raquel Welch's fur bikini for Hammer's sequel to *One Million Years B.C.*, *When Dinosaurs Ruled the Earth*, supplanting the sizzling saurians sculpted by Jim Danforth, who inherited the stop-motion animation chores from Ray Harryhausen. The biggest problem was that Danforth's superb creations did not have nearly as much screen time as Harryhausen's, and so Vetri was forced to carry more of the film, a chore which she was not up to. She's certainly beautiful, and even gets her prehistoric kit off a time or two, but her willowy portrayal hardly seems the stuff that prehistoric women were made of, and she lacks Welch's presence. So the fur bikini did not work the same wonders for her career as it did for her predecessor. She made her last film, *Invasion of the Bee Girls*, only three years later, and performed her last role, period, in the television series *Lucas Tanner* just two years after that. In 1980, she was brutally attacked in her home, and was left bloodied but unbowed, returning to pose for *Playboy* again in 1984. She married four times, and it was her fourth marriage which led to the most scandalous chapter in her story: In 2010, she shot her fourth husband Bruce Rathgeb at close range and stood trial on charges of attempted murder. In September of 2011, she pled no contest to a reduced charge of attempted voluntary manslaughter, and was sentenced to nine years in prison.

Victoria Vetri (middle), Imogen Hassall (right) and Magda Konopka (left) form a titanic trio of prehistoric pulchritude in *When Dinosaurs Ruled the Earth*.

Other genre credits: FILMS: *Rosemary's Baby*, William Castle Productions, 1968 (Terry Gionoffrio); *Invasion of the Bee Girls*, Sequoia Pictures, 1973 (Julie Zorn)

TELEVISION: *The Man from U.N.C.L.E.*: "The Indian Affairs Affair," 1966 (Charisma Highcloud); *Batman*: "I'll Be a Mummy's Uncle," 1968 (Florence of Arabia); *Star Trek*: "Assignment Earth," 1968 (Isis—Human Form); *Land of the Giants*: "The Marionettes," 1970 (Lisa)

Villiers, Caroline (1949–)

BIRTHPLACE: London, England.
FILM: *Captain Kronos, Vampire Hunter*, 1974 (Petra)

Villiers, Mavis (1911–1976)

REAL NAME: Mavis Clare Cooney; BIRTHPLACE: Sydney, Australia.
FILM: *Straight on Till Morning*, 1972 (Indian Princess)

Visitor, Nana (1957–)

REAL NAME: Nana Tucker; BIRTHPLACE: New York City, New York, USA.
FILM: *The Resident*, 2011 (Real Estate Agent)
Other genre credits: FILMS: *End Girl/The Sentinel*, Universal Pictures, 1977 (End Girl); *Babysitter Wanted*, Big Screen Entertainment, 2008 (Linda Albright); *Friday the 13th*, New Line Cinema, 2009 (Pamela Voorhees) TELEVISION: *The Twilight Zone*: "Dead Woman's Shoes," 1985 (Lori); *Alfred Hitchcock Presents*: "Happy Birthday," 1986 (Doris); *The Spirit* (Movie), 1987 (Ellen Dolan); *The Outer Limits*: "In Our Own Image," 1998 (Cecilia Fairman); *Star Trek: Deep Space Nine*: 179 Episodes 1993–1999 (Major Kira/Colonel Kira); *They Are Among Us* (Movie), 2004 (Colette); *Battlestar Galactica*: "Faith," 2008 (Emily); *Grimm*: Melissa "Bee-Ware," 2011 (Melissa Wincroft)

Wagstaff, Elsie Lilian (1899–1985)

BIRTHPLACE: London, England.
FILMS: *Celia: The Sinister Affair of Poor Aunt Nora*, 1949 (Poor Aunt Nora); *Frankenstein and the Monster from Hell*, 1974 (Wild One)
Other genre credits: FILMS: *The Snake Woman*, Caralan Productions, 1961 (Aggie Harker); *Dr. Syn, Alias the Scarecrow*, Walt Disney Productions, 1963 (Mrs. Ransley) TELEVISION: *Walt Disney's Wonderful World of Color*: "The Scarecrow of Romney Marsh" (Part One), 1963 (Mrs. Ransley); *Thriller*: "A Place to Die," 1973 (Old Woman)

Walker, Zena (1934–2003)

BIRTHPLACE: Birmingham, England.
TELEVISION: *Journey to the Unknown*: "Girl of My Dreams," 1968 (Carrie Clark)
BIOGRAPHY—Lovely Zena Walker, the daughter of a grocer, attended RADA, turning down a Hollywood contract to remain there. She had an illustrious stage career, winning a Tony award; her TV career began in 1957 in *Sword of Freedom*. She played the female lead in the *Journey to the Unknown* episode "Girl of My Dreams," which was about a woman who has dreams with very specific details as to when people will die; she is exploited by an abusive American ne'er do well who marries her and uses her dreams to warn and reap rewards from the potential victims. She gives a very touching performance, caught between the rock of her nightmares and the hard place of her husband, who obviously doesn't want them to end. Her last role came in 2003, the year she passed away.
Other genre credits: TELEVISION: *Thriller*: "Murder in Mind," 1973 (Betty Drew)

Wallis, Jacquie

FILM: *The Kiss of the Vampire*, 1963 (Sabena Ravna)
BIOGRAPHY—Her career lasted little more than a dozen years, with not even as many credits to her name as years, but like many a "one-hit wonder," she had one great song in her,

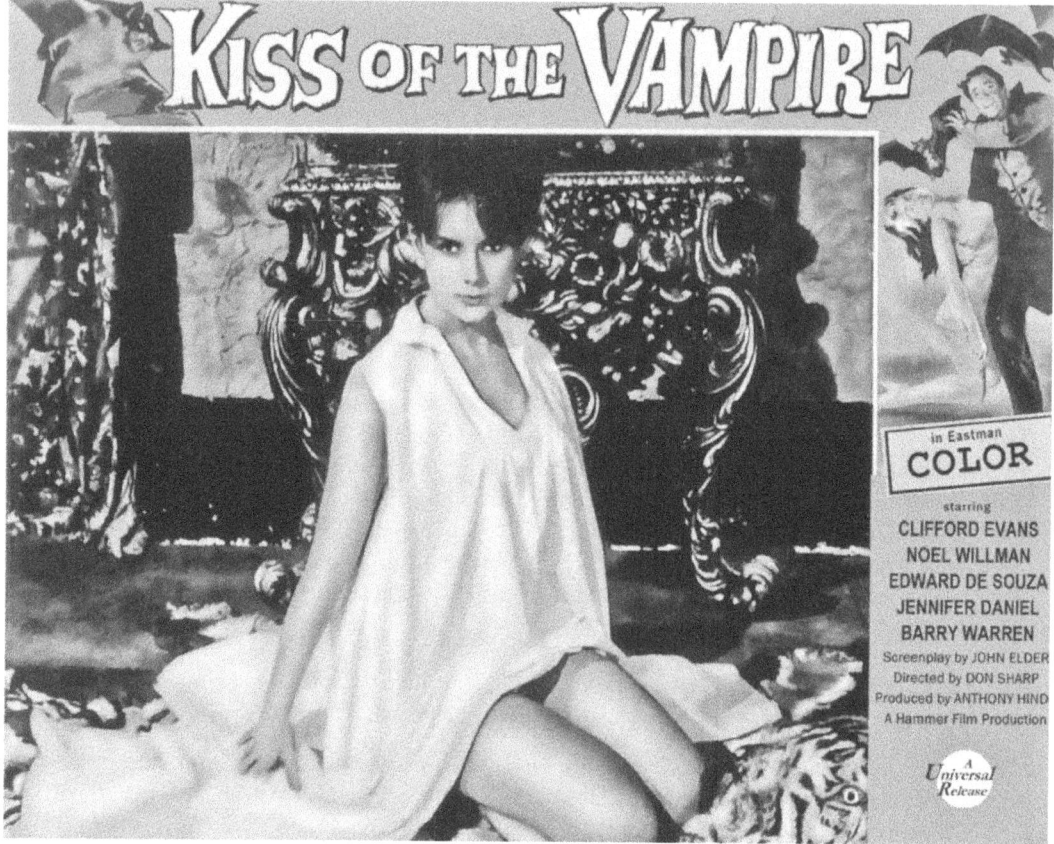

Jacquie Wallis offers a great deal of incentive to become one of the undead, lookin' for *The Kiss of the Vampire* (courtesy Mel Bridgeman).

and that was sung as the sexy vampiress Sabena Ravna in *The Kiss of the Vampire*; she becomes visually aroused as her brother musically seduces star Jennifer Daniel. Like the rest of her clan, she comes to a nasty end, but does so beautifully.

Walmsley, Anna

FILM: *The Revenge of Frankenstein*, 1958 (Vera)

Walsh, Kay (1911–2005)

BIRTHPLACE: Chelsea, London, England.
FILMS: *The Witches*, 1966 (Stephanie Bax); *Journey to the Unknown*, 1969 (Mrs. Joan Walker)
TELEVISION: *Journey to the Unknown*: "The Last Visitor," 1969 (Mrs. Joan Walker)
BIOGRAPHY—This veteran British character actress began her career as a music hall dancer, and made her first film in 1934. She married David Lean in 1940 and contributed to the screenplays of several of his films, including *Oliver Twist*; she later divorced him due to his serial womanizing. In *The Witches*, she was simply marvelous as Stephanie Bax, the writer who is in reality the head of the witches' coven, and upstages star Joan Fontaine. She's cheerful, confident, incredibly charming and charismatic, even when discussing the sacrifice of a young

virgin, and she plays the satanic orgy scene with an unbridled joy, belting out her incantations with a gusto not seen since George Zucco in thrall to the Great God Ramboona in *Voodoo Man* (1944). Unfortunately, the scene is marred by the fact that the "satanic orgy" looks more like drunken idiots about to pass out in a bar at three in the morning, but Walsh more than makes up for all of them with this delightful piece of scenery-chewing. Her second effort for Hammer was equally delightful: a *Journey to the Unknown* episode in which she plays a washed-up old actress who owns a small hotel. She also likes to dress up as her dead husband and become a knife-wielding maniac, thoroughly ruining Patty Duke's stay with her. Walsh later married the psychologist who invented the term "mid-life crisis" and retired in 1982; she died from multiple burns following an accident in 2005.

Other genre credits: FILMS: *Dr. Syn, Alias the Scarecrow*, Walt Disney Productions, 1963 (Mrs. Waggett) TELEVISION: *Alfred Hitchcock Presents*: "I Spy," 1961 (Mrs. Morgan); *Walt Disney's Wonderful World of Color*: "The Scarecrow of Romney Marsh," 1963 (Mrs. Waggett)

Walsh, Sally

FILM: *The Curse of Frankenstein*, 1957 (Young Elizabeth)

BIOGRAPHY— The daughter of Hazel Court, she portrayed Hazel's character of Elizabeth as a young girl in *The Curse of Frankenstein*, her only film. She is now a successful artist.

Ward, Sarah "Lalla" (1951–)

BIRTHPLACE: London, England.

FILM: *Vampire Circus*, 1972 (Helga)

BIOGRAPHY— Sarah Ward attended the Central School of Speech and Drama, and her first feature was the Hammer film *Vampire Circus*, in which she plays vampire acrobat Helga, who puts on quite a show for the unsuspecting villagers with a spectacular routine that is climaxed with her and her partner changing into bats (at which point you would think that the villagers would begin to suspect something). She is best remembered for her role as Romana, one of the Doctor's more endearing assistants in *Doctor Who*; she also endeared herself to star Tom Baker, resulting in a short-lived marriage. She retired in 1993, after her second (and lasting) marriage to evolutionary biologist Richard Dawkins, and now concentrates on her family and her career as an illustrator, often for her husband's books.

Other genre credits: FILMS: *Doctor Who: Shada*, British Broadcasting Corporation, 1992 (Romana) TELEVISION: *Doctor Who*: "The Armageddon Factor," 1979 (Princess Astra); "Destiny of the Daleks," "City of Death," "The Creature from the Pit," "Nightmare of Eden," "The Horns of Nimon," 1979–80; "The Leisure Hive," "Meglos," "Full Circle," "State of Decay," 1980; "Warrior's Gate," 1981 (Romana); *Doctor Who: Dimensions in Time* (Short), 1993 (Romana)

Warne, Jo

TELEVISION: *Hammer House of Horror*: "The House That Bled to Death," 1980 (First Mother)

Warner, Patricia

FILM: *Lust for a Vampire*, 1971 (Schoolgirl)

Washbourne, Mona (1903–1988)

BIRTHPLACE: Birmingham, England.

FILMS: *The Gambler and the Lady*, 1952 (Miss Minter); *The Brides of Dracula*, 1960 (Frau Helga Lang)

BIOGRAPHY— Beloved British character actress Washbourne began her career as a concert pianist, and in the middle of a performance decided she wanted to be an actress (she did finish the performance). Her first role was in 1934, but her career didn't begin in earnest until 1948, and ran uninterrupted for another 40 years. In her second film for Hammer, *The Brides of Dracula*, she's the wife of the unctuous headmaster of the girls' school where Yvonne Monlaur goes to teach, telling one young charge if she leaves her mouth hanging open, she'll be catching flies in it. She won the 1981 Boston, New York, Los Angeles, and National Board of Review Film Critics' awards for Best Supporting Actress for her performance in *Stevie*.

Watford, Gwendoline (1927–1994)

BIRTHPLACE: London, England.
FILMS: *Never Take Sweets from a Stranger*, 1960 (Sally Carter); *Taste the Blood of Dracula*, 1970 (Martha Hargood)
BIOGRAPHY— Gwen Watford was a British character actress active for over 40 years, until her death from cancer in 1994. Both of her Hammer roles are mothers of girls whose lives are being threatened. The first is the harrowing *Never Take Sweets from a Stranger*, in which she must deal with a child molester who also happens to be one of her town's leading citizens. Her powerlessness in the face of the cover-up is agonizingly real. In *Taste the Blood of Dracula*, the situation has been reversed: She is married to a "leading citizen" who conceals monthly exercises in debauchery behind a mask of respectability and abuses his wife and daughter. Again, she gives a nuanced portrayal, torn between her love for her daughter and her sense of duty to her husband that makes her unable to defy his wishes. The quality of performances such as hers that lift the Hammer films above the level of so many inferior potboilers.
Other genre credits: FILMS: *The Fall of the House of Usher*, G.I.B., 1949 (Lady Usher); *The Ghoul*, Tyburn Film Productions, 1975 (Ayah)

Watts, Gwendolyn (1932–2000)

BIRTHPLACE: Carhampton, Somerset, England.
FILM: *Fanatic*, 1965 (Gloria)
Other genre credits: TELEVISION: *Alfred Hitchcock Presents*: "The Impromptu Murder," 1958 (Mrs. Arnold); *The Avengers*: "Man with Two Shadows," 1963 (Julie); *Mystery and Imagination*: "Uncle Silas," 1968 (Sarah Mangles)

Watts, Stephanie

FILM: *The Brides of Dracula*, 1960 (Foxy Girl)

Way, Ann (1915–1993)

BIRTHPLACE: Wiveliscombe, England.
FILM: *Hands of the Ripper*, 1971 (Seamstress)
Other genre credits: FILMS: *The Hands of Orlac*, Pendennis Films, 1960 (Seamstress); *Jabberwocky*, Python Films, 1977 (Merchant's Wife); *Haunted Honeymoon*, Orion Pictures, 1986 (Rachel)

Webster, Joy (1934–)

BIRTHPLACE: Birmingham, England.
FILMS: *The Two Faces of Dr. Jekyll*, 1960 (Jenny); *The Curse of the Werewolf*, 1961 (Isabel)
Other genre credits: FILMS: *The Woman Eater*, Fortress Film Productions, 1958 (Judy) TELEVISION: *The Avengers*: "Diamond Cut Diamond," 1961 (Stella Creighton)

Webster-Brough, Jean

FILM: *Spaceways*, 1953 (Mrs. Daniels)

Wehle, Brenda

FILM: *Let Me In*, 2010 (Principal)

Weir, Mary "Molly" (1910–2004)

BIRTHPLACE: Glasgow, Scotland.

FILMS: *Family Affair*, 1954 (Aggie); *The Lyons Abroad*, 1955 (Aggie); *Hands of the Ripper*, 1971 (Maid)

BIOGRAPHY— The career of veteran Scottish character actress Weir encompassed the stage, radio, television and films such as *The Prime of Miss Jean Brodie*; she also authored a number of books, including *Shoes Were for Sunday*. One of her first successes was as the housekeeper Aggie in the *Life with the Lyons* comedy series, first on radio and then on TV. This led to her reprising the role in two very successful pictures for Hammer. She returned in 1971, still a domestic, for *Hands of the Ripper*.

Other genre credits: FILMS: *The Hands of Orlac*, Pendennis Films, 1960 (Maid); *One of Our Dinosaurs Is Missing*, Walt Disney Productions, 1975 (Scots Nanny) TELEVISION: *Mystery and Imagination*: "The Open Door," 1966 (Mrs. Jarvis); *Out of the Unknown*: "Random Quest," 1969 (Nurse MacLean); *Thriller*: "Come Out, Come Out, Wherever You Are," 1974 (Miss Pendy); *Rentaghost*: 1978–1980 (Hazel the McWitch); *Tales from the Crypt*: "Last Respects," 1996 (Grandma Oakfist)

Welch, Raquel (1940–)

REAL NAME: Jo Raquel Tejada; BIRTHPLACE: Chicago, Illinois, USA.

FILM: *One Million Years B.C.*, 1966 (Loana)

BIOGRAPHY— Probably one of the most beautiful women of all time, Raquel Welch wanted to be a performer from a very early age, originally a ballet dancer. She worked odd jobs, including a stint as a TV weather girl, before she finally started to get bit parts on TV shows (*McHale's Navy* and *Bewitched*), as well as in the movie *Roustabout* with Elvis. Her first lead role came in the sci-fi thriller *Fantastic Voyage*, which got her noticed, but it was her soon-after appearance for Hammer that literally put her on the map — and on magazines, newspapers and bedroom walls the world over. Remember the ubiquitous Farrah Fawcett poster from the 1970s? The pose of Raquel Welch in the most famous fur bikini of filmland from *One Million Years B.C.* was the 1960s equivalent; more so, really, and it had a similar career-launching effect, as much as Ms. Welch is loath to admit. But it's not just the way she physically fills that fur bikini; other buxom actresses did that and got nowhere near as giddy a reaction. No, as much as she hated the role, she gave as much as one can give when uttering nonsense syllables, in a role that's hardly designed to test anyone's acting abilities and intended for one thing only, and that's to get pulses racing; and, as in *Fantastic Voyage* she showed that special something that enabled her to rise above the similar efforts by Victoria Vetri and Julie Ege. It helps that she's surrounded by some of Ray Harryhausen's best animation, wonderful natural scenery, a great musical score and able support from the likes of John Richardson (*She*) and Martine Beswick, things that, for the most part, were conspicuously missing from Hammer's other prehistoric pictures. But none of these things would have mattered if Welch had not been up to the task, and she turned what could have been a movie remembered as simply another Ray Harryhausen film into a pop culture favorite. Welch went on to experience both the lows (*Myra Breckenridge*) and highs (a Golden Globe for *The Three Musketeers*) of the film

Raquel Welch in the outfit that launched a million fantasies, prehistoric and otherwise, in *One Million Years B.C.*

business, and is still quite active. She is also an author and businesswoman with her own line of wigs, jewelry and skincare products, still stunningly beautiful, one of the last true studio system sex symbols — and all because of a "silly dinosaur movie" that she thought no one would ever see.

Other genre credits: FILMS: *Fantastic Voyage*, 20th Century–Fox, 1966 (Cora); *Bedazzled*, 20th Century–Fox, 1967 (Lust/Lillian Lust) TELEVISION: *Bewitched*: "Witch or Wife," 1964 (Stewardess); *Mork and Mindy*: "Mork vs. the Necrotons," 1979 (Captain Nirvana); *Lois and Clark—The New Adventures of Superman*: "Top Copy," 1995 (Diana Stride); *Sabrina, the Teenage Witch*: "Third Aunt from the Sun," 1996 (Vesta Spellman)

Wells, Sheilah

FILM: *The Kiss of the Vampire*, 1963 (Teresa in U.S. Television Version)
Other genre credits: TELEVISION: *Tarzan*: "The Ultimate Weapon," 1966 (Carrie Haines); *The Green Hornet*: "Crime Wave," 1966 (Laura Spinner)

Westcott, Helen (1928–1998)

BIRTHPLACE: Los Angeles, California, USA.
TELEVISION: *Tales of Frankenstein*, 1958 (Christine Halpert)

BIOGRAPHY— The daughter of actor Gordon Westcott, beautiful Helen Westcott was one of the busiest American character actresses in film in the 1950s, and then later on television in the 1960s. She began her career at age four with her mother on the stage, to which she would return later in her career. Her most prominent film role came in *The Gunfighter* with Gregory Peck, and she starred with Boris Karloff in *Abbott and Costello Meet Jekyll and Hyde*. Her lone effort for Hammer was the female lead in the television pilot *Tales of Frankenstein*, which pits her against a very good Anton Diffring and a very bad Frankenstein Monster, which looks like a cross between Glenn Strange and the Sta-Puft Marshmallow Man. Westcott is not Frankenstein's love interest; she plays a woman who brings her sick husband to Diffring in the hopes that he can be cured, and we all know how those things turn out, especially in a half-hour show. Oddly, Westcott comes to see Diffring because of his "reputation," which he hasn't had time to build yet because he hasn't even built his first monster yet — and she doesn't even mind when he robs her husband's grave, if it brings him back to her. She doesn't anticipate his brain finding a new home in the skull of the Monster (which she should have, given his "reputation"). But other than that slight lapse of logic, she does well, as does Diffring, and it's somewhat of a shame the show (and this episode) didn't have time to develop. Westcott retired in 1977, and passed away in 1998.

Other genre credits: FILMS: *Abbott and Costello Meet Dr. Jekyll and Mr. Hyde*, Universal International Pictures, 1953 (Vicky Edwards); *The Invisible Avenger*, Republic Pictures, 1958 (Tara O'Neill); *Monster on the Campus*, Universal International Pictures, 1958 (Molly Riordan) TELEVISION: *The Alfred Hitchcock Hour*: Mrs. Fletcher, "Diagnosis: Danger," 1963 (Mrs. Fletcher); *The Twilight Zone*: "You Drive," 1964 (Lillian Pope)

Wetherell, Virginia (1943–)

BIRTHPLACE: Farnham, Surrey, England.
FILMS: *Dr. Jekyll and Sister Hyde*, 1971 (Betsy); *Demons of the Mind*, 1972 (Inge)
BIOGRAPHY— Virginia Wetherell has very fond recollections of *Dr. Jekyll and Sister Hyde* for many reasons, but the uppermost was that's where she met her future husband, Ralph Bates: "The first day I met him, he stabbed me in the back. Two years later, I married him. Well, you know, you win some, lose some." (*Memories of Hammer*, Midnight Marquee Publishing, 2002) She and Bates were married until his death from pancreatic cancer in 1991, and she now manages a research fund in his name, along with their two children (Daisy and Will Bates, both in the acting profession) and three doctors. She doesn't really have that much to do in *Sister Hyde* except get killed. In her next Hammer, *Demons of the Mind*, she again gets killed, but she has a lot more opportunity to display her talent beforehand as the brassy town slore who agrees to impersonate Gillian Hills for the crazy Shane Briant to "cure" him of his more-than-brotherly love for Hills. She takes her clothes off, but then freaks out as soon as Briant comes down the stairs with 1,000-watt eyes and makes tracks, which can only end badly and does, with her corpse covered in roses. Wetherell is an authentic genre presence; outside of her Hammer films, she is probably best known for her role in *A Clockwork Orange* as the actress who comes out on stage completely nude to test the effect of Malcolm McDowell's "cure" with sickening (for him) results. She also appeared in one of Boris Karloff's last films *Curse of the Crimson Altar*, as well as the Dan Curtis *Dracula* with Jack Palance. Her last screen appearance was in 1998; she is now retired, manages the fund and makes an occasional appearance at fan conventions.

Other genre credits: FILMS: *The Solarnauts*, Wonderama Productions, 1967 (The Woman with No Name); *Curse of the Crimson Altar*, Tigon British Film Productions, 1968 (Eve Morley); *A Clockwork Orange*, Warner Brothers Pictures, 1971 (Stage Actress); *Disciple of Death*, AVCO Embassy Pictures, 1972 (Ruth) TELEVISION: *Doctor Who*: "The Escape," "The Ambush," "The

Expedition," "The Ordeal," "The Rescue," 1964 (Dyoni); *Bram Stoker's Dracula* (Movie), 1974 (Dracula's Wife)

White, Carol Joan (1943–1991)

BIRTHPLACE: London, England.
FILM: *Slave Girls*, 1967 (Gido)
BIOGRAPHY—The daughter of a scrap merchant, blonde and beautiful Carol White trained at the Corona Stage Academy, played her first role as a child in 1949, and was soon working very regularly. At one point she was considered among Britain's most promising young actresses. Her only Hammer film appearance was as the rebellious cave girl Gido who squares off against Martine Beswick in the opening reels of *Slave Girls*; the only thing she gets out of it is a memorable death scene (Martine maneuvers her into impaling herself on a large pointed stick). But soon her career would begin to decline due to drug and alcohol abuse, coupled with a number of disastrous affairs with high-profile stars, and it never recovered. She died in 1991, either as the result of an overdose or the cumulative effects of all those wasted days and wasted nights that resulted in liver disease.
Other genre credits: TELEVISION: *The Avengers*: "Brought to Book," 1961 (Jackie)

White, Joanne

TELEVISION: *Hammer House of Horror*: "The House That Bled to Death," 1980 (Older Sophia)
Other genre credits: FILM: *Silent Night, Deadly Night 2*, Silent Night Releasing Corporation, 1987 (Paula)

White, Liz (1979–)

BIRTHPLACE: Rotherham, South Yorkshire, England.
FILM: *The Woman in Black*, 2012 (Jennet Humfrye)
Other genre credits: FILM: *Franklyn*, Recorded Picture Company, 2008 (Laura)

Wiggins, Rebekah

FILM: *Let Me In*, 2010 (Nurse)
Other genre credits: FILM: *Fright Night*, Albuquerque Studios/DreamWorks SKG, 2011 (Passing Nurse)

Wilcocks, Shelagh

FILMS: *The Vampire Lovers*, 1970 (Housekeeper); *Twins of Evil*, 1971 (Lady in Coach)
Other genre credits: FILM: *Deviation*, Saga Film, 1971 (Auntie) TELEVISION: *Dr. Jekyll and Mr. Hyde* (Movie), 1980 (Mrs. Willoughby)

Wild, Jeanette

FILM: *Dr. Jekyll and Sister Hyde*, 1971 (Jill)
Other genre credits: FILM: *Zeta One*, Tigon British Film Productions, 1969 (Angvisa Girl)
Note: She also appeared in *Monty Python's Flying Circus*.

Wild, Katy (1941–)

BIRTHPLACE: London, England.
FILM: *The Evil of Frankenstein*, 1964 (Beggar Girl)

BIOGRAPHY—Born at the height of World War II, Katy Wild survived the Blitz to become a familiar face to British film and television viewers for over 30 years she featured in 107 episodes of the long-running soap opera *Sons and Daughters*. She made three features for Amicus, the well-regarded *Dr. Terror's House of Horrors* and the not-so-well-regarded *They Came from Beyond Space* and *The Deadly Bees*. Actually, her one film for Hammer wasn't that well-regarded either; *The Horror of Frankenstein* is generally viewed as the black sheep of Hammer's Frankenstein series, due to the casting of Ralph Bates as Frankenstein rather than Peter Cushing (ignoring the fact that Cushing was too old for the role of a young Frankenstein), but it is really *The Evil of Frankenstein* that is the odd monster out. At least *The Horror of Frankenstein* was a remake of *Curse*; financed by Universal, *Evil* is much less a true Hammer Frankenstein than it is an odd compendium of bits and bobs from the Universal series, with absolutely no connection to the continuity of the series except for Cushing personally. Wild appears in a scene inspired by *The Ghost of Frankenstein*; in the Universal film, a little girl is bullied by a gang of boys who kick her ball; in *Evil* the girl is considerably more grown-up, and she is a mute beggar whose bowl has been stolen and tossed around in the same manner. The difference is that in the Universal film, Lon Chaney Jr.'s Monster comes to her rescue; in the Hammer version, she beats the crap out of one of the boys herself. Her origin provides interesting grounds for speculation: Although she simply seems to appear out of nowhere as a separate character, she bears such an amazing facial resemblance to the little girl (Michelle Scott) in the scene at the beginning of the movie that she could be that little girl grown up; struck dumb by witnessing her brother's body being snatched and reduced to begging, orphaned by her parents who were killed by the same shock. Her beggar girl is, like Yvonne Romain in *The Curse of the Werewolf*, not only mute but nameless, and also figures in another prominent bit of *déjà vu* when she inadvertently leads Cushing to the monster preserved in a "glacial ice cavern" *à la House of Frankenstein*. After a (very short) time, one doesn't watch the film to see what happens, one watches it to spot the sources of the bits and bobs: *Frankenstein* (the spectacular electrical fireworks of the creation scene and the monster's kindness towards the childlike girl); *Bride of Frankenstein* (the Monster drinks — only this time, he's a mean drunk); *Son of Frankenstein* (Zoltan the hypnotist is Ygor, only much less charming); *Ghost* (see above); *Frankenstein Meets the Wolf Man* (instead of Chaney losing it at the Festival of the New Wine, it's Frankenstein who loses it at the carnival); and *House* (the aforementioned ice cavern and the traveling carnival). Wild winds up in the arms of Sandor Eles (*The Vampire Lovers*) as they watch Frankenstein's castle explode and burn. Her last role was in the TV series *G.P.* in 1991.

Other genre credits: FILMS: *Dr. Terror's House of Horrors*, Amicus Productions, 1965 (Valda); *The Deadly Bees*, Amicus Productions, 1967 (Doris Hawkins); *They Came from Beyond Space*, Amicus Productions, 1967 (Girl in Street) TELEVISION: *Suspense* (ATV): "Payment in Full," 1960 (Brigitte); *The Avengers*: "Traitor in Zebra," 1962 (Linda); *Suspense* (BBC): "The Honest Man," 1963 (Anita); "Souvenir," 1963 (Michele)

Wilding, April (1941–)

FILM: *Hands of the Ripper*, 1971 (Catherine)
BIOGRAPHY—The stepdaughter of glass-made millionaire Lord Harry Pilkington was active from 1959 to 1971, and *Hands of the Ripper* was her last feature film.

Willard, Lola

FILM: *Straight on Till Morning*, 1972 (Customer)

Williams, Lou
FILM: *Beyond the Rave*, 2008 (Hotel Girl)

Wilson, Sue
FILM: *Creatures the World Forgot*, 1971 (Noo)

Wimbush, Mary (1924–2005)
BIRTHPLACE: Kenton, Middlesex, England.
FILM: *Vampire Circus*, 1972 (Elvira)
Other genre credits: TELEVISION: *Thriller*: "Lady Killer," 1973 (Mrs. Bradley); *K-9 and Company: A Girl's Best Friend* (Movie), 1981 (Aunt Lavinia Smith)

Winstone, Lois (1982–)
BIRTHPLACE: London, England.
FILM: *Beyond the Rave*, 2008 (Lilith)
Other genre credits: FILMS: *Uncut*, Circumcised Films, 2009 (Clarice); *Basement*, Paperknife Productions, 2010 (Saffron) TELEVISION: *When Evil Calls* (Mini-Series): 2005 (Kirsty)

Wojtczak, Tessa (1958–)
BIRTHPLACE: London, England.
TELEVISION: *Hammer House of Mystery and Suspense*: "Czech Mate," 1985 (Girl on Bridge)

Wood, Virginia
TELEVISION: *Hammer House of Horror*: "Children of the Full Moon," 1980 (Sophie)

Woolf, Vicki (1945–)
BIRTHPLACE: Brighton, East Sussex, England.
FILMS: *The Vampire Lovers*, 1970 (Landlord's Daughter); *Hands of the Ripper*, 1971 (Second Cell Whore)
BIOGRAPHY— The film career of buxom character actress Vicki Woolf began in 1960 when she was a companion cell whore to Anne Clune in *The Hands of Orlac*. She had bit parts in two Hammer films as eye candy; her last screen appearance was in 1989.
Other genre credits: FILM: *The Hands of Orlac*, Pendennis Films, 1960 (Cell Whore)

Woollard, Emma
FILM: *Beyond the Rave*, 2008 (Anais)

Wren, Joyce
FILM: *The Two Faces of Dr. Jekyll*, 1960 (Nurse)

Wrigg, Ann
TELEVISION: *Journey to the Unknown*: "Stranger in the Family," 1969 (Miss Payne)
Other genre credits: TELEVISION: *Suspense*: "Sense of Occasion," 1963 (Second Woman)

Wright, Julia

FILM: *Dr. Jekyll and Sister Hyde*, 1971 (Street Singer)

Wright, Maggie (1944–)

BIRTHPLACE: London, England.

FILMS: *Rasputin, the Mad Monk*, 1966 (Second Tart); *Twins of Evil*, 1971 (Alexa)

BIOGRAPHY— Vivacious Maggie Wright began her acting career in 1964, and she managed to bag a big one the first time out, playing the squadron leader of Pussy Galore's Flying Circus in *Goldfinger*. She worked for 20 years in television and films, including *Hammerhead*, which also featured fellow Hammer Heroines Veronica Carlson, Diana Dors, Judy Geeson and Tracy Reed. She is responsible for a couple of firsts: She was the first woman to appear fully nude on the legitimate British stage, and *Twins of Evil* was the first Hammer film to utilize lower frontal nudity. *Twins* was her second Hammer; she'd had a bit part (fully clothed) in *Rasputin, the Mad Monk*, but in *Twins* she was central to the plot as the girl whom Count Karnstein sacrifices in order that her blood may revive his infamous female ancestor. She continued to act until 1983. In 1992, she and her husband were running a bar in Phuket, Thailand; they adopted a Thai girl and moved to Malaysia for a spell, and now live in Australia.

Other genre credits: FILMS: *Goldfinger*, Eon Productions, 1964 (Pussy Galore's Flying Circus Leader) TELEVISION: *The Martian Chronicles*: "The Martians," "The Settlers," "The Expeditions," 1980 (Ylla)

Wyeth, Katya; a.k.a. Kathja Wyeth (1948–)

BIRTHPLACE: Wilhelmshaven, Germany.

FILMS: *Twins of Evil*, 1971 (Countess Mircalla); *Hands of the Ripper*, 1971 (First Pub Whore); *Straight on Till Morning*, 1972 (Caroline)

BIOGRAPHY— Teutonic beauty Katya Wyeth was a model before her brief film and television career in the late 1960s and '70s, and had a number of satisfying bits in genre pictures and shows, most notably as the girl in Alex's final fantasy in *A Clockwork Orange*, riding him like a bucking bronco with nothing on but a smile and stockings as he intones, "I was cured, all right." She also did three turns in Hammer films. The first, *Twins of Evil*, was definitely the most significant, as she is the actress chosen to embody the Carmilla/Mircalla/Marcilla character first brought to un-life by Ingrid Pitt and then Yutte Stensgaard. She's only got one name this time around, because she doesn't have that much screen time; the character has been reduced to little more than a cameo, although it is significant, as she is the one who initiates her descendant into the ranks of the undead. Yutte Stensgaard's blond beauty had deviated from the image established by Ingrid Pitt, but here Mircalla once again recalls Pitt. Wyeth is very sexy and depraved, but she's also the victim of certifiably silly symbolism when, in her lovemaking with the young count, she strokes a candlestick, which rather destroys the mood. The second didn't amount to much; in *Hands of the Ripper*, she has just a few minutes of screen time as one of the trio of pub whores. She's back to a featured role in *Straight on Till Morning*, as the buxom blonde Caroline who takes in Rita Tushingham, is seduced by pretty-boy psycho killer Shane Briant, and then takes in a knife 'twixt the shoulder blades. Her career ended just five years later with a part in *Space: 1999*.

Other genre credits: FILMS: *A Clockwork Orange*, Warner Brothers Pictures, 1971 (Ascot Fantasy Girl); *Burke & Hare*, Armitage, 1972 (Natalie) TELEVISION: *The Avengers*: "Requiem," 1969 (Jill); *Dead of Night*: "Death Cancels All Debts," 1972 (Vanessa); *Space: 1999*: "Devil's Planet," 1977 (Guard) (See photograph on page 200.)

Need a date, Luv? Katya Wyeth, Beulah Hughes, and Tallulah Miller proposition Eric Porter in *Hands of the Ripper*.

Young, Joan (1903–1984)

REAL NAME: Joan Wragge; BIRTHPLACE: Newcastle-upon-Tyne, Tyne and Wear, England.
FILM: *Blood from the Mummy's Tomb*, 1971 (Mrs. Caporal)
Other genre credits: TELEVISION: *Doctor Who*: "Bell of Doom," "Priest of Death," 1966 (Catherine de Medici)

Hammer Film Credits

Actresses profiled in this book are in **bold**.

The Abominable Snowman, 1957; Crew: Executive Producer: Michael Carreras; Associate Producer: Anthony Nelson-Keys; Producer: Aubrey Baring; Director: Val Guest; Story: Nigel Neale ("The Creature"); Screenplay: Nigel Kneale, Val Guest; Music: Humphrey Searle; Cinematography: Arthur Grant; Film Editor: Bill Lenny; Production Designer: Bernard Robinson; Art Director: Ted Marshall; Costume/Dress Design: Beatrice Dawson; Makeup: Phil Leakey; Hair Stylist: Henry Montsash; Production Manager: Don Weeks; Assistant Director: Robert Lynn; Third Assistant Director: Hugh Harlow; Sound Recordist: Jock May; Camera Operator: Len Harris; Gaffer: Steve Birtles; Wardrobe: Molly Arbuthnot; Musical Director: John Hollingsworth; Continuity: Doreen Soan

Cast: Peter Cushing (Dr. Rollason), Forrest Tucker (Tom Friend), **Maureen Connell** (Helen Rollason), Richard Wattis (Fox), Robert Brown (Shelley), Michael Brill (Andrew), Wolfe Morris (Kusang), Arnold Marle (Llama), Fred Johnson (Yeti), John Rae (Yeti-Eyes)

The Anniversary, 1968; Crew: Producer: Jimmy Sangster; Director: Roy Ward Baker; Screenplay: Jimmy Sangster, based on the stage play by Bill MacIlwraith; Music/Musical Supervisor: Philip Martell; Cinematography: Harry Waxman; Film Editor: Peter Weatherley; Production Design: Reece Pemberton; Wardrobe: Mary Gibson; Makeup: Ben Nye, George Partleton, Hugh Richards; Hair Stylist: A.G. Scott; Production Manager: Victor Peck; Assistant Director: Bert Batt; Third Assistant Director: Paddy Carpenter; Painter: Michael Finlay; Sound Recordist: Les Hammond; Sound Editor: Charles Crafford; Sound Recording Supervisor: A.W. Lumkin; Camera Operator: Gerry Anstiss; Supervising Editor: James Needs; Continuity: June Randall

Cast: **Bette Davis** (Mrs. Taggart), **Sheila Hancock** (Karen), Jack Hedley (Terry), James Cossins (Henry), Christian Roberts (Tom), **Elaine Taylor** (Shirley), Timothy Bateson (Mr. Bird), **Sally-Jane Spencer** (Florist), Arnold Diamond (Headwaiter), Albert Shepherd, Ralph Watson (Construction Workers)

Beyond the Rave, 2008; Crew: Producer: Ben Grass: Co-Producer: Alan Raistrick; Executive Producers: Simon Oakes, Marc Shipper; Line Producer: Wendy Bevan-Mogg; Director: Matthias Hoene; Writers: Tom Grass, Jon Wright; Cinematography: Ben Moulden; Film Editor: Lucas Roche; Production Design: Alex Lowde; Art Director: Melanie Light; Assistant Art Directors: Ryan Haysom, Mia Summerville; Makeup Artist: Beth Roberts-Miller; Special Makeup Effects Artists: Robbie Drake, Tristan Versluis, Jo Wand; Special Effects Hair Technician: Maria Cork; Production Manager: James Harris; First Assistant Director: Richard Newman; Second Assistant Director: James Nunn; Third Assistant Director: Ernest Riera; Storyboard Artist: James Husbands; Prop Maker: Lee Fenton-Wilkinson; Sound Recordist: Ashok Kumar; Additional Sound Recordist: Haresh Patel; Sound Editors: Matt Baird, Scott Laing; Sound Mixer: Kumar; Additional Sound Mixer: Jamie Gambell; Post-Production Sound: Finn Curry; Boom Operator: John Crossland; Additional Boom Operators: Jamie Gambell, Simon Bysshe; Foley Editor: Cristina Aragon; Special Effects: Haysom; Special Effects Makeup: Versluis; Pyrotechnician: Neil Jenkins; Visual Effects Supervisor: John D. Bell; Compositor:

Robert A. Willis; Stunt Coordinator: Dave Judge; Stunts: Jude Poyer; Stunt Performers: James Nicholas Fuller, Kerry Kisses Dunne, Ian van Temperley; Assistant Camera: Jon Britt; Still Photographer: James Nicholas Fuller; Electricians: Sam Alberg, Arsenio Assin, Michael Franklin, James Leckey, Eren Ozkural; Gaffers: Pawel Polak, Martin Taylor; Grip: Pete Nash; Sparks: James Harverson; Casting: Hannah Birkett, Sue Pocklington; Casting Assistant: James Nunn; Costumer: Lesette Ormond-King; Additional Costume Designer: Rebecca Gore; Assistant Editor: Richard Deeb; Production Coordinator: Kate Glover; Production Assistants: Mark Evans, Benjamin Harris, Peter McLeod, Richard May, Mark Stein; Location Manager: Jacques Groenewald; Unit Publicist: Axelle Carolyn; Script Editor: Nic Ransome; Dialogue Coach: Mel Churcher; Floor Runner: Hugh Kerrigan; Special Thanks: Eddie Dias

CAST: **Ingrid Pitt** (Tooley's Mother), **Nora-Jane Noone** (Jen), Jamie Doman (Ed), Tamer Hassan (Rich Crocker), Sebastian Knapp (Melech), **Lois Winstone** (Lilith), Trevor Byfield (Leopold), Mark Wingett (Ed's Dad), Jody Halse (Big Jim), Steve Sweeney (Tooley), **Sadie Frost** (Fallen Angel), Alexander Newland (Faustino), Leslie Simpson (Belial), Jake Maskall (Strigoi), Matthew Forrest (Necro), Neil Newbon (Nikolai), Lee Long (Danny Crocker), Lee Whitlock (Terry Crocker), **Katie Borland** (Tina), Oliver Milburn (Sgt.), **Lauren Gold** (Lucretia), **Emma Woollard** (Anais), Ruaraidh Murray (Dave), Danny Tennant (Idiot), Tristan Matthie (Adonis), **Sophie Holland** (Lydia), Jackson Scott (Botz), **Vivienne Harvey** (Tess), Oliver Gilbert (David), Arron West (Kevin), **Elizabeth Elvin** (Bea), Colin Dent (Bazarov), **Lou Williams** (Hotel Girl), **Caroline Acosta** (DJ), Gethin Anthony (Noddy), **Lucy Barker** (Psychiatrist), David Doyle (Detective), Paul T. T. Easter, Ryan Haysom, James Nunn, Pete Tong (Ravers), Alexander Ellis (Army Mate), Mark Evans (Ripped Throat Man), Dave Fire Tusk (Vampire Fire Clown Gimp), Norman Gregory (Angry Farmer), James Harris (Soldier), George Hilton (Punter), **Irene Lacak** (Vampire Sword Girl), **Taylor Morgan** (Girl One), Luke Nash (Pipsqueak Chav), Beeny Royston (DJ Black Cat), Jeff Rudom (Bouncer), **Nicole Verdugo** (Iraqi Girl)

BLOOD FROM THE MUMMY'S TOMB, 1971; CREW: Producer: Howard Brandy; Directors: Seth Holt, Michael Carreras; Screenplay: Christopher Wicking, based on the novel *Jewel of the Seven Stars* by Bram Stoker; Music: Tristram Cary; Cinematography: Arthur Grant; Film Editor: Peter Weatherley; Production Design: Scott MacGregor; Makeup Supervisor: Eddie Knight; Hairdressing Supervisor: Ivy Emmerton; Production Supervisor: Roy Skeggs; Production Manager: Christopher Neame; Assistant Director: Derek Whitehurst; Second Assistant Director: Lindsey Vickers; Third Assistant Director: Michael Murray; Scenic Artist: Bill Beavis; Draughtsman: Tony Baines; Construction Manager: Bill Greene; Assistant Art Director: Don Picton; Print Boy: "Jimmy" Carreras; Sound Editor: Roy Hyde; Recording Director: A.W. Lumkin; Sound Recordists: Claude Hitchcock, Tony Dawe; Dubbing Mixer: Dennis Whitlock; Sound Maintenance: Dan Grimmel; Sound Camera Operator: Jack Harris; Boom Operator: Mike Silverlock; Special Effects: Michael Collins; Camera Operator: Neil Binney; Clapper Loader: Rod Barron; Camera Grip: Peter Woods; Focus Puller: Bob Jordan; Wardrobe Supervisor: Rosemary Burrows; Wardrobe Mistress: Diane Jones; Musical Supervisor: Philip Martell; Continuity: Betty Harley; Production Secretary: Sally Pardo; Stand-In/Valerie Leon: Sarah Mathieson; Unit Runner: Phil Campbell

CAST: **Valerie Leon** (Margaret Fuchs/Queen Tara), Andrew Keir (Prof. Julian Fuchs), James Villiers (Corbeck), Hugh Burden (Geoffrey Dandridge), George Couloris (Prof. "Bunny" Berrigan), Mark Edwards (Tod Browning), **Rosalie Crutchley** (Helen), Aubrey Morris (Dr. Putnam), David Markham (Dr. Burgess), **Joan Young** (Mrs. Caporal), James Cossins (Old Male Nurse), David Jackson (Young Male Nurse), Jonathan Burns (Saturnine Young Man), Graham James (Museum Youth), **Tamara Ustinov** (Veronica), **Penelope Holt**, **Angela Ginders** (Nurses), Tex Fuller (Patient), Harry Fielder (Local Bloke); Madina Luis, Omar Amoodi, Abdul Kader, Oscar Charles, Ahmed Osman, Soltan Lalani, Saad Ghazi (Priests)

THE BRIDES OF DRACULA, 1960; CREW: Executive Producer: Michael Carreras; Associate Producer: Anthony Nelson-Keys; Producer: Anthony Hinds; Director: Terence Fisher; Screenplay: Jimmy Sangster, Edward Percy, Peter Bryan, Anthony Hinds; Music: Malcolm Williamson; Cinematography: Jack Asher; Film Editor: Alfred Cox; Art Director: Tom Goswell; Production Design:

Bernard Robinson; Wardrobe Mistress: Molly Arbuthnot; Casting: Dorothy Holloway; Makeup: Roy Ashton; Hair Stylist: Freda Steiger; Production Manager: Don Weeks; Assistant Director: John Peverall; Second Assistant Director: Hugh Harlow; Props Buyer: Eric Hillier; Assistant Art Director: Don Mingaye; Property Master: Tom Money; Sound Recordist: Jock May; Sound Editor: James Groom; Special Effects: Sydney Pearson; Stunts: Peter Diamond; Lighting Technician: Steve Birtles; Camera Operator: Len Harris; Still Photographer: Tom Edwards; Editorial Supervisor: James Needs; Musical Supervisor: John Hollingsworth; Continuity: Tilly Day

CAST: Peter Cushing (Van Helsing), David Peel (Baron Meinster), **Yvonne Monlaur** (Marianne Danielle), **Martita Hunt** (Baroness Meinster), **Freda Jackson** (Greta), Michael Ripper (Coachman), Miles Malleson (Dr. Tobler), Henry Oscar (Lang), **Mona Washbourne** (Frau Lang), **Andree Melly** (Gina), Victor Brooks (Hans), Fred Johnson (Father Stepnik), Norman Pierce (Landlord), **Vera Cook** (Landlord's Wife), **Marie Devereux** (Village Girl), **Susan Castle** (Elsa), Michael Mulcaster (The Man in Black), Harry Pringle (Karl), Harold Scott (Severin), **Stephanie Watts** (Foxy Girl)

CAPTAIN CLEGG (a.k.a. *Night Creatures*), 1962; CREW: Producer: John Temple-Smith; Director: Peter Graham Scott; Screenplay: "John Elder" (Anthony Hinds), based on the novel *Dr. Syn* by Russell Thorndyke; Additional Dialogue: Barbara S. Harper; Music: Don Banks; Cinematography: Arthur Grant; Film Editor: Eric Boyd-Perkins; Production Designer: Bernard Robinson; Art Director: Don Mingaye; Wardrobe Design: Molly Arbuthnot; Wardrobe Mistress: Rosemary Burrows; Makeup: Roy Ashton; Hair Stylist: Frieda Steiger; Production Manager: Don Weeks; Assistant Director: John Peverall; Sound: Jock May; Sound Editor: Terry Poulton; Special Effects: Les Bowie; Special Effects Assistant: Ian Scoones; Still Photographer: Tom Edwards; Camera Operator: Len Harris; Chief Electrician: Jack Curtis; Editorial Supervisor: James Needs; Musical Director: Philip Martell; Continuity: Tilly Day

CAST: Peter Cushing (The Reverend Doctor Blyss), Patrick Allen (Capt. Collier), Oliver Reed (Harry), Michael Ripper (Jeremiah Mipps), **Yvonne Romain** (Imogene), Martin Benson (Mr. Rash), David Lodge (Bos'un), Derek Francis (Squire Cobtree), **Daphne Anderson** (Mrs. Rash), Milton Reid (The Mulatto), Jack MacGowran (Frightened Man), Terry Scully (Dick Tate), Sydney Bromley (Old Tom Ketch), Peter Halliday (Jack Pott), Rupert Osborne (Gerry), Gordon Rollings (Wurzel), Bob Head (Peg-Leg), Colin Douglas (Pirate Bos'un), Gerry Crampton (Tattooed Swab), Harold Gee (Fiddler)

CAPTAIN KRONOS, VAMPIRE HUNTER, 1974; CREW: Producers: Brian Clemens, Albert Fennell; Director/Screenplay: Brian Clemens; Music/Conductor: Laurie Johnson; Music Supervisor: Philip Martell; Director of Photography: Ian Wilson; Film Editor: James Needs; Casting: James Liggat; Production Design: Robert Jones; Makeup: Jimmy Evans; Hair Stylist: Barbara Ritchie; Production Supervisor: Roy Skeggs; Production Manager: Richard F. Dalton; Assistant Directors: Nick Farnes, David Tringham; Second Assistant Director: Terry Hodgkinson; Assistant Art Director: Kenneth McCallum Tait; Sound Editor: Peter Lennard; Recording Director: A.W. Lumkin; Dubbing Mixer: Bill Rowe; Sound Recordist: Jim Willis; Camera Operator: Godfrey A. Godar; First Assistant Camera: David Wynn-Jones; Wardrobe Supervisors: Dulcie Midwinter, Margie Midwinter; Final Colorist: Donald Freeman; Fight Supervisor: William Hobbs; Continuity: June Randall; Stand-In for Caroline Munro: Glenda Allen; Processing: Humphreys Laboratories; Sound System: RCA

CAST: Horst Janson (Captain Kronos), John Cater (Grost), **Caroline Munro** (Carla), John Carson (Dr. Marcus), Shane Briant (Paul Durward), **Lois Daine** (Sara Durward), Ian Hendry (Kerro), **Wanda Ventham** (Lady Durward), William Hobbs (Hagen), Brian Tully (George Sorell), Robert James (Pointer), Perry Soblosky (Barlow), Paul Greenwood (Giles), **Lisa Collings** (Vanda Sorell), John Hollis (Barman), **Susanna East** (Isabella Sorell), Stafford Gordon (Barton Sorell), **Elizabeth Dear** (Ann Sorell), **Joanna Ross** (Myra), Neil Seiler (Priest), **Olga Anthony** (Lilian), **Gigi Gurpinar** (Blind Girl), Peter Davidson (Big Man), Terence Sewards (Tom), Trevor Lawrence (Deke), **Jacqui Cook** (Barmaid), **Penny Price** (Whore), B.H. Barry, Michael Buchanan, Steve James, Ian McKay, Barry Smith, Roger Williams (Villagers), **Linda Cunningham** (Jane), **Caroline Villiers** (Petra), Julian Holloway (Voice of Kronos)

Countess Dracula, 1971; Crew: Producer: Alexander Paal; Director: Peter Sasdy; Screenplay: Jeremy Paul; Story: Alexander Paal, Peter Sasdy; Idea: Gabriel Ronap; Based on the novel *The Bloody Countess* by Valentine Penrose; Music: Harry Robinson (Robertson); Additional Music/Music Supervisor: Philip Martell; Director of Photography: Kenneth (Ken) Talbot; Film Editor: Henry Richardson; Art Director: Philip Harrison; Costume Design: Raymond Hughes; Makeup Supervisor: Tom Smith; Hairdressing Supervisor: Patricia (Pat) McDermott; Production Manager: Christopher Sutton; Assistant Director: Ariel Levy; Construction Manager: Arthur Banks; Set Designer: Tim Hutchinson; Dubbing Mixer: Ken Barker; Sound Recordists: Terry Poulton, Kevin Sutton; Sound Editor: Alban (Al) Streeter; Sound Re-Recording Mixers: Graham V. Hartstone, Otto Snel; Special Effects: Bert Luxford; Camera Operator: Kenneth J. (Ken) Withers; Wardrobe Master: Brian Owen-Smith; Continuity: Gladys Goldsmith; Choreographer: Mia Nardi

Cast: **Ingrid Pitt** (Countess Elizabeth Nadasdy), Nigel Green (Capt. Dobi), Sandor Eles (Lt. Imre Toth), Maurice Denham (Master Fabio), **Patience Collier** (Julie Sentash), Peter Jeffrey (Capt. Balogh), **Lesley-Anne Down** (Ilona Nadasdy), Leon Lissek (Sgt. of Bailiffs), **Jessie Evans** (Rosa), **Andrea Lawrence** (Zita), **Susan Brodrick** (Teri), Ian Trigger (Clown), **Nike Arrighi** (Fortune Teller), Peter May (Janco), John Moore (Priest), **Joan Haythorne** (Cook), **Marianne Stone** (Kitchen Maid), **Sally Adcock** (Bertha), **Anne Stallybrass** (Pregnant Woman), Paddy Ryan (Man), Michael Cadman (Young Man), **Hulya Babus** (Belly Dancer), **Lesley Anderson**, **Biddy Hearne**, **Diana Sawday** (Gypsy Dancers), Andrew Burleigh, Gary Rich (Boys), Albert Wilkinson, Ismed Hassan (Circus Midgets)

Creatures the World Forgot, 1971; Crew: Producer/Screenplay: Michael Carreras; Director: Don Chaffey; Music: Mario Nascimbene; Cinematography: Vincent Cox; Film Editor: Chris Barnes; Casting: James Liggat; Production Design: John Stoll; Makeup: Colin Garde; Hairdressing Supervisor: Jeanette Freeman; First Assistant Director: Ferdinand Fairfax; Assistant Art Director: Josie MacAvin; Sound Editors: Roy Hyde, Terry Poulton; Sound Recordist: John Streeter; Sound Re-Recording Mixers: Ken Barker, Graham V. Hartstone; Special Effects: Syd Pearson; Stunts: Frank Hayden; Director of Photography/Second Unit: Ray Sturgess; Costume Supervisor: Rosemary Burrows; Musical Director: Philip Martell; Animal handler: Uwe Schulz

Cast: **Julie Ege** (Nala), Brian O'Shaughnessy (Mak), Tony Bonner (Toomak), Robin "Robert" John (Rool), **Marcia Fox** (Mute Girl), **Rosalie Crutchley** (Old Crone), Don Leonard (Old Leader), **Beverly Blake** (Young Mistress), **Sue Wilson** (Noo), Doon Baide (Young Lover), Ken Hare (Honest Leader), Derek Ward (Hunter), Fred Swart (Marauder Leader), **Josje Kiesouw** (Young Dumb Girl), Hans Kiesouw (Young Dark Boy), Gerard Bonthuys (Young Fair Boy), Frank Hayden (Zen), **Rosita Moulan** (Dancer), Leo Payne, **Tamsin Millard**, **Christine Hudson**, **Heinke Thater**, **Cheryl Stewardson**, **Trudy Inns**, **Samantha Bates**, **Debbie Aubrey-Smith**, **Joan Boshier**, **Audrey Allen**, **Vera P. Crosdale**, **Mildred Johnston**, **Lilian M. Nowag**, Jose Rozendo, Jose Manuel, Mark Russell, Dick Swain, Alwyn Van Der Merwe, Manuel Nito, Mike Dickman

Crescendo, 1970; Crew: Producer: Michael Carreras; Director: Alan Gibson; Screenplay: Jimmy Sangster, Alfred Shaughnessy; Music: Malcolm Williamson; Cinematography: Paul Beeson; Film Editor: Chris Barnes; Art Director: Scott MacGregor; Assistant Art Director: Don Picton; Wardrobe: Rebecca "Jackie" Breed; Makeup: Stella Morris; Hair Stylist: Ivy Emmerton; Production Manager: Hugh Harlow; Assistant Director: Jack Martin; Property Buyer: Ron Baker; Construction Manager: Arthur Banks; Painter: Michael Finlay; Set Dresser: Freda Pearson; Sound Editor: Roy Hyde; Sound Mixer: Claude Hitchcock; Dubbing Mixer: Len Abbott; Recording Supervisor: A.W. Lumkin; Camera Operator: John Winbolt; Conductor: Philip Martell; Saxophone Solo: Tubby Hayes; Piano Solo: Clive Lithgoe; Continuity: Lilian Lee; Production Secretary: Sally Pardo

Cast: **Stefanie Powers** (Susan Roberts), James Olson (Georges/Jacques Ryman), **Margaretta Scott** (Danielle Ryman), **Jane Lapotaire** (Lillianne), Joss Ackland (Carter), **Kirsten Betts** (Catherine)

The Curse of Frankenstein, 1957; Crew: Executive Producer: Michael Carreras; Associate Producer: Anthony Nelson-Keys; Producers: Anthony Hinds, Max Rosenberg; Director: Terence Fisher; Screenplay: Jimmy Sangster; Music: James Bernard; Cinematography: Jack Asher; Film Editor:

James Needs; Assistant Editor: Roy Norman; Casting: Dorothy Holloway; Production Designer: Bernard Robinson; Art Director: Ted Marshall; Costume Design: Molly Arbuthnot; Makeup: Phil Leakey, Roy Ashton, George Turner; Hair Stylist: Henry Montsash; Production Manager: Don Weeks; Executive in Charge of Production: James Carreras; Assistant Director: Derek Whitehurst; Second Assistant Director: Jimmy Komisarjevsky; Third Assistant Director: Hugh Harlow; Property Master: Tom Money; Construction Manager: Fred Ricketts; Draughtsman: Don Mingaye; Master Plasterer: Arthur Banks; Sound: W.H. (Jock) May; Boom Operator: Jim Perry; Sound Camera Operator: Michael Sale; Matte Painter: Les Bowie; Stunt Double/Christopher Lee: Jock Easton; Lighting Technician/Second Unit: Steve Birtles; Still Photographers: Tom Edwards, John Jay; Camera Operator: Len Harris; Chief Electrician: Jack Curtis; Focus Puller: Harry Oakes; Electricians: Harold Marland, Bob Palmer; Musical Director: John Hollingsworth; Continuity: Doreen Soan; Production Secretary: Faith Frisby

CAST: Peter Cushing (Victor Frankenstein), Christopher Lee (The Creature), Robert Urquhart (Paul Krempe), **Hazel Court** (Elizabeth), Melvyn Hayes (Young Vic), **Valerie Gaunt** (Justine), Paul Hardtmuth (Prof. Bernstein), **Noel Hood** (Aunt), Fred Johnson (Grampa), Claude Kingston (Boy), Alex Gallier (Priest), Michael Mulcaster (Warder Street), Andrew Leigh (Moribund the Burgomaster), **Ann Blake** (Wife), **Sally Walsh** (Young Elizabeth), Middleton Woods (Lecturer), Raymond Ray (Uncle), Josef Behrmann (Fritz), Henry Caine (Schoolmaster), Trevor Davis (Third Uncle), **Marjorie Hume** (Mother), Ernest Jay (Undertaker), Eugene Leahy (Second Priest), Bartlett Mullins (Tramp), Raymond Rollett (Father Felix)

THE CURSE OF THE MUMMY'S TOMB, 1964; CREW: Associate Producer: Bill Hill; Producer/Director: Michael Carreras; Screenplay: "Henry Younger" (Michael Carreras); Music: Carlo Martelli; Casting: David Booth; Musical Supervisor & Additional Music: Philip Martell; Cinematography: Otto Heller; Film Editor: Eric Boyd-Perkins; Production Design: Bernard Robinson; Wardrobers: Betty Adamson, John Briggs; Makeup: Roy Ashton; Hair Stylist: Iris Tilley; Assistant Director: Bert Batt; Painter: Michael Finlay; Sound Recordist: Claude Hitchcock; Sound Editor: James Groom; Sound Assistant: Alan Thorne; Stunts: Peter Diamond; Camera Operator: Bob Thompson; Gaffer: Steve Birtles; Supervising Editor: James Needs; Continuity: Eileen Head; Technical Advisor: Andrew Low

CAST: Terence Morgan (Adam Beauchamp), Ronald Howard (John Bray), **Jeanne Roland** (Annette Dubois), Fred Clark (Alexander King), George Pastell (Hashmi Bey), Jack Gwillim (Sir Giles), John Paul (Inspector Mackenzie), Dickie Owen (The Mummy), Michael Ripper (Achmed), **Jill Mai Meredith** (Jenny), Harold Goodwin (Fred), Jimmy Gardner (Fred's Pal), Vernon Smythe (Jessop), **Marianne Stone** (Landlady), **Olga Dickie** (Housekeeper), **Nora Gordon** (Sir Giles' Housekeeper), Pat Gorman (Reporter), George Leech (Assailant on Ship), Michael McStay (Ra-Antef), Eddie Powell (Arab), Bernard Rebel (Prof. Dubois), Roy Stewart (Bearer), Larry Taylor (Swordsman)

THE CURSE OF THE WEREWOLF, 1961; CREW: Executive Producer: Michael Carreras; Associate Producer: Anthony Nelson-Keys; Producers: Anthony Hinds; Director: Terence Fisher; Screenplay: "John Elder" (Anthony Hinds), based on the novel *The Werewolf of Paris* by Guy Endore; Music/Conductor: Benjamin Frankel; Stock Music: Leonard Salzedo; Cinematography: Arthur Grant; Film Editor: Alfred Cox; Casting: Stuart Lyons: Production Designer: Bernard Robinson; Art Directors: Don Mingaye, Thomas Goswell; Wardrobe: Molly Arbuthnot; Makeup: Roy Ashton, Colin Garde; Hair Stylist: Frieda Steiger; Production Manager: Clifford Parkes; Assistant Director: John Peverall; Second Assistant Director: Dominic Fulford; Sound: Jock May; Sound Editor: Alban Streeter; Special Effects: Les Bowie; Stunts: Jack Cooper; Still Photographer: Tom Edwards; Camera Operator: Len Harris; Supervising Editor: James Needs; Continuity: Tilly Day

CAST: Oliver Reed (Leon), Clifford Evans (Don Alfredo), **Yvonne Romain** (Servant Girl), **Catherine Feller** (Christina Fernando), Anthony Dawson (Marques Siniestro), **Josephine Llewellyn** (Marquesa), Richard Wordsworth (Beggar), **Hira Talfrey** (Teresa), Justin Walters (Young Leon), John Gabriel (Priest), Warren Mitchell (Pepe Valiente), **Anne Blake** (Rosa Valiente), George Woodbridge (Dominique), Michael Ripper (Drunken Sod), Ewen Solon (Don Fernando), Peter Sallis (Don Enrique), Martin Matthews (Jose), David Conville (Rico), Denis Shaw (Jailer), Charles Lamb (Chef), **Serafina Di Leo** (Senora Zumara), **Sheila Brennan** (Vera), **Joy Webster** (Isabel), **Renny Lister** (Yvonne), **Kitty Atwood** (Midwife), John Bennett (Policemen), Hamlyn Benson (Landlord), Ray

Browne (Official), Rodney Burke, Francis De Wolff, Richard Golding, Alan Page (Customers), Max Butterfield (Cheeky Sodbuster), **Loraine Carvana** (Servant Girl as Child), Howard Lang (Irate Sodbuster), Michael Lewis (Page), Desmond Llewellyn, Gordon Whiting (Footmen), Michael Peake (Cantina Sodbuster), Stephen Scott (Random Sodbuster), Frank Sieman (Gardener), Alister Williamson (John Law).

THE DAMNED (a.k.a. *These Are the Damned*), 1963; CREW: Executive Producer: Michael Carreras; Associate Producer: Anthony Nelson-Keys; Producer: Anthony Hinds; Director: Joseph Losey; Screenplay: Evan Jones, based on the novel *The Children of Light* by H.L. Lawrence; Music: James Bernard; Cinematography: Arthur Grant; Film Editor: Reginald Mills; Production Design: Bernard Robinson; Art Director: Don Mingaye; Costume Design/Wardrobe Supervisor: Molly Arbuthnot; Makeup: Roy Ashton; Hair Stylist: Frieda Steiger; Production Manager: Don Weeks; Assistant Director: John Peverall; Second Assistant Director: Dominic Fulford; Master Plasterer: Stan Banks; Master Carpenter: Charles Davis; Props Buyer: Eric Hillier; Construction Manager: Arthur Banks; Sculptor: Frink; Property Master: Tom Money; Master Painter: Lawrence Wren; Sound Recordist: Jock May; Sound Editor: Malcolm Cooke; Special Effects: Les Bowie; Special Effects Assistants: Ian Scoones, Kit West; Stunts: Jack Cooper; Camera Operator: Anthony Heller; Master Electrician: Jack Curtis; Focus Puller: Harry Oakes; Gaffer: Steve Birtles; Musical Supervisor: John Hollingsworth; Supervising Editor: James Needs; Continuity: Pamela Davies; Master Rigger: Ronald Lenoir; Production Layout: Richard Macdonald

CAST: Macdonald Carey (Simon Wells), **Shirley Anne Field** (Joan), **Viveca Lindfors** (Freya), Alexander Knox (Bernard), Oliver Reed (King), Walter Gotell (Major Holland), James Villiers (Capt. Gregory), Thomas Kempinski (Ted), Kenneth Cope (Sid), Brian Oulton (Barry Dingle), **Barbara Everest** (Miss Lamont), Allan McClelland (Mr. Stuart), James Maxwell (Mr. Talbot), **Rachel Clay** (Victoria), **Caroline Sheldon** (Elizabeth), **Rebecca Dignam** (Anne), **Siobhan Taylor** (Mary), Nicholas Clay (Dick), Kit Williams (Henry), David Palmer (George), John Thompson (Charles), **Fiona Duncan** (Control Room Guard), Edward Harvey (Sawbones), Neil Wilson (Guard), Leon Garcia, David Gregory, Larry Martyn, Geremy Phillips, Anthony Valentine (Teddy Boys), Victor Gorf, Tommy Trinder

DEMONS OF THE MIND, 1972; CREW: Producers: Michael Carreras, Frank Godwin; Producer: Wilbur Stark; Director: Peter Sykes; Screenplay: Christopher Wicking; Story: Frank Godwin; Music: Harry Robinson (Robertson); Cinematography: Arthur Grant; Film Editor: Chris Barnes; Casting: James Liggat; Production Design: Michael Stringer; Costume Design: Rosemary Burrows; Makeup: Trevor Crole-Rees; Hairdresser: Maud Onslow; Production Supervisor: Roy Skeggs; Production Manager: Christopher Neame; Assistant Director: Ted Morley; Second Assistant Director: Graham Fowler; Third Assistant Director: Roger Stock; Construction Manager: Bill Greene; Assistant Art Director: Bill Brodie; Sound Editor: Terry Poulton; Sound Recordist: John Purchese; Dubbing Mixer: Len Abbott; Recording Director: A.W. Lumkin; Camera Operator: Neil Binney; Wardrobe Mistress: Eileen Sullivan; Colorist: David Block; Music Supervisor: Philip Martell; Continuity: Gladys Goldsmith; Production Secretary: Caroline Langley; Unit Publicist: Edna Thomas

CAST: Robert Hardy (Zorn), Shane Briant (Emil), **Gillian Hills** (Elizabeth), **Yvonne Mitchell** (Hilda), Paul Jones (Carl Richter), Patrick Magee (Falkenberg), Kenneth J. Warren (Klaus), Michael Hordern (Priest), Robert Brown (Fischinger), **Virginia Wetherell** (Inge), **Deirdre Costello** (Magda), Barry Stanton (Ernst), **Sidonie Bond** (Mrs. Zorn), Thomas Heathcote (Coachman), John Atkinson, George Cormack (Villagers), **Mary Hignett** (Matronly Woman), **Sheila Raynor** (Old Crone), **Jan Adair** (First Girl), **Jane Cardew** (Second Girl), Richard Beaumont (Young Emil)

THE DEVIL RIDES OUT (a.k.a. *The Devil's Bride*) 1968; CREW: Producer: Anthony Nelson-Keys; Director: Terence Fisher; Screenplay: Richard Matheson, based on the novel by Dennis Wheatley; Music: James Bernard; Cinematography: Arthur Grant; Film Editor: Spencer Reeve; Production Design: Bernard Robinson; Makeup: Eddie Knight; Special Makeup Artist/Black Mass: Roy Ashton; Hair Stylist: Patricia McDermott; Production Manager: Ian Lewis; Assistant Director: Bert Batt; Second Assistant Director: Christopher Neame; Painter: Michael Finlay; Sound Editor: Arthur Cox;

Sound Recordist: Ken Rawkins; Sound Recording Supervisor: A.W. Lumkin; Special Effects: Michael Staiver-Hutchins ; Stunt Coordinator: Eddie Powell; Stunt Drivers: Mike Reid, Jack Silk; Camera Operator/Assistant Editor: Moray Grant; Gaffer: Steve Birtles; Focus Puller: Bob Jordan; Casting: Irene Lamb; Wardrobe Supervisor: Rosemary Burrows; Wardrobe Mistress: Janet Lucas; Supervising Editor: James Needs; Music Supervisor: Philip Martell; Continuity: June Randall; Choreographer: David Toguri

CAST: Christopher Lee (Duc de Richleau), Charles Gray (Mocata), **Nike Arrighi** (Tanith Carlisle), Leon Greene (Rex Van Ryn), Patrick Mower (Simon), **Gwen Ffrangcon-Davies** (Countess), **Sarah Lawson** (Marie), Paul Eddington (Richard), **Rosalyn Landor** (Peggy), Russell Waters (Malin), Yemi Ajibade (African), Patrick Allen (Voice of Rex), John Bown (Receptionist), Ahmid Khalil (Indian), Willie Payne, Mohan Singh (Servant), Eddie Powell (The Goat of Mendes), Keith Pyott (Max), **Zoe Starr** (Indian Girl); **Liane Aukin**, John Falconer, **Anne Godley**, Richard Scott, Peter Swanwick, Bert Vivian (Satanists); John Brown, Richard Huggett

DICK BARTON AT BAY, 1950; CREW: Producer: Henry Halstead; Director: Godfrey Grayson; Screenplay: Jackson Budd, Olafur Haukar Grayson, Emma Trechmann; Music: Rupert Grayson, Frank Spencer; Cinematography/Camera Operator: Stanley Clinton; Film Editor: Max Brenner; Art Director: James Marchant; Makeup: Teddy Edwards; Assistant Director: Eric Veendam; Camera Operator: Jack Rose; Conductor/Music Arranger: Frank Spencer; Continuity: Prudence Sykes

CAST: Don Stannard (Dick Barton), **Tamara Desni** (Anna), George Ford (Snowy White), Meinhart Maur (Serge Volkoff), **Joyce Linden** (Mary Mitchell), Percy Walsh (Professor Mitchell), Patrick Macnee (Phillips), Campbell Singer (Inspector Cavendish), Richard George (Inspector Slade), John Arnatt (Jackson), **Beatrice Kane** (Betsy Horrock), George Crawford (Boris), Paddy Ryan (Fingers), Ted Butterfield (Tommy), Fred Owens (Gangster), Yoshihide Yanai (Chang), Ben Williams (Submarine Captain)

DICK BARTON STRIKES BACK, 1949; CREW: Producers: Anthony Hinds, Mae Murray; Director: Godfrey Grayson; Screenplay/Story: Ambrose Grayson, Elizabeth Baron; Music: Rupert Grayson, Frank Spencer; Cinematography: Cedric Williams; Casting: Edgar Blatt; Casting Manager: Mary Harris; Art Director: Ivan King; Assistant Art Director: Ken Adam; Makeup: Jack Smith; Production Manager: Donald Wynne; Assistant Director: Dicky Leeman; Second Assistant Director: Jimmy Sangster; Camera Operator: Peter Newbrook; Clapper Loader: Neil Binney; Focus Puller: Gerry Turpin; Supervising Electrician: Jack Curtis; Supervising Editor: Ray Pitt; Continuity: Prudence Sykes

CAST: Don Stannard (Dick Barton), Sebastian Cabot (Alfonso Delmonte Fourcada), **Jean Lodge** (Tina), James Raglan (Lord Sir James Armadale), Bruce Walker (Snowy White), Humphrey Kent (Col. Gardner), John Harvey (Major Henderson), Morris Sweden (Agent Creston), Tony Morelli (Nicholas), George Crawford (Alex), Sidney Vivian (Inspector Burke), Jimmy O'Dea, Laurie (Larry) Taylor

DR. JEKYLL AND SISTER HYDE, 1971; CREW: Producers: Brian Clemens, Albert Fennell; Director: Roy Ward Baker; Screenplay: Brian Clemens, based on the novel *The Strange Case of Dr. Jekyll and Mr. Hyde* by Robert Louis Stevenson; Music: David Whitaker; Composer/Song, "He'll Be There": Brian Clemens; Cinematography: Norman Warwick; Film Editor: James Needs; Casting: Jimmy Liggat; Production Design: Robert Jones; Makeup Supervisor: John Wilcox; Makeup: Trevor Crole Rees; Hair Stylist: Bernadette "Bernie" Ibbetson; Production Supervisor: Roy Skeggs; Production Manager: Don Weeks; Assistant Director: Bert Batt; Construction Manager: Bill Greene; Assistant Art Director: Len Townsend; Sound Editor: Charles Crafford; Recording Director: A.W. Lumkin; Sound: Bill Rowe; Special Effects: Michael Collins; Camera Operator: Godfrey Godar; Costume Design/Wardrobe Supervisor: Rosemary Burrows; Wardrobe Mistress: Kathleen Moore; Assistant Editor: Sue Kingsley; Colorist: David Block; Music Supervisor: Philip Martell; Continuity: Sally Ball; Script Supervisor: Sally Jones

CAST: Ralph Bates (Dr. Jekyll), **Martine Beswicke** (Sister Hyde), Gerald Sim (Prof. Robertson), Lewis Fiander (Howard), **Susan Brodrick** (Susan), **Dorothy Alison** (Mrs. Spencer), Ivor Dean (Burke), Philip Madoc (Byker), **Irene Bradshaw** (Yvonne), Neil Wilson, Geoffrey Kenion (Policemen),

Paul Whitsun-Jones (Sgt. Danvers), Tony Calvin (Hare), Dan Meaden (Town Crier), **Virginia Wetherell** (Betsy), **Anna Brett** (Julie), **Jackie Poole** (Margie), **Rosemary Lord** (Marie), **Petula Portell** (Petra), **Pat Brackenbury** (Helen), **Liz Romanoff** (Emma), Will Stampe (Mein Host), Roy Evans (Knife Grinder), Derek Steen, John Lyons (Sailors), **Jeanette Wild** (Jill), Booby Parr (Boy Apprentice), **Julia Wright** (Street Singer), Harry Fielder (Local Bloke)

DRACULA (a.k.a. *Horror of Dracula*), 1958; CREW: Executive Producer: Michael Carreras; Associate Producer: Anthony Nelson-Keys; Producer: Anthony Hinds; Director: Terence Fisher; Screenplay: Jimmy Sangster, based on the novel *Dracula* by Bram Stoker; Music: James Bernard; Cinematography: Jack Asher; Film Editor: Bill Lenny; Production Design/Art Direction: Bernard Robinson; Costume Design/Wardrobe: Molly Arbuthnot, Rosemary Burrows; Makeup: Phil Leakey, Roy Ashton; Hair Stylist: Henry Montsash; Production Manager: Don Weeks; Assistant Director: Robert Lynn; Master Plasterer: Arthur Banks; Master Carpenter: Charles Davis; Props Buyer: Eric Hillier; Construction Manager: Mick Lyons; Draughtsman: Don Mingaye; Property Master: Tom Money; Master Painter: Lawrence Wren; Sound Recordist: Jock May; Boom Operator: Claude Hitchcock; Special Effects: Sydney Pearson, Les Bowie; Stunts: Nosher Powell, Peter Diamond; Camera Operator: Len Harris; Chief Electrician: Jack Curtis; Still Photographer: Tom Edwards; Focus Puller: Harry Oakes; Musical Director: John Hollingsworth; Supervising Editor: James Needs; Continuity: Doreen Dearnaley

CAST: Peter Cushing (Van Helsing), Christopher Lee (Dracula), Michael Gough (Arthur), **Melissa Stribling** (Mina), **Carol Marsh** (Lucy), **Olga Dickie** (Gerda), John Van Eyssen (Jonathan Harker), **Valerie Gaunt** (Vampire Woman), **Janine Faye** (Tania), **Barbara Archer** (Inga), Charles Lloyd Pack (Dr. Seward), George Merritt (John Law), George Woodbridge (Landlord), George Benson (Official), Miles Malleson (Undertaker), Geoffrey Bayldon (Porter), Paul Cole (Lad), Guy Mills (Coach Driver), Richard Morgan (Coach Driver's Companion), John Mossman (Hearse Driver); Stedwell Fulcher, Humphrey Kent, **Judith Nelmes**, William Sherwood (Scenes Deleted)

DRACULA A.D. 1972, 1972; CREW: Producer: Josephine Douglas; Director: Alan Gibson; Screenplay: Don Houghton; Director of Photography: Dick Bush; Camera Operator: Bernie Ford; Art Director: Don Mingaye; Assistant Art Director: Bill Benton; Film Editor: James Needs; Continuity: Doreen Dearnaley; Sound Editor: Roy Baker; Recording Director: A.W. Lumkin; Dubbing Mixer: Bill Rowe; Sound Recordist: Claude Hitchcock; Casting: James Liggat; Music: Mike Vickers; Music Supervisor: Philip Martell; Songs: "Alligator Man"/Sal Valentino, "You Better Come Through"/Tim Barnes; Production Supervisor: Roy Skeggs; Production Manager: Ron Jackson; Special Effects: Les Bowie; Makeup: Jill Carpenter; Hair Stylist: Barbara Ritchie; Wardrobe Supervisor: Rosemary Burrows; Assistant Director: Robert Lynn; Construction Manager: Bill Greene.

CAST: Christopher Lee (Dracula), Peter Cushing (Prof. Van Helsing), **Stephanie Beacham** (Jessica Van Helsing), **Caroline Munro** (Laura Bellows), Michael Coles (Inspector Murray), Christopher Neame (Johnny Alucard), William Ellis (Joe Mitchum), **Marsha Hunt** (Gaynor), **Janet Key** (Anna), Philip Miller (Bob), Michael Kitchen (Greg), David Andrews (Detective Sergeant Pearson), **Lally Bowers** (Matron); Tim Barnes, Sal Valentino, **Annie Sampson**, John Blakely, Brian Godula, **Lynn Hughes**, **Deirdre La Porte**, Cory Lerios, **Lydia Mareno**, Steve Price (Stoneground), **Jane Anthony** ("Debby" Girl), **Flanagan** (Go-Go Girl), John Franklin-Robbins (Minister), **Constance Luttrell** (Mrs. Donnelly), Michael Daly (Charles), Arturo Morris (Police Sergeant), **Jo Richardson** (The Crying Woman), **Penny Brahms** (Hippie Chick), Brian John Smith (Hippie Dude)

DRACULA HAS RISEN FROM THE GRAVE, 1968; CREW: Producer: Aida Young; Director: Freddie Francis; Screenplay: "John Elder" (Anthony Hinds), based on the character created by Bram Stoker; Music: James Bernard; Cinematography: Arthur Grant; Film Editor: Spencer Reeve; Production Design: Bernard Robinson; Makeup: Heather Nurse, Rosemarie McDonald Peattie; Hair Stylist: Wanda Kelley; Production Manager: Christopher Sutton; Assistant Director: Dennis Robertson; Construction Manager: Arthur Banks; Sound Editor: Wilfred Thompson; Sound Recordist: Ken Rawkins; Boom Operator: Harry Fairbairn; Special Effects: Frank George, Bert Luxford, James Snow; Matte Artists: Peter Melrose, Bob Cuff; Stunts: Eddie Powell, Peter Diamond; Camera Operator: Moray Grant; Wardrobe Mistress: Jill Thompson; Supervising Editor: James Needs; Music Supervisor: Philip Martell; Continuity: Doris Martin; Runner: Kevin Francis

CAST: Christopher Lee (Dracula), Rupert Davies (Monsignor Ernest Mueller), **Veronica Carlson** (Maria Mueller), **Barbara Ewing** (Zena), Barry Andrews (Paul), Ewan Hooper (Priest), **Marion Mathie** (Anna Mueller), Michael Ripper (Max), John D. Collins (Student), George A. Cooper (Landlord), Chris Cunningham (Farmer), Norman Bacon (Mute Boy), **Carrie Baker** (First Victim)

DRACULA, PRINCE OF DARKNESS, 1966; CREW: Producer: Anthony Nelson-Keys; Director: Terence Fisher; Idea/Story: Anthony Hinds; Screenplay: "John Sansom" (Jimmy Sangster), based on characters created by Bram Stoker; Music: James Bernard; Cinematography: Michael Reed; Film Editor: Chris Barnes; Art Director: Don Mingaye; Production Design: Bernard Robinson; Wardrobe: Rosemary Burrows; Makeup: Roy Ashton; Hair Stylist: Frieda Steiger; Production Manager: Ross Mackenzie; Assistant Director: Bert Batt; Second Assistant Director: Hugh Harlow; Painter: Michael Finlay; Sound Recordist: Ken Rawkins; Sound Editor: Roy Baker; Special Effects: Les Bowie; Stunts: Peter Diamond, Eddie Powell; Camera Operator: C. Cooney; Editorial Supervisor: James Needs; Music Supervisor/Orchestrator: Philip Martell; Continuity: Lorna Selwyn

CAST: Christopher Lee (Dracula), Andrew Keir (Father Sandor), **Barbara Shelley** (Helen Kent), Francis Matthews (Charles), **Suzan Farmer** (Diana), Charles Tingwell (Alan), Thorley Walters (Ludwig), Philip Latham (Klove), Walter Brown (Brother Mark), George Woodbridge (Landlord), Jack Lambert (Linebacker), Philip Ray (Priest), **Joyce Hemson** (Mother), John Maxim (Coach Driver), Peter Cushing (Van Helsing — Archive Footage)

THE EVIL OF FRANKENSTEIN, 1964; CREW: Producer: Anthony Hinds; Director: Freddie Francis; Screenplay: "John Elder" (Anthony Hinds); Music: Don Banks; Cinematography: John Wilcox; Art Director: Don Mingaye; Wardrobe Mistress: Rosemary Burrows; Makeup: Roy Ashton; Hair Stylist: Frieda Steiger; Production Manager: Don Weeks; Assistant Directors: Hugh Harlow, William P. Cartlidge; Sound Recordist: Ken Rawkins; Sound Editor: Roy Hyde; Camera Operator: Ronnie Maasz; Special Effects: Les Bowie; Stunts: Peter Diamond; Music Supervisor: Philip Martell; Musical Director: John Hollingsworth; Supervising Editor: James Needs; Continuity: Pauline Harlow (formerly Wise)

CAST: Peter Cushing (Baron Frankenstein), Kiwi Kingston (The Creature), Peter Woodthorpe (Prof. Zoltan), Duncan Lamont (Police Chief), Sandor Eles (Hans), **Katy Wild** (Beggar Girl), David Hutcheson (Burgomaster), James Maxwell (Priest), Howard Goorney (Drunk), Anthony Blackshaw, David Conville (Policemen), Tony Arpino (The Body Snatcher), Timothy Bateson (Hypnotized Chap), Frank Forsyth (Manservant), Patrick Horgan (David), Kenneth Kove (Cure), **Michelle Scott** (Little Girl), Alister Williamson (Landlord); Robert Flynn, James Garfield, Derek Martin, Anthony Poole (Roustabouts); Additional Sequence — United States: Steven Geray (Dr. Sergado), **Maria Palmer** (Rena's Mother), William Phipps (Rena's Father), **Tracy Stratford** (Rena as Child)

FANATIC (a.k.a. *Die! Die! My Darling!*) 1965; CREW: Producer: Anthony Hinds; Director: Silvio Narizzano; Screenplay: Richard Matheson, based on the novel *Nightmare* by Anne Blaisdell; Music: Wilfred Josephs; Cinematography: Arthur Ibbetson; Film Editor: John Dunsford; Production Design: Peter Proud; Wardrobe Mistress: Mary Gibson; Makeup: Phil Leakey, Richard Mills; Hair Stylist: Olga Angelinetta; Production Manager: George Fowler; Assistant Director: Claude Watson; Second Assistant Directors: Peter Beale, Stuart Black; Third Assistant Director: Nigel Wooll; Sound Recordist: Ken Rawkins; Sound Editor: Roy Hyde; Camera Operator: Paul Wilson; Still Photographer: Tom Edwards; Supervising Editor: James Needs; Musical Supervisor: Philip Martell; Continuity: Renee Glynne

CAST: **Tallulah Bankhead** (Mrs. Trefoile), **Stefanie Powers** (Patricia), Peter Vaughn (Harry), Maurice Kaufmann (Alan), Donald Sutherland (Joseph), **Gwendolyn Watts** (Gloria), **Yootha Joyce** (Anna), Robert Dorning (Ormsby), Philip Gilbert (Oscar), **Winifred Dennis** (Shopkeeper), **Diana King** (Shopper), Henry McGee (Rector)

FEAR IN THE NIGHT, 1972; CREW: Producer/Director: Jimmy Sangster; Screenplay: Jimmy Sangster, Michael Syson; Music: John McCabe; Cinematography: Arthur Grant; Film Editor: Peter Weatherley; Casting: James Liggat; Art Director: Don Picton; Makeup: Bill Partleton; Production Supervisor: Roy Skeggs; Production Manager: Christopher Neame; Assistant Director: Ted Morley; Set

Dresser: Penny Campbell; Third Assistant Director: Phil Campbell; Sound Editor: Roy Hyde; Sound Recordist: Claude Hitchcock; Recording Director: A.W. Lumkin; Dubbing Recordist: Dennis Whitlock; Camera Operator: Neil Binney; Focus Puller: Bob Jordan; Wardrobe: Rosemary Burrows; Music Supervisor: Philip Martell; Continuity: Gladys Goldsmith

CAST: Peter Cushing (Headmaster Michael Carmichael), **Joan Collins** (Molly Carmichael), **Judy Geeson** (Peggy Heller), Ralph Bates (Robert Heller), James Cossins (The Doctor), **Gillian Lind** (Mrs. Beamish), John Bown, Brian Grellis (Policemen)

FOUR SIDED TRIANGLE, 1953; CREW: Producers: Michael Carreras, Alexander Paal; Director/Screenplay: Terence Fisher; Screenplay/Adaptation: Paul Tabori, from the novel *Four-Sided Triangle* by William Temple; Music: Malcolm Arnold; Cinematography: Reginald H. Wyer; Film Editor: Maurice Rootes; First Assistant Editor: Bill Lenny; Art Direction: J. Elder Wills; Makeup: Dick Bonnor-Morris; Hair Stylist: Nina Broe; Production Manager: Victor Wark; Assistant Director: Bill Shore; Second Assistant Director: Aida Young; Sound Recordists: Bill Salter, Percy Britten; Camera Operator: Len Harris; Clapper Loader: Tom Friswell; Still Photographer: John Jay; Focus Puller: Manny Yospa; Conductor: Muir Mathieson; Continuity: Rene Glynne; Dialogue Director: Nora Roberts

CAST: Stephen Murray (Bill), John Van Eyssen (Robin), **Barbara Payton** (Lena/Helen), James Hayter (Dr. Harvey), Percy Marmont (Sir Walter), **Jennifer Dearman** (Little Lena), Glyn Dearman (Boy Bill), Sean Barrett (Li'l Robin), Kynaston Reeves (Lord Grant), John Stuart (Solicitor), **Edith Saville** (Lady Grant)

FRANKENSTEIN AND THE MONSTER FROM HELL, 1974; CREW: Producer: Roy Skeggs; Director: Terence Fisher; Screenplay: "John Elder" (Anthony Hinds), based on the character created by Mary Shelley; Music: James Bernard; Cinematography: Brian Probyn; Film Editor: James Needs; Casting: James Liggat; Art Director: Scott MacGregor; Makeup: Eddie Knight; Hairdresser: Maude Onslow; Production Manager: Christopher Neame; Assistant Director: Derek Whitehurst; Second Assistant Director: Chris Carreras; Third Assistant Director: Roy Stevens; Construction Manager: Arthur Banks; Assistant Art Director: Don Picton; Sound Editor: Roy Hyde; Sound Recordist: Les Hammond; Dubbing Mixer: Maurice Askew; Sound Re-Recording Mixer: Lionel Strutt; Special Effects: Les Bowie; Camera Operator: Chick Anstiss; Assistant Camera: Cedric James; Focus Puller: Bob Jordan; Wardrobe Supervisor: Dulcie Midwinter; Musical Supervisor/ & Composer/Additional Music: Philip Martell; Violin Solos: Hugh Bean; Continuity: Kay Rawlings

CAST: Peter Cushing (Baron Victor "Dr. Carl Victor" Frankenstein), Shane Briant (Simon Helder), David Prowse (The Monster), **Madeline Smith** (Sarah), John Stratton (Asylum Director), Michael Ward (Transvest), Elsie Wagstaff (The Wild One), Norman Mitchell (Police Sgt.), Clifford Mollison (The Judge), Patrick Troughton (The Body Snatcher), Philip Voss (Ernst), Chris Cunningham (Hans), Charles Lloyd Pack (Prof. Durendel), **Lucy Griffiths** (Old Hag), Bernard Lee (Tarmut), Sydney Bromley (Muller), **Andrea Lawrence** (Brassy Girl), Jerold Wells (Landlord), **Sheila D'Union** (Gerda), Norman Atkyns (Smiler), Mischa De La Motte (Twitch), Victor Woolf (Letch), **Winifred Sabine** (Mouse), **Janet Hargreaves** (Chatter), Peter Madden (Coach Driver), Nicolas Smith (Death Wish), Gordon Richardson (Aggressive); Hugh Cecil, Ron Eagleton, **Lianne Gilmore**, **Beatrice Greek**, **Toni Harris**, Peter Macpherson (Inmates)

FRANKENSTEIN CREATED WOMAN, 1967; CREW: Producer: Anthony Nelson-Keys; Director: Terence Fisher; Screenplay: "John Elder" (Anthony Hinds); Music: James Bernard; Cinematography: Arthur Grant; Film Editor: Spencer Reeve; Casting: Irene Lamb; Art Director: Don Mingaye; Production Design: Bernard Robinson; Wardrobe Mistress: Rosemary Burrows; Wardrobe Master: Larry Stewart; Makeup: George Partleton; Hair Stylist: Frieda Steiger; Production Manager: Ian Lewis; Assistant Director: Douglas Hermes; Second Assistant Director: Joe Marks; Third Assistant Director: Christopher Neame; Draughtsman: Thomas Goswell; Scenic Artist: Felix Sergejak; Master Painter: Sound Recordist: Ken Rawkins; Sound Editor: Roy Hyde; Sound Re-Recording Mixer: Gerry Humphreys; Special Effects: Les Bowie; Special Effects Assistants: Ray Caple, Ian Scoones; Stunts: Peter Diamond; Camera Operator: Moray Grant; Focus Puller: Bob Jordan; Music Supervisor: Philip Martell; Supervising Editor: James Needs; First Assistant Editor: Elizabeth Redstone; Second Assistant Editor: Chris Brennan; Continuity: Eileen Head

CAST: Peter Cushing (Baron Frankenstein), **Susan Denberg** (Christina), Thorley Walters (Dr. Hertz), Robert Morris (Hans), Duncan Lamont (The Prisoner), Peter Blythe (Anton), Barry Warren (Karl), Derek Fowlds (Johann), Alan MacNaughton (Kleve), Peter Madden (Chief of Police), Philip Ray (Mayor), Ivan Beavis (Landlord), Colin Jeavons (Priest), Bartlett Mullins (Bystander), Alec Mango, Anthony Vickers (Spokesmen), Patrick Carter, Howard Lang (Guards), Kevin Flood (Jailer), **Lizbeth Kent** (First Woman), John Maxim (Sergeant), Mark McMullins (Body-Toting Villager), Stuart Middleton (Young Hans)

FRANKENSTEIN MUST BE DESTROYED, 1969; CREW: Producer/Story: Anthony Nelson-Keys; Director: Terence Fisher; Screenplay/Story: Bert Batt, based on the character created by Mary Shelley; Music: James Bernard; Cinematography: Arthur Grant; Film Editor: Gordon Hales; Supervising Art Director: Bernard Robinson; Casting: Irene Lamb; Wardrobe Supervisor: Rosemary Burrows; Wardrobe Mistress: Lottie Slattery; Makeup: Eddie Knight; Hair Stylist: Pat McDermott; Production Manager: Christopher Neame; Assistant Director: Bert Batt; Second Assistant Director: Bill Wesley; Construction Manager: Arthur Banks; Sound Recordist: Ken Rawkins; Sound Editor: Don Ranasinghe; Boom Operator: Harry Fairbairn; Sound Supervisor: Tony Lumkin; Stunts: Peter Diamond; Camera Operator: Neil Binney; Musical Director: Philip Martell; Continuity: Doreen Dearnaley

CAST: Peter Cushing (Baron Frankenstein), Freddie Jones (Richter), **Veronica Carlson** (Anna), Simon Ward (Karl), Thorley Walters (Inspector Frisch), **Maxine Audley** (Ella), George Pravda (Dr. Brandt), Geoffrey Bayldon (Police Doctor), **Colette O'Neil** (Mad Woman), Frank Middlemass (Plumber Guest), George Belbin (Chess-Playing Guest), Norman Shelley (Pipe-Smoking Guest), Michael Gover (Newspaper-Reading Guest), Peter Copley (Principal), Jim Collier (Dr. Heidecke), Alan Surtees, Windsor Davies (Police Sergeants), Timothy Davies (Cop), Robert Davis (Official), Harry Fielder (Angry Villager), **Caron Gardner** (Passer-By), Robert Gillespie (Mortuary Attendant), Michael Goldie (Warder Street), Harold Goodwin (Burglar), Edward Higgins (Workman), **Elizabeth Morgan** (Christina), **Daphne Oxenford** (Lady in Garden), **Dorothy Smith** (Anna's Neighbor), Meadows White (Night Watchman)

THE GORGON; 1964; CREW: Producer: Anthony Nelson-Keys; Director: Terence Fisher; Screenplay: John Gilling; Story: J. Llewellyn Devine; Music/Musical Director: James Bernard; Cinematography: Michael Reed; Film Editor: Eric Boyd-Perkins; Production Design: Bernard Robinson; Wardrobe Supervisor: Molly Arbuthnot; Wardrobe Mistress: Rosemary Burrows; Makeup: Roy Ashton; Hair Stylist: Frieda Steiger; Assistant Makeup: Richard Mills; Production Manager: Don Weeks; Assistant Director: Bert Batt; Second Assistant Director: Hugh Harlow; Third Assistant Director: Stephen Victor; Master Plasterer: Stan Banks; Props Buyer: Eric Hillier; Property Master: Tom Money; Construction Manager: Arthur Banks; Art Director: Don Mingaye; Master Painter: Lawrence Wren; Sound Recordist: Ken Rawkins; Sound Editor: Roy Hyde; Sound Assistant: Alan Thorne; Special Effects: Syd Pearson; Special Effects Assistant: Ray Caple; Stunt Coordinator/Fight Arranger: Peter Diamond; Camera Operator: C. Cooney; Chief Electrician: Jack Curtis; Still Photographer: Tom Edwards; Camera Grip: Albert Cowlard; Focus Puller: John Shinerock; Supervising Editor: James Needs; Musical Supervisor: Marcus Dods; Continuity: Pauline Harlow; Accountants: W.H.V. Able, Ken Gordon; Studio Manager: Arthur Kelly

CAST: Peter Cushing (Doctor Namaroff), Christopher Lee (Prof. Meister), **Barbara Shelley** (Carla Hoffman), **Prudence Hyman** (The Gorgon), Richard Pasco (Paul Heitz), Michael Goodliffe (Prof. Heitz), Patrick Troughton (Inspector Kanof), Joseph O'Connor (Coroner), Jack Watson (Ratoff), Redmond Phillips (Hans), Jeremy Longhurst (Bruno Heitz), **Joyce Hemson** (Martha), **Toni Gilpin** (Sascha Cass), Alister Williamson (Janus Cass), **Ellen Cohen** (Mama Cass), Michael Peake (Constable), **Sally Nesbitt** (Nurse)

HANDS OF THE RIPPER, 1971; CREW: Producer: Aida Young; Director: Peter Sasdy; Screenplay: Screenplay: L.W. Davidson; Story: Edward Spencer Shew; Music: Christopher Gunning; Cinematography: Kenneth Talbot; Film Editor: Chris Barnes; Art Director: Roy Stannard; Makeup Supervisor: Bunty Phillips; Special Makeup Effects: Roy Ashton; Hair Styles Supervisor: Pat McDermott; Production Manager: Christopher Sutton; Assistant Director: Ariel Levy; Sound Editor: Frank Goulding;

Sound Recordist: Kevin Sutton; Dubbing Mixer: Ken Barker; Sound Maintenance: Dan Grimmel; Sound Re-Recording Mixers: Graham V. Hartstone, Otto Snel; Special Effects: Cliff Culley; Camera Operator: Bob Kindred; Wardrobe Supervisor: Rosemary Burrows; Wardrobe Mistress: Eileen Sullivan; Musical Supervisor: Philip Martell; Continuity: Gladys Goldsmith

CAST: Eric Porter (Dr. John Pritchard), **Angharad Rees** (Anna), **Jane Merrow** (Laura), Keith Bell (Michael Pritchard), Derek Godfrey (Dysart), **Dora Bryan** (Mrs. Golding), **Marjorie Rhodes** (Mrs. Bryant), **Lynda Baron** (Long Liz), **Marjie Lawrence** (Dolly), **Margaret Rawlings** (Madame Bullard), **Elizabeth MacLennan** (Mrs. Wilson), Barry Lowe (Mr. Wilson), A.J. Brown (The Reverend Anderson), **April Wilding** (Catherine), **Anne Clune**, **Vicki Woolf** (Cell Whores), **Katya Wyeth**, **Beulah Hughes**, **Tallulah Miller** (Pub Whores), Peter Munt (Mr. Pleasants), Philip Ryan (Constable), **Molly Weir** (Maid), Charles Lamb (Guard), Norman Bird (Inspector), **Ann Way** (Seamstress).

THE HORROR OF FRANKENSTEIN, 1969; CREW: Producer/Director: Jimmy Sangster; Screenplay: Jimmy Sangster and Jeremy Burnham, based on the characters by Mary Shelley; Music: Malcolm Williamson; Cinematography: Moray Grant; Film Editor: Chris Barnes; Art Director: Scott MacGregor; Assistant Art Director: Don Picton; Wardrobe Mistress: Laura Nightingale; Makeup Supervisor: Tom Smith; Hair Styles Supervisor: Pearl Tipaldi; Production Manager: Tom Sachs; Assistant Director: Derek Whitehurst; Second Assistant Director: Nick Granby; Third Assistant Director: Lindsey Vickers; Construction Manager: Arthur Banks; Draughtsman: Tony Baines; Props: Wally Hockings; Set Dresser: Penny Struthers; Sound Recordist: Claude Hitchcock; Sound Editor: Terry Poulton; Recording Director: A.W. Lumkin; Dubbing Editor: Bill Rowe; Boom Operator: Keith Batten; Camera Operator: Neil Binney; Clapper Loader: Rod Barron; Focus Puller: Bob Stilwell; Camera Grip: Peter Woods; Assistant Editors: B. Baker, Larry Richardson; Music Supervisor: Philip Martell; Continuity: Betty Harley; Unit Driver: George Andrews; Unit Runner: Philip Campbell

CAST: Ralph Bates (Victor Frankenstein), David Prowse (The Monster), **Veronica Carlson** (Elizabeth Heiss), **Kate O'Mara** (Alys), Dennis Price (Graverobber), Jon Finch (Lt. Becker), Bernard Archard (Prof. Heiss), Graham James (Wilhelm Kassner), James Hayter (Bailiff), **Joan Rice** (Graverobber's Wife), Stephen Turner (Stefan), Neil Wilson (Schoolmaster), James Cossins (Dean), **Glenys O'Brien** (Maggie), Geoffrey Lumsden (Instructor), C. Lethbridge Baker (Priest), Terry Duggan (Bandit), George Belbin (Baron Frankenstein), Hal Jeayes (Woodsman), **Carol Jeayes** (Woodsman's Daughter), Michael Goldie (Workman), **Sue Hammer** (Maid), Alain Schlockoff

THE HOUND OF THE BASKERVILLES, 1959; CREW: Executive Producer: Michael Carreras; Associate Producer: Anthony Nelson-Keys; Producers: Anthony Hinds, Kenneth Hyman; Director: Terence Fisher; Screenplay: Peter Bryan, based on the novel by Sir Arthur Conan Doyle; Music: James Bernard; Cinematography: Jack Asher; Film Editor: Alfred Cox; Production Design: Bernard Robinson; Wardrobe: Molly Arbuthnot; Makeup: Roy Ashton; Hair Stylist: Henry Montsash; Hound Mask: Margaret Robinson; Production Manager: Don Weeks; Assistant Director: John Peverall; Third Assistant Director: Hugh Harlow; Master Plasterer: Arthur Banks; Master Carpenter: Charles Davis; Props Buyer: Eric Hillier; Construction Manager: Mick Lyons; Draughtsman: Don Mingaye; Property Master: Tom Money; Dog Model Maker: Frank Pannicelli; Scenic Artist: Gilbert Wood; Master Painter: Lawrence Wren; Sound Recordist: Jock May; Boom Operator: Jim Perry; Special Effects: Sydney Pearson; Camera Operator: Len Harris; Camera Operator/Second Unit: Teddy Catford; Still Photographer: Tom Edwards; Focus Puller: Harry Oakes; Gaffer: Steve Birtles; Musical Director: John Hollingsworth; Supervising Editor: James Needs; Continuity: Shirley Barnes

CAST: Peter Cushing (Sherlock Holmes), Andre Morell (Dr. Watson), Christopher Lee (Sir Henry Baskerville), **Marla Landi** (Cecile), David Oxley (Sir Hugo), Francis De Wolff (Dr. Mortimer), Miles Malleson (Bishop), Ewen Solon (Stapleton), John Le Mesurier (Barrymore), **Helen Goss** (Mrs. Barrymore), Sam Kydd (Perkins), Michael Hawkins (Lord Caphill), **Judi Moyens** (Servant Girl), Michael Mulcaster (Convict), David Birks (Servant), **Elizabeth Gott** (Mrs. Goodlippe), Ian Hewetson (Lord Kingsblood)

HYSTERIA, 1965; CREW: Producer/Screenplay: Jimmy Sangster; Director: Freddie Francis; Music: Don Banks; Cinematography: John Wilcox; Production Design: Edward Carrick; Wardrobe

Mistress: Maude Churchill; Makeup: Alex Garfath; Hair Stylist: Alice Holmes; Production Manager: Don Weeks; Assistant Director: Basil Rayburn; Sound Recordist: Cyril Swern; Sound Editor: Roy Hyde; Camera Operator: David Harcourt; Music Supervisor: Philip Martell; Supervising Editor: James Needs; Continuity: Yvonne Axworthy

CAST: Robert Webber (Chris), **Jennifer Jayne** (Gina McConnell), Anthony Newlands (Dr. Keller), Maurice Denham (Hemmings), **Lelia Goldoni** (Denise), Peter Woodthorpe (Marcus), **Sandra Boize** (English Girl), **Sue Lloyd** (French Girl), John Arnatt (Mr. James), **Marianne Stone** (Miss Grogan), **Irene Richmond** (Mrs. Keller), Kiwi Kingston (French Girl's Husband)

JOURNEY INTO DARKNESS, 1969; CREW: Executive Producer: Joan Harrison; Producer: Anthony Hinds; Directors: Peter Sasdy, James Hill; Writers: Charles Beaumont, Leslie P. Davies, John Gould, Oscar Millard

CAST: Patrick McGoohan (Host), Robert Reed (Hank Prentiss), **Jennifer Hilary** (Anne Prentiss), Michael Tolan (Craig), **Nanette Newman** (Jill), Michael Ripper (Albert Cole), **Melissa Stribling** (Helen Ames), **Dorothy Alison** (Mrs. Latham), Patrick Allen (Luther), George Benson (Vicar), **Adrienne Corri** (Woman), **Catherine Finn** (Elsie Cole), Edward Hardwicke (Dr. Yarrow), **Hazel Hughes** (Mrs. Biddle), **June Jago** (Emily), Milo O'Shea (Matt), Roderick Shaw (Rodney), Damien Thomas (Bloke), Kenneth J. Warren (Joe), Jerold Wells (Mayhew), John Welsh (Bart)

JOURNEY TO MIDNIGHT, 1971; CREW: Executive Producer: Joan Harrison; Producer: Anthony Hinds; Directors: Roy Ward Baker, Alan Gibson; Writers: William Abney, Robert Bloch, Jeremy Paul; Music: Harry Robinson; Film Editor: James Needs

CAST: Sebastian Cabot (Host), Chad Everett (Steve Miller), Bernard Lee (Ben Loker), **Fay Compton** (Queen Victoria), Edward Fox (Robert), **Susan Brodrick** (Rose), **Susan Richards** (Mrs. Loker), **Marty Cruikshank** (Diana), Norman Chappell (Friar Tuck), Antony Webb (Nelson), Donald Gee (Aviator), Michael Nightingale (Butler), **Linda Cole** (Lady Hamilton), **Ann Lancaster** (Red Queen), Terence Duff (March Hare), Roy Hanlon (Jimmy), **Maggie Don** (Barbara), **Julie Harris** (Leona), Tom Adams (Jerry Crown), **Tracy Reed** (Joyce), **Catherine Lacey** (Sarah), Marne Maitland (Chardur), Dennis Ramsden (Mrs. Hubbard), Julian Sherrier (Bright Arrow), Geoff Winslip (Knife Thrower)

JOURNEY TO MURDER, 1971; CREW: Executive Producer: Joan Harrison; Producer: Anthony Hinds; Directors: John Gibson, Gerry O'Hara; Writers: Julian Bond, L.P. Hartley, Stanley Miller, Frederick Rawlings; Film Editor: James Needs

CAST: **Joan Crawford** (Hostess), Joseph Cotten (Jeff Wheeler), **Judy Parfitt** (Faith Wheeler), Douglas Wilmer (Harry Vantese), Kenneth Haigh (Dirk), **Joyce Blair** (Betty), David Warbeck (Chris), David Baxter (The Assistant Director), Hugh Futcher (Wardrobe Dresser), **Carol Cleveland** (Lisa), Tom Gill (Golfer), Roddy McDowall (Rollo), **Ingrid Boulting** (Vera), Barry Evans (Jimmy), William Marlowe (Randolph), Eddie Byrne (Copper), John Rudling (Hodgson)

THE KISS OF THE VAMPIRE, 1963; CREW: Producer: Anthony Hinds; Director: Don Sharp; Screenplay: "John Elder" (Anthony Hinds); Music: James Bernard; Cinematography: Alan Hume; Production Design: Bernard Robinson; Wardrobe Supervisor: Molly Arbuthnot; Wardrobe Mistress: Rosemary Burrows; Casting: Dorothy Holloway; Makeup: Roy Ashton; Hair Stylist: Frieda Steiger; Assistant Makeup: Reginald Mills; Production Manager: Don Weeks; Assistant Director: Douglas Hermes; Second Assistant Director: Hugh Harlow; Master Plasterer: Stan Banks; Master Carpenter: Charles Davis; Construction Manager: Arthur Banks; Art Director: Don Mingaye; Assistant Art Director: Kenneth Ryan; Master Painter: Lawrence Wren; Sound Recordist: Ken Rawkins; Sound Editor: James Groom; Special Effects: Les Bowie; Special Effects Assistants: Ian Scoones, Ray Caple, Brian Johnson, Kit West; Stunts: Peter Diamond; Camera Operator: Moray Grant; Chief Electrician: Jack Curtis; Still Photographer: Tom Edwards; Focus Puller: David Osborne; Supervising Editor: James Needs; Musical Supervisor: John Hollingsworth; Continuity: Pauline Wise; Master Rigger: Ronald Lenoir

CAST: Clifford Evans (Prof. Zimmer), Edward de Souza (Gen. Harcourt), **Jennifer Daniel** (Marianne Harcourt), Noel Willman (Dr. Ravna), Barry Warren (Carl Ravna), Brian Oulton, **Dolly Read**,

Elizabeth Valentine (Disciples), Noel Howlett (Fr. Xavier), **Jacquie Wallis** (Sabena Ravna), Peter Madden (Bruno), **Isobel Black** (Tania), **Vera Cook** (Anna), John Harvey (Police Sergeant), Carl Esmond (Anton, U.S. Television Version), **Virginia Gregg** (Rosa, U.S. Television Version), **Sheilah Wells** (Theresa, U.S. Television Version), **Olga Dickie** (Woman at Graveyard), Stan Simmons (Servant), Horst Ebersberg

THE LEGEND OF THE 7 GOLDEN VAMPIRES (a.k.a. *The 7 Brothers meet Dracula*) 1974; CREW: Executive Producers: Run-Run Shaw, Runme Shaw; Producers: Don Houghton, Vee King Shaw; Directors: Roy Ward Baker, Cheh Chang; Screenplay: Don Houghton; Music: James Bernard; Cinematography: Roy Ford, John Wilcox; Film Editor: Chris Barnes; Assistant Editor: Larry Richardson; Art Director: Johnson Tsau; Costume Design: Liu Chi-Yu; Makeup: Wu Hsu Ching; Hairdresser: Peng Yen-Lien; Production Manager: Lam Chua; Unit Manager: Shen Chung; Assistant Directors: Feng Erh, Godfrey Ho; Props Master: Li Wu; Sound Editor: Frank Goulding; Sound Recordist: Les Hammond; Sound Maintenance: Dan Grimmel; Boom Operator: Tommy Staples; Special Effects: Les Bowie; Stunts: Frank Hayden; Camera Operator: Roy Ford; Focus Puller: Keith Jones; Music Supervisor: Philip Martell; Continuity: Renee Glynne; Assistant to Producer: Christopher Carreras; Martial Art Sequences Staging: Liu Chia-Liang, Tang Chia; Floor Manager: Cheng Peng; Production Secretary: Jean Walter

CAST: Peter Cushing (Prof. Laurence Van Helsing), John Forbes-Robertson (Dracula), Chan Shen (Kah/Dracula), **Julie Ege** (Mrs. Vanessa Buren), David Chiang (Hsi Ching/His Tien-An), Robin Stewart (Leyland Van Helsing), **Shih Szu** (Mei Kwei), Robert Hanna (British Consul), James Ma (Hsi Ta), Liu Hiu Ling (Hsi Hong), Liu Chia Yung (Hsi Kwei), Wong Han Chan (Leung Hon), Chen Tien Loong (Hsi San), Hark-On Fung (Hsi Sung), David de Keyser (Voice of Dracula), Wai Lo (Lo Blo), Te Hsiang Teng (Doomed Rickshaw Driver); Pai-Chen Yang, Chuan Chen, Chi Cheng Ho, Hsia Hsu, Ha Huang, Pei Chi Huang, Chun Fai Lau, Hoi Sang Lee, Chiang Wang

LET ME IN, 2010; CREW: Executive Producers: Philip Elway, Frederick Malmberg, John Ptak, Nigel Sinclair; Co-Executive Producers/Exclusive Media Group & Hammer Films: Andy Mayson, Marc Schipper; Associate Producer for Exclusive Media Group & Hammer Films: Jillian Longnecker; Producers: Tobin Armbrust, Alex Brunner, Guy East, Donna Gigliotti, Carl Molinder, John Nordling, Simon Oakes; Co-Producer: Vicki Dee Rock; Production Executive: Robert Kessel; Director: Matt Reeves; Screenplay: Matt Reeves and John Ajvide Lindqvist, from his novel *Lat den ratte komma in*; Music: Michael Giacchino; Director of Photography: Greig Fraser; Film Editor: Stan Salfas; Casting: Avy Kaufman; Production Design: Ford Wheeler; Art Director: Guy Barnes; Set Decorator: Wendy Barnes; Costume Design: Melissa Bruning; Makeup Department: Janessa Bouldin, Andy Clement, Tarra D. Day, Jake Garber, Kelly Golden, Jennifer McDaniel, Bart Mixon, Jessica Nelson, JoAnn Stafford-Chaney, Sheila Trujillo, Georgia Allen, Cristina Patterson Ceret, Chad Washam; Production Management: Anne Johns, Bruce Markoe, Tiffany Tiesiera; Second Unit/Assistant Directors: Jai James, Sarah Lemon, Rip Murray, Chemen Ochoa, Bradley Parker, Katie Pruitt; Art Department: Brett Andrews, R.A. Arancio-Parrain, David D. Baumann, Vince Perardi, Mike Blatner, Patrick Boyles, Craig Butterman, Jason Critchfield, Brooke Fair, Doug Gray, Richard Hughes, Richard Hurff, Janice B. Jacobson, Ronald O. Jaynes, Lelan Keffer, George Kruft, Amahl Lovato, Jason Mack, Jose Mendoza, Matthew Miller, Lawrence Morales, Jesus A. Murillo, Jodi Nichols, Paul Ortega, Randy Ortega, Robert Ortega, P.A. Palladini, Rhonda Paynter, Christina Pizzala, Scott Plunket, Rosario Provenza, Chip Radaelli, Billy Ray, Jorge Reyes, Macario Rivera, Leonard Sanchez, Craig Sears, Josh Sheppard, Kris Strube, Angelo Tomarchio, Omar Villarreal, Keith Walters, Cisco Whitson-Brown, Steven Maies, Lucas Stein; Sound Department: Marco Alicea, Antony Bayman, David Brownlow, John Countryman, Jenna Dalla Riva, Luke D. Gielmuda, Will Files, Kim Focato, Andrew S. Gard, Howie Hammerman, Jack Herren, Bobby Johanson, Rick Kline, Goro Koyama, Andy Malcolm, Steve Morris, Douglas Murray, Chris Navarro, Kurt Peterson, Jack Rametta, Eduardo Santiago, Tony Sereno, Robert Shoup, Clint Smith, Daniel Sperry, Don White, Ed White, Noah Katz, Zach Martin; Special Effects: Brett Cole, Dan Flannigan, David Greene, Werner Hahnlein, Roland Hathaway, Daniel Holt, Mark Noel, Arnold Peterson, Mike Prawitz, Ryan Roundy, Yoichi Art Sakamoto, Arthur G. Schlosser, Richard Terry Tjelmeland, Terry Tjelmeland, Michael S. Walter; Visual Effects: Jeff

Allen, Eric Almeras, Elizabeth Asai, Bryan Baker, Jamie Baxter, Tim Bowman, Kyle Boylen, Shannan Burkley, Sal Castellanos, Pedro Castro, Korey J. Cauchon, Chad Collier, Sean Coonce, Robin D'Arcy, Oliver de Gante, Joseph DiValerio, Traci Duran, Theresa Ellis, Sean Andrew Faden, Christine Felman, Erin Ferguson, Jeremy Fernsler, Ken Finlayson, Brenda Finster, Mark Forker, Antonio Gallardo, Julio Galvan, Stephanie Gilgar, Daniel Solozabal, Gabby Gourrier, Jason Greenblum, Carlos Guillen, Matthew Hackett, Noel Hooper, Chris Hunt, Charlie Iturriaga, Nick Jushchyshyn, David Kashevaroff, Viviana Kim, James T. Kirk, Alberto Landeros, Peter Lang, Martin Lazaro, Tram Le, Seong Joon Lee, Juan Carlos Lepe, Miguel Lizarraga, Bob Lowery, Michael Maker, Haydn Masuda, Ed Mendez, Anton Moss, Masa Narita, Jorge Navarete, Damian O'Farrill, Hiroyuki Okubo, Bradley Parker, Edgar Patron, Edgar Pina, Raul Prado, Tom Quinn, Nordin Rahhali, Ruben Rodas, Sean Rowe, Juan-Luis Sanchez, Casey Schatz, Crystle Schrecengost, Christina Sidoti, Marion Spates, Christa Tazzeo, Cecile Tecson, Messrob Torikian, Arturo Tovar, Salvador Tovar, John-Michael Trojan, Mike Ugucionni, Nancy Wallis, Craig Whitaker, Andy Williams, Malik Williams, Thorsten Wolf, Fiedler Zoltan, Paco Castillo, Brian Delmonico, A. Djordjevic, Graham Dunglinson, Omar Garcia, Pam Gonzales, Kerry Graham, Jonah Hall, Thomas Kuo, Mark Laszlo, Julia MacMullen, Kristen Millette, Andy Mower, Eddie Offermann, Sean Penberthy, Wendy Pirotte, Ryan Reeb, Michael Rogers, Raechel Rowland, Marc Steinberg; Stunts: Emily Brobst, Bobby Burns, Al Goto, Steven Lambert, Angelique Midthunder, Dana Reed, John Robotham, Roger Stoneburner, Deborah Mazor, Ashton Moio, Rowbie Orsatti; Camera/Electrical Department: Saeed Adyani, Mark Anderson, Liza Bambenek, Jeff Bettis, Mike Biss, Ted Bott, Waylon Brady, Chip Byrd, Erick Castillo, Tom D'Amour, Will Emery, Harland Espeset, Ben Estrada, Ryan Eustis, Frank Eyers, Mike Fernandez, Tyler Fletcher, Adam Flores, Raphael Freud, Sean Gilbert, Ian Hanna, Andy Harris, Justin Hartery, Juergen Heinemann, John Hyeoma, Chris Joehnk, Derek Johnson, Jay Kemp, Kurt Kornemann, Frank Larson, C.C. Lee, Christopher Lee, Ben Lobato, Lynn Lockwood, Brian Malone, Dave Midthunder, Mark Miller, Louis Nelson, Lauren Petzke, Mr. Pink, John Stearns, Mark Steinig, Bela Trutz, Asa-Luke Two Crow, James Wilkerson, Peter Zuccarini, Phil Abeyta, Brad Barnes, Dwight Dollins, Chris Norris, J.A. Oliver; Casting: Jo Edna Boldin, Liz Gabel, Barbara Harris, Sabrina Hyman, Marie Kohl, Hanna Macpherson, Christina Ortega, Leeba Zakharov; Costume/Wardrobe: Bradford Booth, John Deering, Juliet Hyde-White, Roberta S. Langhofer, Nancy Molleur, Daniela Moore, Allyson Traub, Molly K. Whitson, Deborah Andrews; Editorial Department: Des Carey, Shane Harris, Mo Henry, David Kashevaroff, Rudy Lopez, Larry McGinley, Stefan Sonnenfeld, Arthur Tremeau, Lee Wimer, Jeff Smithwick; Music Department: Paul Apelgren, Joe Crnko, Andrea Datzman, George Drakoulias, Liz Gallacher, Kathleen Hasay, Simon James, Kory Kruckenberg, Jeff Kryka, Philip Moross, David Sabee, Joel Sill, Steve Smith, Nathan Stoltzfus, Chris Tilton, Brian Valentino; Transportation Department: Pedro Amaya, Linda D. Anderson, Dan Berryman, Kent Boyer, Benette Cantu, Bob Carter, Mike Chavez, Robert Chavez, Arthur Claunch, Christy Claunch, Cindy Claunch, Vincent Cordova, 'Fleet' Eakland, D. Estrada, Kenny Flores, Jason Fujita, Carl Goodwin, Ofisa Isaia, Sherman Jackson, Laura James, Jimmy Lopez, James Lujano, Jared Mangano, Mike McKenny, Colin Meador, Jared Meador, Mario Medina, Dan Miller, Mingo Nazara Jr., Arturo Padilla, Jade Peterson, Robert Rabelo, Patrick Reynolds Jr., Crystal Reynolds, Josh Reynolds, Tommy Rivera, Jesse Romero, Walter Russell, Paul Salard III, Jose Salazar, Bruce Simballa, Paul Walker, Richard Woods; Rest of Crew: Steve Aguino, Kazim Aminy, Phil Arnold, Kristen Blodget, Rob Corlew, Rafi Crohn, J.J. Dalton, Ben Eisenstein, Michael Feldman, Daniel Fisch, Sara Jo Fisher, Jay Floyd, Jackie Fuchs, Colin Garza, 'Roland' Gonzalez, Julie Harris, Krista Harris, Ben Holden, Allegro Hopkins, Rachel Horwitz, Jean Jacobson, Aliza James, Allison Jandreau-Heil, Pablo Kelly, Melanie Kirschbaum, Ron Levin, Clay Lilley, Barbara Long, Colette Longo, Jennifer Mancuso, Carmen Matthews, Elizabeth McMullan, Jacy Merson, Diane Minfa, Freddy Miramahti, Grant Mitchell, Elizabeth Muir, Arturo Padilla, Cora Palfrey, Carrie Parks, Hilton Clay Peres, Ryan Pzedirc, Lynn Raines, Trudy Ramirez, Luke Randall, Emily Rice, Lucy Kim Robertson, Jenessa Rose, Lauren Schoel, Ian Simon, Amanda Smith, Chloe Stagner, Kate Stephenson, Billy Stratton, Amanda Sutton, Jason Tamasco, Victoria Thompson, Suzanne Tierney, Laura Torrance, Richard Vertell, Douglas Weerts, Dana Wilkey, Brian Wilkinson, Emily Zambello, Monika Agorelius, Sebastien Betsch, Erik Chase, Sam Childs, Ashley Davis, Nathan Davis, Sean Furst, Pam Green, Joe Griffenberg, Jason Hariton, Cohl Klop, Ariel Lopez, Grant MacAllister, Walt Myal, Andrea Redder, G.Q. Sanchez, Matthew Taylor, Wyatt Turner, Jarik Van Sluijs, Daniel Villagomez; Special Thanks: Lance Hool, John Ajvide Lindqvist, Chris McGurk

CAST: Kodi Smit-McPhee (Owen), **Chloe Grace Moretz** (Abby), Richard Jenkins (The Father), **Cara Buono** (Owen's Mother), Elias Koteas (The Policeman), **Sasha Barrese** (Virginia), Dylan Kenin (Larry), Chris Browning (Jack), Richie Coster (Mr. Zoric), Dylan Minnette (Kenny), Jimmy Jax Pinchak (Mark), Nicolai Dorian (Donald), **Rebekah Wiggins** (Nurse), Seth Adkins (High School Kid), Ashton Moio (Lanky Kid), Brett DelBuono (Kenny's Brother), **Gwendolyn Apple** (Girl in Pool), Colin Moretz (Arcade Counterperson), Rowbie Orsatti (Scottie), Brenda Wehle (The Principal), Galen Hutchison, Dean Satriano (Football Players), **Rachel Hroncich** (Admitting Nurse), **Deborah Mazor** (Day Nurse), Frank Bond (The Conductor), **Kayla Anderson** (Newscaster); Tobin Espeset, Ben Bode, **Juliet Lopez**, Jon Kristian Moore (Paramedics); David T. Quan (Hospital Gawker), Ronald Reagan (Himself, Archive Footage)

THE LOST CONTINENT, 1968; CREW: Producer: Michael Carreras; Associate Producer: Peter Manley; Executive Producer: Anthony Hinds; Directors: Michael Carreras, Leslie Norman; Screenplay: "Michael Nash" (Michael Carreras), based on the novel *Uncharted Seas* by Dennis Wheatley; Music: Gerard Schurmann; Cinematography: Paul Beeson; Film Editor: Chris Barnes; Casting: Irene Lamb; Art Director: Arthur Lawson; Assistant Art Director: Don Picton; Costume Design: Carl Toms; Makeup: George Partleton; Hair Stylist: Elsie Alder; Assistant Director: Dominic Fulford; Model Maker: Arthur Fehr; Painter: Michael Finlay; Sound Editors: Roy Baker, Carl Mahakian; Sound Mixer: Denis Whitlock; Recording Supervisor: A.W. Lumkin; Special Effects: Robert Mattey, Cliff Richardson; Special Effects Assistant: Peter Hutchinson; Special Effects Consultant: Arthur Hayward; Camera Operator: Russell Thompson; Wardrobe: Mary Gibson; Supervising Editor: James Needs; Musical Supervisor: Philip Martell; Arranger/Source Music: Howard Blake; Continuity: Doreen Soan

CAST: Eric Porter (The Captain), **Suzanna Leigh** (Unity Webster), **Hildegard Knef** (Eva Peters), Tony Beckley (Harry), Nigel Stock (Dr. Webster), Michael Ripper (Sea Lawyer), Neil McCallum (Hemmings), Benito Carruthers (Ricaldi), Jimmy Hanley (Bartender), James Cossins (Chief Engineer), **Dana Gillespie** (Sarah), Victor Maddern (Mate), Reg Lye (Helmsman), Norman Eshley (The Prisoner), Frank Hayden (Sergeant); Mark Heath, Horace James, Michael Heath (Customs Agents), Charles Houston, Alf Joint (Crewmen), Eddie Powell (The Grand Inquisitor), Darryl Read (El Diablo), Shivendra Sinha (Hurri Curri), Donald Sumpter (Sparks), **Sylvana Henriques** (Boat Traveler), **Cynthia Myers** (Native Girl)

LUST FOR A VAMPIRE, 1971; CREW: Producers: Harry Fine, Michael Style; Director: Jimmy Sangster; Screenplay: Tudor Gates; Characters: J. Sheridan Le Fanu ("Carmilla"); Music: Harry Robinson (Robertson); Song: "Strange Love," Performer: Tracy, Lyrics: Frank Godwin; Director of Photography: David Muir; Film Editor: Spencer Reeve; Art Director: Don Mingaye; Makeup Supervisor: George Blackler; Production Manager: Tom Sachs; Assistant Director: David Bracknell; Third Assistant Director: Terry Pearce; Construction Manager: Bill Greene; Props: Wally Hockings; Sound Recordist: Ron Barron; Sound Editor: Terry Poulton; Recording Director: A.W. Lumkin; Dubbing Mixer: Len Abbott; Dubbing Mixer: Len Shilton; Camera Operator: R. Chic Anstiss; Boom Operator: John Hall; Wardrobe Mistress: Laura Nightingale; Music Supervisor: Philip Martell; Continuity: Betty Harley; Hairdressing Supervisor: Pearl Tipaldi; Choreographer: Babbie McManus; Unit Publicist: Geoff Freeman

CAST: **Yutte Stensgaard** (Carmilla/Mircalla Karnstein), Ralph Bates (Giles Barton), **Barbara Jefford** (Countess Herritzen), **Suzanna Leigh** (Janet Playfair), Michael Johnson (Richard Lestrange), **Helen Christie** (Miss Simpson), **Pippa Steel** (Susan Pelley), David Healy (Raymond Pelley), Harvey Hall (Insp. Heinrich), Mike Raven (Count Karnstein), Michael Brennan (Landlord), Jack Melford (Bishop), Christopher Cunningham (Coachman), **Judy Matheson** (Amanda), Christopher Neame (Hans), Eric Chitty (Prof. Herz), Caryl Little (Isabel), Jonathan Cecil (Biggs), **Kirsten (Betts) Lindholm** (Peasant Girl), **Luan Peters** (Trudi), Nick Brimble, David Richardson (Villagers), **Vivienne Chandler, Erica Beale, Melinda Churcher, Melita Clarke, Jackie Leapman, Sue Longhurst, Patricia Warner, Christine Smith** (Schoolgirls); Valentine Dyall (Voice of Count Karnstein)

The Man Who Could Cheat Death, 1959; Crew: Executive Producer: Michael Carreras; Associate Producer: Anthony Nelson-Keys; Director: Terence Fisher; Screenplay: Jimmy Sangster, based on the play "The Man in the Half Moon Street" by Barre Lyndon; Music: Richard Bennett; Cinematography: Jack Asher; Film Editor: John Dunsford; Production Design: Bernard Robinson; Wardrobe Supervisor: Molly Arbuthnot; Makeup: Roy Ashton; Hair Stylist: Henry Montsash; Production Manager: Don Weeks; Assistant Director: John Peverall; Sound Recordist: Jock May; Special Effects: Sydney Pearson; Camera Operator: Len Harris; Musical Director: John Hollingsworth; Supervising Editor: James Needs; Continuity: Shirley Barnes

Cast: Anton Diffring (Dr. Bonner), Christopher Lee (Dr. Gerrard), **Hazel Court** (Janine Du Bois), Arnold Marle (Dr. Weiss), **Delphi Lawrence** (Margo Philippe), Francis De Wolff (Inspector), Michael Ripper (Morgue Attendant), Ronald Adam, Barry Shawzin, Lockwood West (Doctors), **Marie Burke** (Woman at Private View), Charles Lloyd Pack (Man at Private View), John Harrison (Servant), Ian Hewetson (Roget), **Gerda Larsen** (Street Girl), Frederick Rawlings (Footman), Middleton Woods (Little Geezer), Denis Shaw (Tavern Customer)

Maniac, 1963; Crew: Producer/Screenplay: Jimmy Sangster; Director: Michael Carreras; Music/Conductor: Stanley Black; Cinematography: Wilkie Cooper; Film Editor: Tom Simpson; Production Design: Bernard Robinson; Art Director: Edward Carrick; Wardrobe Supervisor: Molly Arbuthnot; Wardrobe Mistress: Jean Fairlie; Makeup: Basil Newall; Assistant Makeup: Stella Morris; Hair Stylist: Patricia McDermott; Production Manager: Bill Hill; Assistant Director: Ross Mackenzie; Second Assistant Director: Terry Lens; Carpenter: Tommy Westbrook; Props Buyer: Marjory Whittington; Assistant Art Director: Jean Peyre; Sound Recordist: Cyril Swern; Sound Editor: Roy Baker; Boom Operator: Jim Perry; Sound Camera Operator: Alan Thorne: Sound Maintenance: Peter Martingell; Sound Camera Operator: Claude Hitchcock; Special Effects: Bill Warrington; Stunts: Eddie Powell; Camera Operator: Harry Gilliam; Still Photographer: James Swarbrick; Camera Focus: Tommy Fletcher, Trevor Wrenn; Clapper Loader: Ray Andrew; Supervising Editor: James Needs; Continuity: Kay Rawlings; Production Secretary: Marguerite Green; Assistant to Producer: Ian Lewis

Cast: Kerwin Matthews (Paul Farrell), Donald Houston (Georges), **Nadia Gray** (Eve Beynat), **Liliane Brousse** (Annette), George Pastell (Inspector Etienne), Arnold Diamond (Janiello), Norman Bird (Salon), **Justine Lord** (Grace), Jerold Wells (Giles), Leon Peers (Blanchard), Andre Maranne (Voice of Salon)

Moon Zero Two, 1969; Crew: Producer: Michael Carreras; Director: Roy Ward Baker; Screenplay: Michael Carreras, adapted from an original story by Gavin Lyall, Frank Hardman, and Martin Davison; Music: Don Ellis; Cinematography: Paul Beeson; Film Editor: Spencer Reeve; Casting: Sue Whatmough; Art Director: Scott MacGregor; Assistant Art Director: John Lague; Costume Design: Carl Toms; Makeup: Ernest Taylor; Hair Stylist: Ivy Emmerton; Wigs: Leonard; Production Manager: Hugh Harlow; Assistant Director: Jack Martin; Construction Manager: Arthur Banks; Sound Editor: Roy Hyde; Recording Director: A.W. Lumkin; Sound Mixer: Claude Hitchcock; Dubbing Mixer: Len Abbott; Special Effects: Les Bowie; Special Effects Assistants: Colin Chilvers, Peter Dawson, Brian Johnson, Terry Schubert, Mike Tilly, Wally Veevers; Special Effects Photographers: Nick Allder, Kit West; Stunt Advisor: Bill Weston; Camera Operator: John Winbolt; Wardrobe: Larry Stewart; Music Supervisor: Philip Martell; Title Song: Julie Driscoll; Continuity: Josie Fulford; Choreographer: Jo Cook; Titles: Stokes Cartoons

Cast: James Olson (Capt. Bill Kemp), **Catherine Schell** (Clementine Taplin), Warren Mitchell (J.J. Hubbard), **Adrienne Corri** (Elizabeth Murphy), Michael Ripper (First Card Player), Ori Levy (Kaminski), Dudley Foster (Whitsun), Neil McCallum (Captain), Joby Blanshard (Smith), Robert Tayman (Second Card Player), Sam Kydd (Len), Keith Bonnard, Leo Britt (Customs Officers), **Carol Cleveland** (Hostess), Roy Evans (Workman), Tom Kempinski (Second Officer), Lew Luton (Immigration Officer), **Claire Shenstone** (Hotel Clerk), **Chrissie Shrimpton** (Boutique Attendant), **Amber Dean Smith**, **Simone Silvera** (Hubbard's Girlfriends), Athol Coats (Mercer), Tim Condren (Yellow Killer), Martin Grace (Red Killer), Bill Weston (Green Killer), Freddie Earlle (Little Chap), Robert Lee (Hotel Employee); **Michelle Barry**, **Sue Baumann**, **Jane Cunningham**, **Irene Gorst**, **Sally Graham**, **Brenda Krippen** (Bar Dancers), The GoJos

THE MUMMY, 1959; CREW: Executive Producer: Michael Carreras; Associate Producer: Anthony Nelson-Keys; Director: Terence Fisher; Screenplay: Jimmy Sangster; Music: Franz Reizenstein; Cinematography: Jack Asher; Film Editors: Alfred Cox, James Needs; Assistant Editor: Chris Barnes; Production Design: Bernard Robinson; Wardrobe Supervisor: Molly Arbuthnot; Wardrobe Assistant: Rosemary Burrows; Casting: Dorothy Holloway; Makeup: Roy Ashton; Hair Stylist: Henry Montsash; Production Manager: Don Weeks; Assistant Director: John Peverall; Second Assistant Director: Tom Walls; Third Assistant Director: Hugh Harlow; Master Plasterer: Arthur Banks; Master Carpenter: Charles Davis; Props Buyer: Eric Hillier; Construction Manager: Mick Lyons; Assistant Art Director: Don Mingaye; Property Master: Tom Money; Master Painter: Lawrence Wren; Sound Recordist: Jock May; Sound Editor: Ron Hyde; Boom Operator: Jim Perry; Sound Camera Operator: Alan Thorne: Sound Maintenance: Charles Bouvet; Sound Department: Claude Hitchcock; Special Effects: Bill Warrington; Stunts: Eddie Powell; Camera Operator: Len Harris; Chief Electrician: Jack Curtis; Still Photographer: Tom Edwards; Focus Puller: Harry Oakes; Clapper Loader: Alan McDonald; Musical Supervisor/Conductor/Orchestrator: John Hollingsworth; Studio Manager: Arthur Kelly; Continuity: Marjorie Lavelly; Cashier: Ken Gordon; Egyptian Mask Maker: Margaret Robinson; Egyptologist: Andrew Low; Publicist: Colin Reid

CAST: Peter Cushing (John Banning), Christopher Lee (Kharis), **Yvonne Furneaux** (Isobel Banning/Princess Ananka), Eddie Byrne (Inspector Mulrooney), Felix Aylmer (Stephen Banning), Raymond Huntley (Whemple), George Pastell (Mehemet Bey), Michael Ripper (Poacher), George Woodbridge (Constable), Harold Goodwin (Pat), Denis Shaw (Mike), Gerald Lawson (Irish Customer), Willoughby Gray (Dr. Reilly), John Stuart (Coroner), David Browning (Police Sergeant), Frank Sieman (Bill), Stanley Meadows (James), Frank Singuineau (Head Porter), James Clarke, John Harrison (Priests), Frederick Rawlings

THE MUMMY'S SHROUD, 1967; CREW: Producer: Anthony Nelson-Keys; Director/Screenplay: John Gilling; Story: "John Elder" (Anthony Hinds); Music: Don Banks; Cinematography: Arthur Grant; Film Editor: Chris Barnes; Casting: Irene Lamb; Production Design: Bernard Robinson; Art Director: Don Mingaye; Wardrobe Mistress: Molly Arbuthnot; Wardrobe Master: Larry Stewart; Makeup: George Partleton; Hair Stylist: Frieda Steiger; Production Manager: Ed Harper; Assistant Director: Bluey Hill; Sound Recordist: Ken Rawkins; Sound editor: Roy Hyde; Special Effects: Les Bowie; Special Effects Assistant: Ian Scoones; Camera Operator: Moray Grant; Focus Puller: Bob Jordan; Music Supervisor: Philip Martell; Supervising Editor: James Needs; Continuity: Eileen Head

CAST: Andre Morell (Sir Basil Walden), John Phillips (Stanley), **Maggie Kimberly** (Claire De Sangre), David Buck (Paul), **Elizabeth Sellars** (Barbara), Michael Ripper (Longbarrow), **Catherine Lacey** (Haiti), Roger Delgado (Hasmid), Eddie Powell (The Mummy), Dickie Owen (Prem), Tim Barrett (Harry), Richard Warner (Inspector), Bruno Barnabe (Pharaoh), **Toni Gilpin** (Pharaoh's Wife), Toolsie Persaud (Kah-To-Bey), Andreas Malandrinos (Curator), John Garrie (Cleaner), Darroll Richards (Sage); Pat Gorman, Michael Rothwell, Terence Sewards, Roy Stephens, George Zenios (Reporters)

THE NANNY, 1965; CREW: Producer: Jimmy Sangster; Director: Seth Holt; Screenplay: Jimmy Sangster, based on the novel by Evelyn Piper; Music: Richard Rodney Bennett; Cinematography: Harry Waxman; Film Editor: Tom Simpson; Production Design: Edward Carrick; Wardrobe Consultant: Molly Arbuthnot; Wardrobe Mistress: Mary Gibson; Makeup: Tom Smith; Hair Stylist: A.G. Scott; Production Manager: George Fowler; Assistant Directors: Christopher Dryhurst, Ariel Levy; Painter: Michael Finlay; Sound Recordist: Norman Coggs; Sound Editor: Charles Crafford; Sound Recording Supervisor: A.W. Lumkin; Camera Operator: Kelvin Pike; Supervising Editor: James Needs; Musical Supervisor: Philip Martell; Continuity: Renee Glynne

CAST: **Bette Davis** (The Nanny), **Wendy Craig** (Virginia Fane), **Jill Bennett** (Aunt Pen), James Villiers (Bill), William Dix (Joey), **Pamela Franklin** (Bobbie), Jack Watling (Dr. Medman), Maurice Denham (Dr. Beamaster), Alfred Burke (Dr. Wills), Harry Fowler (Milkman), **Angharad Aubrey** (Suzy), **Nora Gordon** (Mrs. Griggs), **Sandra Power** (Sarah), Gary Graham (Boy)

NIGHTMARE, 1963; CREW: Producer/Screenplay: Jimmy Sangster; Director: Freddie Francis; Music: Don Banks; Cinematography: John Wilcox; Production Design: Bernard Robinson; Art

Director: Don Mingaye; Wardrobe Mistress: Rosemary Burrows; Makeup: Roy Ashton; Hair Stylist: Frieda Steiger; Production Manager: Don Weeks; Assistant Director: Douglas Hermes; Sound Recordist: Ken Rawkins; Sound Editor: James Groom; Camera Operator: Ronnie Maasz; Special Effects: Les Bowie; Musical Supervisor: John Hollingsworth; Supervising Editor: James Needs; Continuity: Pauline Wise

CAST: David Knight (Henry Baxter), **Moira Redmond** (Grace Maddox), **Jennie Linden** (Janet), Brenda Bruce (Mary), George A. Cooper (John), **Clytie Jessop** (Woman in White), **Irene Richmond** (Mrs. Gibbs), John Welsh (Doctor), Timothy Bateson (Barman), **Elizabeth Dear** (Janet as Child), **Isla Cameron** (Mother), **Julie Samuel** (Maid), Hedger Wallace (Sir Dudley)

THE OLD DARK HOUSE, 1963; CREW: Associate Producer: Dona Holloway; Producers: William Castle, Anthony Hinds; Director: William Castle; Screenplay: Robert Dillon, based on the novel by J.B. Priestley; Music/Conductor: Benjamin Frankel; Cinematography: Arthur Grant; Film Editor: James Needs; Production Design: Bernard Robinson; Wardrobe Supervisor: Molly Arbuthnot; Wardrobe Mistress: Rosemary Burrows; Makeup: Roy Ashton; Hair Stylist: Frieda Steiger; Production Manager: John Draper; Assistant Director: Douglas Hermes; Sound Recordist: Jock May; Sound Editor: James Groom; Special Effects: Les Bowie; Camera Operator: Moray Grant; Supervising Editor: James Needs; Continuity: Pauline Wise; Drawings/Title Backgrounds: Charles Addams

CAST: Tom Poston (Tom), Robert Morley (Roderick Femm), **Janette Scott** (Cecily Femm), **Joyce Grenfell** (Agatha Femm), Mervyn Johns (Potiphar Femm), **Fenella Fielding** (Morgana Femm), Peter Bull (Casper/Jasper Femm), Danny Green (Morgan Femm), John Harvey (Club Receptionist), **Amy Dalby** (Gambler), Charles Addams (Hand in Title Sequence)

ONE MILLION YEARS B.C., 1966; CREW: Producer: Michael Carreras; Associate Producers: Aida Young, Hal Roach; Director: Don Chaffey; Screenplay: Michael Carreras, adapted from an original screenplay by Michael Novack, George Baker and Joseph Frickert; Music & Composer/Special Music Effects: Mario Nascimbene; Cinematography: Wilkie Cooper; Film Editor: Tom Simpson; Assistant Editor: Robert C. Dearberg; Art Director: Robert Jones; Assistant Art Director: Kenneth McCallum Tait; Costume Design: Carl Toms; Makeup Supervisor: Wally Schneiderman; Hairdressing Supervisor: Olga Angelinetta; Production Manager: John Wilcox; Assistant Director: Denis Bertera; Second Assistant Director: Colin Lord; Scenic Artist: Bill Beavis; Draughtsman: Colin Monk; Sound Editors: Roy Baker, Alfred Cox; Recording Director: A.W. Lumkin; Sound Mixers: Bill Rowe, Len Shilton; Matte Painter: Bob Cuff; Special Visual Effects Creator: Ray Harryhausen; Special Effects: George Blackwell; Cameraman/Second Unit: Jack Mills; Gaffer: Steve Birtles; Still Photographers: Pierre Luigi, Ronnie Pilgrim; Camera Operator: David Harcourt; Clapper Loader: Ken Nicholson; Key Grip: Martin O'Connor; Wardrobe Mistress: Ivy Baker; Music Supervisor: Philip Martell; Prologue Designer: Les Bowie; Continuity: Gladys Goldsmith, Marjorie Lavelly; Production Accountant: John Trehy

CAST: **Raquel Welch** (Loana), John Richardson (Tumak), Percy Herbert (Sakana), Robert Brown (Akhoba), **Martine Beswicke** (Nupondi), Jean Wladon (Ahot), **Lisa Thomas** (Sura), **Malya Nappi** (Tohana), Richard James (Teenage Caveman), William Lyon Brown (Payto), Frank Hayden (Rock Man), Terence Maidment (Shell Man), **Micky De Rauch** (Shell Girl), **Yvonne Horner** (Ullah), James Payne (Caveman), Vic Perrin (Narrator), **Nikki Van der Zyl** (Voice of Loana)

PARANOIAC, 1963; CREW: Associate Producer: Basil Keys; Producer: Anthony Hinds; Director: Freddie Francis; Screenplay: Jimmy Sangster, based on the novel *Brat Farrar* by Josephine Tey; Music: Elizabeth Lutyens; Cinematography: Arthur Grant; Production Design: Bernard Robinson; Art Director: Don Mingaye; Assistant Art Director: Kenneth Ryan; Wardrobe: Molly Arbuthnot; Wardrobe Mistress: Rosemary Burrows; Makeup: Roy Ashton; Assistant Makeup: Richard Mills; Hair Stylist: Frieda Steiger; Production Manager: John Draper; Assistant Director: Ross Mackenzie; Second Assistant Director: Hugh Harlow; Third Assistant Director: Ray Corbett; Construction Manager: Arthur Banks; Property Master: Tom Money; Sound Recordist: Ken Rawkins; Boom Operator: Ken Nightingall; Sound Editor: James Groom; Sound Camera Operator: Alan Thorne; Special Effects: Les Bowie, Kit West; Camera Operator: Moray Grant; Camera Grip: Albert Cowlard; Focus Pullers: Robin Higginson, David Osborne; Music Supervisor: John Hollingsworth; Editorial Supervisor/Supervising Editor: James Needs; Continuity: Pauline Wise; Production Secretary: Maureen White

CAST: Oliver Reed (Simon Ashby), **Janette Scott** (Eleanor Ashby), **Sheila Burrell** (Aunt Harriet), Maurice Denham (John), Alexander Davion (Tony), **Liliane Brousse** (Francois), Harold Lang (RAF Type), John Bonney (Keith), John Stuart (Williams), Sydney Bromley (Bum), **Laurie Leigh**, **Marianne Stone** (Women), Colin Tapley (Vicar), Jack Taylor (Sailor), Arnold Diamond

THE PHANTOM OF THE OPERA, 1962; CREW: Producer: Anthony Hinds; Associate Producer: Basil Keys; Director: Terence Fisher; Screenplay: "John Elder" (Anthony Hinds), based on the novel by Gaston Leroux; Music/Conductor: Edwin Astley; Cinematography: Arthur Grant; Film Editor: Alfred Cox; Production Designer: Bernard Robinson; Art Director: Don Mingaye; Wardrobe Design: Molly Arbuthnot; Wardrobe Mistress: Rosemary Burrows; Makeup: Roy Ashton; Hair Stylist: Frieda Steiger; Production Manager: Clifford Parkes; Assistant Director: John Peverall; Second Assistant Director: Peter Medak; Sound: Jock May; Sound Editor: Jim Groom; Stunts: Jack Cooper; Still Photographer: Tom Edwards; Camera Operator: Len Harris; Editorial Supervisor: James Needs; Singing Voice/Heather Sears: Patricia Clark; Continuity: Tilly Day; Staging/Opera sequences: Dennis Maunder

CAST: Herbert Lom (The Phantom), **Heather Sears** (Christine Charles), Edward de Souza (Harry), Thorley Walters (Latimer), Michael Gough (Lord d'Arcy), Harold Goodwin (Bill), Martin Miller (Rossi), **Liane Aukin** (Maria), **Sonya Cordeau** (Yvonne), Marne Maitland (Prof. Xavier), **Miriam Karlin** (Charwoman), Patrick Troughton (Rat Catcher), **Renee Houston** (Mrs. Tucker), Keith Pyott (Weaver), John Harvey (Sgt. Vickers), Michael Ripper, Miles Malleson (Cabbies), Ian Wilson (Dwarf), **Leila Forde** (Teresa), Geoffrey L'Oise (Frenchman), John Maddison (Inspector Dawson), Laurie Main (Forbes), **Jane Merrow** (Chorus Girl), Liam Redmond (Inspector Ward)

PHANTOM SHIP, 1935; CREW: Producer/Supervisor: Henry Passmore; Director: Denison Clift; Story: Denison Clift; Scenario: Charles Larkworthy; Cinematography: Eric Cross, Geoffrey Faithfull; Film Editor: John Seabourne Sr.; Art Director: J. Elder Wills; Musical Director: Eric Ansell; Continuity: Tilly Day

CAST: Bela Lugosi (Anton Lorenzen/Gottlieb), Arthur Margetson (Capt. Briggs), **Shirley Grey** (Sarah Briggs), Edmund Willard (Toby), Dennis Hoey (Tom Goodschild), George Mozart (Tommy Duggan), Johnnie Schofield (Peter Tooley), Gunnar Moir (Ponta Katz), Ben Welden ("Sailor" Hoffman), Clifford McLaglen (Capt. Morehead), Bruce Gordon (Ollie), Gibson Gowland (Andy), Terence de Marney (Charlie), Edgar Pierce (Arian), Herbert Cameron (Grot), Wilfred Essex (Horatio), James Carew (James), Alec Fraser (Cmdr. Mahon), Charles Mortimer (Attorney General), Graham Soutten (Jack), J. B. Williams (Judge)

THE PLAGUE OF THE ZOMBIES, 1966; CREW: Producer: Anthony Nelson-Keys; Director: John Gilling; Screenplay: Peter Bryan; Music: James Bernard; Cinematography: Arthur Grant; Film Editor: Chris Barnes; Art Director: Don Mingaye; Production Design: Bernard Robinson; Wardrober: Rosemary Burrows; Makeup: Roy Ashton; Hair Stylist: Frieda Steiger; Assistant Makeup: Richard Mills; Production Manager: George Fowler; Assistant Director: Bert Batt; Second Assistant Director: Hugh Harlow; Sound Recordist: Ken Rawkins; Sound Editor: Roy Baker; Special Effects: Les Bowie; Stunts: Peter Diamond; Camera Operator: Moray Grant; Focus Puller: Bob Jordan; Editorial Supervisor: James Needs; Musical Supervisor: Philip Martell; Continuity: Lorna Selwyn

CAST: Andre Morell (Dr. James Forbes), **Diane Clare** (Sylvia Forbes), Brook Williams (Dr. Tompson), **Jacqueline Pearce** (Alice Mary Tompson), John Carson (Squire Hamilton), Michael Ripper (Sgt. Jack Swift), Alex Davion (Denver), Marcus Hammond (Tom), Dennis Chinnery (Constable), Louis Mahoney (Servant), Roy Royston (Vicar), Ben Aris (John); Tim Condron, Bernard Egan, Norman Mann, Francis Willey (Young Bloods); Jerry Verno (Landlord), Jolyan Booth (Coach Driver); Peter Diamond, Reg Harding, Keith Peacock, Del Watson (Zombies)

QUATERMASS AND THE PIT (a.k.a. *Five Million Years to Earth*), 1967; CREW: Producer: Anthony Nelson-Keys; Director: Roy Ward Baker; Story/Screenplay: Nigel Kneale; Music: Tristram Cary; Cinematography: Arthur Grant; Film Editor: Spencer Reeve; Supervising Art Director: Bernard

Robinson; Art Director: Ken Ryan; Wardrobe Mistress: Rosemary Burrows; Makeup: Michael Morris; Hair Stylist: Pearl Tipaldi; Production Manager: Ian Lewis; Assistant Director: Bert Batt; Second Assistant Director: Christopher Neame; Third Assistant Director: Bill Westley; Construction Manager: Arthur Banks; Sound Recordist: Sash Fisher; Sound editor: Roy Hyde; Special Effects: Les Bowie; Special Effects Assistants: Ian Scoones, Kit West, Roy Field, Bill Warrington; Camera Operator: Moray Grant; Focus Puller: Bob Jordan; Lighting Technician: Steve Birtles; Casting: Irene Lamb; Music Supervisor: Philip Martell; Composer/Stock Music: Frederic Curzon; Supervising Editor: James Needs; Continuity: Doreen Dearnaley

CAST: Andrew Keir (Prof. Bernard Quatermass), **Barbara Shelley** (Barbara Judd), James Donald (Dr. Roney), Julian Glover (Col. Breen), Duncan Lamont (Sladden), Bryan Marshall (Capt. Potter), Peter Copley (Mr. Howell), Edwin Richfield (Minister), Grant Taylor (Police Sgt. Ellis), Maurice Good (Sgt. Cleghorn), Robert Morris (Jerry); **Sheila Steafel**, Hugh Morton, William Ellis, Leslie Southwick, Brian Walton (Journalists), Hugh Futcher (Sapper West), Thomas Heathcote (Vicar), Noel Howlett (Abbey Librarian), Hugh Manning, Joseph Grieg (Pub Customers), **June Ellis** (Blonde), Keith Marsh (Johnson), James Culliford (Corporal Gibson), **Bee Duffell** (Miss Dobson), Roger Avon, Peter (Bette) Bourne (Electricians), Brian Peck (Technical Officer), John Graham (Inspector), Charles Lamb (Newsvendor), Peter Bennett, John Rutland (London Transport Officials), John Bown (TV Interviewer), Simon Brent (Orderly Officer), David Crane (Institute Attendant), Mark Elwes (Technician), Harry Fielder (Possessed Man), Walter Horsbrugh (Messenger), Alastair Hunter (Institute Doorkeeper), Elroy Josephs (Black Workman), James Payne (The Running Man), Michael Poole, Gareth Thomas (White Workmen), David Savile (Army Officer), Albert Shepherd (Loader), Ian White (TV Announcer)

QUATERMASS 2 (a.k.a. *Enemy from Space*), 1957; CREW: Executive Producer: Michael Carreras; Producer: Anthony Hinds; Director: Val Guest; Story: Nigel Neale; Screenplay: Nigel Kneale, Val Guest; Music: James Bernard; Cinematography: Gerald Gibbs; Film Editor: James Needs; Assistant Editors: Alfred Cox, Michael Hart; Production Designer: Bernard Robinson; Makeup: Phil Leakey; Production Manager: John Workman; Production Supervisor: Anthony Nelson-Keys; Assistant Director: Don Weeks; Second Assistant Director: Stanley Goulder; Third Assistant Director: Hugh Harlow; Property Master: Tom Money; Construction Manager: Fred Ricketts; Draughtsmen: Don Mingaye, David Butcher; Master Plasterer: Arthur Banks; Sound: Cliff Sandell; Sound Editor: Alfred Cox; Boom Operator: Claude Hitchcock; Special Effects: Frank George, Henry Harris, Bill Warrington; Special Effects Assistant: Brian Johnson; Still Photographer: John Jay; Camera Operator: Len Harris; Chief Electrician: Jack Curtis; Focus Puller: Harry Oakes; Electrician: Steve Birtles; Clapper Loader: Alan Gatward; Wardrobe: Rene Coke; Conductor: John Hollingsworth; Continuity: June Randall; Publicist: Bill Batchelor

CAST: Brian Donlevy (Quatermass), John Longdon (Lomax), Sid James (Jimmy), Bryan Forbes (Marsh), **Vera Day** (Sheila), William Franklyn (Brand), Charles Lloyd Pack (Dawson), Tom Chatto (Vincent), John Van Eyssen (P.R.O.), Percy Herbert (Paddy), Michael Ripper (Ernie), John Rae (Mac), **Marianne Stone** (Secretary), Ronald Wilson (Young Bloke), **Jane Aird** (Mrs. McLeod), **Betty Impey** (Kelly), Lloyd Lamble (Inspector), John Stuart (Commissioner), Gilbert Davis (Banker), **Joyce Adams** (Female MP), Edwin Richfield (Peterson), Howard Williams (Michaels), Phillip Baird, Robert Raikes (Lab Assistants), John Fabian (Intern), George Merritt (Super), Arthur Blake (Constable), Michael Balfour (Harry), Leslie Crawford (Guard), Vernon Greeves (First Man), **Jan Holden** (Young Girl), Alistair Hunter (Labour MP), Barry Lowe (Chris), Henry Rayner (Drunkard), **Joan Schofield** (Woman Shopper)

THE QUATERMASS XPERIMENT (a.k.a. *The Creeping Unknown*) 1955; CREW: Producers: Anthony Hinds, Robert Lippert; Director: Val Guest; Screenplay: Richard Landau, Val Guest, based on the television play by Nigel Kneale; Music: James Bernard; Director of Photography: Walter Harvey; Film Editor: James Needs; Assistant Editor: Henry Richardson; Art Director: J. Elder Wills; Makeup: Phil Leakey; Hair Stylist: Monica Hustler; Production Manager: T.S. Lyndon-Haynes; Assistant Director: Bill Shore; Second Assistant Director: Aida Young; Props: Tom Money; Construction Manager: Fred Ricketts; Props Buyer: Jim Day; Master Plasterer: Arthur Banks; Recordist:

H.C. Pearson; Sound Recordist: J. Woodiwiss; Sound Camera Operator: Don Alton; Boom Operator: Percy Britten; Dubbing Sound: Ken Cameron; Special Effects: Les Bowie; Special Effects Assistants: Ray Caple, Roy Field, Vic Margutti; Camera Operator: Len Harris; Visual Effects Assistant Camera: Roy Field; Stunts: Nosher Powell; Chief Electrician: Jack Curtis; Clapper Boy: Tom Friswell; Still Photographer: John Jay; Focus Puller: Harry Oakes; Electricians: Steve Birtles, George Robinson, Charles Stanbridge; Wardrobe: Molly Arbuthnot; Conductor: John Hollingsworth; Unit Driver: Len Ingram; Continuity: Renee Glynne; Accountant: Larry Edmonds; Cashier: Ken Gordon; Receptionist: Pauline Harlow; Production Secretary: Dora Thomas

CAST: Brian Donlevy (Quatermass), Jack Warner (Lomax), Richard Wordsworth (Victor Caroon), **Margia Dean** (Judith Caroon), **Thora Hird** (Rosemary Wrigley), Gordon Jackson (BBC TV Producer), David King-Wood (Briscoe), Harold Lang (Christie), Lionel Jeffries (Blake), Sam Kydd (Police Sergeant), **Jane Aird** (Mrs. Lomax), **Margaret Anderson** (Maggie), **Jane Asher** (Little Girl), Harry Brunning (Night Porter), Eric Corrie (Boyfriend), Edward Dane (Cop), Gron Davies (Green), Basil Dignam (Sir Lionel), James Drake (Sound Engineer), **Mollie Glessing** (Zoo Mother), Michael Godfrey (Fireman), Donald Gray (Announcer), Ernest Hare (Fire Chief), **Betty Impey**, **Marianne Stone** (Central Clinic Nurses), Fred Johnson (Inspector), Maurice Kaufman (Marsh), John Kerr (Technician), Henry B. Longhurst (George), Arthur Lovegrove (Sgt. Bromley), Barry Lowe (Tucker), Mayne Lynton (Zoo Super), Bartlett Mullins (Zookeeper), Frank Phillips (Announcer), George Roderick (Bull), John Stirling (Major), Toke Townley ("Chemist"), Stanley Van Beers (Dr. Reichenheim), John Wynn (Sgt. Pete Best).

RASPUTIN, THE MAD MONK, 1966; CREW: Producer: Anthony Nelson-Keys; Director: Don Sharp; Idea/Story: Anthony Hinds; Screenplay: "John Elder" (Anthony Hinds); Music/Musical Director: Don Banks; Cinematography: Michael Reed; Film Editor: Roy Hyde; Art Director: Don Mingaye; Production Design: Bernard Robinson; Costume Design: Rosemary Burrows; Makeup: Roy Ashton; Hair Stylist: Frieda Steiger; Production Manager: Ross Mackenzie; Assistant Director: Bert Batt; Second Assistant Director: Hugh Harlow; Sound Recordist: Ken Rawkins; Sound Editor: Roy Baker; Stunts/Fight Arranger: Peter Diamond; Camera Operator: C. Cooney; Editorial Supervisor: James Needs; Music Supervisor: Philip Martell; Continuity: Lorna Selwyn

CAST: Christopher Lee (Rasputin), Richard Pasco (Dr. Zargo), Francis Matthews (Ivan), **Barbara Shelley** (Sonia), **Suzan Farmer** (Vanessa), Dinsdale Landen (Peter), **Renee Asherson** (Tsarina), Derek Francis (Innkeeper), Joss Ackland (The Bishop), Robert Duncan (Tsarvitch), Alan Tilvern (Patron), John Welsh (The Abbott), John Bailey (The Physician), Michael Ripper (Comrade Mikhail), **Mary Barclay** (Superior Lady), Michael Cadman (Michael), **Helen Christie**, **Maggie Wright** (Tarts), **Lucy Fleming** (Wide Eyes), Michael Godfrey (Doctor), **Fiona Hartford** (Tania), **Prudence Hyman** (Chatty Woman), Bryan Marshall (Vasily), Bridget McConnell (Gossip), Jay McGrath, Robert McLennan (Dancers), Bartlett Mullins (Porter, the Waggoner), **Veronica Nicholson** (Young Girl), Robert Rowland (Bin Man/Drunk), **Celia Ryder** (Fat Lady), Cyril Shaps (Foxy Face), Leslie White (Cheeky Bastard), Brian Wilde (Father), Jeremy Young (Court Messenger)

THE REPTILE, 1966; CREW: Producer: Anthony Nelson-Keys; Director: John Gilling; Screenplay: "John Elder" (Anthony Hinds); Music: Don Banks; Cinematography: Arthur Grant; Film Editor: Roy Hyde; Art Director: Don Mingaye; Production Design: Bernard Robinson; Wardrobe Supervisor: Rosemary Burrows; Makeup: Roy Ashton; Hair Stylist: Frieda Steiger; Production Manager: George Fowler; Assistant Director: Bill Cartlidge; Sound Recordist: William Bulkley; Sound Editor: Roy Baker; Special Effects: Les Bowie; Stunts: Peter Diamond; Camera Operator: Moray Grant; Focus Puller: Bob Jordan; Editorial Supervisor: James Needs; Musical Supervisor: Philip Martell; Continuity: Lorna Selwyn

CAST: Noel Willman (Dr. Franklyn), **Jacqueline Pearce** (Anna Franklyn, The Reptile), **Jennifer Daniel** (Valerie Spalding), Ray Barrett (Harry), Michael Ripper (Tom Bailey), John Laurie (Mad Peter), Marne Maitland (The Malay), David Baron (Charles), Charles Lloyd Pack (Vicar), Harold Goldblatt (Solicitor), George Woodbridge (Old Garnsey).

THE RESIDENT, 2011; CREW: Executive Producers: Alex Brunner, Renny Harlin, Tom Lassally, Nigel Sinclair, Hilary Swank; Producers: Tobin Armbrust, Cary Brokaw, Guy East, Simon Oakes;

Co-Producers: Vicki Dee Rock, Jillian Longnecker; Director: Antti Jokinen; Screenplay: Antti Jokinen, Robert Orr; Music: John Ottman; Cinematography: Guillermo Navarro; Film Editors: Stuart Levy, Bob Murawski; Casting: Matthew Barry, Nancy Green-Keyes; Production Design: J. Dennis Washington; Art Director: Guy Barnes; Set Decoration: Wendy Ozols-Barnes; Costume Design: Ann Roth; Makeup Department: Vivian Baker, Elizabeth Gallegos, Tony Gardner, Patricia Greer, Blair Leonard, Ashlynne Padilla, Justin Raleigh, Scott Wheeler; Production Management: Anne Johns, Lucille Smith, Tiffany Tiesiera; Second Unit/Assistant Directors: Trish "The Dish" Stanard, Jane Chase Wells, X. Sydney Ng; Art Department: Brett Andrews, R.A. Arancio-Parrain, Jesse Benson Mike Biskupski, Denise Ciarcia, Lisa Corradino, Dan Fitzgerald, Amy Giedraitis, Linda Gore, Libbe Green, Richard Hurff, Ronald O. Jaynes, Amahl Lovato, Ben Lowney, Nichole Miller, Wilhelm Phau, Billy Ray, Dennis Reiwerts, Graham Robertson, Bret Ross, Loren Schoel, Leonard Sanchez, Cisco Whitson-Brown, Jon De Pabon; Sound Department: Ryan Collins, Laura Dale, Chris Collins, Brian Dunlop, David Esparza, Robert Jackson, Tim Limer, Travis MacKay, Tom Marks, Michael Miller, Matthew Nicolay, Jan Petrov, Josh Reinhardt, Will Riley, Edwardo Santiago, Gabe Serrano, Paul Soucek, Callie Thurman, Miles Vedder, James Wright; Special Effects: Werner Hahnlein, Koji Ohmura; Visual Effects: Amy Hollywood Wixson, Ciril Koshyk, Schuyler Pappas; Stunts: Jacob Chambers, Deborah Mazor, John Robotham; Camera/Electrical Equipment: Greg Argarin, Liza Bambenek, Chip Byrd, Erick Castillo, Joe Chess, Jacob Cottrell, Lamont Crawford, Morgan Davis, Andrew Engert, Harland Espeset, Tyler Fletcher, John Gorman, Timothy Kane, Kurt Kornemann, Nikki LeBlanc, David lee, Jason Linebaugh, Mark Mele, David Midthunder, David Jaxx Nagro, Jeremy Antonio Oliver, Laurie Sebastian, Mark Steinig, Mark Stribling, Rick Stribling, Paige Thomas, Scott Wetzel; Storyboard Artist: Ted Boonthanakit; Casting: Judy Cook, Liz Gabel; Costume/Wardrobe Department: John Deering, Yulia Gershenzon, Kourtney Lawlor, Brandy Marrs, Daniela Moore, Frank Trotta Jr., Lauren Warkentien; Editorial Department: Tony Bacigalupi, Philip Beckner, John Daro, Paul Lavoie, Christine Park, Bill Schultz, Kay Sievert, Christos Voutsinas; Music Department: Michelle Belcher, Joseph Bonn, Jason Livesay, Philip Moross, Edwin Wendler; Transportation Department: Mark Dometrovich, J.W. Ray, Pat Reynolds Jr.; Rest of Crew: Monika Agorelius, Steve Aguino, Pam Bertini, Kristen Blodget, Zoe Bower, Cristal Calderon, Ellen Athena Catsikeas, Joann Connolly, Rob Corlew, Trevor Daniel, Tana David, Ashley Elizabeth Davis, Katherine DeJesus, Leandro Di Salvo, Claire Dore, Glenn Feig, Daniel Fisch, Sara Jo Fisher, Lucas Francy, Dominic Garcia, Adrienne Graves, Jason Hariton, Ben Holden, Jean Jacobson, Allison Jandreau-Heil, Susan Kaufman, Stefan Kende, Brandon Leonard, Barbara Long, Jennifer Mancuso, Theresa Marsh, Gary Martyn, Michael McGrail, Hilton Clay Peres, J. Tom Pogue, Emily Rice, Lauren Schoel, Dimitris Soukos, Mitch Spacone, Robert Vertrees, Shannon Walker, Molly Kimball Whitson, James Wilkerson, Dana Wilkey; Thanks: Christopher Lee, Lance Hool, Paavo Jokinen

Cast: **Hilary Swank** (Dr. Juliet Devereaux), Christopher Lee (August), Jeffrey Dean Morgan (Max), Lee Pace (Jack), **Aunjanue Ellis** (Sydney), Sean Rosales (Carlos), **Deborah Martinez** (Mrs. Portes), **Sheila Ivy Traister** (ER Nurse), Michael Showers, **Sandi K. Shelby** (ER Doctors), **Nana Visitor** (Real Estate Agent), Arron Shiver (Architect), Michael Badalucco (Mover), Michael Masse (Security Tech), **Penny Balfour** (Drug Addict), Mark Vincent Morocco (ER Surgeon), **Veronica Hool** (Nurse), Steven Ray Bird (Paramedic), Elli (Rabbi Elli), Cliff Gravel (ER Patient), **Peggy Miley** (Mrs. Rosenbaum), **Alexandria Morrow** (Art Model), **Kisha Sierra** (Good-Looking Girl)

THE REVENGE OF FRANKENSTEIN, 1958; Crew: Executive Producer: Michael Carreras; Associate Producer: Anthony Nelson-Keys; Producer: Anthony Hinds; Director: Terence Fisher; Screenplay: Jimmy Sangster; Additional Dialogue: Hurford Janes, George Baxt; Music: Leonard Salzedo; Cinematography: Jack Asher; Film Editor/Sound Editor: Alfred Cox; Production Design: Bernard Robinson; Wardrobe Mistress: Rosemary Burrows; Casting: Dorothy Holloway; Makeup: Phil Leakey; Hair Stylist: Henry Montsash; Production Manager: Don Weeks; Assistant Director: Robert Lynn; Second Assistant Director: Tom Walls; Third Assistant Director: Hugh Harlow; Master Plasterer: Arthur Banks; Master Carpenter: Charles Davis; Props Buyer: Eric Hillier; Construction Manager: Mick Lyons; Draughtsman: Don Mingaye; Property Master: Tom Money; Master Painter: Lawrence Wren; Sound Recordist: Jock May; Camera Operator: Len Harris; Chief Electrician: Jack

Curtis; Still Photographer: Tom Edwards; Focus Puller: Harry Oakes; Grip: Albert Cowland; Musical Director: John Hollingsworth; Conductor: Muir Matheson; Studio Manager: Arthur Kelly; Chimp Trainer: Molly Badham; Supervising Editor: James Needs; Second Assistant Editor: Alan Corder; Continuity: Doreen Dearnaley; Cashier: Ken Gordon

CAST: Peter Cushing (Dr. Victor Stein), Francis Matthews (Dr. Kleve), Michael Gwynn (Karl), **Eunice Gayson** (Margaret Conrad), John Welsh (Dr. Bergman), Lionel Jeffries (Fritz), Oscar Quitak (Dwarf), Richard Wordsworth (Up Patient), Charles Lloyd Pack (Medical Council President), John Stuart (Inspector), Arnold Diamond (Dr. Malke), **Marjorie Gresley** (Countess), **Anna Walmsley** (Vera), George Woodbridge (Janitor), Michael Ripper (Kurt), Ian Whittaker (Gerda's Boy), **Avril Leslie** (Girl Gerda), Alex Gallier (Execution Priest), John Gayford (Footman), Raymond Hodge (Exhumation Official), Eugene Leahy (Kline), Michael Mulcaster (Tattoo Harry), Gordon Needham (Male Nurse), **Julia Nelson** (Inga), Robert Brooks Turner (Groom), George Hirste, Gerald Lawson, Freddie Watts, Middleton Woods (Patients).

THE SATANIC RITES OF DRACULA (a.k.a. *Count Dracula and His Vampire Brides*), 1973; CREW: Producer: Roy Skeggs; Associate Producer: Don Houghton; Director: Alan Gibson; Screenplay: Don Houghton, based on characters created by Bram Stoker; Music: John Cacavas; Cinematography: Brian Probyn; Film Editor: Chris Barnes; Casting: James Liggat; Art Director: Lionel Couch; Makeup: George Blackler; Hairdressing Supervisor: Maude Onslow; Production Manager: Ron Jackson; Assistant Director: Derek Whitehurst; Second Assistant Director: Chris Carreras; Third Assistant Director: Graham Easton; Construction Manager: Ken Softley; Assistant Art Director: Don Picton; Props: Wilf France; Chargehand Dresser: Arthur Jacobs; Stand-By Carpenter: D. Clarke; Stand-By Rigger: J. Fleetwood; Stand-By Stagehand: R. Race; Sound Editor: Terry Poulton; Sound Recordist: Claude Hitchcock; Dubbing Mixer: Dennis Whitlock; Sound Camera Operator: Chris Munro; Boom Operator: Keith Batten; Special Effects: Les Bowie; Camera Operator: C. Anstiss; Clapper Loader: Peter Carmody; Camera Grip: Stan Patton; Focus Puller: Malcolm Vinson; Wardrobe Supervisor: Rebecca Breed; First Assistant Editor: Larry Richardson; Musical Supervisor: Philip Martell; Continuity: Elizabeth Wilcox

CAST: Christopher Lee (Count Dracula), Peter Cushing (Prof. Lorrimer Van Helsing), **Joanna Lumley** (Jessica Van Helsing), Michael Coles (Inspector Murray), William Franklyn (Torrence), Freddie Jones (Prof. Julian Keeley), Richard Vernon (Col. Matthews), **Barbara Yu Ling** (Chin Yang), Patrick Barr (Lord Carradine), Richard Mathews (John Porter), Lockwood West (Gen. Sir Arthur Freeborne), **Valerie Van Ost** (Jane), Maurice O'Connell (Hanson), Peter Adair (The Doctor), John Harvey (Commissionaire); **Maggie Fitzgerald, Pauline Peart, Finnuala O'Shannon, Mia Martin** (Vampire Girls); Marc Zuber, Paul Weston, Ian Dewar, Graham Rees (Guards)

SCARS OF DRACULA, 1970; CREW: Producer: Aida Young; Director: Roy Ward Baker; Screenplay: "John Elder" (Anthony Hinds), based on the characters by Bram Stoker; Music: James Bernard; Cinematography: Moray Grant; Film Editor: James Needs; Art Director: Scott MacGregor; Assistant Art Director: Don Picton; Wardrobe Mistress: Laura Nightingale; Wardrobe Assistant: Don Mothersill; Makeup Supervisor: Wally Schneiderman; Assistant Makeup: Heather Nurse; Hairdresser: Pearl Tipaldi; Production Manager: Tom Sachs; Assistant Director: Derek Whitehurst; Second Assistant Director: Nick Granby; Third Assistant Director: Lindsey Vickers; Construction Manager: Arthur Banks; Draughtsman: Tony Baines; Props Buyer: Edward Rodrigo; Scenic Artist: Bob White; Sound Recordist: Ron Barron; Sound Editor: Roy Hyde; Recording Supervisor: A.W. Lumkin; Dubbing Mixer: Dennis Whitlock; Assistant Dubbing Editor: Colin Needs; Sound Maintenance: Barry Reed; Sound Camera Operator: David Tappenden; Boom Operator: David Crozier; Special Effects: Roger Dicken; Stunts: Eddie Powell; Camera Operator: Neil Binney; Clapper Loader: Rod Barron; Still Photographer: Joe Woods; Focus Puller: Bob Stilwell; Camera Grip: Peter Woods; Assistant Editors: Adrian McDonald, Stephen Hyde; Music Supervisor: Philip Martell; Continuity: Betty Harley; Unit Publicist: Chris Nixon; Production Accountant: Ken Gordon; Assistant Production Accountant: Stuart King; Unit Runner: Philip Campbell

CAST: Christopher Lee (Count Dracula), Patrick Troughton (Klove), Michael Ripper (Landlord), **Jenny Hanley** (Sarah Framsen), Michael Gwynn (Priest), Dennis Waterman (Simon Carlson), Chris

Matthews (Paul Carlson), **Wendy Hamilton** (Julie), **Anouska Hempel** (Tania), **Delia Lindsay** (Alice), Bob Todd (Burgomaster), Toke Townley (Old Waggoner), David Leland, Richard Durden (Policemen), Morris Bush (Sodbuster), **Margo Boht** (Landlord's Wife), Clive Barrie (Young Fat Chappie), **Olga Anthony** (Party Girl), George Innes (Servant), **Nikki Van der Zyl** (Voice of Sarah Framsen)

SCREAM OF FEAR, 1961; CREW: Executive Producer: Michael Carreras; Producer/Screenplay: Jimmy Sangster; Director: Seth Holt; Music: Clifton Parker; Musical Supervisor: John Hollingsworth; Director of Photography: Douglas Slocombe; Editor: Eric Boyd-Perkins; Supervising Editor: James Needs; Assistant Editor: John Crome; Production Design: Bernard Robinson; Art Director: Thomas Goswell; Assistant Art Director: Bill Constable; Makeup: Basil Newall; Hair Stylist: Eileen Bates; Production Manager: Bill Hill; Assistant Director: David Tomblin; Second Assistant Director: Terry Lens; Sound Editor: James Groom; Sound Recordists: Leslie Hammond, E. Mason, Len Shilton; Special Effects: Les Bowie; Special Effects Assistant: Ian Scoones; Camera Operator: Desmond Davis; Second Unit Camera Operators: Len Harris, Harry Oakes; Still Photographer: George Higgins; Underwater Camera Operators: John Jordan, E.S. Woxholt; Casting: Stuart Lyons; Wardrobe Mistress: Dora Lloyd; Publicity Director: Dennison Thornton; Unit Publicist: Colin Reid; Continuity: Pamela Mann.

CAST: **Susan Strasberg** (Penny), Christopher Lee (Dr. Gerrard), Ronald Lewis (Robert); **Ann Todd** (Jane), John Serret (Inspector Legrand), Leonard Sachs (Spratt), **Anne Blake** (Maid), Fred Johnson (Father), Heinz Bernard, Brian Jackson, Frederick Schrecker (Plainclothes Officers), Fred Rawlings (Plainclothes Sergeant), Policemen (Rodney Burke, Gordon Sterne), **Madame Lobegue** (Swiss Air Hostess), Bernard Browne (Gendarme).

THE SHADOW OF THE CAT, 1961; CREW: Producer: John Penington; Director: John Gilling; Screenplay: George Baxt; Music/Conductor: Mikis Theodorakis; Cinematography: Arthur Grant; Film Editors: James Needs, John Pomeroy; Casting: Stuart Lyons: Production Designer: Bernard Robinson; Art Director: Don Mingaye; Makeup: Roy Ashton; Hair Stylist: Frieda Steiger; Production Manager: Don Weeks; Assistant Director: John Peverall; Second Assistant Director: Dominic Fulford; Sound Editor: Alban Streeter; Sound Recordists: Jock May, Ken Cameron; Special Effects: Les Bowie; Special Effects Assistant: Ian Scoones; Stunts: Jack Cooper; Still Photographer: Tom Edwards; Camera Operator: Len Harris; Electrician: Jack Curtis; Wardrobe Supervisor: Molly Arbuthnot; Continuity: Tilly Day; Cat Trainer: John Holmes

CAST: Conrad Phillips (Michael Latimer), Andre Morrell (Walter Venable), **Barbara Shelley** (Beth Venable), Richard Warner (Edgar), William Lucas (Jacob), Andrew Crawford (Andrew), **Freda Jackson** (Clara), **Vanda Godsell** (Louise), Alan Wheatley (Inspector Rowles), **Catherine Lacey** (Ella), Henry Kendall (The Doctor), Kynaston Reeves (The Grandfather), **Vera Cook** (The Mother), **Angela Crow** (The Daughter), Howard Knight (The Son), Rodney Burke (Oppressed Tool of the Ruling Class), John Dearth (Constable), George Doonan, Fred Stone (Ambulance Men), Charles Stanley (Dobbins), Kevin Stoney (Father)

SHE, 1965; CREW: Producer: Michael Carreras; Associate Producer: Aida Young; Director: Robert Day; Screenplay: David T. Chantler, based on the novel by H. Rider Haggard; Music: James Bernard; Cinematography: Harry Waxman; Film Editor: Eric Boyd-Perkins; Art Director: Robert Jones; Assistant Art Director: Don Mingaye; Wardrobe Mistress: Jackie Cummins; Special Makeup Effects: Roy Ashton; Makeup: John O'Gorman; Hair Stylist: Eileen Warwick; Production Manager: R.L.M. Davidson; Assistant Director: Bruce Sharman; Construction Manager: Arthur Banks; Sound Recordist: Claude Hitchcock; Sound Editors: James Groom, Roy Hyde, Vernon Messenger; Recording Director: A.W. Lumkin; Special Effects: Les Bowie, George Blackwell; Special Effects Assistants: Ian Scoones, Kit West; Special Processes: Les Bowie; Prop Maker: Joy Cuff; Camera Operator: Ernest Day; Gaffer: Steve Birtles; Costumes/Ursula Andress: Carl Toms; Music Supervisor: Philip Martell; Supervising Editor: James Needs; Continuity: Eileen Head; Location Manager: Yoski Hausdorf; Choreographer: Christine Lawson; Assistant to Producer: Ian Lewis; Researcher: Andrew Low

CAST: **Ursula Andress** (Ayesha, "She Who Must Be Obeyed"), Peter Cushing (Ludwig Horace

Holly), Christopher Lee (Billali), Andre Morell (Haumeid), John Richardson (Leo), Bernard Cribbins (Job), **Rosenda Monteros** (Ustane), **Princess Soraya** (Soraya), **Julie Mendez, Lisa Peake** (Night Club Dancers), George Pastell (Voice of Haumeid), **Bula Coleman, Cherry Larman** (Handmaidens), George Lane Cooper, Roy Stuart (Guards), John Maxim (Captain of the Guards), **Oo-Bla-Da Dancers** (Native Dancers), Eddie Powell (Thug), Nosher Powell (British Soldier), **Nikki van der Zyl** (Voice of Ayesha)

SLAVE GIRLS (a.k.a. *Prehistoric Women*), 1967; CREW: Producer/Director: Michael Carreras; Associate Producer: Aida Young; Screenplay: "Henry Younger" (Michael Carreras); Music: Carlo Martelli; Cinematography: Michael Reed; Film Editor: Roy Hyde; Art Director: Robert Jones; Costume Design: Carl Toms; Makeup Supervisor: Wally Schneiderman; Hairdressing Supervisor: Olga Angelinetta; Production Manager: Ross Mackenzie; Assistant Director: David Tringham; Third Assistant Director: Nigel Wooll; Sound Editor: Roy Baker; Sound Mixers: Len Shilton, Sash Fisher; Dubbing Editor: Charles Crafford; Recording Director: A.W. Lumkin; Special Effects: George Blackwell; Camera Operator: Robert Thomson; Focus Puller: Mike Roberts; Wardrobe Mistress: Jackie Breed; Supervising Editor: James Needs; Music Supervisor & Composer/Additional Music: Philip Martell; Continuity: Eileen Head; Choreographer: Denys Palmer

CAST: **Martine Beswicke** (Kari), **Edina Ronay** (Saria), Michael Latimer (David), **Stephanie Randall** (Amyak), **Carol White** (Gido), **Alexandra Stevenson** (Luri), **Yvonne Horner, Sally Caclough** (Amazons), Sydney Bromley (Ullo), Frank Hayden (Arja), Robert Raglan (Col. Hammond), Louis Mahoney (Head Boy), Bari Johnson (High Priest), Danny Daniels (Jakara), Steven Berkoff (John)

SPACEWAYS, 1953; CREW: Producer: Michael Carreras; Director: Terence Fisher; Screenplay: Richard Landau, Paul Tabori; Freely adapted by Paul Tabori from the radio play by Charles Eric Maine; Musical Director/Music: Ivor Slaney; Cinematography: Reginald Wyer; Film Editor: Maurice Rootes; Art Director: J. Elder Wills; Makeup: Dick Bonnor-Morris; Hair Stylist: Polly Young; Production Manager: Victor Wark; Assistant Director: Jimmy Sangster; Sound Recordist: Bill Salter; Special Effects: The Trading Post Ltd; Visual Effects (Process Shots): Les Bowie, Vic Margutti; Camera Operator: Len Harris; Colorist: David Block; Continuity: Renee Glynne; Dialogue Director: Nora Roberts

CAST: Howard Duff (Dr. Stephen Mitchell), **Eva Bartok** (Dr. Lisa Frank), Alan Wheatley (Smith), Philip Lever (Koepler), Michael Medwin (Dr. Andrews), Andrew Osborn (Dr. Crenshaw), **Cecile Chevreau** (Vanessa Mitchell), Anthony Ireland (Gen. Hayes), Hugh Moxie (Col. Daniels), David Horne (Minister), Leo Phillips (Sgt. Peterson), **Marianne Stone** (Mrs. Rogers), **Jean Webster-Brough** (Mrs. Daniels)

STRAIGHT ON TILL MORNING, 1972; CREW: Executive Producer: Michael Carreras; Producer/Director: Peter Collinson; Screenplay: John "Michael" Peacock; Music: Roland Shaw; Cinematography: Brian Probyn; Film Editor: Alan Pattillo; Art Director: Scott MacGregor; Makeup: George Blackler; Production Manager: Tom Sachs; Assistant Director: Clive Reed; Third Assistant Director: Michael Murray; Sound Editor: Alan Bell; Sound Recordist: Claude Hitchcock; Dubbing Mixer: Ken Barker; Sound Re-Recordist: Dennis Whitlock; Focus Puller: Keith Blake; Musical Director: Philip Martell

CAST: **Rita Tushingham** (Brenda Thompson), Shane Briant (Peter Clive), James Bolam (Joey), **Katya Wyeth** (Caroline), **Annie Ross** (Liza), Tom Bell (Jimmy), **Clare Kelly** (Margo), Harold Berens (Mr. Harris), John Clive (Newsagent), Tommy Godfrey (Mr. Godfrey), **Mavis Villiers** (Indian Princess), **Lola Willard** (Customer), Paul Brooke (Uneasy Chap), Mike Mungarvan (Client)

TALES OF FRANKENSTEIN, 1958; CREW: Producer: Michael Carreras; Associate Producer/Director/Story: Curt Siodmak; Teleplay: Henry Kuttner, Catherine Kuttner, Jerome Bixby; Cinematography: Gert Anderson; Film Editor: Tony DiMarco; Art Director: Carl Anderson; Set Decoration: James M. Crowe; Makeup: Clay Campbell; Hair Stylist: Helen Hunt; Assistant Director: Floyd Joyer; Gaffer: Steve Birtles; Supervising Editor: Richard Fantl; Production Assistant: Seymour Friedman

CAST: Anton Diffring (Baron Frankenstein), Don Megowan (The Monster), Ludwig Stossel (Wilhelm), **Helen Westcott** (Christine Halpert), Richard Bull (Halpert), Raymond Greenleaf (Doctor), Peter Brocco (Gottfried), Sydney Mason (Police Chief)

TASTE OF FEAR (a.k.a. *Scream of Fear*), 1961; CREW: Executive Producer: Michael Carreras; Producer/Screenplay: Jimmy Sangster; Director: Seth Holt; Music: Clifton Parker; Cinematography: Douglas Slocombe; Film Editor: Eric Boyd-Perkins; Assistant Editor: John Chrome; Casting: Stuart Lyons: Production Designer: Bernard Robinson; Art Director: Thomas Goswell; Assistant Art Director: Bill Constable; Makeup: Basil Newell; Hair Stylist: Eileen Bates; Production Manager: Bill Hill; Assistant Director: David Tomblin; Second Assistant Director: Terry Lens; Sound Editor: Jim Groom; Sound Recordists: Leslie Hammond, E. Mason, Len Shilton; Special Effects: Les Bowie; Special Effects Assistant: Ian Scoones; Still Photographer: George Higgins; Camera Operator: Desmond Davis; Camera/Second Unit: Len Harris, Harry Oakes; Underwater Camera: John Jordan, E.S. Woxholt; Wardrobe Mistress: Dora Lloyd; Supervising Editor: James Needs; Musical Supervisor: John Hollingsworth; Continuity: Pamela Mann; Unit Publicist: Colin Reid; Publicity Director: Dennison Thornton

CAST: Christopher Lee (Dr. Gerrard), **Susan Strasberg** (Penny Appleby), Ronald Lewis (Robert), **Ann Todd** (Jane), John Serret (Inspector Legrand), Leonard Sachs (Solicitor), **Anne Blake** (Marie), Fred Johnson (Father); Heinz Bernard, Brian Jackson, Frederick Schrecker (Plainclothes Officers), Bernard Browne (Gendarme), Rodney Burke, Gordon Sterne (Policemen), Richard Klee, Frederick Rawlings (Plainclothes Sergeants), **Madame Lobegue** (Swiss Air Hostess)

TASTE THE BLOOD OF DRACULA, 1970; CREW: Producer: Aida Young; Director: Peter Sasdy; Screenplay: "John Elder" (Anthony Hinds), based on the character created by Bram Stoker; Music: James Bernard; Cinematography: Arthur Grant; Film Editor: Chris Barnes; Production Design: Scott MacGregor; Makeup Supervisor: Gerry Fletcher; Hairdressing Supervisor: Mary Bredin; Production Manager: Christopher Sutton; Assistant Director: Dennis Robertson; Second Assistant Director: Nick Granby; Third Assistant Director: Lindsey Vickers; Construction Manager: Arthur Banks; Sound Editor: Roy Hyde; Sound Recordist: Ron Barron; Boom Operator: Keith Batten; Dubbing Editor: Dennis Whitlock; Recording Supervisor: A.W. Lumkin; Special Effects: "Brian Johncock" (Brian Johnson); Special Effects Assistants: Bob Archer, Terry Schubert; Special Effects Team: Mike Tilley; Matte Painter: Les Bowie; Stunts: Eddie Powell, Peter Diamond, Peter Brace; Camera Operator: Neil Binney; Focus Puller: Bob Jordan; Wardrobe Master: Brian Owen-Smith; Music Supervisor: Philip Martell; Continuity: Geraldine Lawton

CAST: Christopher Lee (Dracula), **Linda Hayden** (Alice Hargood), Geoffrey Keen (William Hargood), **Gwen Watford** (Martha Hargood), Peter Sallis (Samuel Paxton), Anthony Higgins (as Anthony Corlan) (Paul Paxton), **Isla Blair** (Lucy Paxton), John Carson (Jonathan Secker), Michael Ripper (Inspector Cobb), **Madeline "Maddy" Smith** (Dolly), Martin Jarvis (Jeremy Secker), Roy Kinnear (Paul Weller), Russell Hunter (Felix), **Shirley Jaffe** (Betty), Keith Marsh (The Father), Peter May (His Son), Reginald Barratt (Their Vicar), **Lai Ling** (Chinese Girl), **Malaika Martin** (Snake Girl), **Amber Blair**, **Vicky Gillespie** (Bordello Girls), **June Palmer** (Redheaded Prostitute)

THE TERROR OF THE TONGS, 1961; CREW: Executive Producer: Michael Carreras; Associate Producer: Anthony Nelson-Keys; Producer: Kenneth Hyman; Director: Anthony Bushell; Screenplay: Jimmy Sangster; Music: James Bernard; Cinematography: Arthur Grant; Film Editor: Eric Boyd-Perkins; Assistant Editor: Chris Barnes; Casting: Dorothy Holloway; Art Director: Thomas Goswell; Assistant Art Director: Don Mingaye; Production Design: Bernard Robinson; Costume Design: Molly Arbuthnot; Makeup: Roy Ashton; Assistant Makeup: Colin Garde; Hair Stylist: Frieda Steiger; Production Manager: Clifford Parkes; Assistant Director: John Peverall; Second Assistant Director: Joe Levy; Third Assistant Director: Dominic Fulford; Sound Recordist: Jock May; Sound Editor: Alban Streeter; Boom Operator: Jim Perry; Sound Camera Operator: Alan Thorne; Focus Puller: Harry Oakes; Camera Operator: Len Harris; Still Photographer: Tom Edwards; Supervising Editor: James Needs; Music Supervisor: John Hollingsworth; Continuity: Tilly Day; Assistant Continuity: Pauline Harlow; Production Secretary: Ann Skinner

CAST: Christopher Lee (Chung King), **Yvonne Monlaur** (Lee), Geoffrey Toone (Capt. Sale), Marne Maitland (Beggar), Brian Worth (Harcourt), Ewen Solon (Tang How), Roger Delgado (Tang Hao), Richard Leech (Inspector Dean), Charles Lloyd Pack (Dr. Fu Chao), **Marie Burke** (Maya), **Barbara Brown** (Helena Sale), Burt Kwouk (Ming), Tom Gill (Beamish), Eric Young (Confucius), **Bandana Das Gupta** (Anna Chang), Michael Hawkins (Priest), Andy Ho (Lee Chung), Milton Reid (Guardian), **Anne Scott** (Girl), **June Barry, Mary Rose Barry, Audrey Burton, Ruth Calvert, Marialla Capes, Katy Cashfield, Patty Dalton, Louise Dickson, Pauline Dukes, Hazel Gardner, Valerie Holman, Julie Shearing, Valerie Shevaloff, Barbara Smith** (Tong Room Girls), **Julie Alexander**, Johnny Arlen, Harold Goodwin, Peter Gray, Ronald Ing, Jules Ki-Ki, Arnold Lee, **Sui Lin**, Michael Peake, Walter Randall, Poing Ping Sam, Steven Scott, Cyril Shaps, Santso Wong, Vincent Wong.

TO THE DEVIL A DAUGHTER, 1976; CREW: Producer: Roy Skeggs; Director: Peter Sykes; Screenplay: Chris Wicking; Adaptation: John Peacock; Novel: Dennis Wheatley; Additional Material: Gerald Vaughn-Hughes; Music: Paul Glass; Cinematography: David Watkin; Film Editor: John Trumper; Casting: Irene Lamb; Art Director: Don Picton; Wardrobe Supervisor: Laura Nightingale; Makeup: George Blackler, Eric Allwright; Hairdressing Supervisor: Jeanette Freeman; Production Manager: Ron Jackson; Assistant Director: Barry Langley; Second Assistant Director: Mike Higgins; Third Assistant Director: Roy Stevens; Construction Manager: Wag Hammerton; Sound Editor: Mike Le Mare; Sound Recordist: Dennis Whitlock; Dubbing Mixer: Bill Rowe; Recording Director: A.W. Lumkin; Special Effects: Les Bowie; Stunts: Eddie Powell; Camera Operator: Ron Robson; Gaffers: Steve Birtles, Ted Hallows; Music Supervisor: Philip Martell; Continuity: Sally Jones; Production Accountant: Ken Gordon; Publicist: Mike Russell
CAST: Richard Widmark (John Verney), Christopher Lee (Father Michael), **Honor Blackman** (Anna), Denholm Elliott (Henry Beddows), Michael Goodliffe (George de Grass), **Nastassja Kinski** (Catherine), **Eva Maria Meineke** (Eveline de Grass), Anthony Valentine (David), Derek Francis (Bishop), **Isabella Telezynska** (Margaret), Constantin de Goguel (Kollde), **Anna Bentinck** (Isabel), **Irene Prador** (German Matron), Brian Wilde (Black Room Attendant), **Petra Peters** (Sister Helle), William Ridoutt (Air Porter), Howard Goorney (Critic), **Frances de la Tour** (Salvation Army Major), Ed Devereaux (Reporter), Bill Horsley (Curator), Peter Sykes (Airport Man); **Zoe Hendry, Lindy Benson, Jo Peters, Bobby Sparrow** (Girls)

TWINS OF EVIL, 1971; CREW: Producers: Harry Fine, Michael Style; Director: John Hough; Screenplay: Tudor Gates; Characters: J. Sheridan Le Fanu ("Carmilla"); Music: Harry Robinson (Robertson); Director of Photography: Dick Bush; Film Editor: Spencer Reeve; Art Director: Roy Stannard; Makeup: George Blackler, John Webber; Production Manager: Tom Sachs; Production Supervisor: Roy Skeggs; Assistant Director: Patrick Clayton; Second Assistant Director: David Munro; Third Assistant Director: Chris Carreras; Construction Manager: Arthur Banks; Sound Recordist: Ron Barron; Sound Editor: William Trent; Dubbing Mixer: Ken Barker; Sound Re-Recording Mixers: Graham V. Hartstone, Otto Snel; Camera Operator: Dudley Lovell; Wardrobe Mistress: Rosemary Burrows; Music Supervisor: Philip Martell; Continuity: Gladys Goldsmith; Hairdressing: Pearl Tipaldi; Casting: James Liggat; Special Effects: Bert Luxford; Special Effects Photography/Second Unit Photographer: Jack Mills; Stunt Coordinator: Joe Dunne; Dialogue Coach: Ruth Lodge
CAST: Peter Cushing (Gustav Weil), **Madeline Collinson** (Frieda Gellhorn), **Mary Collinson** (Maria Gellhorn), Inigo Jackson (Woodsman), **Judy Matheson** (Woodsman's Daughter), Harvey Hall (Franz), Alex Scott (Hermann), **Sheela Wilcox** (Lady in Coach), **Kathleen Byron** (Katy Weil), Roy Stewart (Joachim), **Luan Peters** (Gerta), Damien Thomas (Count Karnstein), Dennis Price (Dietrich), **Maggie Wright** (Alexa), **Katya Wyeth** (Countess Mircalla), David Warbeck (Anton Hoffer), **Isobel Black** (Ingrid Hoffer), **Kristen Lindholm** (Staked Girl), Peter Thompson (Jailer), Roy Boyd (Dying Man), **Maxine Casson, Vivienne Chandler, Doreen Chanter, Irene Chanter, Jackie Leapman, Janet Lynn, Annette Roberts** (Schoolgirls), George Claydon (Midget), John Fahey, Harry Fielder, Kenneth Gilbert, Derek Glynne-Percy, Jason James, Sebastian Graham-Jones, Bill Sawyer (Puritans), **Cathy Howard** (Tomb Girl), Peter Stephens (Brotherhood Member), Garth Watson (Chief Priest)

THE TWO FACES OF DR. JEKYLL (a.k.a. *House of Fright*), 1960; CREW: Executive Producers: Michael Carreras, Anthony Nelson-Keys; Director: Terence Fisher; Screenplay: Wolf Mankowitz, based on the novel *The Strange Case of Dr. Jekyll and Mr. Hyde* by Robert Louis Stevenson; Music: Monty Norman, David Heneker; Cinematography: Jack Asher; Film Editor: Eric Boyd-Perkins; Art Director: Don Mingaye; Production Design: Bernard Robinson; Wardrobe Supervisor: Molly Arbuthnot; Costume Design: Mayo; Makeup: Roy Ashton; Hair Stylist: Ivy Emmerton; Production Manager: Clifford Parkes; Assistant Director: John Peverall; Second Assistant Director: Hugh Harlow; Sound Recordist: Jock May; Sound Editor: Archie Ludski; Camera Operator: Len Harris; Still Photographer: Tom Edwards; Editorial Supervisor: James Needs; Musical Supervisor: John Hollingsworth; Continuity: Tilly Day; Choreographer: Julie Mendez

CAST: Paul Massie (Dr. Jekyll/Dr. Hyde), Christopher Lee (Paul), **Dawn Addams** (Kitty Jekyll), David Kossoff (Dr. Litauer), **Norma Marla** (Maria), Francis De Wolff (Inspector), **Joy Webster** (Jenny), **Maria Andipa** (Gypsy Girl), Frank Atkinson (Groom), Archie Baker, Ralph Broadbent, Alex Miller, Laurence Richardson (Singers); Glenn Beck, Alan Browning, Rodney Burke, Clifford Earl (Young Bloods), John Bonney (Renfrew), Percy Cartwright (Coroner), Dennis Cleary (Waiter), **Bandana Das Gupta, Pauline Dukes, Hazel Graeme, Carole Haynes, Doreen Ismail, Josephine Jay, Jean Long, Magda Miller, Marilyn Ridge, Gundel Sargent, Patricia Sayers, Shirli Scott-James, Moyna Sharwin** (Sphinx Girls), J. Trevor Davies, John Moore (Officers), Roy Denton, Kenneth Firth, George McGrath, Mackenzie Ward (Business Men), **Janina Faye** (Jane), Felix Felton, Walter Gotell, Anthony Jacobs (Gamblers), **Helen Goss** (Nanny), **Lucy Griffiths, Prudence Hyman** (Tavern Women), William Kendall (Clubman), **Roberta Kirkwood** (Second Brass), Arthur Lovegrove (Cabbie), Anthony Pendrell, Fred Stone (Cabinet Ministers), Oliver Reed (Tough Bloke), Doug Robinson (The Boxer), Joe Robinson (Corinthian), Denis Shaw (Tavern Customer), **Pauline Shepherd** (Mary), Donald Tandy (Rogers), **Joan Tyrrell** (The Majordomo), **Joyce Wren** (Nurse)

VAMPIRE CIRCUS, 1972; CREW: Executive Producer: Michael Carreras; Producer: Wilbur Stark; Director: Robert William Young; Screenplay: Justin Kinberg; Story: George Baxt, Wilbur Stark; Music: David Whitaker; Cinematography: Moray Grant; Film Editor: Peter Musgrave; Casting: James Liggat; Art Director: Scott MacGregor; Makeup: Jill Carpenter; Hairdresser: Anne McFadyen; Production Supervisor: Roy Skeggs; Production Manager: Tom Sachs; Assistant Director: Derek Whitehurst; Second Assistant Director: Lindsey Vickers; Third Assistant Director: Graham Easton; Chief Draughtsman: Richard Rambaut; Construction Manager: Arthur Banks; Assistant Art Director: Don Picton; Art Department Runner: "Jimmy" Carreras; Props Buyer: Edward Rodrigo; Chargehand Props: Danny Skundric; Stand-By Props: Peter Wallis; Sound Editor: Roy Hyde; Sound Recordist: Claude Hitchcock; Dubbing Mixer: Ken Barker; Sound Re-Recording Mixers: Ken Barker, Graham V. Hartstone; Sound Camera Operator: Laurie Reed; Boom Operator: Mike Silverlock; Assistant Boom Operator: Chris Munro; Special Effects: Les Bowie; Stunts: Bradforts-Amaros; Camera Operator: Walter Byatt; Clapper Loader: Peter Carmody; Camera Grip: Ted Lockhart; Focus Puller: Bob Smith; Gaffer: Vic Smith; Wardrobe Supervisor: Brian Owen-Smith; Musical Director/Supervisor: Philip Martell; Continuity: June Randall; Publicity Director: Frank Law; Animal Adviser: Mary Chipperfield; Unit Runner: Adrian Delahaye

CAST: Thorley Walters (The Burgermeister), **Adrienne Corri** (Gypsy Woman), Anthony Corlan (Emil), John Moulder-Brown (Anton), Laurence Payne (Prof. Mueller), Richard Owens (Dr. Kersh), **Lynne Frederick** (Dora Mueller), **Domini Blythe** (Anna Mueller), **Elizabeth Seal** (Gerta Hauser), Roderick Shaw (Jon Hauser), Barnaby Shaw (Gustav Hauser), Robin Hunter (Duggie Hauser), Robert Tayman (Count Mitterhaus), John Bown (Schilt), **Jane Darby** (Jenny Schilt), **Sibylla Kay** (Mrs. Schilt), **Dorothy Frere** (Grandma Schilt), **Mary Wimbush** (Elvira), **Christine Paul-Podlasky** (Rosa), Robin Sachs (Heinrich), **Lalla Ward** (Helga), Skip Martin (Michael), Dave Prowse (The Strongman), Milovan (Male Dancer), **Serena** (Female Dancer), Sean Hewitt (Soldier), Giles Phibbs (Sexton), Jason James (Foreman), Arnold Locke (Villager), Bradforts-Amaros (Themselves), David de Keyser (Voice of Mitterhaus Curse), **Anna Bentinck, Nina Francis, Drina Pavlovic, Jenny Twigge** (Schoolgirls)

THE VAMPIRE LOVERS, 1970; CREW: Producers: Harry Fine, Michael Style; Associate Producer: Louis M. Heyward; Director: Roy Ward Baker; Screenplay: Tudor Gates; Story: J. Sheridan

Le Fanu ("Carmilla"); Adaptation: Harry Fine, Michael Style, Tudor Gates; Music: Harry Robinson (Robertson); Director of Photography: Moray Grant; Film Editor: James Needs; Art Director: Scott MacGregor; Costume Design: Brian Cox; Makeup Supervisor: Tom Smith; Hair Stylist: Pearl Tipaldi; Production Manager: Tom Sachs; Assistant Director: Derek Whitehurst; Construction Manager: Bill Greene; Sound Recorder: Claude Hitchcock; Sound Editor: Roy Hyde; Recording Director: Tony Lumkin; Dubbing Mixer: Dennis Whitlock; Camera Operator: Neil Binney; Wardrobe Mistress: Laura Nightingale; Music Supervisor: Philip Martell; Continuity: Betty Harley

CAST: **Ingrid Pitt** (Carmilla/Mircalla/Marcilla Karnstein), Peter Cushing (General Spielsdorf), George Cole (Roger Morton), **Kate O'Mara** (Mme. Perrodon), Ferdy Mayne (Doctor), Douglas Wilmer (Baron Joachim von Hartog), **Madeline Smith** (Emma Morton), **Dawn Addams** (The Countess), Jon Finch (Carl Ebhardt), **Pippa Steel** (Laura), **Kirsten (Lindholm) Betts** (1st Vampire), **Janet Key** (Gretchen), Harvey Hall (Renton), John Forbes-Robertson (The Man in Black), Charles Farrell (Landlord), **Shelagh Wilcocks** (Housekeeper), Graham James (1st Young Man), Tom Browne (2nd Young Man), **Joanna Shelley** (Woodsman's Daughter), Jill Easter (Woodsman's Wife), **Olga James** (Village Girl), Lindsay Kemp (Jester), Sion Probert (Young Man in Tavern), **Vicki Woolf** (Landlord's Daughter)

THE VENGEANCE OF SHE, 1968; CREW: Producer: Aida Young; Director: Cliff Owen; Screenplay: Peter O'Donnell, based on the novel *Ayesha: The Return of She* by H. Rider Haggard; Music/Special Musical Effects: Mario Nascimbene; Director of Photography: Wolfgang Suschitzky; Film Editor: Raymond Poulton; Production Design: Lionel Couch; Costume Design: Carl Toms; Wardrobe Mistress: Rosemary Burrows; Makeup: Michael Morris; Hair Stylist: Mervyn Medalie; Production Manager: Dennis Bertera; Assistant Director: Terry "Captain" Clegg, Ariel Levy; Painter: Michael Finlay; Sound Recordist: Bill Rowe; Sound Editors: Roy Hyde, Jack Knight; Recording Director: A.W. Lumkin; Camera Operator: Ray Sturgess; Special Effects: Bowie Films Ltd., Bob Cuff; Model Maker: Joy Cuff; Supervising Editor: James Needs; Musical Supervisor: Philip Martell; Continuity: Phyllis Townshend; Ritual Sequences Designer: Andrew Low; Solo Saxophone: Tubby Hayes

CAST: **Olinka Berova** (Carol/Ayesha), John Richardson (Killikrates), Edward Judd (Philip), Colin Blakely (George), **Jill Melford** (Sheila), Andre Morell (Kassim), Noel Willman (Za-Tor), George Sewell (Harry), Derek Godfrey (Men-Hari), **Daniele Noel** (Sharna), Gerald Lawson (Seer), Derrick Sherwin (Number One), William Lyon Brown (Magus), Charles O'Rourke (Servant), **Zohra Segal** (Putri), **Christine Pockett** (Dancer), Dervis Ward (Peter, Leering Lorry Driver), Harry Fielder (Caveman), **Dana Gillespie** (Girl at Party)

THE VIKING QUEEN, 1967; CREW: Producer/Story: John Temple-Smith; Director: Don Chaffey; Screenplay: Clark Reynolds; Music: Gary Hughes; Cinematography: Stephen Dade; Film Editor: Peter Boita; Production Design: George Provis; Costume Design: John Furniss; Wardrobe Supervisor: Hilda Geerdts; Wardrobe Master: Jack Gallagher; Makeup: Charlie Parker; Hair Stylist: Bobbie Smith; Production Manager: Rene Dupont; Assistant Director: Dennis Bertera; Second Unit Director: Jack Causey; Third Assistant Director: Mike Higgins; Sound Editor: Stan Smith; Sound Mixers: Bob Jones, H.L. Bird; Special Effects: Allan Bryce; Stunts: Tim Condren, Steve Emerson; Camera Operator: David Harcourt; Photographer/Second Unit: John Harris; Gaffer: Bernie Prentice; Music Supervisor & Composer/Additional Music: Philip Martell; Supervising Editor: James Needs; Continuity: Ann Skinner; Production Liaison: William O'Riley; Horse Master: Frank Hayden

CAST: **Carita** (Salina, the Viking Queen), Don Murray (Justinian), Donald Houston (Maelgan), Andrew Keir (Octavian), **Adrienne Corri** (Beatrice), Niall MacGinnis (Tiberian), **Nicola Pagett** (Talia), Percy Herbert (Catus), Patrick Troughton (Tristram), Sean Caffrey (Fergus), Denis Shaw (Osiris), Philip O'Flynn (Merchant), Brendan Matthews (Nigel), Gerry Alexander (Fabian), Patrick Gardiner (Benedict), Paul Murphy (Dalon), Arthur O'Sullivan (Old Bloke at Tax Enquiry), Cecil Sheridan (Shopkeeper), **Anna Manahan** (Shopkeeper's Wife), **Nita Lorraine** (Nubian Girl Slave), Bryan Marshall (Dominic), Scott McGinnis (Man)

WAKE WOOD, 2011; CREW: Executive Producers: Simon Oakes, Marc Schipper; Co-Executive Producers: Ben Holden, Patrick Irwin, Allan Niblo, Rupert Preston; Producers: Brendan McCarthy,

John McDonnell; Co-Producer: Magnus Paulsson; Line Producer/Sweden: Natasha Banke; Director/Screenplay: David Keating; Screenplay/Story: Brendan McCarthy; Music: Michael Convertino; Cinematography: Chris Maris; Film Editor: Tim Murrell; Production Design: John Hand; Art Director: Owen Power; Costume Design: Louise Stanton; Makeup: Katarina Kovacs; Makeup Assistant: Liz Byrne; Makeup Designer: Kaj Gronberg; Prosthetic Makeup: Deirdre Fitzgerald; Production Manager: Steven Davenport; Assistant Director: Jonathan Quinlan; First Assistant Director: Nick McCarthy; Second Assistant Director: Marcus Lynch; Third Assistant Directors: Anna Harrison, Rosai McCarthy; Training Assistant Director: M. Johnstone; Property Master: Chan Kin; Sound Department: Felix Andriessens, Buster Blaesild, Naomi Dandridge, Tom Deane, Anders Degerberg, Adele Fletcher, Michael Muller, John Nilsson, Martin Schinz, Dominik Schleier, Lionel Strutt; Swedish Special Effects: Magnus Gillberg; Visual Effects: Florian Obrecht; Visual Effects Supervisor: Andreas Schellenberg; Title Designer: Britt Dunse; Stunt Coordinator: Donal O'Farrell; Camera Operator: Ed Lindsley; Second Assistant Camera: Ewa Gerstrom; Swedish Grip: Set Jonasson; Still Photographer: Jesper Lindgren; Crane Operator: Adam Tsan; Costume Supervisor: Jo Mapp; Swedish Wardrobe: Josefin Sandling; Colorist: Kevin Shaw; Music Editor & Composer/Additional Music: P. Daniel Newman; Script Supervisor: Anna-Maria Ni Chathasaigh; Location Manager: Brendan O'Sullivan; Assistant Location Manager: Rossa O'Neill; Production Coordinator: Rachel Lysaght; Production Assistants: Susann Chandler, Lucinda Glynn; Swedish Production Assistants: Jurate Kaminskaite, David Nilsson, Jonas Tarestad, Tobias Thuresson; Thanks: Nic Ransome

CAST: Aidan Gillen (Patrick), **Eva Birthistle** (Louise), Timothy Spall (Arthur), **Ella Connolly** (Alice), **Ruth McCabe** (Peggy O'Shea), Brian Gleeson (Martin O'Shea), **Amelia Crowley** (Mary Brogan), Dan Gordon (Mick), Tommy McArdle (Tommy), John McArdle (Ben), **Aoife Meagher** (Deirdre), **Siobhan O'Brien** (Pharmacy Customer), **Alice McCrea** (Lady Customer), Johnny Fortune (Mechanic), John Hand, Darragh Hand (Arthur's Helpers), Steven McDonnell (Field Boy), Simple the Bull (The Bull)

WHEN DINOSAURS RULED THE EARTH, 1970; CREW: Producer: Aida Young; Director: Val Guest; Screenplay: Val Guest, adapted from an original treatment by J.G. Ballard; Music & Composer/Special Music Effects: Mario Nascimbene; Cinematography: Dick Bush; Film Editor: Peter Curran; Assistant Editor: Robert C. Dearberg; Art Director: John Blezard; Costume Design: Carl Toms; Makeup Supervisor: Richard Mills; Hair Styles Supervisor: Joyce James; Production Manager: Christopher Sutton; Assistant Director: John Stoneman; Second Unit Director: Jim Danforth; First Assistant Director: Carlos Gil; Co-First Assistant Director/Spain: Miguel Gil; Construction Manager: Albert Blackshaw; Sound Recordist: Kevin Sutton; Sound Re-Recordist: Ted Karnon; Dubbing Editor: Frank Goulding; Special Visual Effects/Effects Cameraman/Matte Artist/Process Projectionist/Stop-Motion Animator/Visual Effects Designer & Director: Jim Danforth; Visual Effects Assistant: Dave Allen; Special Effects: Allan Bryce, Roger Dicken, Brian "Johncock" Johnson, Martin Gutteridge, Brian Humphrey, Garth Inns; Camera Operator: Ronnie Fox Rogers; Camera Operator/Second Unit: Johnny Cabrera; Gaffer: Steve Birtles; Still Photographers: Pierre Luigi, Ronnie Pilgrim; Camera Operator: David Harcourt; Clapper Loader: Ken Nicholson; Key Grip: Martin O'Connor; Wardrobe Master: Brian Owen-Smith; Music Supervisor: Philip Martell; Continuity: Josephine Knowles; Continuity/Second Unit: Susanna Merry

CAST: **Victoria Vetri** (Sanna), Robin Hawdon (Tara), Patrick Allen (Kingsor), Drewe Henley (Khaku), Sean Caffrey (Kane), **Magda Konopka** (Ulido), **Imogen Hassall** (Ayak), Patrick Holt (Ammon), **Jan Rossini** (Rock Girl), **Carol-Anne Hawkins** (Yani), **Maria O'Brien** (Omah), **Connie Tilton** (Sand Mother), **Maggie Lynton** (Rock Mother), Jimmy Lodge (Fisherman), Billy Cornelius, Ray Ford (Hunters)

THE WITCHES, 1966; CREW: Producer: Anthony Nelson-Keys; Director: Cyril Frankel; Screenplay: Nigel Kneale, based on the novel *The Devil's Own* by "Peter Curtis" (Norah Lofts); Music: Richard Rodney Bennett; Cinematography: Arthur Grant; Film Editors: Chris Barnes, James Needs; Casting: Irene Lamb; Production Design: Bernard Robinson; Art Director: Don Mingaye; Wardrobe Supervisor: Molly Arbuthnot; Wardrobe Master: Harry Haynes; Makeup: George Partleton; Hair Stylist: Frieda Steiger; Production Manager: Charles Permane; Assistant Director: David Tringham;

Second Assistant Director: Terence Churcher; Sound Recordist: Ken Rawkins; Sound Editor: Roy Hyde; Boom Operator: Charles Wheeler; Stunts: Peter Diamond; Camera Operators: C. Cooney, David Harcourt; Still Photographer: Tom Edwards; Focus Puller: Bob Jordan; Assistant Editor: Tony Lenny; Music Supervisor: Philip Martell; Continuity: Anne Deeley; Choreographer: Denys Palmer

CAST: **Joan Fontaine** (Gwen Mayfield), **Kay Walsh** (Stephanie), Alec McCowen (Alan), **Ann Bell** (Sally), **Ingrid Boulting** (Linda), John Collin (Dowsett), **Michele Dotrice** (Valerie), **Gwen Davies** (Granny), Duncan Lamont (Bob), Leonard Rossiter (Dr. Wallis), Martin Stephens (Ronnie), **Carmel McSharry** (Mrs. Dowsett), **Viola Keats** (Mrs. Curd), **Shelagh Fraser** (Mrs. Creek), Bryan Marshall (Tom), Yemi Ajibade (Mark), **Kitty Atwood** (Mrs. McDowall), John Barrett (Mr. Glass), **Catherine Finn** (Nurse), **Prudence Hyman** (Maid), **Lizbeth Kent** (Villager), Artro Morris (Porter), Willie Payne (Adam), Charles Rea (Sergeant), Rudolph Walker (Mark II), Roy Desmond, Ken Robson, Brian Todd, Don Vernon, Terry Williams (Dancers)

THE WOMAN IN BLACK, 2012; CREW: Producers: Vic David, Guy East, Ben Holden, Richard Jackson, Roy Lee, Simon Oakes, Brian Oliver, Paul Ritchie, Nigel Sinclair, Todd Thompson, Tyler Thompson, Sean Wheelan; Director: James Watkins; Screenplay: Jane Goldman, from the novel by Susan Hill; Music: Marco Beltrami; Cinematography: Tim Maurice-Jones; Film Editor: Jon Harris; Casting: Karen Lindsay-Stuart; Production Design: Kave Quinn; Art Director: Paul Ghirardani; Set Direction: Niamh Coulter; Costume Design: Keith Madden; Hair & Makeup: Jeremy Woodhead, Paul Hyett, Sidony Etherton; Production Manager: Jennifer Wynne; Post-Production Supervisor: Jeanette Haley; First Assistant Director: Dominic Fysh; Second Assistant Director: Emma Stokes; Third Assistant Director: Tom Browne; First Assistant Director/New York: Eric Berkal; Art Department: Huw Arthur, Tina Charad, Quentin Davies, Simon Duric, John Fox, Stella Fox, Jack Garwood, Daniel Nussbaumer, Andrew Palmer, Alan Payne, Mary Pat Sheahan, Jessica Sinclair, Anthony Szuch, Toby Wagner, Damian Leon Watts, Craig Whiteford, Ian Whiteford, Jamie Wilkinson, Simon Wilkinson; Sound Department: Hugo Adams, Niv Adiri, Mark Appleby, Ben Barker, Sandy Buchanan, Andrew Caller, Simon Diggins, Gillian Dodders, Glenn Freemantle, Michael Gassert, James Hyde, James Kum, Emilie O'Connor, Richard Pryke; Timothy Siddall, Ivor Talbot, Ian Tapp, Tarn Willers; Special Effects Fabricator: Elle Baird; Special Effects Makeup: Chris Fitzgerald; Visual Effects: Fiorenza Bagnariol; Alan Banis, Hakan Blomdahl, Tim Caplan, Peter Collins, Mitch Crease, Urban Forsberg, Adam Gascoyne, Marcus Hindborg, Andreas Hylander, Tim Jones, Elin Lindahl, Linus Lindbalk, Martin Malmqvist, Kaveh Montazer, Mervyn New, Daniel Nielsen, Timo Nahri, John Palmer, Damian Pawle, Malin Persson, Rob Pizzey, Aurora Shannon, Ruchira Sharma, Noga Alon Stein; Stunts: Gary Arthurs, Andy Bennett, Nellie Burroughes, Paul Lowe, Marc Mailley, Sam Parham; Camera/Electrical Department: David Armstrong, Graham Baker, Jeremy Braben, Luke Cairns, Martin Conway, Rana Darwish, Darren Flindall, Ian Franklin, Rob Gilmour, David Holliday, Alex Howe, Nathan Mann, Cassius McCabe, Tom McFarling, Sean Monesson, Julian Morson, Brett Parnham, Gary Parnham, James Perry, Felix Pickles, Clive Prior, Nuria Perez, Maiya Rose, Basil Smith, Kat Spencer, Alan Stewart, Pat Sweeney, Alex Teale, Robert Walisko, Nick Wall, Terry Williams; Child Casting: Carolyn McLeod, Wardrobe Mistress: Emma Hutton; Wardrobe Supervisor/New York: Nikia Nelson; Principal Standby: Holly Smart; Editorial Department: Rob Farris, Cheryl Goodbody, Emily Greenwood, Patrick Malone, Erline O'Donovan, Jamie Payne, Rose-Ellen Saunders, Jon Ellis; Music Department: John Kurlander, Tony Lewis, Tyson Lozensky, Brandon Roberts, Joel Sill, Marcus Trump, John Warhurst; Minibus Driver: Mark Cutler; Rest of Crew: Giles Barron, Caroline Bowker, Daniel Budd, Annie Clapton, Joel Clarke, Rosanne Coker, Dan Connolly, Jon Croker, Matt Curtis, Nazmeen Dhansey, John Doherty, Elton Farla, Lee Francis, Holly Gardner, Sasha Gibson, Harry Greaves, Vinnie Jassal, Kevin Jenkins, Sheerin Khosrowshahi-Miandoab, Jillian Longnecker, Lottie Mason, John Miles, Chris Moore, David Seaton, Adele Steward, Alice Syed, Edward Taroghion, Sam Weeden

CAST: Daniel Radcliffe (Arthur Kipps), **Sophie Stuckey** (Stella Kipps), **Janet McTeer** (Mrs. Dailey), Misha Handley (Joseph Kipps), **Lucy May Barker** (Nursemaid), Shaun Dooley (Fisher), **Mary Stockley** (Mrs. Fisher), **Alexia Osborne** (Victoria Hardy), Daniel Cerqueira (Keckwick), **Liz White** (Jennet Humfrye), **Aoife Doherty** (Lucy Jerome), Sidney Johnston (Nicholas Daily), **Indira**

Ainger (Little Girl on Train), **Emma Shorey**, **Molly Harmon** (Fisher Girls), **Jessica Raine** (The Nanny), Roger Allam (Mr. Bentley), Andy Robb (The Doctor), Ciaran Hinds (Daily), Alfie Field (Tom), Victor McGuire (Harold), **Cathy Sara** (Mrs. Jerome), Tim McMullan (Mr. Jerome), **Alisa Khazanova** (Mrs. Drablow), Ashley Foster (Nathaniel), David Burke (PC Collins)

X: THE UNKNOWN, 1956; CREW: Executive Producer: Michael Carreras; Associate Producer: Mickey Delamar; Producer: Anthony Hinds; Director: Leslie Norman; Story/Screenplay/Production Manager: Jimmy Sangster; Music: James Bernard; Director of Photography: Gerald Gibbs; Film Editor: James Needs; Casting: Joseph Losey; Art Director: Ted Marshall; Makeup/Special Makeup Effects: Phil Leakey; Assistant Director: Chris Sutton; Third Assistant Director: Hugh Harlow; Draughtsman: Don Mingaye; Sound Mixer: Jock May; Sound Editor: Alfred Cox; Boom Operator: Jim Perry; Special Effects: Les Bowie, Jack Curtis, Vic Margutti; Camera Operator: Len Harris; Still Photographer: Tom Edwards; Focus Puller: Harry Oakes; Wardrobe Supervisor: Molly Arbuthnot; Conductor: John Hollingsworth; Continuity: June Randall; Publicist: Bill Batchelor

CAST: Dean Jagger (Dr. Royston), Edward Chapman (John Elliott), **Marianne Brauns** (Zena), Leo McKern (Inspector McGill), Anthony Newley (Spider Webb), Jameson Clark (Jack), William Lucas (Peter Elliott), Peter Hammond (Lt. Bannerman), Ian McNaughton (Haggis), Michael Ripper (Sgt. Harry Grimsdyke), John Harvey (Maj. Cartwright), Edwin Richfield (Burnt Soldier), **Jane Aird** (Vi Harding), Norman Macowan (Old Tom), Neil Hallet (Unwin), Kenneth Cope (Sapper), Michael Brooke (Willie), Fraser Hines (Ian), Max Brimmell (Hospital Director), Robert Bruce (Dr. Kelly), **Angela Crow** (Woman), Brown Derby (Vicar), Raymond Dudley (Bloke), Archie Duncan (Sgt. Yeardye), Lawrence James (Gerard), Edward Judd, Brian Peck, Barry Steele (Soldiers), **Stella Kemball** (Woman), Jack Lambert (Man), Stevenson Lang (Reporter), Philip Levene (Security), Anthony Sagar (Gateman), John Stirling (Police Driver), John Stone (Jerry), French Taylor (PC Williams), Shaw Taylor (Police Radio Operator), Neil Wilson (Russell)

Bibliography

Books

Briggs, Joe Bob. *Joe Bob Goes to the Drive-In*. New York: Delacorte Press, 1987.
Brosnan, John. *James Bond in the Cinema*. London: Tantivy Press and S. Brunswick, NJ: A.S. Barnes, 1972.
Eisner, Joel. *The Official Batman Batbook*. Chicago: Contemporary Books, 1986.
Flynn, John. *50 Years of Hammer Horror*. Owings Mills, MD: Galactic Books, 2007.
Guralnick, Peter. *Careless Love: The Unmaking of Elvis Presley*. Boston: Little, Brown, 1999.
_____. *Last Train to Memphis: The Rise of Elvis Presley*. Boston: Little, Brown, 1994.
Haining, Peter. *Doctor Who: A Celebration*. London: W.H. Allen, 1986.
Harryhausen, Ray. *Film Fantasy Scrapbook*. London: Tantivy Press and S. Brunswick, NJ: A.S. Barnes, 1972.
Hearn, Marcus. *Hammer Glamour*. London: Titan Books, 2009.
Johnson, Tom, and Deborah Del Vecchio. *Hammer Films: An Exhaustive Filmography*. Jefferson, NC: McFarland, 1996.
Kinsey, Wayne. *Hammer Films: The Bray Studio Years*. Surrey, UK: Reynolds & Hearn, 2002.
_____. *Hammer Films: The Unsung Heroes*. Sheffield, UK: Tomahawk Press, 2010.
Marrero, Robert. *Horrors of Hammer*. Key West, FL: RGM Publications, 1984.
_____. *Vampires: Hammer Style*. Key West, FL: RGM Publications, 1982.
Pitt, Ingrid. *The Ingrid Pitt Bedside Companion for Vampire Lovers*. London: Batsford, 1998.
Sachs, Bruce, and Russell Wall. *Greasepaint and Gore: The Hammer Monsters of Roy Ashton*. Sheffield, UK: Tomahawk Press, 1999.
Svehla, Gary, and Susan Svehla. *Memories of Hammer: The Fanex Interviews*. Baltimore: Midnight Marquee Press, 2002.

Periodicals

Dark Terrors # 16. Cornwall, UK. Mike Murphy, 1998.
007 Magazine Archive Files: Bond Girls of the 1960s—Martine Beswicke. London: Graham Rye, 2011.
Flesh and Blood # 1, 2. Surrey, UK. Harvey Fenton, 1997.
The House That Hammer Built # 3, 5, 6, 7, 17, and 20. London: Wayne Kinsey, 1997–2005.
Little Shoppe of Horrors # 13, 14, 16, 17, 18, 20, 22, 21, 23, 26. Des Moines: Richard Klemensen, 1991–2011.

Index

Numbers in ***bold italics*** indicate pages with photographs.

The Abominable Snowman 47, 201
Acosta, Carolina 7
Adair, Jan 7
Adams, Joyce 7
Adcock, Sally 7
Addams, Dawn 7–***8***, ***130***
Adderley, Diane 8
Ainger, Indira 8
Aird, Jane 8–9
Aitchison, Peggy 9
Alexander, Julie 9
Alison, Dorothy 9
Allen, Audrey 9
Anderson, Daphne 9–10
Anderson, Kayla 10
Anderson, Lesley 10
Anderson, Margaret 10
Andipa, Maria 10
Andress, Ursula 10–***11***
The Anniversary 58, 95, ***183***, 201
Anthony, Jane 11
Anthony, Olga 11
Apple, Gwendolyn 12
Archer, Barbara 12
Arrighi, Nike ***12***–13
Asher, Jane 13
Asherson, Dorothy 13
Atwood, Kitty 13–14
Aubrey, Angharad 14
Aubrey-Smith, Debbie 14
Audley, Maxine 14
Aukin, Liane 14

Babus, Hulya 14
Baddeley, Hermione 14–15
Baker, Carrie 15
Balfour, Penny 15
Bankhead, Tallulah 15–17
Barclay, Mary 17
Barker, Lucy 17
Barker, Lucy May 17

Baron, Lynda 17
Barrese, Sasha 17–18
Barry, June 18
Barry, Mary Rose 18
Barry, Michelle 18
Bartok, Eva 18
Bates, Samantha 19
Baumann, Sue 19
Beacham, Stephanie ***19***–20
Beale, Erica 19
Bel Geddes, Barbara 20–21
Bell, Ann 21
Bennett, Jill 21, ***57***
Benson, Lindy 21
Bentinck, Anna 21
Benton, Barbi 22
Berova, Olinka ***22***–23
Beswick, Martine 23–25, ***156***
Betts, Kirsten 25–26, ***143***
Beyond the Rave 141–142, 201–202
Birthistle, Eva 26
Black, Isobel 26–***27***
Blackman, Honor 27–29
Blair, Isla 29–30, ***99***
Blair, Joyce 30
Blake, Ann 30
Blake, Anne 30
Blake, Beverly 30
Blare, Amber 30
Blood from the Mummy's Tomb ***122***, 202
Blythe, Domini 30
Boht, Margo 30
Boize, Sandra 31
Bond, Sidonie 31
Borgo, Marianne 31
Borland, Katie 31
Boshier, Joan 31
Boulting, Ingrid 31
Bowers, Lally 31
Brackenbury, Pat 32

Bradshaw, Irene 32
Brahms, Penny 32
Brandon-Jones, Una 32
Brauns, Marianne 32
Brennan, Sheila 32
Brett, Anna 32
Briars, Shevaun 32
The Brides of Dracula ***62***, ***134***, ***137***, 202–203
Brodrick, Susan 32–33
Brody, Estelle 33
Brousse, Liliane 33, ***91***
Brown, Barbara 33
Bruce, Angela 33
Bruce, Brenda 33–34
Bryan, Dora 34
Buono, Cara 34
Burgess, Vivienne 34
Burke, Marie 34
Burnett, Ruth 35
Burrell, Sheila 35
Burton, Audrey 35
Butler, Shirley 35
Byron, Kathleen 35–36

Caclough, Sally 36
Calder-Marshall, Anna 36
Calvert, Ruth 36
Cameron, Isla 36
Capes, Marialla 36
Captain Clegg 9, 161, 203
Captain Kronos, Vampire Hunter 54, 139, ***186***, 203
Carby, Fanny 37
Cardew, Jane 37
Carita 37–38
Carlson, Veronica 38–40, ***70***
Carvana, Lorraine 40
Cashfield, Katy 40
Casson, Maxine 40
Castle, Susan 40
Chandler, Vivienne 41
Chanter, Doreen 41

Chanter, Irene 41
Chasan, Debbie 41
Chevreau, Cecile 41
Chilcott, Barbara 41
Christie, Helen Mary 41
Church, Suzanne 42
Churcher, Melinda 42
Cilento, Diane 42
Clare, Diane 42–43
Clarke, Melita 43
Clay, Rachel 43
Clayton, Lynn 43
Cleveland, Carol 43
Clune, Anne 43
Cole, Linda 43
Coleman, Bula 44
Collier, Patience 44
Collings, Lisa 44
Collins, Joan ***44***–45
Collinson, Madeline 45–***46***
Collinson, Mary 45–***46***
Compton, Fay 46
Connell, Maureen 47
Connolly, Ella 47
Cook, Jacqui 47
Cook, Vera 47
Cordeau, Sonya 47
Corri, Adrienne 47–49
Costello, Deidre 49
Countess Dracula 64, 151, 204
Court, Hazel 49–51
Cowling, Brenda Rose 51
Craig, Wendy 51
Crane, Hilary 51–52
Crawford, Joan 52
Creatures the World Forgot ***68***, 204
Crescendo 153, 204
Crosby, Mary 52
Crosdale, Vera P. 53
Crow, Angela 53
Crowley, Amelia 53
Cruikshank, Marty 53
Crutchley, Rosalie 53

Index

Cuka, Frances 53–54
Cunningham, Jane 54
Cunningham, Linda 54
The Curse of Frankenstein 49, 204–205
The Curse of the Mummy's Tomb **160**, 205
The Curse of the Werewolf 73, **161**, 205–206
Cushing, Peter **39**

Daine, Lois 54
Dalby, Amy Mary 54
Dalton, Patty 54
The Damned **74**, 206
Daniel, Jennifer 54–56
Danielle, Suzanne 56
Darby, Jane 56
Das Gupta, Bandana 56
Davies, Rachel 57
Davis, Bette **57–58**
Day, Vera 58–59
Dean, Margia 59
Dear, Elizabeth 60
Dearman, Jennifer 60
Delany, Pauline 60
De la Tour, Frances 59
Demons of the Mind 102, 206
Denberg, Susan **60–61**
Dennis, Winifred 61
De Rauch, Micky 59
De Sain, Monique 59
Desni, Tamara 61
Devereux, Marie **61–62**
The Devil Rides Out **12**, 13, 206–207
Devil-Ship Pirates 71
Dick Barton at Bay 61, 207
Dick Barton Strikes Back 125, 207
Dickie, Olga 63
Dickson, Louise 63
Dignam, Rebecca 63
Di Leo, Serafina 62
Dr. Jekyll and Sister Hyde 9, 26, 32, 207–208
Doherty, Aoife 63
Don, Maggie 63
Donnelly, Elaine 63
Donovan, Erin 63
Dors, Diana 63–64
Dotrice, Michele 64
Douglas, Katya 64
Down, Lesley-Anne 64–65
Dracula (Horror of Dracula) **82**, 129, 181, 208
Dracula A.D. 1972 **19**, 139, 208
Dracula Has Risen from the Grave 39, **70**, 208–209

Dracula, Prince of Darkness 70, 171, 209
Drake, Gabrielle 65
Duffell, Bee 66
Duke, Patty 66
Dukes, Pauline 66
Duncan, Fiona 67
Dunion, Sheila 67
Dunlop, Lesley 67
Du Sautoy, Carmen 65–66
Dyson, Anne 67

East, Susanna 67
Easter, Jill 67
Edwards, Jeillo 67
Ege, Julie 67–69
Ellis, Aunjanue 69
Ellis, June 69
Elvin, Elizabeth 69
Evans, Jessie 69
Everest, Barbara 69
The Evil of Frankenstein 196–197, 209
Ewing, Barbara 69–**70**

Fanatic **16**, 152, 209
Farmer, Suzan 70–72
Faye, Janina 72
Fear in the Night 44, **85**, 209–210
Feller, Catherine 72–**73**
Field, Shirley Anne 73–**74**
Fielding, Fenella 74, **166**
Fielding, Janet 74–75
Finlay, Marilyn 75
Finn, Catherine 75
Fitzgerald, Maggie 75
Flanagan, Maureen 75
Fleming, Lucy 75–76
Fontaine, Joan **76–77**
Forde, Leila 77
Foster, Julia **77–78**
Four Sided Triangle 146, 210
Fox, Marcia 78
Fox, Sonia 78
Francis, Jan 78–79
Francis, Nina 79
Frankenstein and the Monster from Hell 176, 210
Frankenstein Created Woman **61**, 210–211
Frankenstein Must Be Destroyed **39**, 211
Franklin, Gretchen 79
Franklin, Pamela 79
Fraser, Shelagh 79
Frederick, Lynne **48**, 80
Frere, Dorothy 80
Frost, Sadie 80
Fuller, Toria 80

Furneaux, Yvonne 80–**81**
Fussey, Sharon 81

Gardner, Caron 82
Gardner, Geraldine 82
Gardner, Hazel 82
Gaunt, Valerie **82**–83
Gayson, Eunice **83**
Gee, Prunella 83–**84**
Geeson, Judy 84–86
George, Susan 86
Gilan, Yvonne 86
Gillespie, Dana 86–**87**
Gillespie, Vicky 87
Gilmore, Lianne 87
Gilpin, Toni 87–**88**
Ginders, Angela 88
Glessing, Mollie 88
Goddard, Daphne 88
Godley, Anne 88
Godsell, Vanda 88
Gold, Lauren 88
Goldoni, Lelia 89
Gordon, Hannah 89
Gordon, Nora 89
The Gorgon **106**, 171, 211
Gorst, Irene 90
Goss, Helen 90
Gott, Elizabeth 90
Graeme, Hazel 90
Graham, Sally 90
Grant, Angela 90
Gray, Nadia 90, **91**
Greco, Mary 90
Greek, Beatrice 91
Green, Frances 91
Green, Libertad 91
Green, Wilhelmina 91
Gregg, Virginia 92
Gregory, Celia 92–93
Grenfell, Joyce 93
Gresley, Marjorie 93
Grey, Shirley 93
Griffiths, Lucy 93–94, **130**
Gurpinar, Gigi 94
Gutteridge, Lucy 94

Hale, Georgina 94–95
Hamilton, Gay 95
Hamilton, Wendy 95
Hammer, Sue 95
Hammer House of Horror (TV series) 10, 33, 36, 51, 54, 56, 57, 60, 63, 64, 67, 70, 74, 78, 84, 92, 94, 101, 111, 112, 117, 150, 154, 167, 174
Hammer House of Mystery and Suspense (TV series) 20, 22, 29, 31, 35, 41, 42, 52, 66, 67, 78, 80, 82, 86, 89, 99, 100, 104, 112, 128, 149, 154, 155, 168

Hancock, Sheila 95–96
Hands of the Ripper 158, **200**, 211–212
Hanley, Jenny 96
Hargreaves, Janet 96
Harmon, Molly 97
Harris, Julie 97
Harris, Toni 97
Hartford, Fiona 97
Harvey, Vivienne 97
Hassall, Imogen 97–98, **188**
Hawkins, Carol 98
Hayden, Linda 98–**99**
Hayes, Patricia 99–100
Haynes, Carol 100
Haythorne, Joan 100
Hearne, Biddy 100
Hempel, Anouska **100–101**
Hemson, Joyce 101
Hendry, Zoe 101
Henriques, Sylvana 101
Heywood, Pat 101
Hignett, Mary 101–102
Hilary, Jennifer 102
Hills, Gillian 102
Hird, Thora 102–103
Holden, Jan 103
Holland, Sophie 103
Holman, Valerie 103
Holt, Penelope 103
Hood, Noel 103
Hool, Veronica 104
Horner, Yvonne 104
The Horror of Frankenstein 40, 143, 212
Horton, Helen 104
The Hound of the Baskervilles 116–117, 212
Houston, Renee 104
Howard, Cathy 104
Hroncich, Rachel 104
Hubley, Season 104
Hudson, Christine 105
Hughes, Beulah 105
Hughes, Hazel 105
Hughes, Lynne 105
Hume, Marjorie 105
Hunt, Marsha **19**, 105
Hunt, Martita 105–106
Hylton, Jane 106
Hyman, Prudence **106–107**, **130**
Hysteria 108, 212–213

Impey, Betty 107
Inns, Trudy 107
Ismail, Doreen 107

Jackson, Frieda 107
Jacobs, Paula 108
Jaffe, Shirley 108
Jago, June 108

James, Olga 108
James, Sally 108
Jay, Josephine 108
Jayne, Jennifer 108
Jeayes, Carol 108
Jefford, Barbara 108–109, **177**
Jennings, Hazel 109
Jessop, Clytie 109
Johnston, Mildred 109
Joseph, Joanna 109
Joshi, Indira 109–110
Joslin, Annis 110
Journey into Darkness 213
Journey to Midnight 213
Journey to Murder 213
Journey to the Unknown (TV Series) 9, 15, 21, 31, 33, 43, 48, 52, 65, 66, 79, 95, 97, 102, 106, 109, 116, 120, 125, 128, 135–136, 153, 157, 164, 181, 189, 191
Joyce, Yootha **16**, 110

Kane, Beatrice 110
Karlin, Miriam 110
Kay, Sybilla 110
Keats, Viola 111
Keller, Sarah 111
Kellerman, Barbara 111
Kelly, Claire 111
Kemball, Stella 111
Kent, Lizbeth 111
Keogh, Barbara 111–112
Key, Janet **19**, 112
Khazanova, Aliza 112
Kiesouw, Josje 112
Kimberly, Maggie 112–**113**
Kind, Sophie 113
King, Ann 113
King, Diana 113–114
Kinski, Nastassja **28**, 114
Kirkwood, Roberta 114
The Kiss of the Vampire 27, **190**, 213–214
Knef, Hildegard 114
Knight, Shirley 115
Konopka, Magda 115, **188**
Krippen, Brenda 115

Lacak, Irene 115
Lacey, Catherine 115–116
Laird, Jenny 116
Lancaster, Ann 116
Landi, Marla 116–117
Landor, Rosalyn 117
Langrishe, Carolyn 117
La Porte, Deirdre 115
Lapotaire, Jane 117–118
Larman, Cherry 118
Larsen, Gerda 118
Lawrence, Andrea 118

Lawrence, Delphi 118–119
Lawrence, Marjie 119
Lawson, Sarah 119
Leapman, Jackie 119
Lee, Christopher **19**, **99**
The Legend of the 7 Golden Vampires 68, 214
Leggatt, Alison 120
Leigh, Laurie 120
Leigh, Suzanna 120–121
Lemoine, Joy 121
Leon, Valerie 121–**122**
Leslie, Avril 122
Let Me In **138**, 214–216
Lind, Gillian 122–123
Linden, Jenny **123**
Linden, Joyce 123
Lindfors, Viveca 124
Lindsay, Delia 124
Ling, Barbara Yu 124
Ling, Lai 124
Lister, Renny 124
Little, Caryl 124
Liu, Hui-Ling 124
Llewellyn, Josephine 124
Lloyd, Sue 125–125
Lobegue, Madame 125
Lodge, Jean 125
Loe, Judy 125–126
Long, Jean 126
Longhurst, Sue 126
Lopez, Juliet 126
Lord, Justine 126
Lord, Rosemary 126
Lorraine, Nita 126
The Lost Continent 87, 114, 120, 216
Lovell, Angela 126
Lumley, Joanna **127**–128
Lust for a Vampire 108, **177**, 216
Luttrell, Constance 128
Lynley, Carol 128–129
Lynn, Janet 129
Lynton, Maggie 129

MacLennan, Elizabeth 129
Malin, Diana 129
The Man Who Could Cheat Death **50**, 118, 217
Manahan, Anna Maria 129
Maniac **91**, 217
Mareno, Lydia 129
Marks, Patricia 129
Marla, Norma 129, **130**
Marsh, Carol 129–130
Marshall-Gardiner, Jessica 131
Martin, Malaika 131
Martinez, Deborah 131

Matheson, Judy 131
Mathie, Marion 131
Maureen, Molly 131–132
May, Dinah 132
Maynard, Patricia 132
Mazor, Deborah 132
McCabe, Ruth 132
McConnell, Bridget 132
McCrea, Alice 132
McSharry, Carmel 132
McTeer, Janet 132–133
Meagher, Aoife 133
Meineke, Eva Maria 133
Melford, Jill 133
Melly, Andree 133, **134**
Mendez, Julie 133–134
Meredith, Jill 134
Merrow, Jane 134–135
Merton, Zienia 135
Miles, Vera 135–136
Miley, Peggy 136
Millard, Tamsin 136
Miller, Magda 136
Miller, Tallulah 136
Mockler, Suzanne 136
Monlaur, Yvonne **134**, **137**
Monteros, Rosenda **11**, 137–138
Moon Zero Two 43, 48, 165, 217
Moretz, Chloe Grace **138**
Morgan, Elizabeth 138–139
Morgan, Taylor 139
Morrow, Alexandria 139
Mort, Patricia 139
Moulan, Rosita 139
Moyens, Judi 139
The Mummy **81**, 218
The Mummy's Shroud **113**, 218
Munro, Caroline **19**, 139–140
Myers, Cynthia 140

Nadasi, Mia 140
The Nanny 21, 51, **57**, 218
Nappi, Malya 140
Neilson, Catherine 140–141
Nelmes, Judith 141
Nelson, Julia 141
Nesbitt, Sally 141
Newell, Joan 141
Newman, Nanette 141
Nicholson, Veronica 141
Nightmare **123**, 218–219
Noel, Danielle 141
Noone, Nora-Jane 141–142
Nowag, Lillian 142

O'Brien, Glenys 142
O'Brien, Maria 142
O'Brien, Siobhan 142
The Old Dark House 74, **166**, 219
O'Mara, Kate 142–144
One Million Years B.C. **194**, 195, 219
O'Neil, Collette 144
Oo-Bla-Da Dancers 144
Osborne, Alexia 144
O'Shannon, Finnuala 144
Oxenford, Daphne 144

Pagett, Nicola 144
Palmer, June 145
Palmer, Maria 145
Paranoiac 166, 219–220
Parfitt, Judy 145
Parsons, Alibe 145
Paul-Podlasky, Christine 145–146
Pavlovic, Drina 146
Payne, Natalie 146
Payton, Barbara 146
Peake, Lisa 146
Pearce, Jacqueline **55**, 146–148
Pearl, Elna 148
Peart, Pauline 148
Perry, Anna 148
Peters, Jo 148
Peters, Luan 149
Peters, Petra 149
The Phantom of the Opera 14, 168, 220
The Phantom Ship 93, 220
Phillips, Michelle 149
Phillips, Sian 149–150
Pinkney, Lynn 150
Pitt, Ingrid **143**, 150–151
Plague of the Zombies 42, 147, 220
Pockett, Christine **151**
Poole, Jackie 152
Pooley, Kirstie 152
Portell, Petula 152
Porter, Sarah 152
Posta, Adrienne 152
Power, Sandra 152
Powers, Stefanie **16**, 152–153
Prador, Irene 153
Pravda, Hana 153–154
Price, Penny 154

Quatermass and the Pit (Five Million Years to Earth) **172**, 220–221
Quatermass 2 221
The Quatermass Xperiment 59, 221–222

Index

Quinn, Mary 154
Quinn, Patricia 154

Raffin, Deborah 154–155
Raines, Cristina 155
Raines, Jessica 155
Randall, Stephanie 155, **156**
Rasputin the Mad Monk 172, 222
Rawlings, Margaret 155
Raynor, Sheila 156
Read, Dolly 156
Reardon, Corinna 157
Redmond, Moira 157
Reed, Oliver **74, 161**
Reed, Tracy 157–158
Rees, Angharad 158
Rennie, Maggie 158
The Reptile **55, 147,** 222
The Resident 182, 222–223
The Revenge of Frankenstein **83,** 223–224
Rhodes, Marjorie 158
Rice, Joan 158
Richards, Lee 159
Richards, Susan 159
Richardson, Beryl 159
Richardson, Jo 159
Richmond, Irene 159
Ridge, Marilyn 159
Ridley, Emma 159
Ripper, Michael **55**
Roberts, Annette 159
Robillard, Elizabeth 159
Robins, Sheila 160
Roland, Jeanne **160**
Romain, Yvonne 160–162
Romanoff, Liz 162
Ronay, Edina **162**–163
Rosay, Francoise 163
Ross, Annie 163
Ross, Joanna 163
Rossini, Jan 163
Royle, Carol 163
Rule, Janice 163–164
Ryder, Celia 164

Sabine, Winifred 164
St. Clement, Pam 164
Sampson, Annie 164
Samuel, Julie 164
Sara, Catherine 164
Sargent, Gundel 164
The Satanic Rites of Dracula 127, 224
Saville, Edith 164
Sawday, Diana 165
Sayers, Patricia 165
Scarf, Donna 165
Scars of Dracula **96, 100,** 224–225

Schell, Catherine 165
Schofield, Joan 165
Scott, Anna 166
Scott, Anne 166
Scott, Janette **166**
Scott, Kathryn Leigh 167
Scott, Margaretta 167
Scott, Michelle 167
Scott-James, Shirli 168
Scream of Fear **179**
Seagrove, Jenny 168
Seal, Elizabeth 168
Sears, Heather 168–169
Seely, Wendy 169
Seghal, Zohra 169
Sellars, Elizabeth 169–170
Serena 170
The Shadow of the Cat 170, 225
Sharwin, Moyna 170
She 10, **11,** 225–226
Shearing, Julie 170
Shelby, Sandy 170
Sheldon, Caroline 170
Shelley, Barbara 106, 170–173
Shelley, Joanna 173
Shenstone, Clare 173
Shepherd, Pauline **130,** 173
Sheridan, Dinah 173–174
Sherman, Marianne 174
Shevaloff, Valerie 174
Shih, Szu 174
Shorey, Emma 174
Shrimpton, Chrissie 174
Sierra, Kisha 174
Silvera, Simone 175
Sinclair, Peggy 175
Slave Girls (Prehistoric Women) 24, **156, 162,** 226
Smith, Amber Dean 175
Smith, Barbara 175
Smith, Christine 175
Smith, Dorothy 175
Smith, Madeline **143,** 175–176
Soraya, Princess 176
Spaceways 18, 226
Sparrow, Bobby 176
Spencer, Sally-Jane 176
Stallybrass, Anne 176
Starr, Zoe 176
Steafel, Sheila 177
Steel, Pippa **143,** 177
Stensgaard, Yutte **177**–178
Stevenson, Alexandra 178
Stewardson, Cheryl 178
Stockley, Mary 178
Stone, Marianne 178–179

Straight on Till Morning 185, 226
Strasberg, Susan **179**–180
Stratford, Tracy 180
Stribling, Melissa 180–181
Stuckey, Sophie 181
Sui Lin 181
Summerfield, Eleanor 181
Swank, Hilary 181–**182**

Tales of Frankenstein 195, 226–227
Talfrey, Hira 183
Taste of Fear 179, 227
Taste the Blood of Dracula **99,** 176, 227
Taylor, Elaine **183**–184
Taylor, Siobhan 184
Telezynska, Izabella 184
The Terror of the Tongs 137, 227–228
Thater, Heinke 184
Thomas, Lisa 184
Thompson, Sophie 184
Tilton, Connie 184
Tirard, Anne 184
To the Devil a Daughter **28,** 114, 228
Todd, Ann 184
Traister, Sheila 185
Tushingham, Rita 185
Twigge, Jenny 185
Twins of Evil **46,** 228
The Two Faces of Dr. Jekyll 7–8, **130,** 229
Tyrell, Joan 185

Ustinov, Tamara 185

Valentine, Elizabeth 185
Vampire Circus **48,** 229
The Vampire Lovers 8, **143,** 150, 229–230
Van der Zyl, Monica 186
Van Ost, Valerie 186
The Vengeance of She **22, 151,** 230
Ventham, Wanda 186–187
Verdugo, Nicole 187
Vetri, Victoria 187–**188**
The Viking Queen **37,** 230
Villiers, Caroline 189
Villiers, Mavis 189
Visitor, Nana 189

Wagstaff, Elsie 189
Wake Wood 230–231

Walker, Zena 189
Wallis, Jacquie 189–**190**
Walmsley, Anna 190
Walsh, Kay **76,** 190–191
Walsh, Sally 191
Ward, Lalla 191
Warne, Jo 191
Warner, Patricia 191
Washbourne, Mona 191–192
Watford, Gwendoline 192
Watts, Gwendolyn 192
Watts, Stephanie 192
Way, Ann 192
Webster, Joy 192
Webster-Brough, Jean 193
Wehle, Brenda 193
Weir, Molly 193
Welch, Raquel 193–**194**
Wells, Sheilah 194
Westcott, Helen 194–195
Wetherell, Virginia 195–196
When Dinosaurs Ruled the Earth **188,** 231
White, Carol **156,** 196
White, Joanne 196
White, Liz 196
Wiggins, Rebekah 196
Wilcocks, Shelagh 196
Wild, Jeanette 196
Wild, Katy 196–197
Wilding, April 197
Willard, Lola 197
Williams, Lou 198
Wilson, Sue 198
Wimbush, Mary 198
Winstone, Lois 198
The Witches **76,** 190–191, 231–232
Wojtczak, Tessa 198
The Woman in Black 132–133, 232–233
Wood, Virginia 198
Woolf, Vicki 198
Woollard, Emma 198
Wren, Joyce 198
Wrigg, Ann 198
Wright, Julia 199
Wright, Maggie 199
Wyeth, Katya 199–**200**

X: The Unknown 32, 233

Young, Joan 200